PEACE AND SURVIVAL

PEACE AND SURVIVAL

West Germany, the Peace Movement,
and European Security

DAVID GRESS

HOOVER INSTITUTION PRESS

Stanford University   Stanford, California

Hoover Press Publication

Copyright 1985 by the Board of Trustees of the
Leland Stanford Junior University

First printing, 1985

Manufactured in the United States of America

89 88 87 86 85   9 8 7 6 5 4 3 2 1

Library of Congress Cataloging in Publication Data

Gress, David, 1953–
Peace and survival.
Bibliography: p. 237
Includes index.
1. Germany (West)–Politics and government.
2. Peace. 3. Europe–Defenses. I. Title.
DD258.75.G74 1985   943   85–12562
ISBN 0-8179-8091-1

Design by P. Kelley Baker

TO SIDNEY HOOK

CONTENTS

Neither the fear of war nor, certainly, the Soviet presence in Eastern Europe and that of the United States in Western Europe are caused by nuclear weapons. A nuclear-free Europe would be a Europe dominated by the Soviet Union and not, therefore, either more peaceful or more free; such a Europe would rather be much more prone to the same dangers of war faced by all other regions of the globe, and from which nuclear arms have so far saved her. Nor would the Finlandization of Western Europe as such alleviate the subjection of Eastern Europe. The first priority is therefore to re-establish the balance which, at first, can only be founded on the recoupling of Western Europe and the United States, and, in the longer term, on an autonomous European defense.

Pierre Hassner, "Pacifisme et terreur."

The choice faced by European nations, according to revolutionary Marxism, "socialism or barbarity?" has been replaced by another, "survival of the democracies or the global establishment of a new form of social and political exploitation, namely totalitarianism?" . . . In recent years, pacifism has revived in the United States and in Western Europe. This phenomenon is a symptom of the spiritual condition of society in industrial countries; the republican and democratic principles made its material prosperity possible, and now that prosperity has undermined those principles . . . In the pacifists, the word of the Psalmist is fulfilled: *oculos habent, et non videbunt.*

Octavio Paz, "Pacifismo, nihilismo, eterno ritorno."

If Europe is not to be a mere fiction, it must realize that its present limits deny the very notion of Europe and represent a deficiency analogous to the deficiency of German history . . . if the concept of Europe is not to be a lie, we must get used to the thought that "Europe" is only a fragment and that it is unendurable that its eastern part should be dominated by its adversary.

Alfred Heuss, *Versagen und Verhängnis*

PREFACE

The idea for this work stemmed from my experiences in Denmark in 1979–1982 as a writer and debater on the issues of NATO, Western defense, Soviet policy, and the attitudes of Western intellectuals. Those were years of increasing tensions and uncertainty in the Atlantic Alliance. Arms control, which had originally been an American idea "rammed down the throat of reluctant or skeptical Europeans," as Pierre Hassner put it, was now an article of faith for some European governments, notably that of the Federal Republic of Germany. For West Germany, the pursuit of arms control and détente with the Soviet and East European regimes, regardless of their behavior, were now political necessities that no responsible politician could question. Furthermore, the official West German attitude in the 1980s was that the division of Europe was an important element, even a precondition, of stability, and that deliberate attempts to overcome it were dangerous and should be avoided. Until the early 1960s, however, it was the position of almost all West German political leaders, from Willy Brandt on the left to Franz-Josef Strauss on the right, that the division of Europe, caused primarily by the Soviet Union, was not only illegitimate and unjust, but the main source of tension and the threat to peace. U.S. efforts in the 1950s and 1960s to achieve détente with the Soviet Union, which involved accepting the status quo of European division, therefore worried West German governments greatly. When the Reagan administration questioned the utility of arms control, denounced Soviet actions as evidence of aggressive intentions, and said what all West Germans believed twenty years before, namely that the division of Europe was intolerable, unjust, and a perpetual source of tension, it helped provoke the rise of what Hassner called an "intense minority" that was in fact a "moral majority." This intense minority, which insisted that the main problem in Europe was not a Soviet threat that it regarded as mythical, but provocative U.S. and NATO policies, included many politicians, mostly, but not exclusively, Social Democrats, as well as academics, writers, and other public figures. It was by no means confined to the peace movement.

During these same years, other changes were taking place in the political culture, attitudes, and social psychology of the West German population as a whole. The violent radicalism of the late 1960s and 1970s had seemingly come to an end, but it was replaced by an equally radical, if generally non-violent, rejection of the political and social organization of the West German republic by large numbers of young people, a rejection manifested in the electoral triumph of the Green movement in 1983. On the other hand, there was little to indicate that the majority of citizens were withdrawing their sympathy or support from their state and society. There was an increasing interest in German history and culture, and to some extent a revival of interest in the idea of the nation and hence in the problem of divided Germany.

These various issues, the rise of what one might call "nationalist neutralism," the ideology of the peace movement, the change in the SPD from an *Ostpolitik* aimed at liberalizing Eastern Europe to one of appeasement of the Soviet Union, and the revival of interest in the national question, are the main themes of this book.

Two points of terminology should be noted. First, whenever the words "Germany" or "German" are used in the text without qualification, they always refer to the country as a whole, that is, the unified German state (1871–1945), all four zones of occupation (1945–1949), or both West and East Germany (including, in principle, the territories east of the Oder-Neisse line). In no case do I use "Germany" or "German" to refer to the Federal Republic alone. The other point is that the phrase "national policy" corresponds to what in German is called *Deutschlandpolitik*, which refers to the policy (whatever its content) of any given West German government for dealing with the problem of the divided nation and its implications. I might also note that all quotations from foreign-language sources are my translations.

I had chosen my title, *Peace and Survival*, before coming across Lawrence Beilenson's work, *Survival and Peace in the Nuclear Age* (Chicago: Regnery Gateway, 1980). The similarity is fortuitous; Beilenson's broad and forthright view of the challenges to Western security and Western defense, while concerned mostly with recommending a new strategic policy for the United States, is one to which I, with some reservations, would subscribe, and I have learned much from it.

The overall focus of Part I is the changes in outlook on the national issue from the early years to the 1980s, and of Part II, philosophical and cultural differences in beliefs about peace, political morality, and legitimate authority between, on the one hand, the peace movement and its academic and political supporters and, on the other, the proponents and defenders of NATO and the West German state. My own opinions and perspectives will be evident from my judgments and conclusions; in terms of general approach and temperament in the study of modern history and international relations, especially East-West relations, I definitely count myself among the traditionalists. I agree with Robert Gilpin that "the exercise of power is still the central feature of international relations"; power, ideology, and the conflict of incompatible interests, as seen by Raymond Aron, Pierre Hassner, Samuel Huntington, and, for Germany specifically, by such as Hans-Peter Schwarz, seem to me to be decisive, not only for the overall future of states and nations, but also for changes in systems of economic and social organization. Specifically, Soviet power by its very existence influences the politics of Western countries, which, when taken together, are potentially far stronger than the Soviet Union. Raymond Aron pondered this paradox in his last works, and one begins to understand a good deal about some of the arguments against NATO policies in West Germany if one sees them, in the words of Hans-Peter Schwarz, as to some extent "an attempt, in view of the decline of American power, to come to terms with the new lord and master."

I owe thanks to a number of individuals for making the book possible. In 1980–1981 I had the pleasure of organizing and directing the two European Congresses on Freedom and the Future held at the European College near Stege, Denmark. The theme of the first was East-West relations and Soviet power, and of the second, the crisis of social democracy in Western Europe. I thank Ingolf Knudsen, principal of the College, and the distinguished guests, especially Michael Hereth, Sidney Hook, Melvin Lasky, Leopold Labedz, and Richard Löwenthal for valuable discussions on the history and policies of the SPD, West German defense and security policy, and the politics and influence of leading intellectual and academic circles in West Germany and other Western countries.

Being on the Stanford campus as a National Fellow of the Hoover Institution in 1982–1983 meant that I had access to what is probably the best collection of material for the study of the strategic debate, West German politics and history, and political change in Western societies. For this opportunity and for the generous financial support that sustained my family and myself during my research I wish to thank the director, Dr. W. Glenn Campbell, and Dr. Dennis Bark, executive secretary of the National, Peace, and Public Affairs Program of the Hoover Institution while this work was in progress. The help of other members of the staff was indispensable, particularly Agnes Peterson, who kept me informed of new accessions in the West European collection, and Mary Bellamy, who found and supplied a considerable amount of relevant press articles and analyses. To the interest and support of Dr. John Moore and Dr. Peter Duignan, I owe the chance to return to the Hoover Institution in 1984 to continue my research and writing on European politics and security. I also thank the Hoover Institution Publications Committee and its chairman, Richard T. Burress, for undertaking to publish the work. Last but not least, the careful editing by Lydia Duncan improved the style and clarified the argument on virtually every page.

At a critical juncture before I left Denmark, support was generously provided by the Egmont H. Petersen Fund and the Tuborg Foundation, both in Denmark. I wish particularly to thank Ole Dahl of the Egmont H. Petersen Fund for his efforts. The Carlsen-Lange Endowment, the Danish-American Foundation, Imerco Inc., and Norsk Hydro Inc. provided grants toward the cost of moving to the United States. A grant from the USA-76 National Committee of Denmark helped defray the cost of travel in the United States in 1982–1983.

In 1983, the Institute of Educational Affairs in New York twice provided travel grants enabling me to spend a total of four months in West Germany, France, and Scandinavia. In addition, Dr. Robert L. Pfaltzgraff, Jr., of the Institute for Foreign Policy Analysis kindly invited me to participate in the conference on the peace movement, European security, and the morality of deterrence organized by the IFPA and the Konrad Adenauer Foundation in Bonn, during which I had the opportunity to discuss these topics with experts from both sides of the Atlantic. Special thanks go to Kim Holmes of the IFPA for showing me his studies of the Green Party and of the new "national neutralism" in West Germany. I also thank Jeffrey Herf for sending me the manuscript of his article on the breakdown of the Atlanticist consensus in the SPD, and for discussing the subject with me.

These periods of study and observation allowed me to keep up-to-date on political developments and currents of public opinion in Western Europe and thus to make significant revisions of the present text, as well as to plan future studies. The flow of analysis and opinion on the issues treated here, however, is vast. My references, therefore, are of two kinds; first, to a selection of general literature on the subject of each chapter or section, and second, to arguments or analyses that supported or diverged from my own on important points. It will be no secret to the careful reader that I am heavily indebted, above all, to the work of Pierre Hassner and Hans-Peter Schwarz.

.   The most important personal inspiration for my work is recorded in the dedication. Sidney Hook has been for me not only a model of philosophical stringency but also, since his attendance at the Second European Congress on Freedom and the Future in 1981, a good and valued friend. Among other scholars and friends at the Hoover Institution and Stanford University, I should like to thank Lewis Gann, who cheerfully read two drafts of the manuscript and contributed important suggestions, ideas, and bibliographic references, and Professor Gordon Craig, for whose comments I am particularly grateful, since we disagree on important aspects of the issues discussed. Alain Besançon, Arnold Beichman, and Albert Wohlstetter also provided ideas, frequently in stimulating conversation. Needless to say, neither they nor anyone else bears any responsibility for the remaining faults or for my personal judgments or proposals.

Finally, I take great pleasure in thanking my wife, Jessica, for bearing with my strange working habits with increasing good humor. The work has benefited more than it deserves from her help and support.

INTRODUCTION

When the United States, Great Britain, and France granted sovereignty to the western zones of occupied Germany in 1949 and permitted their union as the Federal Republic, it was generally assumed that the new state was merely a provisional institution pending a final settlement between the Western Allies and the Soviet Union that would allow the establishment of a democratic constitutional state for all German citizens. The Basic Law of the Federal Republic called on "all Germans to complete the unity of Germany"; some Christian Democrats even suggested that the new federal government should be installed in barracks next to the demarcation line separating the Western and Soviet zones of occupation to demonstrate its provisional character. Even so, there were those, especially in the Social Democratic Party (SPD), who, for various reasons, feared that a West German state per se precluded Soviet acceptance of unification. Thus the debate (which had begun the instant the National Socialist regime was destroyed in 1945) about the political constitution and foreign policy of the new Germany continued on a new level.

West Germany joined the Atlantic Alliance in 1955 and was allowed to establish its own armed forces (under the supervision of the West European Union), though it was specifically forbidden to manufacture or deploy nuclear weapons on its own. This followed a round of agitation and debate between those who agreed with the government and its leader, Konrad Adenauer, that there was no hope of unity without the guarantee of liberty and who therefore put defense and Western solidarity first, and those who believed that Western integration would provoke the Soviet Union and allow it to strengthen its hold on Eastern Europe and particularly East Germany, thus exacerbating the tensions of division and endangering peace. Until 1960, the SPD officially supported the latter argument as well as various disarmament and denuclearization proposals that were forthcoming from Eastern Europe and from neutralist circles in the West.

In the 1960s, both the government and the SPD modified their positions. The essential commitment of the Christian Democratic Union (CDU) to unification but not at the price of liberty was obscured by its increasing focus on domestic issues and on West European integration; the SPD gradually abandoned its insistence on political unification and now hoped only that cultural unity could be preserved by official acceptance of the status quo of division. However, in doing so, the Social Democrats were tacitly accepting the permanent political division of the continent and thereby acquiescing in the foremost aim of Soviet policy in Europe. The question was whether this acquiescence, which included recognition of East Germany as a "separate state on German soil", would not in fact harm the cause of peace and security by legitimating the undemocratic and illegitimate East German regime, merely in return for unilaterally revocable promises of improved contacts.

During their tenure (1969–1982), the Social Democrats nevertheless pursued their *Ostpolitik* (literally, Eastern policy, though now defined substantively as a policy of seeking good official relations with Eastern regimes) and offered the East German government trade, gifts, and ransom money in return for humanitarian improvements. These included promises, not always fulfilled, of easier postal and telephone communications, more frequent permits for old (retired) East Germans to visit relatives in the West, and the easing of restrictions on visits by Germans living in the West to relatives in the East. Ostpolitik, and the Western effort to achieve détente, thus became a one-way street, at least as far as Europe was concerned. The West offered guarantees and concessions designed to reassure the Soviets that the political system established by the Soviet Union in Eastern and Central Europe in 1944–1948 was safe, but was unable to ensure Soviet compliance with Western interests and demands for the respect of human rights.

In the mid-1970s, the issue of national unification resurfaced in new and unexpected forms. Some West German critics, including some individuals who had actively opposed Adenauer's policies in the 1950s, now asserted that the responsibility for division rested at least as much with the United States and with Adenauer as with the Soviet Union. This attitude made agreement between the United States and some of its allies, including the Federal Republic, on the understanding of Soviet purposes and hence of the means and goals of détente, much more difficult. Combined with the revival of debate over the national issue in West Germany, it led, in the wake of NATO's double-track decision of December 1979 (to modernize defense while negotiating arms reductions), to the agitation, demonstrations, recriminations, and increasing mutual irritation of 1980–1983. Although the fear and anger that helped generate the peace movement against the double-track decision seem to have subsided somewhat since then, it is, in my view, a grave mistake to suppose that their causes have disappeared entirely. As long as Germany and Europe remain divided and as long as Central Europe remains a vital zone of East-West confrontation, chronic protests and expressions of impatience and resentment are not only to be expected, but are indeed perfectly comprehensible. What is less comprehensible is why the impatience and resentment are directed so overwhelmingly at the United States and the West German government, rather than at the true author and beneficiary of European division, namely the Soviet Union. The explanation for this is probably to be sought above all in cultural factors, some of which are analyzed in Part II of this book. Though purely psychological explanations for the behavior of the peace movement can be overdone, one particular element is certainly important, namely the mechanism of denial, whereby the true and obvious source of a problem is denied, that is, ignored, because it is either too difficult, fearsome, or hopeless to deal with. Instead, anger and resentment are directed against secondary, but vulnerable, targets, in this case Western governments and policies.

In this book, I begin in Part I by retelling the well-known story of reconstruction and the revival of faith in the possibility of constitutional democracy in West Germany after Hitler, although with a somewhat different emphasis. I try to determine the foundations, the constants, and the requirements of the postwar European order as it had been established by 1948. I then look in particular at the cultural environment of West German politics to determine the presuppositions of the debate over the maintenance of national security from the early 1950s through the 1970s. I focus on the changing national and security policy of the SPD, because it was the major coalition partner in government in 1969–1982 and because of its Ostpolitik and its belief in the combination of détente and deterrence, which is now the object of so much criticism by members of the peace movement (who call it "security conservatism") and by Atlanticists of all parties who worry about Soviet plans and purposes. In this context I also briefly examine the arguments for and against various kinds of deterrence that have been proposed since the founding of NATO, as well as the reasons why the deterrent strategy of NATO is now being criticized. Doubts of its efficacy and reliability are heard, paradoxically, not only from the peace movement, which considers any nuclear defense unacceptable, but from military experts who question the logic of a defense posture that, because it cannot reliably ward off conventional attack, must rely on nuclear weapons that are also overmatched by those of the Soviet Union. As the Soviet conventional and theater-nuclear arms buildup continued through the 1970s and early 1980s, NATO's strategy increasingly came to resemble "a gamble," as Henry Kissinger called it as early as 1961, "that a threat one is not, and one should not be, prepared to implement will never be challenged".[1]

In both subjective and objective ways, a series of factors have operated to create a definite crisis—of confidence, of strategy, of political options, and of Atlantic Alliance solidarity—that was in no way overcome by the victory of the "Union" parties (the Christian Democratic Union and the Christian Social Union, or CSU) in March of 1983. The most important were a deterrent that may be having the primary effect of "deterring the deterrer"; intense agitation by influential groups against the idea of a nuclear-based deterrent; cultural and political currents in West Germany, in which impatience with the established order, utopian ideals, and cool political logic interact; and a powerful intellectual establishment of the left that has never managed to accept the constitutional democratic order as it was constituted. Part II of the book is devoted to examining some of the ideological manifestations of this crisis: the denial of authority as a principle of political order in general and of the legitimacy of the West German state and economic system in particular, the moralization of politics, and the increasing polarization of positions. The most crucial question, however, is probably the question of what the peace movement actually means by "peace." How does the movement's definition and understanding of the word compare with peace as it exists in reality and has been defined at various periods of European history? How realistic are the chances of achieving the peace movement's "total" or "positive" peace, and will the single-minded attempt to pursue it not result instead in a confrontation with the civil authorities of, in this case, West Germany, thereby weakening the defensive posture and, perhaps, increasing the risk of war by indirectly encouraging Soviet moves? This danger has, it seems to me, been overlooked, possibly for diplomatic reasons, in debates on and with the peace movement, which is one more reason to take the movement and its implications seriously. This line of argument does not, of course, mean that I impute to the vast majority of those who march under the banners of the peace movement either the conscious preparation of civil war or subversion in the interests of the Soviet Union.[2]

One reason it is so difficult to predict policy formation and political behavior in West Germany or in any other Western country is that the old foreign policy consensus is gone; the old elites, if they still exist, are unable to command the support (or even sympathy) of large sectors of the populace and of the public media. Until well into the 1970s, policy in these countries was formulated by a small elite whose members had similar backgrounds and experience. Whatever the differences of perception or the political reasons for criticism of prevailing Alliance policies, there were common beliefs, a shared history: World War II and the collapse of the old European state-system; the U.S. role in the Allied victory and in postwar economic and political reconstruction; the realization that democratic systems were vulnerable from both within and without, both economically and politically; and the consequent appreciation of the urgency of West European integration. Few of those involved in active policy formation by the mid-1970s actually remembered the early postwar years; nevertheless, the consensus seemed to be holding. The "long march through the institutions," as West German radicals called their strategy for revolutionary social change beginning in the late 1960s, had resulted by the early 1980s in significant personnel and attitude changes in ministries of culture, education, communications, development aid, social services, health, and housing, but had hardly modified the policymaking core of the foreign ministries.

The enduring stability of the postwar political consensus was partly the legacy of the remarkable group of statesmen of early postwar Western Europe (Konrad Adenauer, Robert Schuman, Jean Monnet, Ludwig Erhard, Alcide De Gasperi, and Paul-Henri Spaak).[3] The tenures of most of these strong leaders had been long enough for them to develop mutual familiarity, if not genuine friendship, and their disagreements were always kept within bounds by the unshaken convictions that theirs was a community of danger, a *Schicksalsgemeinschaft*, and that if they did not stand together, they would most assuredly hang separately. They were not in all cases the heads of government of their respective countries, as was Konrad Adenauer, the archetypal "father of Europe" (he ruled as chancellor from 1949 to 1963, and his political career had begun before World War I). The weak political system of the Fourth French Republic meant that long-term policy formulation and consultation with allies and partners rested not with the head of state but with the leading ministers and civil servants whose positions were more permanent, such as Jean Monnet and Robert Schuman. However, the common commitment of these leaders to European defense, integration, and economic development, the relative absence of bureaucratic constraints, and above all the intimate and restricted nature of foreign policy formulation were the foundations of a political stability and consensus that has not prevailed since in the Alliance.

The explosive rise of the peace movement in West Germany and adjacent Alliance countries that began in 1979 was, in part, the result of changes that destroyed that stability and consensus. Since the mid-1970s, the vast expansion of government bureaucracies, the increasing prominence of issues of social and economic policy (and their cost), the difficulty of securing stable governing majorities and the combined problems of unemployment, inflation, and vastly increased governmental deficits had made policy formulation and execution more difficult. In the mid-1960s, the security of the West was taken for granted by the wider public and, as a problem of policy, had become the concern, in European NATO countries, of only a few high civil servants and ministers, all of whom had shared the experience of wartime and the immediate postwar era. Defense policy in West Germany largely kept this low profile even during the political and cultural conflicts that rent Western Europe in the late 1960s and early 1970s. However, gradually the intellectual (and sometimes physical) onslaught on existing conditions began to affect foreign policy. At first there was an increase in anti-American and anti-NATO propaganda, and many formerly pro-security and pro-defense media adopted a more "critical" line. The focus of controversy shifted to the inside of policymaking institutions when members of the rebellious generation of educators, bureaucrats, politicians, and journalists began their "long march through the institutions." The generation also included a number of politicians (who were less willing to support the existing defense and security policy and more skeptical of the need for either), and the simultaneous expression of new values and beliefs in the media, in higher education, and in public debate, had by the late 1970s largely undermined the policy consensus established by the earlier generation. Sustained only by its inertia, this consensus was vulnerable to the least shock.

What disappeared was not just a broad agreement on foreign and security policy. In West Germany, security as such was simply not an important issue for most people from the 1950s to the 1970s. If it was mentioned at all, it was as a set of general common principles, the most fundamental of which was an acceptance of the need for a defensive alliance to protect the democratic political and social system of Western Europe. What disappeared was also the broad popular consensus on the aims and values of social and economic policy, which had been shaped during the 1950s by the originally Christian Democratic idea of the "social market economy." In its Bad Godesberg program of 1959, the SPD had rejected its last remaining Marxist principles, chiefly the state ownership of the means of production, and when the party came to power in 1969, its chairman, Willy Brandt, declared that his intention was to extend the social market economy, not to destroy it, under the slogan "As much freedom as possible; as much regulation as necessary."

On the philosophical level, this broad consensus on public policy in West Germany had its roots in the revival and coalescence, in the immediate postwar years, of two philosophical and political traditions: the theory of natural law and the economic "neo-liberalism" of the Freiburg school of economic thinkers. Both natural law theory and economic liberalism had been in eclipse since the late nineteenth century, superseded respectively by the new school of legal positivism that rejected natural law as a dangerous form of unscientific metaphysical irrationalism, and by the belief, powerfully reinforced during the recession of 1873–1896, that the economy could and should be organized and directed by the state. Legal positivism, which was favored by socialist legal thinkers, and the state socialism of Germany's economy as it developed during World War I, both helped to prepare the ground for Hitler's regime and national socialism. The experience of Hitler's tyranny and the defeat of his regime, however, led many prominent legal thinkers to reassert natural law theory as not only reasonable but even necessary. As for German economic neo-liberalism (and its associated concept of the social market economy), it was an attempt to come to terms with what its adherents saw as the disasters, not only of collectivism – Nazi or communist – but also of old-fashioned free-market liberalism. In the social market economy, ideally, there is economic freedom, but within an overarching concept of political and social order that ensures that the advantages of the free market would accrue to all citizens.

The philosophy of the social market economy became the official policy of the CDU in 1949, and because Adenauer won the crucial first election of 1949, its principles were indeed applied.[4] The reconstruction of West Germany would certainly have taken a very different course if the SPD had formed the first government, since at the time that party was still committed to outright economic collectivism, as well as to the security and foreign policies that will be described below.

In the late 1970s, the strong anticommunism and the commitments to economic growth and to a broadly egalitarian social policy characteristic of the older generation of Social Democratic, liberal, and Christian Democratic politicians was replaced by a more strident egalitarianism, less faith in the ability of the capitalist system to provide economic satisfaction, and less belief in the value of or the need for collective defense within the Alliance. This is, roughly speaking, the core of the ideology of the "successor generation," defined (in the case of West Germany) as those born after 1950 who, by the mid-1980s, were beginning to achieve influence in government, the media, education, and even business.[5]

The breakdown of political consensus on domestic and foreign policy, distrust of NATO and opposition to the very idea of its existence, and the rise of the peace movement and its associated ideologies are particularly difficult problems in West Germany because of that country's peculiar political, cultural, and geographical situation. In this book I have tried to evaluate these new problems. In doing so, I have adopted a historical and philosophical approach. My main historical focus is the German national question, since it is the mainspring of the current agitation and unease in West Germany (although German observers do not always admit this). I discuss both the national policies and the attitudes of West German governments since the

war and the revival, since around 1978, of discussion of the national issue by
all political parties. In particular, I discuss the revival of the old argument,
first advanced in the late 1940s and early 1950s when the bases of West German foreign policy were being laid, that West German loyalty to the Alliance
is not necessarily in the best German or West German interest. This argument was made explicit in the electoral campaign of 1983, when the SPD
chose as its slogan "In the German Interest" (*im deutschen Interesse*), and
clearly implied that the modernization of intermediate nuclear forces (INF)
and the strengthening of Western defense, the justification of which the SPD
questioned, were not in that interest. The argument of the peace movement
that West Germany should refuse to allow INF modernization on its territory
is closely connected with the movement's agitation against deployment of
the new missiles. The movement claims that such deployment is part of a
NATO strategy aimed at confining nuclear war to Europe and that these missiles by their very existence make such war more likely. The logic of this
position depends on an acceptance of a number of propositions, which I
have summarized in Chapter 9. Its popularity, however, is also a result of
inconsistencies in the existing NATO defense posture and strategies.

As part of my philosophical approach, I have tried to relate the development of these ideas to cultural, political, and intellectual trends in contemporary civilization, which seem particularly marked in West Germany. The
ideas of the new neutralism are part of a *Zeitgeist*, a complex of attitudes and
expectations. This complex includes far more than beliefs about peace and
security. It is a combination of what one commentator has called "the
routinization of radicalism" and what another has called "premature
postindustrialism"–the mistaken belief that the material prosperity and
democratic stability of advanced industrial states no longer depend or
should depend primarily on industry. Consequently, the time has come to
stop worrying about production and to worry instead about distribution,
that is, about equality.[6]

In Chapter 10, I return to the issue of security and ask what the increasing influence of these new attitudes and beliefs in West German politics implies for the future. The collapse of the Atlanticist wing of the SPD, which
is closely paralleled by analogous developments in the British Labour Party,
in Scandinavian Social Democratic parties, and, most important, in the
Democratic Party of the United States, will undoubtedly have far-reaching
effects on the shape of West German foreign and security policy, including
Ostpolitik, relations with Eastern Europe, and relations with the United
States. Since the old security consensus has clearly broken down, the most
promising task for those concerned with European security and transatlantic
relations may well be to work for some form of more autonomous European
defense, an idea that, by the mid-1980s, was being promoted by an impressive

range of experts, military as well as civilian, American as well as European.[7]
Another, equally pressing task is to begin a dialogue with those more
thoughtful critics of the Alliance and of Western strategy who are searching,
however vaguely, for a European identity. Though they are often unrealistic
and unfair in their judgments, their indignation and their hopes can be
shared by all those committed to the peace and survival of Europe.

ACRONYMS

CDU   Christlich-Demokratische Union (Christian Democratic Union, the West German conservative party)

CSU   Christlich-Soziale Union (Christian Social Union, the German conservative party in Bavaria)

DKP   Deutsche Kommunistische Partei (German Communist Party, the reorganized Communist Party in West Germany after 1969)

EDC   European Defense Community

EKD   Evangelische Kirche in Deutschland (Evangelical, that Lutheran, Church in Germany)

FDP   Freie Demokratische Partei (Free Democratic Party, the West German liberal party)

FOFA   Follow-On Forces Attack

ICBM   Intercontinental ballistic missile

INF   Intermediate nuclear forces

IRBM   Intermediate-range ballistic missile

KPD   Kommunistische Partei Deutschlands (Communist Party of Germany, so called until its prohibition by law in West Germany in 1956; in the Soviet Zone, the KPD had merged with the SPD in 1946 to form the SED)

SED   Sozialistische Einheitspartei Deutschlands (Socialist Unity Party of
       Germany, the communist party in the Soviet Zone/East Germany
       after 1946)

SPD   Sozialdemokratische Partei Deutschlands (Social Democratic Party of
       Germany)

I

THE POLITICAL
AND STRATEGIC
CONTEXT

1

THE PREMISES OF
WEST GERMAN NATIONAL
AND SECURITY POLICY

German history since 1945, in East as well as West, has been almost wholly determined by the momentous events of that year, which marked one of the few genuine turning points in world history.[1] Those events, and their results, can usefully be discussed under five headings.

First, there was the fact of the total defeat, not only of Hitler and of National Socialism as an ideology and a political movement, but of the German state and its armed forces. In the Casablanca declaration of February 1943 and in subsequent statements, the Allies had explicitly refused to distinguish between the two and had identified the German state and people with the Nazi regime that deserved to be destroyed. The most important result of this was to deny the German resistance to Hitler, which sought a negotiated end to the war and the survival of a recognizable and legitimate German state, any moral standing in Allied eyes. Furthermore, the Allied identification of people and regime made it far more difficult for the resistance to gain support and operate within Germany since many individuals who might have been willing to join in fact remained loyal to Hitler and the regime. As they saw it, in accordance with the Prussian professional and military ethic that was their moral standard, the Allied position put them in an intolerable dilemma. They would have preferred to overthrow the regime and establish a legitimate German government, even though such an act would be a betrayal of the fundamental Lutheran and Prussian principle that the state, whatever its regime, especially in an emergency such as war, has a presumptive claim on the loyalty of its subjects. However, the Allies were now understood to have said that *any* German government would have to surrender unconditionally to end the war. Therefore, for any German to betray the state would not only be treason—objectively, as well as in the eyes of the Nazis—but also pointless. Most of the adherents of the various resistance groups that flourished in the earlier war years accordingly withdrew, leaving only the men of the Stauffenberg group who tried to assassinate Hitler and stage a coup d'etat on July 20, 1944.

Nazi propaganda also made effective use of the Allied declarations in demanding, and getting, loyalty and sacrifices from a populace that, in 1933, at the time of the last free elections, had only been 43 percent National Socialist. The simple anger and fury inspired by the Allied bomber offensive in ordinary people were obviously important, and certainly the Prussian ethic of solidarity with the state in times of emergency also played a part. Whatever the exact causes in each individual case, the fact was that there was no civil unrest, no massive disaffection, and almost no individual acts of rebellion, at least not until the very last months. The extent to which a different Allied position—one encouraging resistance and opposition—would have changed the situation in Germany itself can, of course, never be known. However, there can be little doubt that the Allied position as it was strengthened and encouraged the identification of the vast majority of ordinary Germans with the regime, until, and only until, the moment it ceased to exist.

When the war ended and the true dimensions of the atrocities perpetrated by the regime began coming to light, this wartime loyalty of the German populace was regarded by most in the West as confirming the demonic picture of the evil German that had been propagated during the fighting. Many American and other writers began to condemn Germans throughout history for their fatal departure from Western ways and denounced German political and cultural figures from Luther to Bismarck as forerunners of Hitler. At the same time, many German writers went beyond the mere rejection of National Socialism and also searched for the roots of the "wrong turn" in the distant past. Ernst Niekisch, the former "National Bolshevik" who had tried to combine Leninism with extreme nationalism, spoke of "Germany's existential failure" (*deutsche Daseinsverfehlung*), which had resulted in Germany's justified annihilation, whereas the historian and former National Socialist Otto Westphal, in a work published posthumously in 1953, repented of his and Germany's ways and claimed that the only future for Germany was as a province of a united Europe.[2] The most celebrated of these early reappraisals was *Die deutsche Katastrophe* (1946), by the aged historian Friedrich Meinecke, who anticipated Western historians by tracing the origins of the fatal departure to Bismarck, whose tremendous political achievement of unification was now seen to be outweighed by his flaws of character, his separation of ethics and politics, and his authoritarianism, which depoliticized the middle classes and reinforced the fatal Romantic concentration on *Bildung* (apolitical, spiritual self-enrichment) at the expense of political involvement and responsibility. Simultaneously, however, some sociologists, believing that Meinecke's intense moral concern was, in fact, itself an example of apolitical romanticism, argued for a supposedly more scientific explanation. They saw the failure of democracy in united Germany as related to Germany's "delayed statehood." The principal work in this tradition was Hellmuth Plessner's *Die verspätete Nation*, subtitled *Studies in the Seducibility of the Bourgeois Spirit*, which he wrote while in exile in Holland in the 1930s and which was reissued in 1959.[3]

Of course, this "ideology of defeat" and its components (the rejection of history, the belief that all native philosophical and political traditions were now tainted or, at best, morally dubious, and the deep suspicion of all authority—or rather, the refusal to distinguish between just and unjust authority) makes a great deal of sense when one recalls the second great fact of 1945: the revelation of the Nazi crimes, the realization that the regime that had just been destroyed and that had commanded the loyalty, if not the affection, of the overwhelming majority of Germans had deliberately organized and carried out the murder of 6 million Jews throughout Europe and had brutally imprisoned and murdered uncounted thousands of others. The impact of this revelation was at least as great as that of the military and political defeat, and was combined with it in the public mind. As one historian put it in the mid-1960s:

> Probably no modern European nation has until now been confronted in its history by as radical a military, political, and spiritual bankruptcy as the Germans have been after the end of the Hitler regime. For here it was not merely a question of a state falling apart (*Staatszerbrechen*) such as France experienced several times since the French Revolution, but of a state falling apart burdened by crimes of state (*Staatsverbrechen*) of an unimaginable dimension.[4]

The reality of the "state falling apart burdened by crimes of state" conferred on West German politics a peculiar moral burden. It is remarkable, however, that this moral burden, far from growing lighter with time and ultimately losing its influence on the political culture, in fact became very much of an issue beginning in the later 1960s. The student activism of 1967 and after, the emergence of dozens of radical sects and groupings, and the slower growth throughout the 1970s of movements against nuclear energy and other forms of industrial activity, and, finally, the peace movement itself, were all powerfully motivated by this moralism. Why was its full effect so delayed? One important reason was that the political leaders of the early postwar years (such as Adenauer, Kurt Schumacher, Ludwig Erhard, and Erich Mende) had all been convinced opponents of the Nazi regime and free of any suspicion of collaboration in its iniquities. Although they shared the moral burden of all Germans and indeed spoke of it with a sense of tragedy and responsibility often lacking in the rhetoric of the 1970s and after, they were able to put it aside and did not let it affect the practical conduct of politics. Twenty years later, the memories of 1945 were growing dim and economic reconstruction had been successfully completed; yet paradoxically this very success, the very stability of the new regime, made the new moralism plausible. As one German critic ironically pointed out, it was an attack, not on the grandparents who voted for Hitler, but on the parents, the rebuilders of Germany (middle-aged by the later 1960s), because they had not revolted themselves.[5] These parents, born in the 1920s and early 1930s, were too young to have helped actively to build or support the regime, but old enough that war, defeat, the loss of close friends and relatives, and, in many cases, of the family's home and property as well were their fundamental, formative experiences. They were shaped by those events, so much so that the sociologist Helmut Schelsky in a famous study of 1955 defined them as the "skeptical generation."[6] The cataclysm of defeat and the subsequent struggle for material survival depoliticized and deideologized them, so much so that their children, the generation of protest, mistakenly assumed that their parents were deficient in political awareness or even morality. The alleged "inability to mourn" of the generation that accomplished the economic miracle was seen by its children—those born in the later 1940s and after—as an attempt at exculpation and as a failure to "overcome the past." In thus distorting history, the successors, in their dissatisfaction with a political situation wholly different from that of the 1940s, overlooked the very real "overcoming" that took place in the immediate postwar years. The final effect of the second fact of 1945—the revelation of the Holocaust—was, then, delayed. In the immediate postwar years, there was the tremendous sense of shock, horror, and shame, and the acceptance of the Nuremberg Trials as a cleansing purification. After reconstruction had got under way in the early 1950s and the "skeptical generation" began to take over in government, education, and business, the dramatic issues of the early years lost their prominence. Then, beginning in the mid-1960s, the student rebels at West German universities reopened the issue of Nazism, its origins, and its deeds. One of the prominent themes of this new moralism was that the West German state and West German society were explicitly accused of being "proto-fascist," that is, not much better, in principle, than the regime of Hitler. In this deliberately provocative comparison of a constitutional democracy with a totalitarian tyranny, the new moralists explicitly denied that the difference between democracy and totalitarianism was meaningful; indeed, many neo-Marxist and other leftist writers denounced "totalitarianism" as a concept invented by American political scientists in order to identify the Soviet Union with Nazi Germany for cold war purposes. The only important feature of a social system, these writers argued, was the economy; since private ownership of the means of production prevailed both in Nazi Germany and in contemporary West Germany, therefore they were alike in essentials, and a new form of Nazi or, as it was always called, "fascist" dictatorship, might emerge at any moment. The peace movement has taken over a good deal of this extreme hostility to the West German social and political system. Not only does this clearly show that the movement is indeed descended from the agitation and activism of the late 1960s; it also helps explain why so many in the peace movement are much more actively and insistently opposed to Western defense and Western policies than they are to the activities of the Soviet Union.

The third fact of 1945, which had a decisive effect on the postwar order in Germany and Europe, was the collapse of the wartime alliance between the United States, Britain, and the Soviet Union, which had been united only by the war against Germany. America and Britain had fought the war to survive and to preserve their own democratic institutions. Postwar aims and plans were deliberately left vague, and when Churchill, who was most concerned to maintain Western interests, attempted to influence the planning and conduct of operations to protect them, he was overruled by Roosevelt, who, mistakenly as it turned out, believed that, if Stalin could be appeased by concessions, he would cooperate with the West in constructing a peaceful postwar order. The latter, however, had far more precise aims, which Adam Ulam has summarized as a "traditional policy of expansion, tempered by the need for coexistence"[7] — the extension of Soviet power and of direct Soviet military control as far westward as possible; the permanent destruction of Germany as an independent political entity and the absolute predominance of the Soviet Union as the main continental European power; the establishment of loyal communist regimes in Eastern Europe and, if possible, in Germany and Western Europe as well, so as to deny the capitalist powers the resources of Europe for the future wars he foresaw. In short, Stalin sought to achieve the greatest possible Soviet influence in the postwar world with a view to the inevitable showdown with capitalism. These aims are evident in hindsight and were so even at the time to some observers. Even before the German surrender in May 1945, the incompatibility of Stalin's plans for postwar Europe with the vague and general principles bequeathed by Roosevelt to Truman was clear. The ruthless efficiency with which the trained cadres unleashed by Stalin established communist rule in Eastern Europe (including the Soviet zone of Germany), within days and weeks of the arrival of the Red Army made it clear that they had no intention of relinquishing or modifying their authority. In general, the political landscape of Europe east of the Elbe that still existed in the mid-1980s had been pretty well established by the end of 1945; the modifications made since then have been trivial. Most important for our purposes, the Soviet hegemony entailed what became the main issue of postwar European history, namely the division of Germany.

The two remaining aspects of the situation of 1945 were, in a sense, derivative of those aspects already mentioned. There was, first, the flight (in 1945) and expulsion (in 1945–1951) of virtually all the native inhabitants of the regions of Germany east of the Oder and Görlitzer Neisse rivers (that is, East and West Prussia, Danzig, Pomerania, East Brandenburg and Upper and Lower Silesia), a total of 11 million people from lands of great economic and industrial significance and rich in cultural heritage and tradition, including the ancient cities of Königsberg, Stettin, and Breslau.[8] Another 5 million were expelled in 1945–1950 with extreme brutality and much bloodshed from the Sudetenland and other areas of East Central Europe with substantial German populations. About 2 million others perished in flight or were killed by Red Army soldiers or local non-Germans. The arrival of this vast number of refugees in the Western zones had, by the end of 1948, increased their population by one-fourth and in the long term permanently changed the demography of what would later become the Federal Republic. In the 1970s, 60 million people inhabited the area formerly inhabited by 40 million. Much of the territory in the Northeast and East that was lost in 1945 was thinly populated, and most of the cultural and industrial centers of old Germany were in what is now the Federal Republic; nevertheless, in the long run, the increase in population density and the loss of access to the East—what the cultural sociologist Alfred Weber called the "loss of breathing room"—undermined the Germans' sense of rootedness, of security, and geographical continuity. Weber saw this loss of physical space as a loss also of *Kulturraum*, cultural space—specifically, the old Central European civilization, which had been based on two elites, now both destroyed: the Jews and the East German aristocracy. It is interesting to note that one of the minor themes of the cultural rebellion against Western integration and Western policies, including defense policy, in the 1980s was a dream of reviving some sort of Central European culture. Needless to say, such a dream is incapable of fulfilment since the two elites cannot be resurrected.[9]

The last aspect was, quite simply, the vast amount of destitution and destruction. The bureaucratic institutions of the ruined Reich ceased to exist after the surrender, and chaos prevailed. What little industry was left could not operate for lack of capital and supplies, the last of the railways stopped moving, and general economic activity came to a virtual standstill. In 1946 and 1947 real poverty and hunger were no mere specters in Germany, and during the harsh winter of 1946–47 many people froze to death. There is general agreement that material conditions were at their worst, not during the war itself, but in 1946–47, when there seemed no way of getting things going again. The strict separation of the occupation zones and the variations in policy of the occupying powers aggravated the situation: in the Soviet zone, there was organized and vindictive looting; in the French zone, harsh prohibitions and regulations were imposed, designed to humble and to punish, albeit much less brutally than in the East; in the British and U.S. zones, an initial policy of strict separation of Germans and occupiers gave way, beginning in 1946, to a more pragmatic approach, the first result of which was the bizonal economic area, established in January 1947, within which movement was relatively unrestricted and even some economic activity was soon allowed.[10] It was not, however, until the French began to lift some of their restrictions and all three Western powers agreed that the Soviets were not interested in any sort of cooperation for mutual benefit that Ludwig Erhard was allowed to prime the engine of reconstruction with the currency reform of June 1948, which at a stroke wiped out all debts (and liquid savings as well), destroyed the black market, and cleaned the slate for serious investment and production.

TOWARDS AUTONOMY

The breakdown of Allied unity after the victory—or rather the basic incompatibility of Western and Soviet strategic and political aims from the beginning—raised two issues for which the British and American leadership and public opinion were very ill prepared. There was, first, the question of how to react to Soviet behavior and Soviet policies in general, a question that for many was still bound up with the general question of understanding what was going on behind the Soviet lines in Europe at all. And second, there was the issue of what to do about Germany: to continue occupation indefinitely, seeking contact and compromise with the Soviets in the hope of achieving a final settlement of the German and European problems acceptable to all parties, or to allow some degree of political autonomy in the Western zones at the risk of an irrevocable break with the East. Throughout 1946 and 1947, adherents of these two views struggled for control of policy in Western governments, while the more general problem of European reconstruction and the desperate need of the continental countries for supplies of food, equipment, and liquid capital became ever more urgent.[11]

Meanwhile, some Germans at least were also beginning to take an interest in their political fate. In the East, German Communists who had spent the war years in exile in Moscow had already set up the framework of rule and were trying to expand it, chiefly by infiltrating the SPD in Berlin and the Western zones.[12] It was clear to the politically aware in the Western zones that the chances of establishing a viable democratic regime in any part of Germany depended on German, and not primarily Allied, action. Already, political parties had been formed: the Christian Democratic Union, composed mainly of remnants of the conservative and confessional parties of the Weimar Republic, who had a pronounced religious and ethical commitment that, for some, notably Jakob Kaiser, verged on a "Christian socialism" inspired by the communitarian ideas of the German Resistance; and the liberal Free Democratic Party (FDP).[13]

Establishing the organizations of a democratic party system was not easy, even in the Western zones. At the outset, political activity was locally and regionally based. This was partly because communication between zones and even between towns and districts within zones was at first forbidden or extremely difficult and remained so until 1948. It was also a result of the absence, since 1933, of a national party system, and of the revival of old regional patterns of loyalty and outlook. The success of Adenauer is partly explained by the fact that he began his career as a municipal politician and mayor of Cologne, and his reputation had therefore not been tarnished by the failure of the national politicians of the late Weimar period (1930–1933). The revival of regionalism was particularly marked in Bavaria, a state with a history far longer than Prussia's that had been eclipsed by the dominant northern state during the period of confederation and imperial unification (1815–1945). Prussia was now territorially, culturally, and politically destroyed, and the system for which it had stood had been discredited. Bavaria was the only German state left intact in 1945 and, moreover, was wholly in the U.S. zone. As a result, a feeling of identity and pride resurfaced among south Germans. To the extent that the Federal Republic had and has a cultural capital, it is the old political capital and royal residence city of Munich. But the very strength of Bavaria as the largest *Land* in West Germany made the early planners wary of locating the political center in Munich as well. They had no intention of repeating the mistake of allowing the largest state to overshadow other regions and provinces, as Prussia had. There was also a fear of Catholic dominance over the Protestants in the northern and southwestern regions of the Western zones. In the old Reich as a whole, Protestants had retained a comfortable majority; after 1945 their numbers, even though increased by the refugees from the eastern territories, barely exceeded those of the Catholics.

The Social Democratic leader, Kurt Schumacher, physically broken by his long imprisonment in concentration camps but intellectually and politically more alive than ever, insisted for a time on the possibility of an all-German democratic, neutral, and socialist regime. He genuinely believed that only a unified Germany could contribute to peace in Europe; he also knew that before 1933 the SPD had never, or rarely, been as predominant in any of the areas in the Western zones as it had been in central Germany—Berlin, Saxony, Thuringia—or in Silesia. The Catholic vote, which had always been found mainly in Bavaria and the Rhineland, and the strength of organized Protestantism were both obstacles to any future success of the SPD. However, Schumacher saw quite soon that in view of communist practices in the Soviet zone, especially the absorption and destruction of the SPD in 1946, the only chance for democratic socialism in Germany lay in a commitment to a West German state in which its ideals might be realized. Schumacher's relations with the Allies, especially the Americans, were truly appalling, not so much because of a conflict of ultimate aims, but rather because of his abrasive personality, his peculiarly German combination of nationalism and socialism, and his impatience with delay.[14] His relations were not much better with the Christian Democratic leaders. For example, Adenauer, a Catholic Rhinelander with a deep suspicion (justified by events) of Prussians and of the military, frequently found Schumacher's Prussian background (he was a World War I officer) and his constant emphasizing of the national issue too much to bear.

These, however, were minor obstacles. By the end of 1947, most British and U.S. administrators in West Germany favored the re-establishment of some degree of political autonomy. Secretary of State James F. Byrnes's Stuttgart speech in late 1946 on the importance of European unity and, even more important in domestic U.S. politics, the former isolationist Senator Vandenberg's speech of March 1948 on the Marshall Plan (or, as it was formally called, the European Recovery Program) emphasized the importance of European integration and recovery for the preservation of democracy in those countries where it was still found. However, hopes that European reconstruction could be effected in cooperation with the Soviets and for the benefit of East Europeans as well, as had been originally proposed, were dashed by Soviet refusals and, more obviously, by Soviet actions.[15]

In Germany particularly, the universal desire that reconstruction and political reorganization take place throughout Germany, and with the active participation of all Germans, was replaced by the somber realization that this was simply not possible, or at least was possible only on the unacceptable condition that the Western Allies yield control of the Western zones to a neutral German administration that would, in fact, be a tool of the Soviet Union. The creation of the Federal Republic in 1949 was a provisional measure; according to the preamble to the Basic Law, officially proclaimed on May 23, 1949, it was established by "the German people in the lands of Baden, Bavaria, Bremen, Hamburg, Hesse, Lower Saxony, North Rhine-Westphalia, the Rhineland-Palatinate, Schleswig-Holstein, Württemberg-

Baden and Württemberg-Hohenzollern . . . acting also for those Germans who have been prevented from taking part. The entire German people remains called to realize the unity and freedom of Germany." The lack of any other real options and the relief with which the British and the Americans returned domestic sovereignty to legitimate native authorities disprove two critical assertions that were made at the time and were being made in the 1980s: first, that the West German state was deliberately established by capitalist interests and parties (Adenauer and the CDU in alliance with the leaders of heavy industry) to prevent a unified, socialist Germany, and second, that the Allied powers helped this process over the heads of and against the will of the German people, intending to use the new state in their conflict with the Soviet Union. Both assertions became stock elements of East German and Soviet propaganda, but they were also occasionally repeated in West Germany by those whose understandable desire for unification was combined with a refusal to face facts.

To be sovereign in international law, a state must have an independent foreign policy and the freedom to establish and maintain armed forces in whatever form and having available whatever weapons are deemed necessary for security. On those two counts, clearly, the Federal Republic was not sovereign when created, nor is it now. Formulation of its foreign policy was restricted by the moral and political heritage of World War II, national division, and the threat from the East.[16] In the matter of national defense, the heritage of the war was an even more sensitive issue, for many Germans had no desire to see their countrymen in uniform ever again. On the other hand, the Americans and the British, and even, in time, the French, admitted that without a contribution from the Germans in the Western zones, the defense and security of Western Europe could scarcely be assured. At the time the Federal Republic was established, therefore, the discussion no longer turned on whether its territory should be defended, but on who should do it and where the ultimate political control of the forces involved should lie. In April 1949, the North Atlantic Treaty was signed in Washington, establishing a supranational military organization—NATO—with military contributions from all member states, whose governments shared jointly in the control of the organization and its forces.[17]

From the very beginning it was clear that if NATO were to guarantee the security of West Germany, some form of West German participation in the defense effort would be necessary. Neither the United States alone, nor a combination of the Allied forces in West Germany, were considered adequate to meet any real emergency. Once NATO was established, therefore, the United States began to press its European allies to allow some West German rearmament. By far the strongest opposition to this came, as one would expect, from France. To avoid the creation of a West German army that might one day come under the sovereign control of the West German government, the French premier, René Pleven, proposed in October 1950 a plan for a European Defense Community (EDC), which would be subsidiary to NATO but would have its own political and command structure.[18] The organization would be concerned entirely with the security of Western Europe, but would, because of its scope, be a more equal partner of the United States than the European allies individually in the general planning and administration of the Alliance. Advocates of the EDC concept also thought that it would help the cause of European integration in general, something that all responsible leaders, including the Americans, strongly supported.[19] What could be more reasonable than that the West German forces to be established be allocated to the EDC, thus eliminating the need for a national command that might disturb other Europeans as well as provide welcome ammunition to Soviet propaganda? The only genuine opposition to this idea in West Germany itself came from former Wehrmacht officers, whose arguments were automatically discredited; the more foresighted of them (such as Hans Speidel) welcomed the idea, however, and were extremely disappointed by its failure.[20] Although the original proposal had been French, it was the French parliament that finally rejected the plan in August 1954, chiefly on the grounds that it would infringe national sovereignty. Having themselves destroyed the EDC, however, the French were now in no position to refuse the other option: direct admission of the Federal Republic to the Atlantic Alliance.

Although admission to NATO meant that the principal responsibility for security devolved on the West German government, which consequently was required to establish an army (the *Bundeswehr*), the military sovereignty of the former occupying powers was not wholly relinquished. All three of them still maintained troops on West German territory in the 1980s. Furthermore, even with the addition of West German forces, NATO was not regarded by its own military and political leaders as capable of repulsing a Soviet conventional attack in kind. This basic inadequacy in conventional forces was voluntarily accepted at the Lisbon conference of 1952, when military experts argued that a reliable conventional defense posture in Europe would require 96 divisions and 9,000 aircraft, which was almost twice what was available at the time. Consequently, NATO decided deliberately to rely for its security guarantee on U.S. nuclear forces and in 1954 decided to deploy tactical nuclear weapons in West Germany. These weapons are ultimately controlled not by NATO, but by the American "national command authorities," that is, the president or his deputy, in accordance with the general principles governing the use of nuclear weapons. Furthermore, a condition of Alliance membership for West Germany was that West Germany would not itself develop or deploy nuclear, chemical, or biological weapons while accepting that its security depended in large part on the deterrent effect of such weapons in the hands of its allies. This self-denial of sovereignty, coupled with acceptance of American-controlled nuclear weapons on West German territory, was one of the two main issues in the security debate in West Germany from the mid-1950s onward. The other was the national issue. The conflict between the belief in *Westintegration* (that is, membership not only in the Alliance but in the Common Market) and a policy aiming at national unity was unavoidable from the outset and has determined the choices and perceptions of politicians as well as of the general public ever since.

THE NATIONAL JUSTIFICATION OF THE HALLSTEIN DOCTRINE

When West Germany joined the Alliance in 1955, Adenauer and his government did not regard it as prejudicial to their national policy or as implying that reunification was not their overarching political goal. The premises of his position were two: first, that the pursuit of unification did not exclude but in fact required the independence of West Germany, and only the Alliance could guarantee this. Unification at the price of neutralization was not a viable option, although it has been presented as such at various times, notably in the early 1950s and again in the 1980s. The belief that the Soviet Union would allow a neutral Germany to possess a free political system and democratic institutions is based, at best, on assumptions about Soviet desires and policies that are, in the nature of things, unprovable. Supporters of this belief have referred above all to Stalin's so-called diplomatic note offensive of 1952, in which he proposed negotiations leading to a peace treaty with a unified, neutral, but not disarmed, Germany, as well as free elections. As Adam Ulam says, "It is impossible to determine the exact proportions of propaganda vs. a serious bargaining offer in the Soviet proposals." Did the Soviets consider the prospect of a large West German army, allied to the United States, so dangerous that they were in fact willing to "throw their East German regime to the wolves" if, as a result, West German rearmament could be prevented? In my opinion, they hoped rather to upset Western planning; if the United States, Britain, and France had chosen to reopen negotiations, plans for the EDC and for organizing West German forces would have come to a halt, and even if a neutral Germany had been established, the Soviets would certainly have used every means available to exploit its neutrality in their interest. Whatever the true Soviet plans and motives, the "note offensive" became the source of a fruitful and enduring West German legend of lost opportunity, which has been resurrected in some quarters of the peace movement as further evidence of Western opposition to the true interests of peace in Europe.[21]

The second premise of Adenauer's position, which followed from the first, was that a delay in deciding West Germany's status and determining its relations with NATO as well as with the Soviet Union could only harm its security by giving the Soviets the impression that the Federal Republic was politically vulnerable.[22] Adenauer took this second premise seriously, as was indicated by his visit to Moscow in the same year (1955) that West Germany joined NATO. The visit had both a general and a particular purpose. The former was to establish diplomatic relations, while demonstrating that the Federal Republic was now an independent actor in international politics and confirming to the Soviets that West Germany's claim to speak for all Germans and its commitment to reunification had not changed. The particular purpose was to secure the release of German prisoners of war who were still being held in the Soviet Union ten years after the end of hostilities. This purpose was largely achieved: virtually all surviving POWs were returned to West Germany the following year. Adenauer rightly regarded bringing home the prisoners, who had suffered horribly in the Soviet camps, as one of his greatest triumphs, and there is no doubt that it contributed mightily to the success of the CDU-CSU in the 1957 elections, in which they obtained a majority of the popular vote.

In accordance with his national policy, Adenauer did not consider it morally or politically justified to grant legitimacy to the East German communist regime. The logic of this refusal was made clear in the Hallstein Doctrine (named after Walter Hallstein, a senior official of the Foreign Ministry), which was first clearly formulated by Adenauer in a speech to the Bundestag in September 1955: "The Federal Republic will view the establishment of diplomatic relations with the so-called German Democratic Republic by third parties as an unfriendly act tending to aggravate the division of Germany."[23] This doctrine flowed from the principle, enunciated in the Basic Law, that the Federal Republic was the sole legitimate representative of the German people and of their national will (*Alleinvertretungsanspruch*, the "claim of sole representation"). The de jure recognition of the East German regime as a political entity could not but harm the credibility of this claim and, in consequence, the cause of national unity as well. West German governments, until the policy changes in the late 1960s, therefore insisted that nonrecognition of the Pankow regime was a condition of friendly relations with them and refrained from establishing diplomatic relations with states of the Soviet bloc that, of course, recognized East Germany (recognition of the Soviet Union, however, could be said to be required for reasons of state). In constitutional theory, the Alleinvertretungsanspruch depended on the further claim that the Federal Republic was the temporary legal representative of the unified German state, the Reich, which had lost its ability to govern and otherwise to exercise its sovereignty in diplomatic relations when the German armed forces surrendered on May 7, 1945, but which continued to exist in principle and in law.[24]

A consequence of this theory was and is the principle that German citizenship is unitary; that is, any German inhabitant of East Germany has all the rights and duties of his compatriots in the West. The East German regime is properly regarded as an illegal organization engaged in depriving those Germans unfortunate enough to live under its domination of their constitutional rights of freedom of thought, expression, and movement. Any German released or escaped from East German territory (or freed by ransom) at once enters into the full enjoyment of these rights, including the right to work and the right to medical and social services. Although this argument was, by the 1980s, no longer officially stressed, even by those who claimed to be acting in the German interest, and West Germany itself had recognized East Germany (though not as an independent state) in 1972, it is hard to see how it could have lost its force, unless the passage of time in itself is assumed to change the principles of constitutional law.[25]

I have described the theory that was the basis of the Hallstein Doctrine and Adenauer's national policy to show the consistency of his position and his loyalty to the letter and spirit of the Basic Law. His national policy can be described as a policy of principle, the principle being unification in freedom through strength, although no one was willing to state the conditions under which the principle might be put into practice. The purpose of the Atlantic Alliance was purely defensive, and the North Atlantic Treaty explicitly excluded any offensive act, even (and perhaps especially) in the cause of German unification. In retrospect, it may well seem that the only real opportunity the West ever had to bring about German unification and the end of Soviet dominance in Eastern Europe (which were, after all, the supposed aims of U.S. policy in the period of "rollback" in the early to mid-1950s) was in the years 1953–1956 (from the death of Stalin and the East German workers' uprising on June 17, 1953, to Khrushchev's consolidation of power at the Twentieth Party Congress in early 1956). The uprising spurred brief hopes of reunification that were as briefly dashed. After the failure of the last Four-Power conference on Germany, held in Berlin in January 1954, and the admission of West Germany to NATO in the following year, the atmosphere began to change perceptibly.

NATIONAL POLICY AND RELATED ISSUES SINCE 1955

In the rest of this chapter, I shall deal briefly with the changes in government policy that preceded the advent of the new Ostpolitik. The attitude of the SPD during this time is the subject of the following chapter.

Adenauer's principles—the demands for reunification and for restoration of the German state within its frontiers of 1937 as a precondition for free elections and a peace treaty—were officially maintained by the government until 1969. Behind the unchanging facade, however, a distinct evolution in attitudes, approaches, and expectations can be detected. This evolution can be divided into three phases.

In the first phase, which ended in 1955, political and security arrangements and policies still had a provisional character that was emphasized by the government. National division, and therefore the Federal Republic and its institutions, including its armed forces, was provisional because, as the government argued, reunification in a democratic, constitutional state would take place soon, provided only that the West did not relax its vigilance. In those early years, as I have stressed, the policy of decisive Westintegration, politically, militarily, and economically, was seen as a necessary precondition of reunification.

In 1955, by the ratification of the Paris accords of 1954, the Federal Republic was admitted to NATO and became, in the full sense, an actor on the international scene as such. In the same year, the Soviet Union organized the Warsaw Pact, which included the GDR. The outlines and limits of the future role of West Germany in the political, economic, and security system of Western Europe were thereby drawn. They have not essentially changed since, and 1955 can therefore be regarded as the watershed year in postwar European history in general and in West German national and foreign policy in particular.[26]

The second phase in the gradual evolution of West German national and security policy ran from 1955 to early 1963. The government, and Adenauer in particular, maintained the Alleinvertretungsanspruch and the policy of strength, including the Hallstein Doctrine, as stringently as before, if not more so. Yet reunification was increasingly seen as a principle, not a goal soon to be achieved. Adenauer's political convictions and his realism were never more in conflict than in those years. As Hans-Peter Schwarz has put it:

> Evidently, he faced the bleak outlook for national unity clearly and without illusions. There is no doubt that, under certain conditions, he would have been prepared to work for a modus vivendi on the German question. This is clear from certain considerations

dating from his last years in office that point ahead in the direction of policy since the late 1960s. Residual patriotism on behalf of
the Reich and sober, political realism were combined in his character in a way that even he himself would not always admit. In all
his thought on the German question, moreover, he was strongly
affected by sympathy for the Germans in the East. He himself
knew what it meant to be the captive of a totalitarian dictatorship,
and understood the feelings of his compatriots in the GDR.

Even he, however, could achieve no more in this area than a
policy of frustrating contradictions. The tragic fate of his people
was also that of his German policy.[27]

Adenauer's reappraisal of his foreign policy was not confined to the
German issue, though it re-emerged in his last years thanks, mainly, to the
second Berlin crisis of 1958–1962, when Khrushchev tried by various means
to force the Western Allies out of the city.[28] The U.S. failure to respond
strongly to the Berlin Wall and to the Soviet violations of the Potsdam and
other Four-Power agreements that it represented confirmed the old
chancellor's fundamental belief that the psychological and political will of
the West, and especially of the Americans, to resist Soviet expansionism was
at best doubtful. The Berlin crisis also reminded all the world, and the
Germans in particular, that they were vulnerable in a way Britain and France
could never be. This had a dampening effect on the justified sense of accom-
plishment prevalent in West Germany in the late 1950s. Another reason for
Adenauer's increasing doubts regarding U.S. aims and policies was the
revival, by President Kennedy, of the "grand design" for global security of
transatlantic cooperation among the United States, Britain, and France–a
design that excluded West Germany.[29] Partly as a reaction to these perceived
uncertainties in the U.S. commitment to European security, and partly out
of long-standing conviction, the chancellor pursued the rapprochement
with France that had begun with the formation of the European Coal and
Steel Community in 1952. In January 1963 Adenauer and de Gaulle signed
a Franco-German friendship treaty that, in the former's mind at least, was to
be the prelude to a West European political and security system based on a
Paris-Bonn axis. In the event, this idea came to nothing. In de Gaulle's
opinion, as expressed in 1966, this was because "Bonn's preferred and ever-
renewed ties to Washington have deprived the treaty of its spirit and its
substance."[30] In actuality, Adenauer's successors, notably Chancellor Ludwig
Erhard and Foreign Minister Gerhard Schröder, as well as the SPD leadership, turned out to be much less worried by what the United States might or
might not do than by the prospect of general European uncertainty that
would inevitably result from a major reorientation of West Germany from
reliance on the United States to Gaullist Europeanism and nationalism.

Although Adenauer's vision of a Franco-German alignment as the foundation of West European political unity and military security led nowhere at the time, it foreshadowed later episodes in French-West German relations: not only the mutual trust and cooperation of Chancellor Helmut Schmidt and French president Valéry Giscard d'Estaing in the years 1976–1981, which was mainly confined to the sphere of economic policy and which did not always display an equal realism regarding the Soviet Union, but also the close agreement of Chancellor Helmut Kohl and President François Mitterrand from 1982 onward, which was focused primarily on security issues. In the longer view, one could argue that it was Kohl who, in this as in other respects, was the true heir of Adenauer, both in his realistic appraisal of the Soviet Union and in his clearly expressed desire to promote West European unity in the military as well as the political and economic areas.

The third phase of West German foreign policy in the period until 1969 began in early 1963, when, after the dramatic events of the Berlin and Cuba crises, the international climate rather suddenly improved. The tendency toward improved East-West relations, détente, and peaceful coexistence seemed permanent and irreversible, at least until the later 1970s. In West Germany, Adenauer's scruples and long-term fears (about U.S. policy, about Soviet aims, and about the loss of moral fiber in an increasingly hedonistic and permissive society) were soon forgotten by his pragmatic successors. They mostly came from the Protestant (or nondenominational) and liberal wing of the CDU under Erhard, Schröder, and Eugen Gerstenmaier. Their main concerns were economic policy, integration in the Common Market, and, as indicated above, good relations with the United States. In other words, they, and their allies in the younger generation of SPD leaders, were Atlanticists. Over against them stood another group, a Catholic and conservative wing, which one might call Gaullist in foreign and national policy, led by Adenauer and others such as Heinrich Krone and Rainer Barzel, and supported by Franz-Josef Strauss of the CSU, who, while convinced Europeanists, maintained a tough line on the reunification question.[31]

The conflict between these two groups broke out in the open in the summer of 1963, when the United States and Britain, having signed the Nuclear Test Ban Treaty with the Soviet Union, tried to obtain West German ratification of it. The problem was that Khrushchev had already obtained East German ratification. If the Federal Republic also ratified the treaty, this might be construed as indirect recognition of East Germany. Khrushchev, of course, knew this perfectly well and was obviously waiting with great interest to see what would happen. In the event, the West German government gave in and ratified the treaty. Adenauer, Krone, and their allies felt, however, just as they had in the wake of the Berlin crisis, that the United States was unilaterally imposing its policy of détente toward the Soviet Union on West

Germany and thereby making it impossible for the West German government to uphold the principles of its national policy. Since Adenauer was also
engaged in a last-ditch struggle to prevent Erhard from becoming his successor, the rift in the party soon became profound. It was never really healed,
although the liberal Protestant wing had the upper hand throughout the
1960s and 1970s and certainly an overwhelmingly greater impact on the
formulation of national and foreign policy.

The struggle between the two groups in the early 1960s thus ended with
the complete victory of the Atlanticists, that is, of those whose highest
priority was good relations with the United States and who were willing to
abandon Adenauer's attempt to make the German question and the demand
for reunification an integral part of Alliance policy. Given the rapid changes
in U.S.-Soviet relations and this pragmatic approach to the German
question, the eventual breakthrough of the new doctrine of Ostpolitik
(recognition of the status quo in Eastern Europe, acceptance of East
Germany as a separate state, abandonment of the demands for reunification
and of claims to the Eastern territories) was no surprise. It was surprising,
rather, that it took so long, once Adenauer, the mainstay of the old position,
had left the scene.

From the perspective of national policy, the period 1963–1969 was one of
reorientation from firm commitment to the letter and the spirit of the
Hallstein Doctrine and the Alleinvertretungsanspruch to the Ostpolitik we
know today and that has been such a source of friction in the Alliance on the
governmental level. The negotiations with East Germany, Poland, and the
Soviet Union, the official repudiation by the Federal government of any
desire to change existing frontiers, notably the Oder-Neisse line, by force, the
treaties of friendship with the Soviet Union and Poland of 1970–1971, and
the Grundlagenvertrag (basic treaty) on relations between the Federal
Republic and the East German regime, now called by its own official designa-
tion, the "German Democratic Republic," of 1972, symbolized the end of an
era. They were not opposed with much vigor by the CDU, and this probably
more than anything else served to allay what criticism there was from those
who remembered Adenauer's firmness and consistency of purpose.

Nor was the national issue prominent in the public mind in the 1960s or
most of the 1970s. This was the time of the "new politics"; the new generation
of bureaucrats, ministers, and educators was ready to implement Social
Democratic plans and hopes for a more thorough transformation of society
and for a change in West Germany's foreign relations, spurred by Chancellor
Willy Brandt's slogan mehr Demokratie wagen (try for more democracy).[32] The
idea that the interests of the East Germans might be best served by West
German intransigence, that recognition of the East German regime and of
the political facts of Soviet power and control was both morally and legally

wrong, had lost all influence.[33] During the 1960s it was argued with increasing frequency and insistence that the Hallstein Doctrine was counterproductive, that East Germany was, after all, a de facto state, however objectionable its system of rule, and that, moreover, its subjects were Germans who deserved whatever humanitarian relief a relaxation of tensions might bring. To the extent that beginning such a relaxation was in the power of the Federal government, therefore, it should be tried. The argument that de facto states deserved recognition regardless of their nature was, however, not evenly applied. The same progressive Social Democrats who argued for this sort of realism vis-à-vis East Germany were equally prepared to eschew it in the case of South Africa or Ian Smith's Rhodesia, nor did anyone suggest that a fair price for recognition as a de facto state by the Federal Republic might, for example, be recognition by East Germany of Israel.

Ostpolitik was proposed as not only necessary, given the realities, but desirable since, it was argued, better relations with the Eastern regimes would have beneficial effects for their subject peoples as well. In other words, *Wandel durch Annäherung* (change through convergence), as Brandt's chief aide, Egon Bahr, stated in a famous speech in 1963, was the way forward. Openness to the East, so went the rationale of Ostpolitik, would allow the Eastern regimes to loosen their controls and would thus benefit especially the Germans, thus fulfilling, if in a different way, the charge contained in the Basic Law.[34] The premises of this position were obvious enough and were indeed quite openly admitted: that East and West had a common interest in peace and security; that accepting the status quo in Europe would remove Soviet fears of revanchism, which were taken seriously and not assumed to be merely propaganda; that unification through strength was not only impossible, but immoral; that the best way to help the Germans in the East was to accept their regime, although one would try to avoid complying with Eastern demands that this take the form of full diplomatic recognition. These ideas had by the mid-1970s obtained the status of obvious truths in West Germany and were rarely criticized, even by the last remnants of the old "national-Gaullist" wing of the CDU. In this sense, one might say that Ostpolitik had changed from being a set of policy principles corresponding to the national interest (as it had come to be understood in the 1960s by all parties) to an ideology, a set of beliefs about Europe, security, the Soviet Union, and the possibilities of national policy that was not susceptible to proof or disproof.[35]

In the early 1980s, when security policy was again the focus of active and polarized political debate as well as mass popular concern, national policy, and hence Ostpolitik, also returned to prominence. A division of opinion and outlook recalling the split of Gaullists and Atlanticists of the early 1960s emerged, but with a dramatic difference. In the 1960s, the national Gaullists, who wanted to keep reunification and the national question as the central focus of policy even at the expense of some disagreement with the United States, were found mostly in the CSU and the Catholic and conservative wing of the CDU. The SPD, most of the CDU, and almost all the politically important opinion makers in the media and the academic world were Atlanticists, whose main priority was good transatlantic relations as the basis for détente and arms control negotiations with the Soviet Union. Both the national Gaullists and the Atlanticists shared a commitment to West European political and economic integration, but whereas the Atlanticists saw such integration as part of a broader Atlantic community and in any case subordinated it to the transatlantic relationship, the Gaullists saw it as a necessary bulwark against Soviet expansion and as a way of stiffening the popular political will to resist in Western Europe. Only this political will, they thought, could in the end bring about German reunification.

In the 1980s, by contrast, the Atlanticists were found mostly in the CDU, with a few survivors in the SPD, such as Helmut Schmidt.[36] The rest of the SPD, along with many influential journalists, academics, and other intellectuals, had become highly critical of U.S. and Alliance policies. In regard to the national question and European security, many of them believed that the primary problem was not a Soviet threat, but rather the superpower confrontation as such, which they tended to blame more on the Reagan administration than on Soviet actions. They consequently also believed that East and West Europeans could, and should, act together to ensure that this confrontation did not disturb détente in Europe, and some of them, such as the writer Peter Bender (of whom more later), even argued that the main task of West German policy ought to be to contribute to "the Europeanization of Europe." Here was a new German Gaullism in the making, which shared with the old variety a suspicion of U.S. policies and a generally pro-European orientation. The difference was that whereas the CDU-CSU Gaullists of the 1960s saw West European unity as a means to resist a Soviet threat that to them was evident, the new SPD and peace movement Gaullists of the 1980s believed in a common West and East European unity as a bulwark against the war-threatening policies and actions of both superpowers. If, as I believe, this idea was a dangerous illusion based on a complete misunderstanding of the international situation in general and of Germany's predicament in particular, the most important task of responsible West German political debate and policy formation in the mid-1980s would then be the resurrection of the idea that West European political and military integration is necessary to resist Soviet pressure, does not imperil good relations with the East Europeans (as opposed to their governments), and is not incompatible with maintaining the goal of reunification in a democratic constitutional state.

2

THE NATIONAL ISSUE
AND THE SPD

Given West Germany's history and strategic situation, the evolution of its politics, particularly in relation to the issues of security and national division, could not be simple. As chancellor, Adenauer followed policies in these two areas that for a time seemed to solve the apparent contradiction between a genuinely national policy and a security consistent with NATO commitments and interests. During that time, however, the SPD, because it was unfettered by the limitations imposed on a ruling party, was able to seem more genuinely concerned with national unity than the government. Though the party officially accepted the government's order of priorities (freedom first, reunification if possible), there was a constant undercurrent of opinion in favor of seeking negotiated mutual security agreements with the Soviet Union that, it was thought, might lead to reunification. In fact, the very belief that such negotiated agreements were not only possible, but that they might actually help further the national interest in unity was a characteristic trait of the Social Democratic outlook throughout the 1950s. Over against it stood Adenauer's equally characteristic belief that security could best be guaranteed in a defensive alliance and not by negotiations with one's potential enemy.

In hindsight it seems clear that even had the SPD been in power and in a position to offer the East some sort of deal involving partial West German neutralization, the Soviet Union would not have reciprocated by abandoning the East German regime and allowing reunification. As things were, however, the SPD was able to propose plans for demilitarization and negotiation with impunity, while blaming the government for immobility and an unreasoning spirit of confrontation. The result was that the SPD seemed to many outsiders to be the party with the more credible national policy and the greater concern for unity. Among these outsiders were political academics, clergymen, journalists, and other intellectuals who formed various associations and published various statements during the 1950s arguing the need for a neutralistic policy of reconciliation with the Soviet Union and a greater distance to the West, especially the United States. Some of these people, such as Gustav Heinemann, died without seeing their ideas gain much ground. Others lived long enough to be honored by the peace movement of the 1980s as elder statesmen, like Martin Niemöller (who died at 91 in 1983), Helmut Gollwitzer, Heinrich Albertz, Ute Ranke-Heinemann or, the most famous, the editor and publisher of *Der Spiegel*, Rudolf Augstein.[1]

The neutralist wing of the SPD shared with these men a conviction that a national policy in the true interest of all Germans could be pursued outside of, and even in opposition to, the West German commitment to NATO and membership in the Atlantic Alliance. This conviction gradually spread throughout the SPD from the late 1970s, so that it was possible, in 1983, for the party to launch its election campaign with the slogan *im deutschen Interesse* (in the German interest). The slogan was deliberately meant to imply that the SPD policy stood against INF deployment and for increased trade, negotiations, and other official relations with the Soviet Union and East Germany that were in the interest, precisely, of all Germans. The difference between this, in my view, dangerous illusion and the illusions of the 1950s is that the latter were still part of a desire for national political unity in one democratic, constitutional state. The Ostpolitik of the period since 1969, on the other hand, is based upon the recognition of the independent statehood of East Germany. For the SPD, the "German interest" is no longer reunification, but disarmament (unilateral if necessary). The shift is decisive. To see reunification as the prime political goal is also to see the division of Europe as the fundamental political problem. To see disarmament as the prime goal, on the other hand, is to see the division of Europe and the mutual deterrence of East and West as conditions of stability, which can be preserved by arms control negotiations, and not sources of tension. The resulting perspective and policy options are radically different, based as they are on diametrically opposed interpretations of the history of Europe since 1945.

It was not popular in West Germany in the 1980s to assert that, so far from being a guarantee of security and mutual deterrence, the division of Europe was in fact the basic problem. In fact, it was almost impossible to find anyone willing to make that assertion.[2] In the 1950s, the opposite was the case. No one argued that division was stabilizing. The difference between the government and the SPD was rather that the former believed that a neutral-ized West Germany would be easy prey for the Soviet Union, and that it was therefore better for most Germans to remain free than to indulge in possibly disastrous experiments. The SPD, on the other hand, hoped by an offensive strategy of disarmament and détente to convince the Soviet Union that NATO and West Germany were no threat and that it was therefore in the Soviet interest to come to a final settlement with the Western powers and with a unified Germany.

The focus of the following sections is the evolution of SPD policy from this strong pro-unity stand to the modified stand of the 1960s and after, when Soviet refusal to concede unification under any circumstances was tacitly accepted as a fact. The results of this change were the Eastern treaties with Poland, East Germany, the USSR, and Czechoslovakia of 1969–1972, which specifically included West German acknowledgment of the inviola-bility of existing borders, and the Conference on Security and Cooperation in Europe (CSCE). The latter began in Helsinki in 1975, and, in the Soviet perspective, it has taken the place of the nonexistent peace treaty and has granted permanent Western, including West German, sanction to the terri-torial and political conditions imposed by force by the Soviet Union on East Central Europe in 1944–1949. The shift in SPD priorities from reunification to disarmament reflects this triumph of Soviet political strategy.

SOCIAL DEMOCRATS AND NATIONAL SECURITY

Since the early postwar years, the SPD has necessarily been more concerned with the problems of national unity and security than any other Western social democratic party. Before 1945, the British Labour Party, the French Socialist Party, and the Social Democratic parties in the Netherlands and Scandinavia were opposed to nationalism and to any intimations of mili-tancy in defense policy, both of which were seen as part of the ideology of the right. After 1945, however, when communism, the alienated brother-enemy of social democracy, was perceived as a threat to Western democracies, these parties overwhelmingly supported the Atlantic Alliance, sometimes more fervently than their conservative opponents. Ernest Bevin, foreign secretary of the British Labour government from 1945 to 1951, personified this new combination of tough anticommunism, belief in the value of nationalization, and economic egalitarianism, as did lesser-known socialists such as the Norwegian Haakon Lie.

The new orientation of most leading socialists was rather a concern for social democratic values threatened by the Soviet Union, whose leaders saw the realization of those values as the ultimate denial of their ideological claims, than for national security pure and simple. The rise of powerful neutralist or anti-NATO elements in some, if not all, of these parties since the 1970s therefore does not mark an abandonment of a commitment to security as such that never existed. Social Democrats basically want to perceive the Soviet Union as a status quo power, that is, a power primarily concerned, not with expansion, but with the protection of its territorial holdings and political system. This view allows them to return to a position with which they have always felt more comfortable, namely the above-mentioned belief in the value of détente and collective security agreements. Their faith that the Soviet Union is not an enemy, but rather feels threatened by aggressive Western policies, also allows them to oppose increased defense budgets, which, in their view, imperil social policies and cause unnecessary tension.[3] The rediscovery of these principles in the SPD is related, of course, to the general disenchantment with Western values and achievements that characterized the political and cultural left throughout Western Europe since the later 1960s, with the legacy of anti-Americanism of the Vietnam War period, and with the resurrection of Marxist and neo-Marxist ideology attacking the social democrats for revisionism and capitulation to capitalism.

The strong pro-NATO stand of the majority of West European social democrats, including the SPD, from the 1950s to the 1970s was, in historical perspective, an anomaly. In general social democratic suspicion, if not fear, of military needs and arguments has been the rule, not the exception. Communist hostility to social democrats ("social fascists") was a powerful legacy of the 1930s, and as long as the social democratic parties were led by men who remembered that era or were willing to learn from it, NATO had their complete support. The change that began in the 1960s in the SPD attitude to security was closely related to the change in national policy. One important reason for it was the gradual rise to prominence in the party of people who did not remember the 1930s or even the early postwar years, and whose view of East-West relations therefore differed markedly from that of their elders. Another reason was that some of those elders themselves, notably Willy Brandt, changed their opinion dramatically. A third reason, finally, was the new view of the Soviet Union. In the political conditions of the 1970s and after, these changes made it much more difficult for those who still believed in the need for NATO to make their case.

SPECIFIC PROBLEMS OF THE SPD

As long as the Soviet Union was seen as a threat, the prime national responsibility of all free Germans, Social Democrats as well as liberals and conservatives, was to uphold the security of West Germany as a democratic state that would be a token of hope for the East Germans. When the era of détente began in the 1960s, this perception changed, as the SPD formulated its new Ostpolitik and reassessed its position regarding NATO and defense. Beginning in the 1950s, a tendency grew in the SPD to perceive no direct Soviet threat and to regard the Soviet Union as an essentially defensive power with legitimate security interests in Europe. By the time the party came to power, first in coalition with the CDU in 1966, and later with the FDP from 1969 to 1982, important SPD leaders, including Brandt, no longer regarded an overriding commitment to security or to the Atlantic Alliance as the chief goal of West German foreign policy. Rather, they wanted to pursue good relations with the Soviets and to avoid any policy that might antagonize them. Regarding East Germany, the SPD gradually abandoned the argument that there was an unbridgeable gulf between the East German regime, which was loyal to the Soviets alone and whose interests were by definition incompatible with those of the West German people. As will be described below, it was in 1962–1963 that senior party spokesmen (Willy Brandt and Egon Bahr) first expressed the opinion that recognition of the East German regime in some form could benefit those Germans who were its subjects. The SPD's firm commitment, in the 1950s, to the principle that there could and should be no communication with, or recognition of, a party and a regime that denied, not only national unity, but all that the SPD stood for, gave way, in the 1960s, to an equally firm commitment to the opposed, and incompatible, belief that acceptance of that same regime would help the people to whose true interests (in national and democratic rights) it remained unalterably opposed. This transition in the SPD led, when the party held power, to the Grundlagenvertrag of 1972, and to the insistence by the SPD and, increasingly, the FDP and the Union parties as well, that Ostpolitik and détente, to the degree that they improved or were believed to improve the lives of East Germans, were, and must be, *unumkehrbar* (irreversible). The thin line between Ostpolitik as policy and as a self-binding ideology, a "self-denying ordinance," is clear here. The justification of Ostpolitik, in part because of its effects on other aspects of policy, particularly transatlantic and European relations, constituted one of the three major interrelated elements of West Germany's foreign, security, and national policy dilemma in the 1980s. The other two were: on the level of political activism, the ideology and activities of the Greens and the peace movement; and on the cultural and academic level, the strong criticism, even rejection, not only of U.S. policies, but of the United States as a social and political model, combined with a hesitant search for positive aspects of native German traditions and modes of thought.

We might further note that, as the ruling party from 1969 to 1982, the SPD became less and less able and willing to produce broad policy statements enjoying the support of the entire party leadership because of increasing internal divisions that were partly caused by, and partly reflected in, the political and personal differences among Willy Brandt, party chairman since 1963 and chancellor from 1969 to 1974; Helmut Schmidt, chancellor from 1974 to 1982, and Herbert Wehner, *Fraktionsvorsitzender* (leader of the party's Bundestag group) from 1969 to 1983. In June 1960, Wehner, in a famous speech to the Bundestag, had openly declared that the SPD was abandoning all neutralist and anti-NATO pretensions and was now firmly committed to a bipartisan foreign and defense policy along with the CDU. Until the early 1980s, this commitment was officially honored by the party leadership, though with increasing difficulty. The loss of a common and binding identity in security matters was poignantly manifested in 1982, when Helmut Schmidt found it necessary to threaten to call a vote of confidence to retain support by the Bundestag group for INF modernization, and even more when Schmidt found himself in a minority of 5 approving the new missiles at the extraordinary party congress of November 1983, against a majority of 389. On the subject of Ostpolitik, however, there continued to be a remarkably large consensus in the SPD, so large, in fact, that it was sometimes hard to tell whether the policy was being justified by reference to a Social Democratic (and Christian Democratic) commitment to the Germans in the East, or increasingly by fear of Soviet displeasure, as Henry Kissinger, Walter Laqueur, and Hans-Peter Schwarz have charged. In other words, it is difficult to ascertain whether the notion of a "self-Finlandization" of West Germany and its governmental policies has any validity.

Here again we find the problem of perceived versus genuine national interests and the question of the standard by which genuine interests can be determined.[4] The arguments for Ostpolitik in the 1970s and 1980s usually defined it as a policy of maintaining negotiations with and financial aid to East Germany despite the general climate of East-West relations and without stressing the constitutional, legal, and national principles affirmed in the Adenauer era, including human rights. This means that it was the perceived political interest of almost all West Germans, and certainly all leading politicians, to maintain these ties first, for humanitarian reasons, and second, because it was desirable to have a channel of contact that would remain open whatever the climate of East-West relations. The events of 1983–1984 were generally believed, in West Germany, to have confirmed the validity of that analysis. Despite the chill in U.S.-Soviet relations, it was argued, the two Germanys were still talking, and Franz-Josef Strauss, formerly a strong critic of SPD Ostpolitik, arranged loans of $700 million to East Germany. However, some observers noted that, while happy enough to take the money, the East German ruler, Erich Honecker, actually did little, if anything, to further peace and security. The automatic shooting devices at the East German border with West Germany, which some in the Bonn government thought would be dismantled, remained in place; and, in September 1984, Honecker at the last moment canceled his planned visit to the Federal Republic. As usual, the leverage that Ostpolitik, specifically economic relations, was supposed to have given West Germany in the East turned out to be largely illusory.[5] Behind the willingness to indulge in this illusion lies, as I have argued above, the post-1960s belief that the division of Germany is a condition of stability and the consequent belief that the East German regime should be appeased and conciliated, not challenged and provoked. The contrary argument is that, in fact, the genuine national and security interests of West Germany are not served by the surrender of principles, such as the claim to be the sole legitimate representative of the German people, or by providing massive loans and gifts to a regime, the very recognition of which would have been regarded virtually as treason only twenty years ago.

This is indeed, in simplified form, part of the argument of this book, and only by making such an argument is it possible to distinguish clearly between the justifications of Ostpolitik and its character and effects when measured against the external standard of German national and security interests in the historical context of Soviet power and the European balance since 1945. As stated above, those interests are best summarized as the survival of a democratic constitutional state in as much of Germany as possible, which for the foreseeable future means in the Federal Republic, a goal that in turn requires a serious and sustained security effort and the maintenance of constitutional principles vis-à-vis the East. The security effort has arguably been maintained, though there is much room for improvement and rationalization, specifically in the direction of wider West European cooperation; the principles have not. The revival of the national issue in popular and academic debate, especially on the left, followed an almost complete disappearance of national rhetoric from official party political statements. This was one effect of the change from an offensive conception of Ostpolitik, reminiscent of the SPD position of the 1950s when political unification was still the goal, to a defensive conception, in which achievements were claimed and defended, but no grandiose plans were developed.[6] The extent to which this change was forced upon the SPD and the West German government by East German and Soviet behavior has rarely been explicitly acknowledged, and this fact again emphasizes the extent to which Ostpolitik seems to have become a domestic political necessity, something that must be pursued regardless of the consequences.

VARIETIES OF NATIONALISM AFTER 1945

Political culture in West Germany shifted decisively leftward in the 1960s, following a general trend in Western countries. The SPD came to power via the "Grand Coalition" with the CDU-CSU in 1966 and then was the dominant partner in the smaller coalition with the FDP in 1969, which lasted until 1982. These two developments meant that traditional nationalism of the right-wing variety, which had been totally discredited by the Nazis, disappeared completely as an issue and as a political option. Even had the Nazis not exploited nationalism, it is still hard to imagine how it could have survived in anything like its original form, even in the free half of a divided nation.[7] What would its purpose and aims be? Not reunification, for that was the basic aim and hope of all political forces, including the Social Democrats. Perhaps nationalists could have advocated reconquest of the provinces of East Prussia, Pomerania, East Brandenburg, and Silesia, unilaterally granted to communist Poland by Stalin in 1945 in return for what he had seized in 1939 under the Hitler-Stalin Pact. Even the most unrealistic ideologue had to admit, in the 1950s, that such ideas were unlikely to win popular support, and even if they did, there were no means of realizing them. West Germany's new army, subject to NATO command, was no match for the Soviet forces in East Germany and Eastern Europe.

Given the political and strategic dead end of such speculations, neo-nationalism in West Germany since the war has turned inward, to an older strand of German national sentiment that emphasizes the *Heimat*, the homeland or home region, including rural values, the uncorrupted virtues of simple people, and a suspicion of foreign ways and values.[8] Because these were also feelings that had been exploited by Hitler, it was not surprising that they failed to arouse much sympathy. They were (and continue to be) of little importance in the political consciousness and culture of the majority of citizens of the Federal Republic; in the 1980s, this majority identified strongly with democratic institutions and ideals. As recently as 1959, only 2 percent of the respondents in a poll conducted by the Allensbach Institute believed that "today was the best time" in German history, as against 42 percent who believed this of the period 1933–1939 (the early years of the Third Reich), and 45 percent who believed it of the Kaiserreich before 1914. By 1981, the figures had changed to 80 percent, 2 percent, and 4 percent, respectively. Belief in and support for defense, as represented by the Bundeswehr, has also been solid; from 1974 to 1980, the number who believed that the Bundeswehr contributes to peace increased from 69 percent to 90 percent.[9] These overall signs of political stability should be borne in mind when discussing the new anti-

Western nationalism of the left and the inconsistencies and potential risks of the Social Democratic understanding of East-West relations and of the Soviet Union. Only in the 1980s did reminiscences of the *antikapitalistische Sehnsucht des deutschen Volkes* (anticapitalist longing of the German people), extolled by Gregor Strasser, head of the Nazi Party organization, in 1932, resurface in certain elements and beliefs of the Green Party and the peace movement.[10] However, it is unlikely that many old nationalists would feel at home at a Green gathering. The desire for power still exists, but it has been transformed, ideologized and moralized, drowned in a sea of sentiment (see Chapters 7 and 9).

After 1945, political debates centered on, and ideologies were shaped by, the international confrontation between Western democracy and Soviet totalitarianism, and neither the old pan-Germanism and anti-Semitism of Vienna nor the authoritarian militarism of Prussia had any meaning or possibility of revival in the new context. Even so, currents of national feeling survived to a greater or lesser extent in all political parties, and the resurgence of such currents since the mid-1970s is understandable as a reaction to the apparently permanent tension caused by national division. First, among liberals and conservatives, nationalism took the form of anti-communism, that is, resentment directed at the ideological enemy that was seen to have caused great suffering, as well as national division. Second, there was the nationalism of the SPD, illustrated in 1914 when the majority of the party voted for the government's war loans and hence for war. This nationalism was a peculiar combination of proletarian solidarity and a strong sense of the role and power of the state. German Social Democrats, after all, were unlikely to forget that it was Bismarck, the architect of the united German state, who introduced social insurance legislation in the 1880s. Opposition to the social, economic, and political hierarchies of the *Kaiserreich* did not mean opposition to a strong state, but rather anticipation of what Social Democrats would do when they took over. Hence, even the Nazi persecutions of the Social Democrats did not destroy their nationalism but rather reinforced more than ever their desire to survive and to create a new, strong, free, and socialist Germany, without aggressive intentions, but able to maintain its political weight in the center of Europe.[11]

The Social Democratic commitment to national unity after 1945 – first its preservation and then its recovery – was thus not a result of the successful exploitation of anticommunism, but of beliefs that were part of the very identity of the party. Another reason, rarely stated, was that SPD and CDU-CSU power were more equally balanced in the Federal Republic than they had been in the old German heartland – the provinces that later became East Germany – which had been the chief bastion of SPD electoral power before

1933. This was partly due to the increased weight of the Catholic element in the Federal Republic as opposed to pre-1945 Germany. Almost all Catholics are Christian Democrats, while the Protestants are divided, with approximately 60 percent supporting the SPD. The vast majority of persons without religious affiliation vote Social Democratic. Social Democratic domination of Germany therefore was, and would be, a consequence of unity. The historical strength of the SPD in central (after 1949, East) Germany was much increased by the party's strong commitment to unity and democratic socialism. During the revolt of June 17, 1953, the East German workers hailed Erich Ollenhauer, the SPD leader, and not Adenauer. Willy Brandt, when mayor of West Berlin from 1957 to 1963 (the "right-wing extremist," as Walter Ulbricht called him), was enormously popular in East Germany. Unofficial polls carried out by journalists indicated that even in the 1980s, 75 percent of the vote in a free East German election would go to the SPD.

One might suppose that, because of the common origins of social democracy and communism in the working-class movement, Social Democrats are sometimes more realistic about communism as an ideological influence, particularly on Soviet power and policy, than conservatives, who tend to view the Soviet Union as "just another great power" or "just a revised version of old Russian imperialism." Certainly, if one compared SPD leaders, such as Fritz Erler, with a conservative like de Gaulle, this theory might be borne out. In West Germany, however, there were few politically important conservatives at any time since 1945 who were tempted to regard the Soviet Union as "just another power," though the tendency certainly existed on the far right.[12] Anticommunism, indeed, became an essential part of the political identity of the CDU-CSU, and understandably so. However, when anticommunism was denounced in the 1960s and 1970s as either unnecessary or hysterical or both, it began to lose its value as an identifying posture, especially among younger voters. By the 1980s, it was clear that unless the Union parties could develop a national policy that identified the interests of all Germans without basing it on general anticommunism, they ran the risk of leaving debate and action on the national issue entirely to the new nationalist left.

THE EARLY PHASE OF
SPD NATIONAL POLICY (1945–1955)

In view of subsequent developments, it is ironic that it was the Soviets who first gave permission to organize political parties in occupied Germany. By early summer of 1945, the first steps had been taken in Berlin toward the creation of the Christian Democratic Union. The leading figure in these efforts was Jakob Kaiser, a member of the Resistance and a Christian socialist who hoped that the ruin and disaster would give rise to a new social order based on Catholic social ethics. His belief in Germany as a potential "bridge between East and West" was sincere, if unrealistic, and was revived in the 1980s by many who had probably never heard of him.[13] However, it was not Kaiser but the Social Democrats who resisted the idea and the reality of division the longest, and the most adamant among them was their leader, Kurt Schumacher. By the end of the war, he was already reconstructing the SPD from his base in Hannover. In July 1945 he stated the SPD position as follows: "Social Democrats will tell the world that living without a unified Germany is not what the other peoples have been fighting for in this war. Without national unity and as a mere object of the most varied foreign political influences, such a great people would be nothing but a mass of rot and apathy."[14]

As indicated above, this argument, that the preservation of unity is not just a necessity for Germans but is a requirement for stability and peace in Europe, remained a cornerstone of the SPD position until at least the early 1960s. It was maintained as a principle if not as a demand likely to be fulfilled. The Communists, who were setting up their rule in the Soviet zone, sounded similar notes, particularly in the early postwar years; such rhetoric from the East did not cease entirely until 1970.[15] For example, Wilhelm Pieck, chairman of the KPD (German Communist Party), arguing for amalgamation of the KPD and the SPD in 1946, declared: "Above all we must prevent the disastrous situation caused by the Hitler war from leading also to the disintegration of the national unity of our people."

The practice of soliciting, cajoling, threatening, or infiltrating democratic socialist and other parties in Soviet-occupied territories after 1945 to create "democratic fronts" and "united workers' parties" was a standard communist tactic. Its success in the Soviet zone of Germany, however, meant that the SPD in the rest of Germany was now on its guard. As a consequence, the repeated propaganda efforts of the SED (the name given to the communist party in the Soviet zone after the SPD there had been taken over and destroyed in 1946) to undermine the national and proletarian credentials of the SPD met with very little success; the SPD immediately established an underground party organization in the Soviet zone (which was maintained until the building of the Berlin Wall in 1961) and consequently claimed to be the true representative of East German workers, who had been defrauded of their rights by the Soviet-imposed regime. This national claim of the SPD was, in a sense, the counterpart of the government's official Alleinvertretungsanspruch, and continued to be asserted forcefully and effectively until it was tacitly abandoned during the 1960s.

The combination of the SPD's intimate knowledge of communist power

and practices and the strong national heritage made it, as I have said, a consistently credible guardian of the principle of national unity and the democratic system in the early postwar period. This did not mean, however, that
it unequivocally supported Adenauer's policy of joining the Alliance and
promoting a West German armament. Indeed, the Social Democrats tended
to see Alliance membership as subordinating the German national
interest—unification—to allied, especially American, interests, which were
primarily security oriented. They feared that any German attempts at unification might be stifled by U.S. plans and policies, either in the sense that
the Americans would be unwilling to risk a conflict with the Soviet Union
or in the sense that they might simply decide that unification was not a
priority. The SPD, in effect, wanted both security from communist infiltration and attack, and a realistic hope of reunification. This contradiction
emerged clearly in a speech by SPD chairman Ollenhauer in the Bundestag
in 1954, when the Paris treaties granting West Germany full sovereignty,
admitting it to the Alliance, and regulating the status of the Saar were being
discussed:

> There are serious signs that the occupying powers subordinate the
> question of German unity to a general policy of decreasing ten-
> sions between East and West . . . It is the *tragedy of the foreign policy*
> *of the Federal Republic* that it has not hitherto been able to free
> itself from the constraints resulting from the chancellor's offer to
> rearm of August 1950, and that, in practical terms, the *integration*
> *of the Federal Republic in the West* has always had *priority over reuni-*
> *fication* . . . The argument that negotiations will be proposed after
> the ratification of the treaties and that the Soviets will then be pre-
> pared to talk is no answer to the present situation . . . The great
> cause, the unity of our people, demands the exploration of all pos-
> sibilities of negotiation . . . our most vital task must be to prevent
> the Soviet-occupied zone of Germany from being included in the
> Soviet security system,
>   (. . . a CDU member: But it already is!)
> and that the Soviet Union should grant that part of Germany its
> freedom . . . the Soviet-occupied zone . . . is happily as yet very far
> from being an integrated part of the Soviet military system.
>   (Euler, CDU: It has been for a long time!)
> . . . This is not merely a national issue. Détente, security, and
> peace in Europe and the world cannot be permanently achieved
> as long as Germany is divided and an Iron Curtain runs through
> Europe.[16]

The commitment to the West was always the ultimate cornerstone of
CDU policy, at the same time flowing from and implying anticommunism,

whereas for the SPD, until the early 1960s, national unity always came first, but Social Democrats ignored the fine line between desire and illusion. In the 1950s, there was considerably less disagreement on the existence of the Soviet threat than on domestic economic and social policy. As previously indicated, the position of the Christian Democrats regarding the two imperatives of security and unification was ambiguous. The general feeling among Social Democrats was that the two were ultimately synonymous since no permanent peace in Europe was possible without universal respect for human rights, including the rights of East Europeans and East Germans. The government shared this view, but also believed that an important aspect of security, which was its highest priority, was West European integration. Toward the end of the 1950s, there was a great deal of hope that some form of real political federation of Western Europe was just around the corner. These feelings, and the extent to which real economic integration had already progressed, disturbed the SPD greatly and confirmed the belief of many critics of the government that Westintegration was, for all its benefits, a hasty and ill-conceived policy devised by politicians with little understanding of or sympathy for national unity.

THE GESTATION OF SOCIAL DEMOCRATIC OSTPOLITIK (1955–1963)

The inauguration of Ostpolitik, and the fairly rapid weakening of domestic opposition to it, was a result of changed perspectives on the national question in all parties. In the previous chapter, I discussed the changes in the CDU-CSU, where the outlook of the new generation of leaders, and even to some extent of Adenauer in his last years, already anticipated the new Ostpolitik of the social-liberal coalition.[17] In the SPD, an analogous change took place, from belief in grand schemes for East-West disarmament as the precondition of a German settlement to belief that direct negotiations with East Germany and the Soviet Union were both necessary and desirable. The beginnings of the change were perceptible in the late 1950s, coinciding, paradoxically enough, with the opening moves in the second Berlin crisis. Although Schumacher had been adamant that the eastern provinces could never be formally surrendered and that all territorial questions had to await the final peace conference, some SPD members had abandoned this position by the mid-1950s. Instead, they focused on the international complications and problems caused by German division, as indeed Schumacher had also done since 1945. The new SPD themes during the period 1955–1960 were détente, disarmament, nuclear-free zones (though they were not called that), and collective security agreements.[18]

The SPD, along with other social democratic parties, had a tradition of believing that collective security arrangements were a better way of securing peace than defensive alliances. This tradition went back to the nineteenth century and had its roots ultimately in socialist internationalism. Its eclipse in the first postwar decade was due to the impact of the Soviet threat and to the all-important influence in the party not only of the chairman, Schumacher, but of the mayor of Berlin, Ernst Reuter.[19] By 1953 both were dead, and the party was in the hands of new men, some of whom were already looking ahead to a time when the Soviet Union could be included in a European settlement that would also help restore German unity. The last element is important. The revival of belief in collective security in the SPD in the later 1950s remained at first within the overall bounds of a strong commitment to reunification.

The new themes emerged in the SPD following the Kennan-Rapacki proposals of 1957 (named after the American diplomat George Kennan and the new Polish foreign minister, Adam Rapacki), which included a nuclear-free zone comprising both Germanys, neutralization of Central Europe, and the convening of a European security conference to make peace with a unified Germany and create a reliable collective security framework for the future. The United States, and Adenauer, rejected the proposals as patent attempts to weaken NATO and expand Soviet influence in Central Europe. They were tailor-made, however, to appeal to many of the new forces in the SPD. Thus Fritz Erler, a rising star in the party and basically a staunch Atlanticist, pleaded strongly for consideration of the Kennan-Rapacki Plan in the Bundestag in 1958.[20] This was at a time when the West German security debate was dominated by the question of nuclear arms for the Bundeswehr, which the SPD opposed. Following the publication of a manifesto entitled *Kampf dem Atomtod* (Fight Atomic Death), signed by many well-known public figures, and a declaration against national nuclear armaments by leading nuclear physicists, including Werner Heisenberg and Carl Friedrich von Weizsäcker, a popular campaign began that lasted for about a year and a half and left a permanent legacy in West German politics.[21] The pacifist and neutralist elements on the left of the SPD were strengthened, and, perhaps more important, the threat of nuclear war became a theme of public debate in a way that exactly prefigured the arguments of 1980 and after.

In 1958–1960, a number of SPD resolutions were introduced in various places around the country demanding negotiations with East Germany, rejection of nuclear weapons deployment, and exploration of what were regarded as clear opportunities for neutral unification. By far the most important of those resolutions, however, was the document known as the *Deutschlandplan*, which was official SPD policy for about a year, until formally abandoned in Wehner's speech to the Bundestag of June 1960. Wehner was its author. He was a former Communist and, unlike some of that breed, did not move to the Atlanticist right of the SPD but stayed decidedly on the left on social and economic issues. The *Deutschlandplan* was more than just a list of rather utopian demands for negotiation and confederation; indeed, the original proposal anticipated the left-wing idea of "taking the best" of both systems in a coming convergence – an idea that became popular in some academic and political circles in the 1970s.

> The SPD proposes:
> 1. The establishment of a zone of reduced tension comprising both parts of Germany, Poland, Czechoslovakia, and Hungary.
> 2. After the completion of the carefully planned and timed "military thinning-out" the zone of reduced tension will be free of foreign troops and of all atomic and hydrogen weapons.
> 3. All agreements on arms limitations and on the simultaneous withdrawal of the forces of NATO and the Warsaw Pact in Central Europe are to be subject from the outset to unhindered air and surface inspection.
> 4. The integrity of the participating states is to be guaranteed by a collective security agreement of all interested parties including the USA and the USSR.
> 5. As soon as the European security system becomes effective, the states in the zone of détente will give up their memberships in NATO and the Warsaw Pact . . .
>
> The aim of all negotiations demanded by the Social Democratic Party of Germany is the conclusion of agreements that serve to realize European security . . . and to bring Germany together politically and economically pending her final reunification.

The similarities to the neutralist and semi-neutralist proposals and beliefs of the 1980s are striking, although we should bear in mind the differences of context. Quite apart from the much more favorable military balance in 1960, the political and cultural atmosphere in general was much more calm than in the 1980s. The threatening and suspicious moralism of much so-called critical agitation of the 1980s was unknown, and proposals such as the Kennan-Rapacki Plan and Wehner's *Deutschlandplan* were not regarded as instruments to ward off evil, but as suggestions for political action to achieve an ultimate goal – the security and freedom of Europe. The division of Europe was still seen as the main obstacle to this goal. The underlying assessments and presuppositions of such plans are open to question, they are certainly a far cry from the mixture of illusions, sentiment and desire presented as solutions to world conflict presented by the peace movement of the 1980s.

Although the Social Democratic version of Ostpolitik was not put into effect until the SPD became the chief governing party in 1969, the change from the uncompromising democratic nationalism of the 1950s to the much more uncertain attitude regarding the national issue evident in Ostpolitik occurred mainly in the early 1960s. The most significant external event that triggered that change was the erection of the Berlin Wall, a unilateral action in flagrant violation of all prevailing agreements, yet one that had the paradoxical consequence of softening, not hardening, the West German (and particularly the Social Democratic) attitude. It is likely that the trauma of seeing the West, especially the United States, demonstrate its impotence when confronted by this act of force played a considerable part in the psychological reorientation of SPD leaders such as Willy Brandt, Fritz Erler, Herbert Wehner, and Egon Bahr. However, the brutality of the Eastern regime, and the particular insult to democratic socialists that its spurious claim to be a "workers' and peasants' state" represents, show that the policy of conciliation and appeasement of that regime might be much more detrimental to Alliance solidarity, the possibility of obtaining political consensus in West Germany, and the long-term strength and credibility of the SPD as a democratic party committed to Western values than the new political strategists of the 1960s anticipated.

At the end of 1960, Herbert Wehner, whose faith in collective security and in the possibilities of rapprochement with the East was already evident in the 1950s, was still able to state that "the Federal Republic . . . cannot undertake to negotiate unification with the usurpers of power beyond the zone frontier . . . it is clear that setting the final seal on German division is the main aim of Soviet policy in Central Europe . . . in the conflict of East and West, the place of the Federal Republic and therefore also that of the Social Democratic Party of Germany is unequivocally on the side of the West." Whenever Wehner or other leaders at the time invoked their party, they were also invoking the silent voices of German workers in the East. The fact that the SPD could maintain a clandestine party organization in East Germany and, most of all, the open statements of striking workers during the 1953 uprising had demonstrated that the SPD commanded a significant, and courageous, following in the Soviet zone.

Uncertainty over the fate of Berlin continued in 1961 and stimulated a rash of initiatives for appeasement of the Soviet Union and East Germany. The German Peace Union (Deutsche Friedens-Union), an organization of left-wing intellectuals, Communists, and leftist Social Democrats, demanded

"the separation of Germany from the opposing military blocs" and direct negotiations with Pankow. These proposals are very reminiscent of the *Deutschlandplan* and were indeed probably inspired by it, although the SPD had officially abandoned such ideas. On the same day in August 1961 that the Berlin
Wall was erected, Willy Brandt, mayor of Berlin, declared to the city fathers:

> The measures ordered and taken by the Ulbricht regime at the be-
> hest of the Warsaw Pact states to close off the Soviet zone and the
> Soviet sector of Berlin are a flagrant breach of justice. As a conse-
> quence, Berlin is being divided not only by a sort of frontier, but
> by the barbed wire fence of a concentration camp . . . I have
> begged the responsible commanders [of Allied forces] and their
> governments to make vigorous representations to the Soviet gov-
> ernment. We believe that the Western powers must insist that
> these illegal actions be reversed . . . and I am sure that I am
> expressing the sense of this House when I say that I do not think
> that mere protests will be enough.

However, protests was all he got, and they were slow in coming.[22] Meanwhile, Walter Ulbricht, the East German ruler, was praising "the glorious
sons and daughters of our workers . . . the glorious young men in the People's
Army and the People's Police" for their "splendid fighting spirit" in "protecting the borders" of the GDR against the imperialists. He claimed that "our
security measures will allow the peace-loving forces in West Germany . . . to
resist the extremists, from Strauss to Brandt." Taking his cue from Goebbels,
who knew that a big enough lie repeated often enough becomes the truth,
Ulbricht even claimed that "Western bourgeois governments" had "encouraged" the East German regime to "get rid of" (*beseitigen*) that "source of
tension," West Berlin.

For a while the reaction of the SPD was what one would expect: dismay,
indignation, and horror. At the annual party conference in 1962, party
leaders declared that the Berlin Wall demonstrated the utter moral and
economic bankruptcy of the Ulbricht regime and affirmed that the "security
and stability of the Federal Republic of Germany are indispensable conditions for overcoming division." This was precisely the government position,
and the SPD was thus reaffirming its commitment of June 1960 to Adenauer's foreign and defense policy.[23] In the same statement, they referred to
the territory of the GDR as *Mitteldeutschland*, or central Germany (a term
used by the CDU-CSU), and claimed that "West Berlin belongs to the Federal Republic," an assertion that has always been anathema to the East German regime, even though it was itself based in East Berlin, in violation of the
Potsdam Agreement of 1945.

This stern stand was soon to change decisively, however. In October, the "extremist" Brandt gave a speech at Harvard University entitled "The Ordeal of Coexistence" (*Koexistenz – Zwang zum Wagnis*). For the most part, it was an eloquent description of the situation and its implications, including the observation that the Soviets, "by obtaining the consent of the West to the division of Germany, are trying to alienate Western Germany from its allies." By imposing his will on Berlin, Khrushchev was trying to "destroy throughout the world the credibility of U.S. guarantees, which would threaten the national security of the U.S. itself." These correct observations were followed by somewhat more vague statements. Brandt "deplored" the fact that attempts at solving the German question and the problem of peace in Europe had not been pursued more vigorously, alluding to the Soviet "note offensive" of 1952. He said that the Berlin Wall made any serious negotiation with the Soviets impossible for free Germans, but nevertheless concluded that "even in Berlin, we must face facts as they are and struggle for every alleviation of human problems, every possible practical solution." This, briefly, was the premise of Ostpolitik.

Brandt's aide Egon Bahr (then the head of the West Berlin Press Office of the SPD), in his famous address of July 1963 to the Evangelische Akademie Tutzing, used the phrase *Wandel durch Annäherung* (change through rapprochement). Referring to Kennedy's suggestion that the West should trade with the East as much as possible without endangering its own security, he called for measures short of actual recognition, including negotiations for increased human contact and economic ties. These measures might also, he pointed out, help the people raise their standard of living so that their frustration would not lead to "uncontrollable developments" that would cause "unavoidable setbacks." He was clearly here expressing fear of a repetition of the June 1953 uprising, which, given the absence, in practice, of a U.S. commitment to German freedom and unity, might lead not only to increased severity on the part of the Pankow regime, but also to Soviet-inspired reprisals against West Berlin. Although Bahr by the late 1970s was promoting views that, on reasonable grounds, could be characterized as detrimental to Western defense, there can be no disputing the fact that, in the unpleasant context of 1962–1963, his stand was fully understandable. The tragedy of the German situation then as in the 1980s was that measures aimed at improving the material life and human rights of East Germans inevitably also aided the regime that was unjustly oppressing them, thus making its collapse, which was a necessary precondition for reunification, more unlikely than ever.

This unpleasant truth was at first fully realized by the proponents of the new national policy. With the course and results of the second Berlin crisis firmly in mind, Brandt, Bahr, Fritz Erler, Helmut Schmidt, and other leading Social Democrats had by 1963 decided that, for the sake of the East Germans, who were not about to be liberated by Western tanks, some level of relations with the regime would have to be tolerated.

THE CHANGING ASSUMPTIONS OF OSTPOLITIK (1963–1983)

To argue for toleration of East Germany as the only realistic means of helping East Germans, however, was not the same thing as an endorsement of that regime, much less a belief that peace and stability in Europe now depended primarily on recognition of the status quo. Until around 1970, Social Democratic arguments for a new approach to the communist regimes of Eastern Europe and the Soviet Union still generally included reassertions of the basic position of earlier times, namely that no genuine peace in Europe was possible until division was ended and East Europeans were granted the free exercise of their human rights.

The change from this, admittedly somewhat paradoxical, position to the outlook of the later 1970s and 1980s, which was that the Eastern regimes, including specifically East Germany, were deserving of understanding and support in themselves, and that they contributed to, rather than hindered, peace in Europe, was a rather lengthy process. Its beginnings may be found in certain of Brandt's speeches and articles from the later 1960s, when he was foreign minister in the CDU-CSU-SPD coalition of 1966– 1969. Thus, at the NATO foreign ministers' conference in June 1968, while acknowledging that the Soviet Union preferred isolation and tension to détente in Eastern Europe, he argued for Western concessions and specifically for an "interim solution" for the two Germanys, a "regulated coexistence" (geregeltes Nebeneinander).[24] Reunification and the solution of the German question were no longer ends in themselves, but should be placed "in the context of a general European peace order." Brandt was expressing the old Social Democratic belief in collective security agreements in these remarks, which also mark the shift in his policy from resistance to appeasement as the preferred way to deal with the facts of Soviet power and intransigence. The trend accelerated rapidly from the moment Brandt became chancellor in 1969. The same man who had fought tooth and nail in the 1950s for the principle that West Berlin was an integral part of the Federal Republic and who had reiterated time and again that the division of Germany, caused by the Soviet Union, was a constant threat to peace now, as chancellor, proved willing to surrender Federal claims to West Berlin and, far more important, to grant recognition of the statehood, sovereignty, and even legitimacy of the East German regime.

That regime had continued to woo the SPD and the West German trade union movement with occasional appeals to national unity until the later

1960s. This was in accordance with the SED party program of 1963 (superseded in 1976), which began:

> The Socialist Unity Party of Germany unshakably holds to its goal, the restoration of the national unity of Germany and the overcoming of division caused by the imperialist Western powers in conspiracy with West German monopoly capitalism. The struggle for a united, democratic, and peace-loving Germany has, since the work of Marx and Engels, been an integral part of the good traditions of the revolutionary German workers' movement.

All this was to change very abruptly in 1970, when Willy Brandt as chancellor traveled to Erfurt in East Germany to see Willi Stoph, chairman of the Council of Ministers of the GDR. As the first visit of a West German chancellor to East Germany, it marked the beginning of a process of modified recognition and acceptance of the communist regime that was a key element of Brandt's Ostpolitik.[25] In January of that year, Walter Ulbricht, the East German ruler, although arguing that the German Democratic Republic and the Federal Republic of Germany were two separate states, still repeated that "the German nation was divided two decades ago by the imperialist Western powers and the forces of West German monopoly capitalism. We, however, desire . . . that one day this nation, divided by imperialism . . . shall draw together again." Exactly two months later in Erfurt, Stoph declared that "the interests of socialism stand above all *alleged* national similarities" (emphasis added) and stressed far more vigorously than Ulbricht had the incompatibility of the socialist and capitalist social systems.[26]

The East German regime was determined that the new Ostpolitik, including the recognition of the political and territorial status quo in Eastern Europe created by Soviet power in 1945, should not lead to any expressions of national solidarity on any level within East Germany. Official recognition, trade privileges, loans, and gifts from West Germany were welcome; attempts to extend the policy to the individual and cultural level were not. Erich Honecker, who succeeded Ulbricht as head of state in 1971, declared to Western journalists in 1972 that "the verdict of history is clear: on German soil two German states with opposing social systems have arisen, which can nevertheless peacefully coexist;" nevertheless, "the ideological opposition means that segregation (*Abgrenzung*), and not rapprochement or convergence, is the order of the day." [27] Whereas a great number of Germans from the West were allowed to visit friends and relatives in the East, beginning in 1972, the number of visits in the other direction was limited to persons outside the work force, who would not deprive the regime of their labor if they chose to stay in the West (they would, in fact, relieve the regime of a charge). East Germany also benefited directly from strength of the West German economy. While the regime's representatives denounced West German monopoly capitalism, "based on the exploitation of man by man," they were busy releasing hundreds of political prisoners to West Germany each year for an average sum per head of about $60,000. Remarkably, the number of such prisoners in Eastern jails and labor camps remained the same (about 13,000). Whenever the number threatened to get too low, the police would round up new victims, thus guaranteeing the regime a permanent and welcome source of hard-currency income.

The first formal result of the new Ostpolitik was the Treaty on Basic Relations (Grundlagenvertrag) between the two Germanys that was signed in 1972 and ratified by the Federal Republic the following year. There now began a period of East-West German relations that, while strictly distinguished in Bonn from normal diplomatic relations with foreign states, provided the opportunity for a good deal of interaction and official contacts. From 1974 to 1981, the representative of the Federal government in East Berlin was a close collaborator of Brandt's named Günter Gaus. Gaus, a former foreign editor of *Der Spiegel* and hence an associate of its rather anti-American publisher, Rudolf Augstein, came to incorporate the second phase of Ostpolitik, in which the Eastern regimes were viewed with sympathy. In a book published in 1983 Gaus openly asserted that in East Germany some positive German values were better preserved and respected than in the West and that the regime was in fact far more humane, reasonable, and enlightened than the death zone at the border and the Berlin Wall might lead uninformed outsiders to suspect. Unfortunately, however, the world situation, the "logic of the blocs," and, especially, the "crusading mentality" of the Reagan administration in the United States had worsened East-West relations. Consequently, East Berlin could no more escape this deteriorating climate than could Bonn.[28]

The underlying message of Gaus's book was the same as that of numerous other speeches, articles, and essays of the early 1980s. If only the two superpowers would stop bothering the Europeans with their quarrel, which was no concern of Europe's anyway, mutually satisfactory arrangements were certainly possible. Gone, at least from the West German public scene, was the old instinctive rejection of a regime (East Germany) and a political situation (the division of Europe) as intrinsically immoral and illegitimate. In the revised version of Ostpolitik, as practiced by the SPD during its last years in power, and promoted by Brandt, Bahr, Oskar Lafontaine, Gaus, and others after its return to opposition in 1982, the thin line separating toleration of the East German regime for the sake of helping its innocent victims from active support in the interests of "mutual stability" and a mythical "security partnership" had been crossed. The image of political danger in the minds of leading politicians was no longer Munich 1938, but 1914; not a situation in which democratic statesmen gave in to the threats of a totalitarian regime, but a crisis of mutual misunderstanding and confusion leading to a war that no one wanted. The reading of postwar European history that saw the Soviet Union, totalitarianism, and the division of the continent as the fundamental political problem had given way to a reading that rejected the categorical distinction of democracy and totalitarian dictatorship, believed in a mutual East-West interest in stability and hence in maintaining division, and, finally, tended increasingly to blame the United States, and not the Soviet Union, for acting in ways that threatened war. As one West German critic put it: "The public is presented the image of the Soviets ready to negotiate at West German request and the Americans unwilling to negotiate despite German urging. The essence . . . is ultimately that the conceptions of threat are shifted. It is not the Soviets that have to be feared, but the Americans. From this altered fear it is not much further to the conclusion that Western Europe has to achieve security not *against* the Soviet Union, but *with* the Soviet Union."[29]

Paradoxically, while this was happening in the Federal Republic, an opposite change was occurring in France. There, in the 1960s, the United States was routinely blamed for East-West tensions, the division of Europe was hailed as a necessary, if unfortunate, condition of peace, and the existence of a Soviet threat was denied. Only a few voices, such as that of Raymond Aron, opposed this consensus. By the 1980s, it had been shattered by the combined influence of East European émigrés and Solzhenitsyn's *Gulag Archipelago*, the growing appreciation of Aron's strategic and philosophical analysis, and the emergence of a remarkable group of native, younger thinkers inspired by a renewed determination to defend liberal democracy.[30] Similar, if more modest, tendencies could be observed in some other Western countries.

Why this difference between West Germany and its allies? Four interrelated factors seem important. First, the almost complete success of the SPD-FDP government of 1969–1982 in convincing the people of the value and success of Ostpolitik. At the price of recognizing what was already the case, namely the territorial and political status quo in Eastern Europe, it was argued, West Germany had obtained humanitarian improvements for East Germans and security guarantees for Berlin from the Soviets; moreover, gifts and loans of money and technology were bound in the end to contribute to a liberalization of the Eastern regimes, including that of East Germany. Second, the gradual growth of Soviet power throughout the 1970s and after exercised a subtle and unacknowledged influence on West German policymaking and public debate. There was a very definite tendency to avoid doing or saying things that might annoy the Soviets. From being a means of leverage in Eastern Europe, therefore, Ostpolitik increasingly became a one-way street of accommodationism and, even, appeasement. Third, the presence of U.S. nuclear-armed forces in West Germany was an unpleasant reminder, not only of the incomplete sovereignty of the Federal Republic, but, more important, of the requirements and realities of deterrence. As these requirements and realities were disregarded or even denied, it became ever more likely that serious disturbances would result when the strategic balance needed restoration. This is precisely what happened in 1980 and after, when the NATO double-track decision, supported by Helmut Schmidt and, until 1983, by the parliamentary group of the SPD, was presented in 1979 as a necessary step to maintain deterrence. For those wide segments of the politically active public for whom there was no longer a Soviet threat and for whom the main cause of tension was U.S. actions, the double-track decision was clearly an intolerable provocation. The fourth factor, finally, was sociological and chronological: the increasing influence in politics, the media, the universities, and public life generally of a new generation that did not share the background and outlook either of the founders of West Germany and NATO or of those who administered both in the 1960s and 1970s. The reasons for this change are complex; some have to do with shifts in social psychology and attitudes common to all industrial societies, some are specific to West Germany and to the way these shifts were manifested in that country. They will be discussed further in Part II.[31]

Were there, by the mid-1980s, any signs that the illusions of Ostpolitik, the faith in the good intentions of the Soviet Union, and the belief that East and West Germany had common interests and goals were threatened? Some there were, but not many. A CDU-CSU-FDP coalition, led by Helmut Kohl, a former associate of Adenauer's, had replaced the Schmidt government in 1982. However, it remained committed to Ostpolitik, and by 1984 it was not yet clear whether this meant Ostpolitik (and national policy) in the manner of Lafontaine, Gaus, and the later Brandt, or the more refined and realistic attitude shared by the SPD and the CDU in the 1960s. The peace movement, though defeated in its attempt to stop the deployment of new U.S. missiles, which began in 1983, remained active. More important, the tone and content of public debate on the issues of defense, national policy, and the condition of Europe had not really changed. The "logic of the blocs," not Soviet actions, was still seen as the main problem. However, in one area there had been a change that might, in time, have some political influence. This was the revival of interest in the German nation as a historical and cultural phenomenon, a revival that must necessarily, if pursued honestly, lead to a confrontation with the actual history of Germany in 1945–1960 and hence to an improved understanding of the issues at stake.

3

THE NATIONAL ISSUE
AND HISTORICAL WRITING
SINCE THE 1960s

Neither outright nationalism nor strong sentiments on behalf of the old unified Reich were forces of any significance at any time in West German politics or public life, and what little there was had largely died out by the early 1960s. The founder generation of the republic, men born and educated in the Wilhelmian Reich, was gone from the political arena by the mid-1960s. It was succeeded in the leadership of the political parties and public life by a much more disparate group of individuals born in the first decade and a half of the twentieth century and ranging from Gerhard Schröder in the CDU to Willy Brandt in the SPD. These were men whose formative political experiences dated from the Weimar Republic, when the democratic forces in the Weimar coalition of parties rejected the overweening nationalism characteristic of the influential antidemocratic forces of the right. None of them were at all inclined to militant nationalism of this sort, nor did they share the modified pride in national unity characteristic of the founders. Their tenure of power in West Germany, from the mid-1960s to, roughly, the later 1970s, was the time of the new Ostpolitik, the abandonment of the Hallstein Doctrine, and the acceptance of the division of Europe as the necessary basis for negotiations and, one hoped, humanitarian improvements for Germans in the East.

There was one important, if short-lived, resurgence of nationalism during this period. In late 1966, a severe economic crisis prompted the formation of the Grand Coalition of CDU-CSU and SPD, with Kurt Georg Kiesinger as chancellor and Willy Brandt as foreign minister. The role of sole opposition party fell to the liberals, the FDP, who had been in government in all but four years of the Federal Republic's history. The collaboration of CDU and SPD, the economic crisis, and the fear aroused in some quarters by what was seen as the excessive weight of the coalition, temporarily drove some hundreds of thousands of voters to the right-wing National Democratic Party (NPD), which during 1967–1968 gained representation in the governments of several Länder. However, in the federal elections of 1969 the NPD failed to clear the 5 percent hurdle and rapidly declined into the insignificance from which it had emerged. There was no repeat of this temporary success in the later economic crises of 1973–1974 and 1980–1981.

The politicians and activists of the NPD seem to have been recruited mainly from the ranks of unrepentant former Nazis and nationalists, and the party could thus be said to represent the last fling of old-style nationalism on the political stage. The revival of interest in the national issue and the question of national identity that began in the late 1970s is of a wholly different stamp and has little, if anything, to do with nationalism or nostalgia for the old Reich.

The period 1967–1974 was marked by a series of domestic political crises, culminating in the fall of Brandt from the chancellorship, and the effects of an international crisis, namely the first oil shock. In 1967 began the period of student unrest, radical agitation, and civil confrontation, which had not really ended even in the mid-1980s, though the type of protest changed during the 1970s. Though this radical activism could certainly be described as an expression of serious and, among the younger generation, widespread disaffection from and dissatisfaction with prevailing social, political, and economic conditions, there was no sign that the national question or the problem of national identity was regarded by the activists as being of any interest or relevance whatever.[1]

In 1969, the formation of the social-liberal SPD-FDP coalition marked the decisive move to the new Ostpolitik. On the federal political level, the government was now faced with the challenge of formulating, presenting, defending, and ratifying the treaties with East Germany, the Soviet Union, and other East European countries. Though the outcome of these struggles was never really in doubt, they were intense and exposed the government to questions, doubts, and criticism from domestic rivals and foreign allies. The challenge reached its high point in the attempt by the Bavarian CSU government in 1973 to have the Grundlagenvertrag with East Germany voided by the Federal Constitutional Court on the grounds that it violated the Basic Law.[2] The attempt failed, and the court, in an ambiguous ruling that was criticized by both sides in the debate, determined that the Grundlagenvertrag, though recognizing the independent statehood of the GDR, did not violate the command of the Basic Law to preserve the unity of Germany or the rights of Germans in the East. West Germany was declared to be still "partially identical" with the German Reich and responsible for the whole of Germany. The GDR could therefore not be regarded as foreign territory. Needless to say, this reading was rejected out of hand by the East German regime, which insisted more than ever before that the idea of a German national identity comprising both states was meaningless and unacceptable.

While the country was busy trying to cope with the effects of the first oil crisis in the spring of 1974, an assistant of Brandt's, Günter Guillaume, was revealed as a spy for the East German State Security Service. Suspicions of Brandt's general political judgment and reliability resurfaced in the CDU, and he resigned the chancellorship, though retaining control of the SPD. He was replaced, from 1974 to 1982, by Helmut Schmidt.

The arrival of Schmidt signaled the rise of yet another generation to the political leadership of West Germany. This was the generation of the soldiers of World War II, which also included the FDP leader, Hans-Dietrich Genscher, and the CSU leader, Franz-Josef Strauss. With the partial exception of Strauss, who was also untypical in that he had achieved a leading position in the 1950s, much earlier than his contemporaries, they were extreme pragmatists, perfect examples of what Schelsky called "the skeptical generation." Consequently, not only national issues, but all broader questions concerning what meaning and purpose might, or should, inform policies and political decisions, were pushed aside. In the "new politics" of the 1970s, what mattered were practical results and technical competence, not such intangibles as Sinn (meaning) or Geist (spirit).[3]

This concentration on practical challenges was characteristic of the government of the economist Schmidt as opposed to that of the journalist and political romantic Brandt. It was successful in dealing with the first oil crisis and the terrorist violence that was one of the outgrowths of late 1960s radicalism. Another outgrowth, however, namely the antinuclear and antiindustrial protest movements and citizens' initiatives of the 1970s, could not be dealt with in the pragmatic manner of the Schmidt-Genscher government. They became permanent fixtures of the political and social landscape and collectively constituted the Szene (scene), a subculture found, by the later 1970s, in every West German city, which included students, dropouts, writers and some academics, and varying numbers of well-wishers, hangerson, and supporters. While generally expressing an overwhelmingly negative attitude to political life and to democratic institutions generally, the Szene was continuing evidence of the disaffection of many of the younger generation with existing conditions.

This disaffection, by the late 1970s, included not only the West German society and polity, but the industrial world as a whole, and in particular the United States as its most powerful and successful part. The Szene, the citizens' initiatives, and their supporters, were gradually becoming politicized or repoliticized, and this time the focus was primarily on the United States and NATO, not on domestic issues or persons perceived as reactionary. The Green movement, and along with it the peace movement, was born out of this process of politicization and had by 1984 established itself as a seemingly permanent element in West German politics.[4]

These developments at first had little to do with the national question. The anti-American and anti-NATO orientation of the Greens and the peaceniks, however, almost automatically drove them to consider the national question, even if superficially. The more intelligent of them easily saw that if one questioned the value of U.S. policies for West Germany, one was obliged to propose alternatives and hence to address the issue of West Germany's special political situation. A vague idea of some sort of federation or reunification between two Germanys, each neutralized and separated from their respective superpower, arose and spread in the early 1980s among certain Greens and left-wing Social Democrats. A number of books, articles, and speeches supported this idea without, however, offering very concrete suggestions on how to implement it.[5]

While this political romanticism was growing within the left and within the Szene from the late 1970s, a much broader and more general revival of interest in the national issue and in the problem of the political and national identity of Germans as a people and West Germany as a country was taking place. This revival could be seen in various ways; in the number of conferences on national identity, Germany, and the implications of the state of U.S.-Soviet relations for West Germany; in the flood of newspaper and magazine articles on all aspects of the national issue; and in the increase of popular interest in German history, an increase that seemed to stand in direct proportion to the decline in the amount and quality of the teaching of German or any other sort of history in the schools. In what follows I shall discuss the latter symptom, primarily because I believe it to be both the most intrinsically interesting and also potentially the most important aspect of the renewed concern with the national issue. The phenomenon of a decline in general historical knowledge among young people and a simultaneous increase in historical interest, expressed in the production of, and the market for, popular historical works, could be observed in other Western countries as well, perhaps most obviously in France. This was obviously not only an educational problem. As the historian Rudolf von Thadden said, it raised "the extra-scientific and in the end political question of historical consciousness."[6] In West Germany, where the consensus on how to view the national past was never as wide as in France, and where the postwar problem of national division made the question of historical identity acute, this question of historical consciousness took on a special significance.

GERMAN HISTORIANS AND NATIONALISM BEFORE 1945

In order to put the revival of historical interest and its implications into perspective, it is necessary not only to look at the external political environment, as I have done above, but also to understand at least the main lines of the internal history of the discipline.[7]

The situation of the German historical profession in 1945 was, in a way, paradoxical. Apart from the very serious loss of its Jewish practitioners, most of whom emigrated to the United States, thereby enriching American academic life, it had been remarkably unaffected by the Nazi regime. However, this general immunity from ideological *Gleichschaltung* (political control) was due less to any special antitotalitarian vigor displayed by historians than to the broad conservative and nationalist consensus in the profession. Historians had largely escaped censorship or exploitation by the regime because, in general, they sympathized with what they saw as its praiseworthy aim of restoring German national dignity and power.[8] The reasons for the dominance of a national-conservative outlook in German historical writing cannot be fully discussed here, where my purpose simply is to provide a background sketch. Still, a few remarks are in order. First, there was the principle, established in the early nineteenth century by the founders of modern historical study, especially Leopold von Ranke, that since nation-states were the main agents of political action, they should be the objects of historical description. The aim of the new historical science, unlike the historiography of the Enlightenment (which usually had a didactic or moral purpose), was to discover "how things actually were" and to describe the unique individuality of past epochs and events. Since the new science also, in the interests of truth and reliability, focused almost exclusively on political history, the appropriate unit of study was the highest form of political organization, the nation-state. Of course, this focus on the political history of nation-states was not unrelated to the fact that the new approach to the study of history, or historicism, as it came to be called, was emerging in the early nineteenth century, when the nation-state was becoming the basis of political life in the West.[9]

Second, as nationalism as a social force and a mass ideology gained ground, some historians began increasingly to see the nation-state not only as the proper object of study, but also as a supreme achievement of civilization. This tendency triumphed in Germany with some suddenness after 1866, when Prussia's victory over the Austro-Hungarian empire marked the end of hopes for a pan-German state (including Austria), and prepared the ground for the *kleindeutsch* (little-German) nation-state of 1871–1945.[10] It culminated in the work of the Prussian historian and nationalist liberal politician Heinrich von Treitschke, who, in his mature work after 1866, not only argued that the only possible political framework for Germany was the very nation-state that came into being in 1871, but also that foreign policy, that is, relations and conflicts with other sovereign states, was the cause of all historical change. With few exceptions, these two arguments, and the political position they implied, remained dominant among German historians until well after 1945.[11]

The defeat of Germany in World War I was a shattering blow to the vast majority of German historians who had identified with the imperial regime of 1871–1918 and its war aims. It affected their political and professional attitudes in two rather different ways. Some historians, like Friedrich Meinecke, accepted the defeat as a demonstration of the failure of the aggressive nationalism of that period and gave the democratic constitution their full support. They, however, were a minority. Their colleagues by and large continued to distrust mass democracy and gave the Weimar Republic of 1918–1933 only conditional support. However, even in this group there were many who did not simply reassert old nationalistic ideas and assumptions; they tended to spiritualize national values and to look for a cultural and moral renewal in German political and social life beyond democracy and capitalism, a renewal based on the idea of a "German path" (*deutscher Sonderweg*) of cultural and political development.[12]

At the end of the Weimar Republic, then, there were three main orientations represented in the mainstream of German historical studies, namely Meinecke's pro-republicanism, the reassertive political nationalism of such as Erich Marcks, and the more ethical nationalism, based on belief in the value of a specific German culture, represented primarily by a group of somewhat younger historians, such as Gerhard Ritter and Hans Rothfels.[13] Meinecke was already an older man in the 1920s, and his particular legacy was continued above all by his students, many of them Jewish, who emigrated in 1933 and after and made their (very successful) careers in the United States. The outright political nationalists had little trouble making their peace with Nazism, which many of them welcomed. The ethical nationalists, finally, reacted to Hitler in different ways. Rothfels, being Jewish, was forced from his chair in Königsberg at the height of his career and went to the United States, but after the war he was one of the few émigré historians to return and enjoyed a delayed second career around 1960. Ritter remained and, some critics claimed, collaborated too closely with the nationalists and ideologues who were allowed to control the profession and its institutions under Nazism; on the other hand, he demonstratively retained contact with some of the émigrés. During the war he joined the resistance group of Carl Goerdeler, the mayor of Leipzig, who was hanged in 1944.[14]

GERMAN HISTORICAL WRITING SINCE 1945

The defeat in 1945 undermined the assumptions and professional beliefs of German historians of all three categories, political nationalist, ethical nationalist, or republican liberal. As for the last group, it was above all that of Meinecke, and his political liberalism and personal blend of political and cultural history, that seemed a dead end in 1945. His best students were teaching and writing in the United States, and he was now too old (83 in 1945) to do much more. His final gesture was to produce, in his work *Die deutsche Katastrophe* (The German catastrophe), an indictment of the very principles and aims of political nationalism as it had developed in Germany since 1866, and to argue, in a lecture in 1948, that perhaps Jakob Burckhardt, the cultural historian and philosopher, was a better guide for the present than Leopold von Ranke, whose glorification of the nation-state Meinecke now saw as a cause of much evil.[15]

Political nationalism had lost credibility and moral justification under the Nazi regime, and even had it survived among historians, the division of Germany in 1947–1949 and the wholly unprecedented international environment of the postwar period would have sufficed to make it irrelevant as a philosophical position. This left ethical nationalism, which in the form of a national conservatism stressing cultural factors indeed became the dominant outlook of West German historians until around 1960. Gerhard Ritter came into his own during the 1950s as the elder statesman of the profession, and his philosophical essays on Nazism and German history in a European context, some written during the war, but all published or reissued after 1945, were popular, not just among other historians, due to their elegant blend of moderate moralism and their interpretation of Nazism as above all a consequence of the political mobilization of the popular masses, and not as evidence of some crucial flaw in German society and culture.[16] There was little attempt to look closely at the economic, political, and social conditions and problems of the period after 1871 or to evaluate Nazism as other than a disaster caused by alien forces. On the other hand, there was a new and considerable professional and popular interest in European political and cultural history, as well as in the history of Germany before industrialization and the establishment of the nation-state of 1871. Medieval studies, where the sharp distinction of social, political, and economic history, and the belief in the nation-state as the agent of change, had never been applicable, flourished, and some of the most interesting philosophical speculation in the period 1945–1960 on the role of historical studies and on the character of German history and culture as a whole came from medievalists such as Hermann Heimpel (one of the few openly repentant former National Socialists), Peter

Rassow, Friedrich Heer, Herbert Grundmann, Albert Mirgeler, Michael Seidlmayer, and Fritz Kern.[17] In a piece written in 1962, Mirgeler argued that political and cultural pluralism, not centralism, had been the historically given condition of Germany since the ninth century. Pointing to the discrepancy between the unitary national histories of West European states and the constant fragmentation of Germany, Mirgeler noted:

> The discrepancy determined not only our external history, that is, our relations to other European peoples, but also the inner-German problem. Let us recall the conception of Charlemagne, in which the Romance and Germanic lands were to balance each other in a central zone that would be both Frankish and Germanic. Whatever the later fate of that central zone, the dynamic border between the older and the younger Europe never coincided exactly with the western limits of the later German empire . . . Even in Charlemagne's conception, therefore, there was not merely one Germany, but two Germanys: the one Germany was a task for the future, the two were historical and geographical facts. It is useless to try to conceal this fundamental fact of German history by an ideology of ill-conceived centralism or by mere force. In any general European conflict, the dynamic border on German soil inevitably reappears, for the simple reason that the German West was European before it was German . . . On this condition rests another, equally important fact, confirmed throughout our history, namely that the German question has always been simultaneously a European question, and that the task of German unity presupposes a common European ground.[18]

Mirgeler's attempts to anchor German history and the contemporary German question in a broad framework of European history were typical of a fruitful trend in West German historical writing in the 1950s that was by no means entirely extinct in the 1980s, as will be seen below. A similar current was represented by Fritz Kern, who moved from a narrow interest in medieval law and theories of power to universal history, and in his last years helped launch the *Historia Mundi*, a multivolume world history with each period or culture treated by a different specialist. Such multivolume projects were characteristic of what seems to be a specifically German blend of professional study and popular culture, which survived the traumatic changes of the 1940s. As I shall argue below, an important indication of the revival of popular interest in history since the mid-1970s was precisely the popularity of new projects of this type.

The fundamental assertion of the national conservative school of the 1950s was that a narrow national interpretation of history, whether as method or as ideology, was illegitimate and morally irresponsible. Whether these historians focused on Germany or on Western Europe, on antiquity, the Middle Ages, or the modern era, they all saw states, cultures, and societies in interaction and balance. The wealth of new insight and understanding they provided is sufficient to refute claims made by some critics that West German historical writing from 1945 to the 1960s was little more than a moralized and spiritualized version of the old nationalistic approach. Rothfels, in particular, though personally of a conservative bent, made great efforts in the 1950s and early 1960s to promote the inclusion of the study of social conditions and social policy in political history. An important outlet for younger historians were the *Vierteljahrshefte für Zeitgeschichte* (a journal of contemporary history), edited, in the 1950s, by Rothfels and Theodor Eschenburg. The main theme of Rothfels's own work was the "importance of the problem of nations and nationalities for national and transnational politics, culture, and order, in the perspective of basic values of political ethics."[19] Few historians felt inclined to pursue this subject, but it nevertheless anticipated some of the themes of debate in the 1980s, notably the renewed interest in *Mitteleuropa* and the hope (or illusion) cherished by a number of peace movement sympathizers that some sort of European political order could be achieved across the East-West divide.

By 1960, the leading spokesmen of the ethical nationalist outlook were at or near retirement age, and younger men, whose professional training had mostly taken place after 1945, were coming to the fore. At the same time, the total number of posts in historical teaching and research was being increased as part of the general expansion of higher education. The early 1960s, therefore, marked a sea change in the historical profession comparable, in its way, to the change in the international and domestic political climate caused by the second Berlin crisis and the U.S.-Soviet détente that immediately followed. However, the dominance of conservative ethical nationalism was not replaced by any single rival outlook. Though political and diplomatic history based on the old principle of nation-states as the primary actors steadily lost ground, it was by no means wholly without practitioners even in the 1980s. On the other hand, while many of the most talented and productive younger historians took the social and economic conditions of Germany in the period of industrialization, war, and dictatorship (1871–1945) as their focus, the approaches and specific interests varied greatly and not until the mid-1970s could one speak of a definite school of what came to be called *Gesellschaftsgeschichte* or "history of society." The new historians did, however, share one characteristic common bias: they all denied that politics and foreign relations were the major causes of change, and some even went so far as to make political developments into mere functions of underlying processes in the social and economic structure. For them, accordingly, questions of national identity, national culture, or the development and contemporary condition of the German nation were of little interest or concern.

The first example of change in the profession that came to wider public attention was, however, not a work of social or economic history, but a methodologically conventional diplomatic history of the origins of World War I. The difference between this work, Fritz Fischer's *Germany's War Aims in the First World War*, first published in 1961, and earlier studies lay in the thesis and not in the method. Against the professional consensus that the war of 1914 was largely an accident in which all parties were equally guilty, Fischer claimed that German military and political leaders had, quite consciously, planned an attack on the rest of Europe with the express purpose of dominating the continent and thus achieving the status of a world power.[20] Although his interpretations have been challenged, there is no doubt that he was able to make a good case that the ideology of expansion was widespread in many military groups, particularly the "new men" of the imperial navy who were competing with the old Junker-dominated army for the emperor's favor.

Fischer's work had a twofold impact on historians and on political debate in West Germany generally. First, it played a decisive part in opening the way to thorough and critical study of the interrelationships of the economy, politics, and nationalist ideology in post-1871 Germany. More important, it introduced a moralistic element into the evaluation of modern German history that coexisted uneasily with the claims made for the new emphasis on social history, claims that stressed the greater objectivity, explanatory force, and methodological rigor of the new approach by comparison with the purely political focus of the older, national-conservative historians. If Fischer could document the existence of beliefs and desires in pre-1914 Germany that were considered morally deficient in the 1960s, this was a powerful help to those historians who now saw their main task as finding the roots of Nazism in the social, economic, and cultural conditions of Germany in the period of industrialization. Since the search for the roots of Nazism was, almost inevitably, a morally charged task, the new social historians, though claiming to be more objective, and hence less judgmental, than the older political history, were often in practice no less, and often far more, prone to judging the past by the standards of the present. To a considerable degree, knowing the conclusion of German national history under Nazism, they allowed themselves to make the mistake of finding, or even inventing, undesirable and morally blameworthy traits in earlier periods.

Generalizing very roughly, then, one can say that from the early 1960s to the late 1970s, political history in a form more or less recognizably similar to that of the old-fashioned nationalists, although without the nationalist bias, survived, though it had lost its dominant position within the profession, whereas a growing number of the younger generation of historians turned to a wide range of problems in the general area of social and economic development. The political history of the twentieth century was particularly well served by the work of Karl Dietrich Bracher and Hans-Peter Schwarz, who were both very productive and, in the 1980s, editors of the *Vierteljahrshefte für Zeitgeschichte*, cofounded by Rothfels. While Schwarz concentrated on the political history of West Germany and on the analysis of East-West problems, Bracher included ideologies and social conditions in a broad perspective of European history in the twentieth century. As to the believers in social and structural history, they were, by the later 1970s, themselves fully established and even, in some cases, approaching retirement. There was little overlap between the two groups, and a good deal of mutual incomprehension, which culminated in the late 1970s in a series of fairly fierce polemics in the professional journals, which spilled over into the mass media.[21]

Even if there had been anyone around to lead it, a simple return to the modified nationalism of the 1950s was impossible. Instead, those who might want to revive the national issue, in historical writing or otherwise, would have to take cognizance, even if unsympathetically, of Brandt's trips to the East, the West German treaties with the Soviet Union, Poland, East Germany, and Czechoslovakia; and the acceptance, at the Conference on Security and Cooperation in Europe in Helsinki in 1975, of the Soviet conquests and the status quo, as interpreted by the Soviet Union, in Eastern Europe. These political developments changed the ways in which the national issue and the question of national identity could be put in contemporary debate, but at the same time, the final end of hopes for political reunification in the near future stimulated a revival of interest in the common national past.

Interest in history in general was on the rise in the 1970s, despite, or perhaps because of, the loss of familiarity with German and European political and cultural history among young people. The social historians denied the importance of the old ruling classes and often argued specifically that social and economic history, as they practiced it, was the only kind of history compatible with a progressive, liberal, or leftist political outlook. Since such an outlook and a comparable, widespread contempt for old-fashioned political history were dominant among the politicians and bureaucrats who designed school and university curricula in the 1970s, young people were exposed to a bewildering array of problems and issues that they had no basis for studying or judging properly without the broad general knowledge of the kind that the old curricula had provided. As educators, the social historians were prone to forget that they were only able to criticize and to go beyond political and diplomatic history because they themselves still remembered the facts and the framework provided by the older tradition. As practiced and taught in the 1970s, history in West Germany was too exclusively critical, as some of its practitioners admitted; the element of tradition, of maintaining and transmitting the knowledge collected by earlier generations, using earlier methods, was neglected. In neglecting to define and transmit a basis of historical knowledge, moreover, those leading historians who regarded themselves as the most progressive and enlightened members of their profession failed adequately to deal with the fact that historical consciousness, as the foundation of the adaptation of individuals and groups to their political and cultural environment, was again becoming an issue.[22]

One practical reason for this failure was the almost complete turning away, by those who regarded themselves as innovative and liberal, from the literary, narrative aspects of historical writing. To write history as a good story, immediately understandable on a human level, was, in the eyes of many social historians, wrong for two reasons. It not only obfuscated and simplified the true complexity of past conditions, but it was also, in a way not easily defined, unscientific, and there was general agreement, in West Germany as elsewhere, that history was a social science, and not, as the historicists of the nineteenth century had claimed, a unique science unlike any other and one that, in its narrative expression at least, partook greatly of art.[23] However, popular demand for history could not be satisfied with the products of social history. Here, narrative and good stories were still required. This meant that the renewal of history as a force in public and cultural life in West Germany, and as a means of returning to the national question in new ways, was, initially at least, the work of historians on the margin of the profession as it appeared in the early 1970s.

Two important works signaling a revival of popular interest in German history in the early 1970s were biographies, namely Golo Mann's life of the seventeenth-century warlord Wallenstein and Joachim Fest's study of Adolf Hitler.[24] Fest's work was the first full-length study of the German dictator to enjoy great popular acclaim in West Germany and opened a phase of discussion of Nazism that was both more nuanced and less colored by personal or political polemics than before. Fest was an editor of the *Frankfurter Allgemeine Zeitung*, one of the three leading daily newspapers in West Germany, and Mann had been a co-editor, in the 1960s, of a multivolume world history of the older type, that is, focusing on political and cultural history, published by Propyläen Verlag, a subsidiary of the newspaper and publishing group owned by Axel Springer that included another leading daily, *Die Welt*.

The Propyläen Verlag, whose publishing policies generally, but not exclusively, followed the conservative inclinations of its owner, played an important part in increasing the exposure of the West German public to historical writing over the next decade and a half. In 1975–1976, the house issued a *Propyläen Geschichte Europas* in six volumes. Some of the authors chosen for this project, such as Theodor Schieder or Bracher, were leading exponents of some of the post-1960 methods and approaches, but at the same time concerned to combine these new approaches with a reasonable concentration on political events and an ability to present large masses of material and broad perspectives in easily understandable ways. Thus, this European history marked a breakthrough to broad public awareness of the new kinds of history, while also showing that it was indeed possible to incorporate new methods and insights into a synthesis in which political and diplomatic history still received its due.

NEO-NATIONALISM AND HISTORICAL CONSCIOUSNESS IN THE 1980s

One of the contributors to the *Propyläen Geschichte Europas* fell wholly outside the categories of social versus political history, although his contribution in this case showed no sign of his eccentricity. This was Hellmut Diwald, a professor at the University of Erlangen and a native of the Sudetenland, the German area of Bohemia annexed by Hitler in 1938. Three years after his volume in the Propyläen series appeared, he shocked the public and the professional world by publishing (also through Propyläen), an 800-page tome entitled *Geschichte der Deutschen* (History of the Germans). Its most striking feature is its narrative structure, which begins in the late 1970s and winds backward to the year 919, the traditional starting point of German history. However, this was not the reason why Golo Mann, in a review, described its contents as "the most outrageous matter I have had occasion to read in a German book since 1945."[25] Rather, it was Diwald's opinions on German history and especially about such sensitive topics as National Socialism, World War II, and the national issue after 1945. He was denounced, and indeed saw himself, as a man of the right; nevertheless, his view concerning national policy was not at all that of Adenauer. Paradoxically, he gave East Germany more credit than West Germany on the grounds that at least the East German regime had no choice and was consistent in its rejection of unification, whereas the West German government was opportunistic and prone to give way to the strongest assertion of political will by allies or adversaries. Inasmuch as this amounts to a criticism of Ostpolitik for not really advancing the cause of unity, it is certainly an arguable proposition. However, in refusing to go along with Adenauer's principled refusal to grant legitimacy to the East German regime and in ridiculing Adenauer's national policy, Diwald also drew perilously near to blaming the West, not the Soviet Union, for division. In a subsequent article, written for the anthology *Die deutsche Einheit kommt bestimmt* (German unity is sure to come), Diwald echoed the anti-American left in asking "what does Germany, what do the Germans, have to do with the motives, arguments, and interests of the two rivals? The United States and the Soviet Union each claims that it alone... guarantees our security. A security that consists of being exposed, as a Central European nuclear battlefield, to certain destruction."[26] In an exhibition of historical blindness, surprising in an historian whose claim was that he was more perceptive than his colleagues, Diwald ignored, first, that the division of Germany was the direct consequence of German aggression under Hitler, and second, that the division of Europe and the East-West conflict were not irrelevant to Germany, but that on the contrary the fate and national interest of all Germans was intimately tied to the survival of the West. To argue, as he did, that the West was primarily to blame for the division of Germany, because it hypocritically claimed to be defending freedom and democracy, whereas the Soviet Union had a legitimate interest in keeping Germany divided and maintaining control in Eastern Europe, was to accept wholesale the simplistic propaganda of the left and the peace movement. He had forgotten, or chose to disregard, the axiom of West German policy for twenty years after 1949, that the pursuit of unification must never jeopardize security or the integrity of democratic institutions. In his anti-Western, and specifically anti-American nationalism, Diwald was ideologically close to left-wing nationalists such as Peter Brandt, another contributor to *Die deutsche Einheit kommt bestimmt*. Brandt's contribution was entitled "Patriotism from the Left." His belief in an anti-Western, anticapitalist nationalism, based on the hope of reunification in a neutral, socialist state, had already been made clear in 1981, when he published the anthology *Die Linke und die nationale Frage* (The left and the national question).[27]

Another, far less overtly political event had in the meantime further stimulated an interest in national history and hence in the question of national identity. This was an exhibition in Stuttgart in 1977, the theme of which was culture and civilization in the Staufen period (1150–1250). The subject was remote enough in time for the exhibition to become, in the experience of many visitors, a reaffirmation of the value of the national past. As such it paved the way for another exhibition, that on Prussia in Berlin in 1981, which provided the occasion for a rich yield of public debate and books about, for, and against Prussia as a state and as a part of German history.[28] The tone of many of the writings included in the five-volume anthology published as a catalogue of and companion to the exhibition on Prussia was highly critical, after the fashion of the no longer so new social history, but there was also, in some contributions, a definite fascination with a subject that had been largely ignored by self-styled liberal and progressive historians. It is noteworthy that volume 3, a richly annotated compilation of original texts, letters, and other sources for Prussian social history was edited by Peter Brandt. That Brandt's interest in German history was closely connected with his political stance was clear from the introduction he provided to the above-mentioned anthology of writings and speeches on the national issue by leaders of the German left, which was published in the same year (1981).[29] While critical of aspects of Prussia that he found objectionable, the young Brandt was openly concerned to see positive elements in Prussian history and to argue that a true German left both could and should take an interest in the national issue as an ideological base from which to attack the hegemony over Germany held by the United States and the Soviet Union.

The interest in Prussia continued to grow after the exhibition. In 1981, an historian who, like Joachim Fest and Golo Mann, was also a journalist, Lothar Gall, published a massive biography of Bismarck, and in 1983 this was followed by a successful study of Frederick the Great by Theodor Schieder.[30] Both were issued by the Propyläen Verlag, which by now had established itself as the dominant producer of historical works of high scientific standard for the educated public. As Schieder was one of the older leaders of those historians who, since the early 1960s, had emphasized social history at the expense of politics and diplomacy, his own turn to biographical work was a significant gesture. His book also confirmed the tendency, established with the *Propyläen Geschichte Europas* in the mid-1970s, for Propyläen, normally considered a fairly conservative house, to invite adherents of the newer schools to try their hand at writing for a broader public. This was further evident in the choice of authors for the first multivolume popular history of Germany to be published since the war, the *Propyläen Geschichte Deutschlands* in eight projected volumes that began appearing in 1983.

By the early 1980s marketing experts in West German publishing must have discovered that national history in massive doses was an idea whose time had returned. In addition to the Propyläen series, the new house of Severin and Siedler (subsequently changed to Siedler alone) in West Berlin launched, in 1982, a six-volume history entitled *Die Deutschen und ihre Nation* (The Germans and their nation), covering the period after 1763. Severin and Siedler was an interesting newcomer in other respects as well. The firm was established in 1981 and quickly made a mark with a selection of political and historical works focusing on various hitherto unfashionable themes related to national history and the national question, such as the German resistance to Hitler, political and religious essays on contemporary culture, biographies of German historical figures, and critical contributions to the political debate of a generally conservative cast. However, the conservatism of Siedler authors was not generally that of the CDU, where the national issue since the 1960s was addressed in subdued tones, if at all, but often of an older and more assertive variety that coexisted quite well with the nationalist or proto-nationalist tendencies on the left as expressed, for example, by Peter Brandt. The six-volume German history, by contrast, was a pluralistic enterprise much like the Propyläen projects; the authors included Atlanticist CDU conservatives like Michael Stürmer (whose political opinions did not prevent him from writing excellent social history), SPD sympathizers like Hagen Schulze, and culturally conservative but politically liberal free spirits like the versatile Heinrich Lutz.

The problem of national identity was addressed only indirectly in the vast bulk of these works; however, all the authors seemed to share a common theme in their attempts to present various segments of the national past to an audience, many of whom were now too young to remember the decade of defeat and division. This theme was that political unity in a single nation-state was neither the ideal nor the typical fate of Germans in history. Simply by virtue of presenting a panorama of political, cultural, social, and economic conditions and developments in the long term, these histories taught their readers that "Germany" and the unified nation-state of 1871–1945 were not synonymous.[31] As such, they accorded well with the post-1969 consensus on Ostpolitik, that it was, among other things, a means of securing the continuity at least of the *Kulturnation* (cultural nation) in the consciousness of West German citizens. One possible consequence of this view, however, was potentially dangerous as a source of complacency regarding the problem of national division and the political conflict that had caused it, namely the idea that since Germany in the past had usually been politically fragmented, the post-1949 situation was not so original or unusual after all and should therefore not be a cause for special alarm or indignation. This idea, of course, ignored the obvious fact that while political disunity was certainly typical of German history, nevertheless there were no minefields and no death traps on the border, say, of Saxony and Bavaria in 1866, nor were attempts to leave any German state forbidden to all inhabitants on principle, as they were in East Germany.

The problem of the national and civic identity of the West German state was perhaps the central theme of a third multivolume historical work of the 1980s, the *Geschichte der Bundesrepublik Deutschland* (History of the Federal Republic of Germany) in five volumes published in 1981–1985, covering the years 1945–1980. The very decision to publish such a work marked the extent to which the Federal Republic was seen, by a majority of its citizens, as a state in its own right, based on a legal and legitimate political order. In that respect it was symptomatic of the new *Staatsbewusstsein* (consciousness of statehood, of the reality of sovereignty) that many professed to see in West Germany in the 1980s, paradoxically enough simultaneously with the *Staatsverdrossenheit* (disgust with the state) that was a common attitude among the Greens. However, it did not mark a denial of the national issue; on the contrary, the detailed exposure, in excellent literary style, of the East-West confrontation of 1945–1955 and of the blend of hopes, illusions, and possibilities on the road to West German independence could only serve to emphasize the premises and principles of West German national and foreign policy. The authorial team included Hans-Peter Schwarz, a leading analyst of contemporary international politics and the acknowledged expert on Adenauer and his time, and Karl Dietrich Bracher. The latter had contributed a prize-winning volume to the *Propyläen Geschichte Europas* and was regarded by Hans-Ulrich Wehler, a leader of the social historical school, as "our best *Zeithistoriker*" (historian of the present era), although he was definitely a practitioner of a type of political and intellectual history that the social historians regarded as conservative. One could say that, compared with the Propyläen or the Siedler series, or indeed with scholarship on modern German history generally, the *Geschichte der Bundesrepublik Deutschland* presented a more conservative image, although this would be unfair; the fact of the matter was that although the polemical struggles over who was right in making the decisions concerning the fate of postwar Germany and why were fierce and long-lasting, nevertheless the consensus on basic interpretations among serious scholars was fairly wide.

Apart from the essays published on the occasion of the Staufen and Prussian exhibitions and the several multivolume works I have mentioned, the number of individual works, general histories of part or all of Germany, or biographies aimed at the educated general reader (a figure many had thought long gone from the public scene) in the 1980s were certainly evidence of a serious and broad revival of historical interest. An obvious task for West Germany's foreign friends, allies, and well-wishers was to respond to this interest in national history, and by extension in the current national question, by producing studies and interpretations of their own. Such a response would show that the outside world was aware that the West German intellectual and political scene in the 1980s consisted of more than the radically anti-Western and anti-NATO peace movement on the one hand and the pro-Atlantic and pro-NATO official circles on the other. It might also convince many of those tempted, in their irritation with U.S. behavior and policies, to support the peace movement, to engage in serious dialogue with foreign friends on matters of mutual concern. Unfortunately, with few exceptions, this foreign response was not forthcoming.

The most important of these exceptions were two American books, *The*

German Problem Reconsidered, by David Calleo, and *The Germans*, by Gordon Craig.[32] Calleo's book, published in 1978 and in an inferior German translation in 1980, was a series of wide-ranging essays on the form, constraints, and principles of German foreign policy from 1870 until the inauguration of the new Ostpolitik in the late 1960s. The arguments were stimulating and sometimes daring, and the view of the motivations and rationale of German policy, even Hitler's, was much more sympathetic and comprehensive than that presented by the vast majority of postwar historians, German or otherwise. German imperialism and totalitarian dictatorship were a result not of any intrinsic philosophical or political flaw in German culture or society, but were rather "the consequence of the intense pressure brought to bear on the society from its external problems . . . If the Germans seemed paranoically concerned with force, they were, in fact, open on all sides to their most powerful military enemies . . . German military fears may have been self-fulfilling, but certainly were not without foundation . . . The lesson is not that Germans are peculiarly wicked, but rather that even a deeply rooted civilization can rapidly descend into barbarism — at home and abroad — if put under intense sustained pressure."[33] Calleo would probably accept Ernst Nolte's brief definition of the "fundamental dilemma" of the Germans since the Middle Ages, namely, that "politically united, they were too strong to live quietly in Europe, and too weak to rule over Europe."[34] Calleo's re-evaluation of German foreign policy also led him to criticize those who condemned that policy from what he saw as a simplistic position. He was not referring to Wehler or the other social historians who described themselves as "critical" historians, although his strictures applied to them as well, but rather to liberal democratic critics such as Ralf Dahrendorf and Bracher, whose exhaustive studies of the breakdown of the Weimar Republic and the Nazi regime are the foundation of any study of the period. Calleo saw their "positivistic" approach as lacking any deep understanding of or respect for the idealist political traditions that inspired German political thought and warned that excessive reliance on technical rationalism in politics, based on a supposedly value-free social science, and an understandable rejection of tainted political metaphysics were not enough: "No set of social mechanisms can long flourish in the absence of creative political imagination."

Gordon Craig's book, *The Germans*, was a very different work. Deliberately conceived as a broad introduction to aspects of modern German history, politics, and culture for the nonspecialist, it was tremendously popular in the United States, but also, perhaps surprisingly, in West Germany, where it appeared in the fall of 1982, only a few months after the original English edition. The first part of the book was devoted to the argument "that the year 1945 represented a caesura in German history that was sharper and more conclusive than any previous break in modern times" and that the establishment and evolution of the two German states since 1949 made "the chances of a reversion to the past," that is, to extreme nationalism, dictatorship, and aggressive war, "all but negligible." In the second part, Craig, in a series of chapters on different subjects, such as "Religion," "Germans and Jews," "Women," and "Literature and Society," "intended to suggest the way in which contemporary German attitudes show the effect of old but stubborn assumptions."[35] To many West Germans, Craig, in the manner of a genial, experienced uncle, seemed to be giving them the same message and advice that was to be found in the great multivolume histories, namely that there were positive as well as negative continuities in postwar Germany and that the democratic, West German state, despite its faults, was both the most successful and the most just state ever to have existed on German soil.

On the national issue, Craig was able to take account of the first stirrings of leftist nationalism, as expressed by Günter Gaus after his return in 1981 from East Berlin, where he had been the Bonn government's permanent representative for seven years. In his judgments, Gaus, a rising star in the SPD, was somewhere between Egon Bahr on the one hand and the leftist neo-nationalists like Peter Brandt on the other. As such, his views were probably representative of a fairly wide segment of the educated public, and Craig's summary of them is worth quoting. Gaus felt

> that West Germans had paid a high price for overcoming the historical gulf that had existed between Germany and the West and for becoming, politically, economically and culturally, part of the Western World. They had . . . lost something of their essential substance in the years that had passed since the end of the Third Reich; the cosmopolitanism and materialism of the West had eroded their individuality as people; and they had sacrificed native cultural values, inwardness and a sense of community and the folkways inherited from the past, to the seductions of the consumer society.[36]

As I said at the end of the previous chapter, Gaus was one of the many who had ceased to see the division of Germany into a constitutional, democratic state and a totalitarian regime as the crucial political problem for Germans and a source of threat to peace. His thinly veiled nostalgia for older and better German habits and values coexisted easily with his anti-Americanism and his opposition to those who, in West Germany, still saw the division of Germany as not only unjust and unacceptable, but as the outward sign of a threat to the Western democracies that required constant vigilance. In denying the reality of that threat, Gaus, Brandt, Diwald, and those who thought like them identified the German national interest, not with the defense of democracy and liberty in Europe, but with independence of the United States and of what they saw as dangerous U.S. policies. Unless supported by armed force and by a will to self-assertion quite beyond anything seen in West Germany since the 1950s, however, such independence could only be a dangerous illusion.

One who saw this clearly was the political scientist Bernard Willms. He was one of the few thinkers in West Germany to appeal openly and without embarrassment to the ideas of the legal theorist Carl Schmitt, who was chiefly notorious for his defense of Nazi totalitarianism; his often perceptive diagnoses of modern politics from the Weimar period were ignored or forgotten.[37] Willms believed that it was possible to separate the sound from the corrupt in Schmitt's thought and proceeded to construct a modified Schmittian political philosophy based on "self-assertion and recognition," that is, recognition of the reality and the seriousness of political conflicts and differences.[38] This recognition of the otherness of one's political opponent, and consequently of the fact that political conflicts were absolute and could not be ended by the adjudication of a third party, was an essential element in Schmitt's famous distinction of friend and enemy as the basic distinction of politics, comparable to that of good and evil in morality or of beautiful and ugly in esthetics. Schmitt was attacked for glorifying struggle and violence in this distinction, although his critics often forgot his all-important corollary, which was that it was precisely the absolutism of the distinction that provided politics with its essential challenge, namely the challenge of limiting political conflicts to avoid mutual destruction.

The postwar East-West conflict seemed to Willms, as it did to Raymond Aron in France, to fit Schmitt's analysis of political struggle. At this point, Willms could very easily have taken the path that led to Diwald's position; he could have maintained that the two Germanys could and should opt out of the struggle and try to achieve reunification based on a common interest in avoiding superpower hegemony. In some of his earlier work, indeed, Willms did seem to be proposing this argument. When he came to write *Die deutsche Nation* (The German nation), his major analysis of the national issue, however, he had clearly changed his mind.[39] In an epigraph, Willms quoted Nietzsche against the leftist neo-nationalists and their illusions: "Because you lie about what is the case, you will have no thirst for what ought to be."

The first part of the book, "A Theory of the Nation," is an application of Willms' philosophy of politics as "self-assertion and recognition." For Willms, all human existence, defined as self-assertion in freedom, must be maintained and defended in constant interaction, friendly or otherwise, with others who in their turn are engaged in self-assertion. All human existence is therefore political existence. The source of conscious motivation for this political self-assertion is the nation; political self-consciousness is therefore inevitably national consciousness, expressed in a common language, a common system of laws, and a common history. The means to secure political existence, furthermore, is the state. Since all existence is political, and since political consciousness is national consciousness, the state, being the necessary framework of concrete existence, and which can no more exist in the abstract than can the individual, is necessarily an incorporation of the nation.

Having established these basic principles, Willms recounts the story of German nationalism from the *Freiheitskrieg* (war of independence from Napoleon in 1808–1813) to the tragic failures of national self-assertion in the attempted coup of July 20, 1944, and the workers' uprising in East Germany on June 17, 1953. After dealing in detail with various philosophical and political objections to nationalism in general, for example, that it is undemocratic, that it denies the reality of the class struggle, or that it is an obstacle to good international relations, he comes to his main subject, namely the question of German national identity, and to his main argument, which is that German nationalism, so far from being dangerous or outdated, is in fact an essential foundation of political independence.

After 1945, a majority of Germans agreed with the victors of World War II that nationalism had been partly responsible for the rise of Hitler and for the atrocities committed by Germans under the Nazi regime. Willms argues that Nazism was not so much an expression of nationalism as a perversion of it. However, he does not rest his justification of German nationalism on moral grounds. Rather, he claims that the permanent state of guilt maintained in West Germany after 1945 was, in its effect, a political weapon used by foreign and domestic enemies to weaken the West German republic and the legitimacy of its legal and moral order. He writes:

> A "guilty society" is weakened and cannot respond decisively to attacks on, say, its legal system. This is the reason that the German left continues its insistence on German guilt for National Socialism in a way that has long since reached the dimensions of a civil war . . . When we see what interests former and present adversaries of the Germans have in maintaining a consciousness or feelings of guilt in the sense of a continued weakening of national consciousness, we have reached the point at which the question of the "guilty nation" can be judged and answered . . . The moralization of history prevents the nation from . . . coming to itself and asserting itself . . . Consciousness of self cannot be received from others; peace cannot come from enemies. Consciousness of self presupposes identity, and identity is not . . . the mere claim of being in accord with even the highest of principles. Identity is correspondence with one's self in knowledge and will

. . . The Germans are identical also with their National Socialist past; they must identify with the victims and with the executioners. This identification must take the form of a construction, not a destruction of national self-consciousness . . . Confessions of national guilt are just as pointless and senseless as they are lacking in credibility . . . What alone makes political sense for the nation is the struggle against tendencies to weaken the "guilty" nation permanently.[40]

Willms goes on to describe the consequences of national division as "political nonidentity," exacerbated, in the East, by a forcibly imposed antinational, and therefore false, identity, and in the West, by the moralizing antinationalists who, in Willms's view, call the political tune in West Germany. Again, at this point he might be expected to have followed Diwald and the neo-nationalist left in attacking the United States, capitalism, or NATO as the chief enemies to be disposed of. He does not do this; his first, and major, conclusion is that "the Soviet Union is the present enemy of the German nation." Although the West bears heavy responsibility for having surrendered Eastern Europe and East Germany to Soviet power, nevertheless, in the political situation of the 1980s, the West is the ally of all Germans, West and East, since reunification and the re-establishment of full national identity are possible only if the Soviet Union is weakened, and this in turn requires above all a strengthening of West European military forces and political will. Willms's second conclusion, therefore, is that "the national interest of Germany is, for the first time in history, identical with that of Europe."[41]

Starting from the same premise, that Germans need to reassert a national identity, Diwald and Willms, who both define themselves as conservative, reach opposite conclusions. In attacking the West, and especially the United States, for standing in the way of a "German national interest," Diwald and such leading SPD politicians as Günter Gaus, Oskar Lafontaine, and Erhard Eppler were, if Willms is right, playing into the hands of the "present enemy," the Soviet Union. Political analysis of the course of East-West relations, and of the question of the survival both of West Germany's national commitment to reunification and of its democratic constitution suggests that Willms, and not Gaus, Lafontaine, and Eppler, is right. In any case, the intense discussion of the issues of national division and national identity, historical consciousness, and future national and defense policies in the 1980s showed that the German question was far from being dead.

4

WEST GERMANY AND THE
NEW STRATEGIC DEBATE

The principal problem of deterrence in Western Europe ever since the origin of NATO has been that a contradiction exists between the political requirement that it be credible to both friend and foe and the lack of sustained political will to maintain force levels and postures that unambiguously fulfill that requirement. There were two main reasons for this lack of will. First, the heads of European NATO governments, including that of West Germany, never believed that their countries could really afford the conventional forces and weaponry required to provide a purely conventional deterrent. Rejecting what Bernard Brodie called the "conventional war thesis," that is the view that the major threat in Europe was a threat of conventional attack and that NATO should not have to bear the risk of first use of nuclear weapons, they relied on the U.S. strategic and tactical nuclear forces as the basic deterrent, a position that was convincing only as long as those U.S. forces were clearly superior, or at least equal, to Soviet strategic forces. Second, and perhaps more important, European politicians, and particularly West German politicians since the early 1960s, simply did not see the Soviet threat in the same way as most U.S. strategists and defense officials, and, in Brodie's words, "they have therefore firmly and consistently refused, despite long and continued prodding by our government, to build up to anything like the levels demanded by the conventional war thesis."[1] This difference in views of Soviet intentions was not, of course, solely a transatlantic difference. The debate in the United States between those who believed that the threat of assured destruction was an adequate deterrent and those who believed that it was unconvincing and that, therefore, a deterrent posture based on the ability and will to employ nuclear weapons in a limited fashion against military targets was essential was also, in essence, a debate about the character of the Soviet Union.[2] Those who took a pessimistic view of the utility or efficacy of the threat of assured destruction and who, on the basis of their judgment of Soviet policies, argued that operational doctrines for the limited use of nuclear weapons were more likely, in the long run, to deter the Soviet Union, however, had few counterparts in Western Europe. West German and other European leaders were less worried about the threat of direct Soviet attack and consequently tended to think less in terms of fighting a possible war than in terms of arms control, East-West contacts, and the chances of pan-European disarmament.

The contradiction between the need for deterrence and the means available was, by the late 1970s, no longer merely academic. Chancellor Helmut Schmidt's request, made in 1977, for INF modernization was, in part, a recognition that a purely conventional deterrence was impossible to achieve.[3] However, his request, and the consequent double-track decision of NATO to modernize INF by withdrawing existing tactical nuclear warheads and replacing them with far fewer, but more accurate missiles were the major external cause of the peace movement of the 1980s and of the intense political, cultural, and philosophical debate on defense strategy, security policy, and the future of the divided nation that was under way in West Germany in the 1980s.

STRATEGY, SECURITY, AND THE NATIONAL QUESTION

The debate on the issues of strategy and security in West Germany was always inseparable from the national issue and Ostpolitik generally. In Chapters 1 and 2 above, I explained why I agree with those, such as Alois Mertes and Hans-Peter Schwarz, who have argued that West Germany's genuine security interests are not really in conflict with the national interest in reunification in a democratic constitutional state. Détente and Ostpolitik, however, as understood and practiced by such leading Social Democrats sympathetic to the peace movement as Willy Brandt, Egon Bahr, Günter Gaus, and Oskar Lafontaine do conflict both with West Germany's security interests in the Atlantic Alliance and, I argue, with the German national interest in reunification. This is because these policies have come to mean the maintenance of relations with Eastern governments rather than the support of human rights in Eastern Europe. Their success in these, limited, terms then necessarily becomes hostage to the good will of the very Eastern regimes who are themselves the principal obstacles to peace and democracy in

Europe, and they thus become self-defeating. The genuine German national interest cannot rationally be served by making good relations with the Soviet Union, the single greatest enemy of that interest, and with East Germany the main criterion of success in foreign or security policy. By accepting the political status quo of division of Germany and Europe as the basis of, and not the obstacle to, peace and democracy, the new leadership of the SPD has created for West German policy planning a previously nonexistent contradiction, namely a contradiction between a perceived "national interest" in negotiations with East Germany and other Eastern regimes and a narrowly conceived "security interest," defined as loyalty to the Atlantic Alliance. Only the West German government itself, aided by intelligent public criticism, can extract itself from this impasse. This is what Henry Kissinger meant when, on the tenth anniversary of the Moscow Treaty of 1970 between the USSR and West Germany, he stated in 1980 that the Federal Republic must choose between loyalty to the idea of détente embodied in that treaty and a policy of actively seeking reunification, calling this choice "a historical imperative" for West Germany.

There were, since the late 1970s, four main reasons for the revival of intense discussion in West Germany of defense, security, and the national issue. First, there was the increase in Soviet armed strength in Eastern Europe: the steady buildup of conventional forces; improvements in technology, communications, and organization; and, beginning in 1977, the deployment of the SS-20 intermediate-range ballistic missile (IRBM), a nuclear system of unprecedented range, survivability, and accuracy, capable of striking targets in Western Europe from movable launchers in the USSR. By early 1984, according to NATO sources, the Soviet Union had deployed 378 SS-20 launchers, each capable of firing three independently targetable 150-kiloton warheads with a range of at least 5,000 kilometers (by comparison, the single-warhead Pershing II U.S. IRBM, of which 108 were to be deployed in 1983–1988, has a maximum yield of 50 kilotons and a range of 1,800 kilometers). Of this number, at least 252 were in European Russia. In late 1984, the U.S. Department of Defense claimed that the number had risen still further, though exact figures were not released. It was reported that the launchers could be reloaded, doubling the number of available warheads to at least 1,512 ($252 \times 3 \times 2$) in the European theater alone. Deployment of the SS-20 marked an increase in tension in the arms race, the reality of which is often hard to define because of the clichés and rhetoric that characterize public debate in the West.[4] However, the initial deployment occurred at a difficult time for Western politicians and planners. As indicated above, the need for a profound revision of NATO strategies and methods and for a restoration of the credibility of deterrence had been clear for some time, but public realization of this need was hampered by the international and domestic atmosphere of détente, the expectation that tensions would lessen, which led to the belief that they were in fact lessening and to an unwillingness on the part of those outside government and military circles (and sometimes by those within such circles), to take cognizance of the Soviet arms buildup and its implications.

The second and third reasons for the change are the international and domestic West German political climate in the later 1960s and 1970s and the relative absence of the issues of security and deterrence from West German public debate during these years. The fourth reason is the general economic crisis since 1973–1974, the growth in social welfare and other nondefense public spending combined with unemployment and inflation. This crisis has on occasion loomed large and has indeed been used by West Germany as an excuse to avoid dealing directly with the implications of growing Soviet power for Ostpolitik and security policy. It led, during the 1970s, to an increasing resistance in public debate to drawing the objective conclusions implied by the changing military balance.

As with Ostpolitik, one must be careful to distinguish between one's own perception of that changing balance and the conclusions that follow from that perception, given one's presuppositions, and the political psychology and motivations of the politicians and analysts one is studying. One of the most significant changes in West German public opinion since approximately the mid-1970s has been the loss of confidence in transatlantic cooperation and in the importance of American strength for peace and security. Whereas the Soviet Union is still perceived as a threat and the Soviet arms buildup is still perceived as a cause of tension, and whereas support in general for membership in the Alliance has not decreased significantly, it is remarkable that there is virtually no support for increased defense spending in West Germany, and not very much support (approximately 30 percent) for deployment of Pershing IIs and ground-launched cruise missiles (GLCMs) as proposed by NATO in 1979 as part of the modernization of its deterrent. Only a small minority absolves the Soviet Union and blames the United States for East-West tension and for insecurity in Europe, but an increasing number blame both sides and do not believe that American policies serve either peace or security. This trend is particularly striking among Social Democratic voters; in 1983, 48 percent of them blamed both superpowers equally for the increase in tension. In 1982, 42 percent blamed the United States and 59 percent blamed the Soviet Union. That West European concessions to the Soviet Union, including certain elements of Ostpolitik as it was practiced since the later 1970s, might be a source of tension was not even considered by West German respondents in this poll.[5]

Beginning around 1980, the argument, last heard in SPD circles in the mid-1950s, that East-West tension in Europe was the fault of both superpowers and of the "logic of the blocs," as it was often called, was revived by a number of journalists and politicians. Most, but not all, were associated with the left wing of the SPD, and their statements and arguments to an extent mediated between the agitation of the peace movement, which began at the same time, and the deliberations of established scholars and government officials. One important consequence of this neo-neutralism, as one could call it, was to obtain respect for the peace movement and its agitation from individuals and political groups that would formerly have rejected the premises and suppositions of that agitation out of hand. There was little effect in the opposite direction; that is, the peace movement did not become just as tolerant and understanding of official policies as defenders of those policies became of the peace movement. By the mid-1980s, nevertheless, a considerable degree of pluralism was evident in the West German defense debate, which had not been the case at the beginning of the decade. While some neo-neutralists, such as Günter Grass and his literary colleagues, the SPD politicians Oskar Lafontaine and Erhard Eppler, or the military analyst Alfred Mechtersheimer, continued their strident attacks on the United States and on NATO strategy, others demonstrated a sincere desire to find alternatives to existing or proposed defense postures that, in their eyes, would contribute to peace in Europe. While one could legitimately quarrel with their hopes and assumptions, there was no doubt of their commitment to Western democracy in general or to the survival of the constitutional democratic system of the Federal Republic in particular.

The attacks on the "logic of the blocs" and the "new cold war" allegedly being waged by Washington frequently took their cue from three influential Hamburg periodicals, the "Hamburg trinity," as it was called, of (in descending order of professional responsibility and respectability) *Die Zeit, Der Spiegel*, and *Stern*. Born of the neo-liberalism of the late 1940s and 1950s, these journals were originally very similar in their editorial policies, and their journalists were more often close friends and allies than rivals. By the early 1960s, they had achieved what Schwarz called "a position of virtual oligopoly" in the production of highbrow reportage for the academically educated middle class.[6] There were no comparable conservative or radical organs of opinion of similar influence, and it is hardly an exaggeration to say that, instead of being merely an element in the formation of a pluralistic public opinion, the Hamburg trinity by the late 1960s was West German public opinion, or at least its intellectually respectable and respected part. When that opinion turned leftward in the late 1960s and 1970s, therefore, it was not always clear whether the Hamburg trinity and its literary and academic allies were following this trend or, in fact, guiding it. However that may be, it was an undeniable fact that by the early 1980s all three journals were distinctly more critical of the Bonn government, of the United States, and of Western values generally, and more inclined to doubt official Western assertions about the need or the value of certain defense policies, particularly the double-track decision.

Die Zeit, which during the chancellorship of Helmut Schmidt was often considered an "unofficial court newspaper," in its editorial line as formulated by Theo Sommer and Marion Gräfin Dönhoff, both stimulated and accompanied the leftward and anti-American drift of the SPD, so that the dominant tendency of the paper on foreign and security policy by the mid-1980s was definitely closer to the positions taken by Willy Brandt, Egon Bahr, Günter Gaus, or even Oskar Lafontaine than to those of Helmut Schmidt and the much-weakened Atlanticist wing of the party. *Der Spiegel*, in appearance a German version of *Time* or *L'Express*, was in fact a quite different publication. In the 1970s, it became increasingly politicized, especially in its foreign reporting and editorial line, and could thus justly be called, in Helmut Schelsky's words, "the left-wing Augstein journal."[7] During the rearmament debate in the early 1950s, its founder, publisher, and sometime editor, Rudolf Augstein, was known as a national-neutralist publicist, and his editorials and comments in the 1980s showed that he had returned to his earlier position. *Stern* has never been a serious journal of opinion, but its circulation was all the larger for that. As with *Der Spiegel*, a slick and Americanized exterior masks extremely politicized and biased reporting, which, in *Stern*, has now become overtly anti-American and sympathetic to the Soviet Union.

By the mid-1980s, a bewildering variety of opinions regarding the proper national and security policy for West Germany were competing for public attention and political influence. Nevertheless, it was possible to distinguish four conceptually different approaches, each of which led to different attitudes, hopes, and proposals in both areas. The first three were primarily political and are dealt with at greater length elsewhere in this book. The fourth, which I call defense revisionism, appeared to be primarily technical and military, though it also had definite political connotations, and it is the main focus of this chapter.

The first of these approaches one could call "old Ostpolitik." It was the government policy of the early 1960s revised to meet the needs of the 1980s and was typified by Franz-Josef Strauss, the CSU leader and Bavarian prime minister, who in 1983–1984 secured $700 million in loans to East Germany from West German banks. His argument for doing so was not that the Eastern regime was now a legitimate government worthy of support in the general interest of East-West détente, but that the loans proved to East Germany that it needed West Germany to survive, and that this would necessarily force East Germany to adopt a less hostile policy than the Soviet Union might otherwise want. Behind these arguments there were probably also some vestiges of Strauss's old "Euro-Gaullism"; his vision that by supporting East European societies and encouraging pluralism, one would eventually undermine the regimes and bring the day of true European unity closer. "Old Ostpolitik" also coexisted with other approaches within the Bonn government of Helmut Kohl, in power since late 1982. Alois Mertes, who had strongly criticized the notion, popular in the SPD, of a "security partnership" of East and West, arguing instead that the only logical such partnership was between the nations of the Atlantic Alliance whose common purpose was to deter attack by the Soviet Union, became a close adviser of the Kohl government on national policy.[8] As such he represented "old Ostpolitik," in that he claimed that the personal and humanitarian improvements for East Germans achieved in the 1970s should be protected and, if possible, expanded, precisely because this was good national policy, the final purpose of which was still reunification.

The second approach, which one could call "new Ostpolitik," differed from the "old Ostpolitik" in not aiming primarily at reunification and in seeing the very process of negotiations with East Germany and other communist states as desirable in and for itself. The new Ostpolitik was the favored approach of those who saw European division as a necessary condition of stability rather than as a threat or a problem and who believed in the fundamental compatibility of Soviet security needs and policies with those of the West. In the mid-1980s, the new Ostpolitik was represented by the overwhelming majority of the SPD, but also had strong support in the FDP and even in certain groups of the CDU. It was thus the government policy from the mid-1970s at the latest until the early 1980s and continued to influence policy and public opinion also after 1982. In regard to NATO and the United States, adherents of this approach were much more skeptical and critical than those who followed what I have called the "old Ostpolitik." Because they believed in a security partnership of East and West (and not just of Europe and the United States) and because their primary aim was East-West stability, they tended to give the Soviet Union and its communist allies the benefit of the doubt when judging such actions as the invasion of Afghanistan or the suppression of democratic movements in Poland. Western reactions aimed at protecting human rights or defending democracy tended to make them uneasy and forced them into such clearly uncomfortable positions as that of defending martial law in Poland on the grounds that it improved stability. There was considerable irony in this since these same believers in new Ostpolitik were often also heard attacking other policies for being morally unjustified or inadequate. Many of them owed their earliest political education to the agitation and activism against the U.S. involvement in Vietnam in the 1960s. However, when it came to applying moral principles to conditions in Eastern Europe, these same people suddenly discovered the virtues of Realpolitik and the need to subordinate ultimate ends to practical needs. There was even a further irony in this, however, since it was possible in the mid-1980s to make a very good case that this sort of "realism" in regard to Eastern Europe was, in fact, the height of unrealism and illusion. Contrary to the arguments of the new Ostpolitik, it could be maintained that acceptance of the coercive maintenance of the status quo by communist regimes, and by extension of the division of Germany by Soviet power, was conducive neither to peace, stability, nor to justice.

Something like the new Ostpolitik was also the standard view of many in the peace movement, and most important, of the most influential segments of the quality press (*Die Zeit* and *Der Spiegel*). This view, its consequences and its political implications, are dealt with throughout this book.[9]

The third general approach to national and security policy was of more recent date than either of the varieties of Ostpolitik. Though it overlapped with the new Ostpolitik, it represented a different attitude, which I call "neo-neutralist." The neo-neutralists went beyond the new Ostpolitik both in their good faith in the Soviet Union and in the possibilities for a general European escape from the superpower confrontation and in their skepticism of, even hostility to, U.S. aims and policies. The neo-neutralists were the intellectuals of the peace movement. They did not constitute the mass of demonstrators or activists, but they were the people whose writings, speeches, and other public statements served to legitimize and justify peace movement actions expressing disapproval and fear of NATO policies, deployments, and intentions.

The neo-neutralists, as I have already indicated, were by no means confined to the extreme left of the political spectrum. They included right-wingers such as Hellmut Diwald as well as members of the nationalist left such as Peter Brandt. One of the best-known neo-neutralists in the 1980s was the journalist Peter Bender, who had made a name for himself in the 1960s advocating recognition of the GDR and an active Ostpolitik as part of what he called "offensive détente." At that time, his policies corresponded closely to "old Ostpolitik"; they were pro-democratic, offensive in character, and aimed at German reunification within a general framework of European peace and the growth of democracy in Eastern Europe. In 1981, in his book *Das Ende des ideologischen Zeitalters*, he appeared to be maintaining his earlier commitment to democracy and European peace, but these things were now to be secured and obtained by a mutual rejection by East and West Europeans of Soviet and U.S. hegemony respectively.[10] He completely disregarded the fact that East Europeans were somewhat less able, to put it mildly, than West Europeans to shake off superpower domination. His extremely optimistic view of Soviet intentions and policies led him to ignore the possible consequences of unilateral Western disarmament or of West European renunciation of U.S. protection. In subsequent articles, Bender returned to this theme, or illusion, of his, namely that there was a genuine possibility of a "Europeanization of Europe" that could be achieved with the consent of the Soviet Union, and described the proper role of West Germany as "a bridge to the East."

Bender's idea of a European peace order was close to that of Willy Brandt, the SPD leader, who by the mid-1980s could well be described as a neo-neutralist. However, neither Bender nor Brandt were as overtly and as consistently hostile to the United States as some. Their primary concern was the creditable one of securing European peace, though their beliefs about how to go about it were, in my view, wholly illusory and therefore dangerous. In the case of Oskar Lafontaine, a leading younger figure in the SPD and one whom many saw as Brandt's heir in the chairmanship of the party, neo-neutralism seemed to be a consequence of a simple, intolerant, and ferocious anti-Americanism. Whether Lafontaine, who in 1983 began advocating West German withdrawal from NATO, indeed feared the United States more than the Soviet Union, as he claimed, or whether this fear was simply a device cynically adopted to curry favor with the peace movement and with younger voters who might otherwise support the Greens, was hard to say, but the political consequences of his position were perfectly clear.[11] If put into practice, they would necessarily amount not merely to rejection by West Germany of the NATO strategy of flexible response, but to unilateral disarmament and to a self-neutralization based solely on hopeful illusions about Soviet intentions. The basic fact, as I see it, of East-West relations in Europe, namely that Soviet restraint is largely a function of Western deterrent strength, and its corollary, that a weakening of the West might very well end that restraint, was not only ignored, but specifically denied by the neo-neutralists. That denial, in fact, was what distinguished them from adherents of both the old and the new Ostpolitik, and from the supporters of the fourth approach, which I call "defense revisionism."

DEFENSE REVISIONISM: THE STARNBERG PROPOSALS

In the mid-1980s, there were several forms of defense revisionism in West Germany. As a widespread trend of thought and debate, it owed its origin to the crisis of NATO strategy and to the renewed questioning of the viability or justifiability of flexible response that surfaced in the later 1970s. However, defense revisionism in the particular form espoused by Carl Friedrich von Weizsäcker and his colleagues at Starnberg went back at least to the early 1970s. In fact, the Starnberg studies drew their philosophical and ethical strength from the early moral, philosophical, and political debate on nuclear weapons that began at the time of their invention and use in 1945. Weiz-säcker himself was one of the "Göttingen Seven" who signed a manifesto pro-testing against plans for the nuclear arming of the Bundeswehr in 1957 and arguing for a denuclearization of Europe along the lines of the Soviet-sponsored Rapacki plan. In 1962, he had argued for recognition of the status quo in Eastern Europe, including East Germany. The actual military and technical proposals of this school of defense revisionists echoed the early, conservative opposition to West German rearmament and membership in NATO, led by former Wehrmacht officers such as Bogislav von Bonin and Hasso von Manteuffel, who argued for an autonomous West German defense relying on many small, conventionally armed units and an active militia.[12] The political hope of people like von Bonin was that a West Germany independent of the United States but capable of mustering a con-vincing conventional deterrent to Soviet attack would be in a better position to negotiate for reunification. Unlike some of his former fellow officers of the Wehrmacht, von Bonin did not actively support Soviet proposals or express greater trust and faith in the Soviet Union than in the United States; never-theless, there was a distinct element of national-neutralism in his ideas that survived in the defense revisionism of the 1980s, though it was certainly less prominent in this approach than in either the new Ostpolitik or in neo-neutralism.

In 1970 Weizsäcker, a distinguished nuclear physicist and philosopher, was named codirector of the Max-Planck-Institut zur Erforschung der Lebensbedingungen der wissenschaftlich-technischen Welt (the Max Planck Institute for the Study of the Conditions of Life of the Scientific-Technical World) in Starnberg near Munich. His colleague as director was the political philosopher and theorist Jürgen Habermas. Weizsäcker, the descendant of a line of southwest German civil servants and scholars, was the last surviving representative of a great German tradition, that of cultural Protestantism. Like his late friend and teacher, Werner Heisenberg, he has been inspired by Goethe, classical Greek thought, Christianity, and the methods and insights of modern physics, and he is able to discuss complex problems of ethics, poli-tics, and religion as well as technical questions of physics, all in a literary style and demonstrating a knowledge of European culture and civilization that must be the envy of even the most widely read philosophical or historical specialist in any American university. The institute to which he came is one branch of the network of research institutions originally created in the nineteenth century (under the name Kaiser-Wilhelm-Institut) to promote ad-vanced study of the cultural, social, and natural sciences. After World War II, the branches remaining in West Germany were renamed in honor of the physicist Max Planck and reorganized, and today they are the sanctuaries of undisturbed research in a great variety of fields. The Starnberg branch was largely a creation of Habermas, one of whose main concerns has always been the social, political, and philosophical consequences of modern science and its methods and, conversely, the effects on science and the scientific method of political, social, and economic thought and conditions. The arrival of Weizsäcker (who remained at Starnberg until he retired in 1980, at which time his section was closed down and that of Habermas renamed the Max Planck Institute for Social Sciences) marked, however, a new departure. Weizsäcker's purpose was to study and, if possible, to understand, the conditions and problems of peace and conflict from a perspective that was to combine philosophy, ethics, politics, strategy, and weapons technology.

The first results of this research project were found in three works, all published in 1976 and all dealing, from three separate perspectives, with the principles and inherent logic of doctrines of deterrence.[13] Weizsäcker's book is a wide-ranging and pessimistic study of the interdependence of economic conditions in Western industrial nations, the availability of energy resources, social stability, and the likelihood of an East-West conflict, given assumed or possible changes in those variables. It is more sophisticated than such analyses as that of Johan Galtung, who is ideologically committed to a position strongly critical of the West; nevertheless, Weizsäcker fails to consider that Soviet policy may have principles and purposes alien to the West and that the immediate Soviet aim may in fact be to establish credible superiority on all levels so as to be able to impose constraints on the West that are short of war, but that would mean the end of the Western democratic capitalist order.[14]

The second work, by Horst Afheldt, is a detailed discussion of NATO's prevailing principles and means of war deterrence, evaluated for their plausibility and implications and compared with a series of norms that Afheldt argues are necessary for a genuine policy of peace. The basic premise follows from the apparent paradox that deterrence is not credible unless it includes a strategy for what to do if it fails, in other words, a war-fighting doctrine.[15] Deterrence, therefore, has two requirements: it must make any attack appear as unattractive and unlikely to succeed as possible; and since nuclear war will be suicidal for all, it must also make nuclear options in the event of failure as unattractive as possible. There must be no "reward" for pre-emptive or first strikes; any posture that invites such strikes is destabilizing. That includes, for Afheldt, the strategy of so-called forward defense (Vorneverteidigung) on the Central Front, an increase in conventional arms levels, or INF modernization. Since the implementation of such measures makes it more probable that early use of nuclear weapons by the Soviets will be needed to overcome them, they are, given Afheldt's unstated but dubious assumptions about Soviet strategy, inherently destabilizing.[16] Afheldt recommends, instead, some unilateral disarmament and a change in West German defense strategy consisting of use of what he calls "autonomous techno-commandos," integrated units equipped with tank-destroying precision-guided munitions that are spread over the countryside so as not to offer obvious and concentrated targets. Such a defensive posture, argues Afheldt, is not destabilizing since it is incapable of offensive coercive action and could not be used or perceived as a threat in a crisis; being decentralized, it does not invite nuclear strikes. Yet it will be a highly credible deterrent in an actual war situation.

He supports his argument by referring to the strategy on which Austrian territorial defense is based, and which is the subject of the third Starnberg book, by Emil Spannocchi, former commander-in-chief of the Austrian army, and Guy Brossolet. This strategy, called *umfassende Landesverteidigung* (comprehensive territorial defense, or ULV), is far more than just a system of military organization. As conceived in Austria, ULV is composed of four integrated elements, military, spiritual, civilian, and economic. The military element is the doctrine of *Raumverteidigung* (area defense), based on a distinction between "key zones," the physical and economic characteristics of which make them prime targets of an invasion and which must therefore be fortified and defended, and "area security zones," where mobility is important and where the defense will maneuver to harass and attack the enemy. The defending forces consist of a territorial militia recalled for frequent training, supported by mobile forces. The spiritual element consists of the readiness and will of the population to defend itself and to make this readiness clear to any potential attacker. It is thus not the same thing as psychological defense, which aims at maintaining popular morale in times of threat or attack. Civilian defense as part of ULV must not be confused with the entirely different notion of "civilian defense" propagated by Gene Sharp and a number of German and Scandinavian theorists and discussed in the following section. Within the ULV, civilian defense consists not only of all the measures commonly included in civil defense, but also of "measures to maintain state and government authority . . . systems of public information . . . the supply of personnel, social welfare measures, traffic, telecommunications, etc." Economic defense, finally, consists of measures to ensure the material supplies needed by industry and the population and thus includes measures for administering food and energy resources, rationing, monetary policy, the work force, care of refugees, and related matters.[17]

The similarity of the ULV concept as actually practiced in Austria, where it was made part of the constitution in 1975, to Afheldt's ideas is obvious. The problem, however, is that while ULV or something like it might work very well in small, socially and culturally homogeneous countries like Austria (population 9 million), Switzerland (6 million), or Sweden (8 million), which are moreover neutral and whose only aim in war is to deter violations of their neutrality, it was not at all certain that such ideas would serve the desired purpose when applied to much larger and less homogeneous countries like West Germany, which, moreover, was a leading member of an international alliance, namely NATO. Spannocchi himself emphasized that ULV was not directly applicable to West Germany (the Central Front), and that Austria would in any case be forced to surrender if threatened with nuclear attack.

In the Starnberg view, deployment of long-range INF, cruise missiles, or other Eurostrategic nuclear or nuclear-capable systems that are mobile and hence likely to be seen as "exploitable options" (uncertain factors in a crisis or if deterrence fails), was destabilizing and would lead inevitably to a continued arms race and to political uncertainty both in the United States and the Soviet Union. Afheldt and Weizsäcker both concluded that new intermediate nuclear systems should not be deployed either on the European or the American mainland.[18] However, since both believed that submarine-based systems had a credible second-strike potential and were thus of value for deterrence, they accepted deployment of new forward-based systems (to replace existing ones) at sea, while opposing the further development of antisubmarine warfare (ASW) technology as tending to reduce that credibility and hence as destabilizing.

CIVILIAN DEFENSE

There were, in the 1980s, other varieties of defense revisionism being discussed in West Germany, of which the most important were the theories of so-called civilian defense (called in German *soziale Verteidigung*, social defense). Civilian defense, as described by its supporters, is not just a method of deterring attack or defeating invasion, but an important element of a vision of a social, economic, and psychological order in which war will not only be banned as policy but virtually outlawed as a concept. Proponents of civilian defense, who tended politically to support the neo-neutralist views outlined above, were not primarily concerned with the Soviet threat or with the balance of forces in Central Europe. In their view, if war broke out, it would be caused not so much by Soviet expansionism as by what they saw as the inherently violent and conflict-prone international system. This view was, in fact, shared by many people who did not believe in the virtues of civilian defense; it was part of the general outlook of those who saw the East-West conflict as characterized by a self-sustaining arms race and who therefore believed that unilateral measures of Western disarmament could "break the spiral" and contribute to a lessening of tensions. In this view, the great problem of East-West relations was misunderstanding and mutual fear, and not the need to deter an inherently expansionist and totalitarian Soviet Union from threatening Western interests.[19] While mainstream supporters of this view usually restricted themselves to calling for arms control negotiations and arguing that lack of such negotiations was in itself highly dangerous, however, supporters of civilian defense called for a transformation of the international system itself and of the internal political and social structure of its member nations.

The first step toward that transformation, in their view, was to undermine the psychology of confrontation typical of government and military circles in East and West. Since the West was easier to influence, that was where the attempt to influence must begin. If unilateral disarmament should result in war, which they considered highly unlikely, the principles of civilian defense and nonviolent civil resistance were to be applied, in the belief that this would mollify the attacker and prove to him the futility of the exercise. These principles were designed "not to stop the attacker from entering your territory, but to deny him access to the political, social, and economic institutions of the occupied country." This was to be done in two ways, by "denial," that is, passive resistance, strikes, insubordination, or sabotage, and by "undermining," that is, attempts to influence the enemy, the establishment of alternative (underground) political institutions ("civil usurpation"), and the denial of money and supplies. These civilian defense principles rested on three hypotheses. The first was the idea that one could successfully deny an enemy enough gain from his conquest to outweigh the costs of invasion and of suppression of the civilian defense activities. The second, which followed from the first, was that the promise of such activities in itself would have a "deterrent effect." The third, finally, was that the practice of civilian defense would "influence militarist and aggressive feelings among enemy forces and in the enemy population," leading to "a total conversion" and, presumably, the abandonment of the attempted occupation.[20]

While including guidelines for action in case of war, however, civilian defense theory in fact assumed that the mere adoption of civilian defense principles would deter attack. By demonstrating commitment to nonviolent principles and to international pacifism, moreover, it would lead to a "disarmament race," in which all parties, given the good example, would rush to divest themselves of outdated and immoral means of coercion. At this point, the conditions for creating "positive peace," the new order, would be present.

As a theory of deterrence, civilian defense was both simple and attractive; as Daniel Frei put it, "with only three variables and three hypotheses, it manages to solve a problem that has plagued mankind for millennia." As Frei also pointed out, however, its major flaw was that it entirely ignored the character, methods, and aims of the potential attacker, that is, the Soviet Union. In other words, it was fundamentally apolitical and lacked any reference to historical experience, surely a necessary precondition of any proposal for dealing with the East-West conflict. Concretely, it contained four crucial assumptions, none of them very plausible and all contradicted by past experience. First, it assumed that the Soviet Union, in attacking the West, would be guided by a crudely material cost-benefit analysis, such that, if the costs were too great, the attack would be called off or never launched. Second, it assumed that the Soviet Union would be guided by humanitarian standards of conduct similar to those obtaining in Western societies and their armed forces. In view of Soviet history from 1917 to the mid-1980s, this assumption was so grotesque as to beggar description. Third, it assumed a degree of cohesion and discipline, even regimentation, in the societies to be defended, that is, in Western Europe, wholly incompatible with the prevailing social structure and the behavior, beliefs, and expectations of the vast majority of citizens. Finally, it assumed that the attacker would be incapable of learning from experience and taking effective countermeasures. The silliness of this assumption was apparent from any comparison of Soviet behavior in Hungary in 1956 with the Soviet tactics of oppression applied to Czechoslovakia in 1968 and to Poland in 1981 and after. Each case showed increasing sophistication, competence, and efficacy on the part of the Soviet leadership and its local allies in the countries concerned. In short, it seemed that civilian defense, while elegant and effective on paper, was likely to be effective only against an enemy as morally rigorous and socially responsible as Western nations themselves on their best behavior. That this was in fact true could be seen from an examination of past attempts to use some or all of the methods of civilian defense against an occupying power. In all of modern history, Frei found only three cases of successful civilian defense in the sense understood by Gene Sharp and other proponents; Great Britain was the enemy/occupier in two of them, and France in the third. Both countries had long traditions of restraint in war and were among the few to insist that principles of justice and legality should apply even in times of emergency and in dealing with subversion. More to the point, perhaps, in both the examples Frei chose of civilian defense against the Soviet Union (Czechoslovakia and Poland), it was abundantly clear that the crucial assumptions of the theory were not borne out. Soviet forces and their local henchmen were not converted, they were not deterred from taking action, and they were perfectly capable of devising and implementing effective countermeasures.[21]

DEFENSE REVISIONISM
AND DEFENSE NEEDS IN THE 1980s

The Starnberg proposals and other ideas for the conventional defense of West Germany, such as those presented by Jochen Löser and other former

Wehrmacht officers, became quite popular in the 1980s because they seemed to describe a strategy that was affordable, technically possible, and likely to be far more popular than the U.S. INF missiles accepted by NATO in the double-track decision of 1979. However, on closer inspection, some of these advantages turned out to be serious liabilities. As pointed out by Gottfried Greiner, the *Inspekteur* (military commander) of the Bundeswehr from 1977 to 1982, this operational strategy was not a strategy of deterrence. Tank traps, a territorial militia, techno-commandos, and in-depth deployment were operational means that could not deter the Soviet Union from attacking, despite Afheldt's theoretical argument that because decentralized deployment offered no nuclear targets, an attacker would have no conceivable rationale for using nuclear weapons and would thus be forced to rely on conventional forces, which could be defeated with this strategy. Greiner struck at the heart of the philosophical assumptions underlying the Starnberg and Löser proposals when he said that "behind the images of an operational in-depth defense or a civilian defense there loom the contours of a neutralized and nuclear-free German state whose security would have to be guaranteed by the two antagonistic superpowers . . . we detect here, supported directly or indirectly by the prevalent political pacifism, the desperate hope that one may without risk, on the basis of personal preferences and introversion, withdraw from international entanglements that have become increasingly incalculable."[22] The echoes of the Kennan-Rapacki Plan, the Deutsch-landplan, and other proposals from the early postwar period for neutralizing Central Europe (and, in particular, keeping nuclear weapons out) were evident here, as they were to a much greater degree in the suggestions made by neutral politicians, such as the Swedish prime minister Olof Palme, in 1982 for a nuclear-free belt of 100 or more kilometers on both sides of the Iron Curtain.

The problem with all these ideas was their failure to take into account political realities and the aims of Soviet policy, which specifically included controlling West European defense decisions for the purposes of exerting political pressure and expanding influence.[23] The assumptions were the same as that underlying what I called new Ostpolitik, namely the idea of the *Sicher-heitspartnerschaft*, that the common interest in preventing war, which no one doubted, was also a common interest in a recognizably similar form of peace, and (specifically in the strategic arguments) the idea that what would deter the West would also deter the Soviet Union, and for the same reasons.[24] Ultimately, this tendency to judge Soviet political and military strategy by Western values (mirror-imaging) is, paradoxically, a form of cultural imperialism, and one, moreover, that could prove fatal to those values themselves.

Military professionals in active service in NATO have tended to reject the ideas of Afheldt, Löser, and their colleagues (some of whom are retired military professionals), but that does not mean that they deny that NATO strategy and the Alliance posture are not in trouble or that the credibility of deterrence is at risk. On the contrary, the leaders of the armed services throughout NATO, including West Germany, have lamented for years the discrepancy between the politically required strategy—forward defense on the Central Front—and the lack of means provided for it. By the mid-1970s, these laments began to be taken seriously by NATO member governments, although there was still very little sign of public concern.

In 1976–1977, the political and military heads of the Alliance established a number of principles and requirements for strengthening NATO's deterrent, given the Soviet arms buildup and its foreseeable consequences. These principles found their first formal expression in the decision of all member-governments in the spring of 1978 to increase defense spending by 3 percent a year (in real terms)—an agreement that only the United States, Britain, Norway, and, paradoxically, France (which, since 1966, has not been integrated in the military organization) have kept. The increased rate of deployment of the SS-20 IRBMs since 1980 and the first appearance of the SS-22 short-range ballistic missile (SRBM), bearing a 500-kiloton warhead with a range of 900 kilometers, in 1979, however, demonstrated that INF modernization in the West was an issue of great urgency, for political as well as for military reasons.

The main political reason was that INF modernization would demonstrate the cohesion of the Alliance and its will to restore some measure of balance in the gray area of Eurostrategic weapons. The military reason was that it would deprive the Soviet Union of the opportunity to confine a conventional or a tactical nuclear war to Europe by guaranteeing immediate U.S. nuclear involvement.[25] The Soviets, fearing precisely this development, staged a propaganda war against the new missiles. To the Americans, they argued that since the new missiles could strike the Soviet Union from Western Europe, they were strategic weapons and their use in a European war would invite strategic retaliation against the United States, unleashing a full-scale exchange of ICBMs. To the Europeans, they argued that the Americans, by deploying the Pershing IIs and GLCMs, hoped to confine nuclear war to Europe and thus to spare their own territory.[26] The idea that the United States planned limited nuclear war in Europe or (more euphemistically) hoped to limit nuclear war to Europe if it broke out, became orthodoxy in the peace movement and throughout that large and diffuse group in West Germany that habitually suspected the designs of their own or the American government. The fact that anyone could possibly believe that a Western government might seriously consider nuclear war as a policy option in peacetime is a measure of how great the distrust and incomprehension had become by the early 1980s. Those holding such a belief ignored not only all relevant differences between Western democratic nations and the Soviet Union, but also the obvious fact that even during the height of the cold war, when the United States alone had an undeniable first-strike strategic capability, it did not exercise this offensive power on any occasion, even to counter aggressive Soviet moves.

The clearest case of this restraint occurred in 1948, when the Soviets, in breach of the Potsdam Agreement of 1945, denied the Western Allies access to West Berlin and began the blockade of that city. The United States would have been entirely justified legally and morally in forcing a path for Western convoys, an act that some historians and others believe might have caused the Soviets to withdraw from the Eastern zone of occupied Germany. However that may be, the vulgar Marxist and anti-American argument has it that the United States fought World War II and implemented the European Recovery Plan (Marshall Aid) for its own economic and political benefit and to shore up global capitalism. There would have been no better time for the United States to deliver a decisive blow against Soviet power and to further its own interests than in 1948. Using the legal and moral justification of the Potsdam Agreement, the Americans could have escalated tensions to an extreme and then launched an atomic first strike. Without a nuclear force of their own, the Soviets would have had no other response than to launch a conventional attack on Western Europe. Such an attack in 1948 would have completed the destruction of West European industry (the potential U.S. competitors), leaving the United States inviolate. The United States would have built up its forces and intervened as in 1941 against the Soviet Union, as it did against Germany in 1941. The Soviets would have been defeated, and with its main political rival gone, the United States would have achieved true global hegemony. That nothing of the sort happened, that the Americans, and their allies, allowed the Soviets a free hand in Eastern Europe— even let them break agreements and promises and actually move forward from their position of 1945 (by establishing the East German regime and, later, letting that regime take over East Berlin and build the Berlin Wall)— flatly contradicted the newly popular vision of an expansionist America careless of peace and security in Europe.

Military concerns about the credibility of the deterrent were made clear by the publication in 1977–1980 of a series of scenarios by former NATO commanding officers, all implying that without considerable improvements in conventional defense, NATO could not possibly defeat the Warsaw Pact without using nuclear weapons.[27] Public opinion in West Germany and elsewhere in Western Europe, however, was aroused less by these imaginative attempts to warn of the relative (and, in some respects, absolute) decline of

Western defensive strength than by NATO's dual-track decision in December 1979 to go ahead with INF modernization while simultaneously negotiating for reductions in the level of INFs on both sides. A combination of misinterpreted and ill-conceived (but hardly ill-intentioned) official U.S. statements, a widespread belief that U.S. strategic doctrine for the first time was moving toward counterforce targeting and plans for limited nuclear war, a general rejection of "military alarmists," and many years of neglect of defense and security issues by politicians and the media resulted in a loss of confidence on the part of large sectors of the public in the peaceful purposes of NATO in general and the Reagan administration in particular. For too long, Western Europe had depended on the U.S. "extended deterrent," which was based on the nuclear umbrella and the guarantee that any Soviet attack in Western Europe would be met with retaliation; as a result it had lost interest in defense and security concerns altogether.[28]

The psychological environment created by this loss of interest (indeed sometimes hostility) was the worst possible context for the reasoned discussion of the problem of maintaining and improving conventional deterrence under conditions of nuclear parity and Soviet intermediate nuclear superiority. The very measures requested by NATO to improve deterrence, that is, INF modernization, seemed to many West Germans to be making war more likely. Yet to go on living with a steadily less credible conventional defense and no intermediate nuclear deterrent between tactical and intercontinental strategic systems was to make Soviet success in a conventional attack and hence the stark choice between NATO surrender and strategic holocaust more likely.

Karl-Peter Stratmann, a sensitive and informed analyst of the dilemma of NATO strategy in the 1980s and the lack of public understanding of its implications, concluded that if the deterrent was still effective, it was so largely for the wrong reasons, and that this discrepancy between what is and what should be provided the Soviets with an opportunity to exercise political and psychological pressure to stop NATO governments, especially West Germany, from taking the necessary measures to improve their defenses. The deterrent effect on the adversary, wrote Stratmann in 1981, "rests above all on military options and potential escalatory compulsions that cause powerful self-deterrent reflexes on the Western side and that moreover, for some years have been exposed to increasing politico-psychological erosion." The prime Soviet aim was to isolate the U.S. government from its European allies, and, Stratmann found, "the realization of increasing Soviet military strength and willingness to take risks, on the one hand, and of the doubtful defensive capabilities of the Western Alliance, on the other, is changing the psychological climate in Western Europe and will continue to do so."[29] In other words, Stratmann was implying that the arguments in *Die Zeit, Der Spiegel,* and *Stern* for more West German independence of the United States, and the beliefs of the neo-neutralists like Eppler, Gaus, and Lafontaine in the SPD, were inspired less by a genuine interest in West German autonomy than by fear of what the Soviet Union could or would do to those who remained loyal to the United States and to the Atlantic Alliance. These people, who professed to believe that fears of Soviet attack were anachronistic, that the Soviet Union was really interested only in maintaining the status quo, and that the United States, not the Soviet Union, was an aggressive power whose actions might provoke war, were, on this view, actually displaying, in the words of Hans-Peter Schwarz, an understandable "tendency, in view of the decline of American power, to come to terms with the new lord and master."[30] It was ironic that if this was indeed their true motivation, their vision of the Soviet Union was in fact far more alarmist than that of the cold warriors whose ideas they claimed to find so unpalatable. The key to understanding this paradox is probably that, on either interpretation of their behavior, the neo-neutralists and peace activists were simply ignorant of the Soviet Union, its history, ideology, aims, and methods. If they meant what they said when they claimed that the Soviets were not dangerous, they were certainly ignoring a good deal of evidence and all the lessons of experience. If, on the other hand, they were really driven by a conscious or unconscious fear, as some have asserted, they were also ignoring all the evidence that could have told them that the one factor most likely to provoke Soviet aggression and violence was the appearance of weakness in potential victims. A modernization of NATO defensive strength, accompanied by a restoration of public morale in Western countries, especially West Germany, was likely to contribute much more effectively than any number of peace demonstrations or anguished public statements to the continued freedom of Western Europe.[31]

As we have seen, however, public support for defense, which was a precondition for restoring morale, did not extend to support of INF modernization, or at least not sufficiently. The solution that would combine adequate defense with broad public understanding would, therefore, have to take the form of a conventional deterrent strong enough not only to convince the Soviets, but also to reassure the West Europeans. As Michael Howard put it in the article that launched the concept of "reassurance" as a necessary element of deterrence:

> What is needed today is a reversal of that process whereby European governments have sought greater security by demanding an ever greater intensification of the American nuclear commitment;

demands that are as divisive within their own countries as they are
irritating for the people of the United States. Instead, we should
be doing all we can to reduce our dependence on American
nuclear weapons by enhancing, so far as is militarily, socially and
economically possible, our capacity to defend ourselves.[32]

This solution had been officially rejected by NATO governments as
politically and economically impossible at the Lisbon meeting in 1952 and
had last been proposed by the United States around 1960, with little effect.[33]
By the mid-1980s, however, most professional military men in West Germany, many politicians (except those on the SPD left), and even some critics
of NATO had come to believe that a convincing conventional deterrent,
which would raise the nuclear threshold to a level more acceptable to the
general public, was in fact within the economic means of NATO governments. In 1982–1983, General Bernard W. Rogers, SACEUR (Supreme
Allied Commander Europe), published two widely read articles presenting
his plan for a conventional deterrent in Europe that would reduce the potential role of nuclear weapons of all types and hence radically modify the
existing strategic doctrine of "flexible response," which included the option of
early (and first) use of nuclear weapons. The Rogers Plan, as it was called, was
subjected to intense scrutiny in *The Economist*, whose experts found it to be
militarily sound and economically possible. Over the next few years, numerous other studies appeared arguing for a conventional deterrent on military
or political grounds. U.S. military experts produced plans for a conventional
defense of Western Europe that relied on so-called "emerging technologies."
These so-called "deep attack" concepts became the basis of the doctrine of
FOFA (Follow-On Forces Attack) on enemy troop concentrations, centers of
supply and communications, traffic chokepoints, and air bases behind the
front, which was officially adopted as part of NATO's defense posture, within
the overarching strategy of flexible response, in late 1984. A somewhat bolder
strategy, involving outright counterattack by NATO forces into Warsaw Pact
territory, was proposed by Samuel P. Huntington under the name of "conventional retaliation" and defended on political grounds; a NATO invasion
of Eastern Europe might lead to the collapse of Soviet power there, and therefore the threat of such a response to Soviet attack would be a highly effective
deterrent. A few voices, such as that of John Mearsheimer, even asserted that
the existing NATO posture constituted an adequate conventional deterrent.
They were, however, in a minority; most political analysts and military experts believed that considerable changes, and some increase in spending,
were necessary to make the conventional forces convincing as a deterrent in
themselves.[34]

These active debates of the mid-1980s clearly showed that, both politically and militarily, conventional deterrence was an idea whose time had come. The peace movement and its sympathizers, however, were by no means entirely satisfied with these new directions in the defense debate. For them, and indeed for many officials of the West German government, conventional defense concepts, by excluding the threat of strategic nuclear retaliation against the Soviet Union by the United States in the case of any attack on Western Europe, decoupled the United States from Western Europe and hence made war more, not less, likely. The moral and political arguments on both sides were weighty and there was little sign of the debate coming to any final conclusion. Provided, however, that sensible leadership in West Germany and other NATO countries was forthcoming, and that those who supported the West's right to self-defense were able to appeal to the emotions, prejudices, and beliefs of those who denied that right, it seemed that there was a reasonable chance of establishing some minimal consensus on security for the rest of the century, a consensus based on some combination of conventional deterrence and continued reliance on flexible response as a necessary element of uncertainty in Soviet calculations.

In order better to judge the possibility for such a consensus, however, it is necessary to examine not only the various attitudes and perceptions in national and security policy in the Federal Republic, as has been done so far, but also the contemporary West German cultural and ideological landscape. How, in particular, do the various sectors of opinion understand the notion of peace? This question cannot be answered without at least a brief survey of various types and definitions of peace in Western history, which is the subject of the following chapter, after which I discuss the rejection, first by a few radical intellectuals, and, in the 1980s, by wider sections of the public, especially among the young, of the idea of legitimate political authority and its replacement by a form of ahistorical and apolitical moralism.

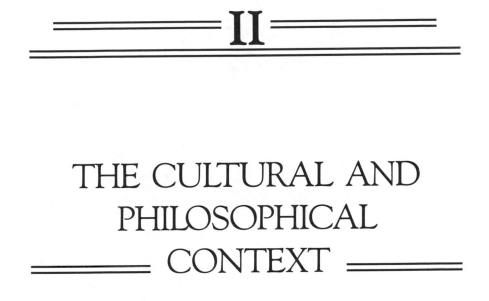

II

THE CULTURAL AND PHILOSOPHICAL CONTEXT

5

THE ISSUE OF PEACE
IN HISTORICAL PERSPECTIVE

PEACE IN THEORY AND PRACTICE

"Peace" is an ambiguous word. If it were not, there would be no peace movement; there would simply be a continuing rational discussion concerning the
best means to preserve (or obtain) peace. Sometimes, indeed, there does seem
to be full agreement on the end to be attained and disagreement only on the
means. The peace movement and many in the SPD argued, as we have seen,
that INF modernization in Western Europe was a threat to peace and not a
way of safeguarding it. Behind this argument lies the idea that the East-West
conflict is in itself a source of danger, and not merely the expression of the
incompatible interests of the United States and the Soviet Union, or of
democracy and communism. Consequently, as I have also argued above, the
most important conflict of opinion in West Germany on the issues of peace
and national survival in the 1980s was between the few who saw the political
division of Europe, maintained by Soviet power, as the chief problem, and
the majority who believed that the threat to peace came not from the
Soviets, but from the East-West conflict itself.

However, it is not enough merely to explain the paradox of deterrence,
that is, the paradox that the security of Western Europe rests ultimately on
a threat that, if carried out, would mean the end of civilization. Behind the
attacks on the morality and legitimacy of deterrence lies something more
than a simple technical disagreement. The impetus of the peace movement
is not just a desire to improve or safeguard an existing peace; the movement

denies that what exists is peace and asserts that "real" peace will prevail only if the international political scene undergoes a radical transformation. This belief is expressed in many forms; in the somewhat inarticulate rhetoric of the demonstrators, who accuse the United States of genocidal mania; in the curious blend of utopian politics and science known as "peace research"; in the philosophical pessimism and moral indignation of Christian socialists such as Eugen Kogon or Helmut Gollwitzer; and in the ethical stand of such as Carl Friedrich von Weizsäcker or Walter Jens. It is this moral charge that makes life so difficult for those who fear the potential political consequences of the new pacifism, partly because they do not always realize that underlying the disagreements is a fundamental difference in the definition of peace, and partly because the moral aggressiveness of the peace movement makes the position of its critics seem, *a priori*, illegitimate and immoral. For reasons derived from strategic, political, and historical analysis, I find myself in opposition to the assertions of the peace movement. Nevertheless, I respect its moral assumptions, and I see clearly that the assertions and even the activism necessarily follow from those moral assumptions. Since I also believe that the debate could be conducted in a much more sophisticated and intellectually productive way than it generally has been, I shall briefly analyze the historical and ideological roots of the differing notions of what is politically possible or desirable in the search for international order.

The first notion is that of peace, a prime example of what the British political philosopher W. B. Gallie has called an "essentially contested concept," that is, a concept capable of a number of mutually incompatible, but equally valid definitions and applications. There are almost as many definitions of peace and how it can be secured as there are thinkers who have explored the problem. The fundamental ambiguity lies in the fact that peace can be both a political condition (as well as a judgment concerning that condition) and a vision to be achieved; that it has a descriptive as well as an emotive dimension. The present problem, in abstract terms, is that those who believe in peace as a vision decline to recognize peace as a political condition and judge that the prevailing condition is not one of peace. As a vision, universal peace (or positive peace or whatever other name is used) has become extremely influential in our century, deriving its strength from the moral impulse of ideological radicalism and the nature of modern war. As a political condition, universal peace has never in fact prevailed, and it is precisely this experience that suggests that attempts to make it prevail by changing the mentality and the behavior of governments in the West are likely to have unintended and potentially disastrous consequences. History offers two quite different examples of peace, corresponding to the two logically possible forms of advanced international order: imperial or hegemonic peace and international or constitutional peace. The former is the peace of a world empire; the latter that of the classical Western state system as it developed in the sixteenth and seventeenth centuries. In addition, since 1945 and the beginning of the nuclear era and global superpower confrontation, nuclear peace, a new and hybrid form of peace, has come into being. The uncertain and complex character of nuclear peace has led to the revival of faith in the possibility of utopian peace and to the denial that nuclear peace is any kind of peace at all.

Both of the two traditional kinds of peace have had the historical effect of limiting violence and reducing the socially and economically harmful consequences of political confrontations. Both have been understood by some as inevitable and by others as desirable. Neither resembles the universal peace of utopian thinkers, for whom the limitation of physical violence can be coupled with the hope for a change of heart, a repentance, which, according to them, will abolish the political confrontations that lead to organized violence.

In the era of modern ideology since the French Revolution, the distinction between the political condition and the utopian goal of peace, and between peace as a description of a prevailing or achievable condition and peace as a moral vision transcending all prevailing conditions, has been further blurred by the exploitation of the moral vision of peace by the Soviet Union, which, more than any other political force, has sought to impose its own version of imperial peace. The belief in a utopian peace beyond politics is shared, at least in theory, by the peace movement in the West and the rulers of the East. The peace movement sees itself as fighting an irrational arms race and a threat of nuclear war caused by the technological system that created nuclear weapons. Consequently, if the ruling powers of modern, Western, industrial society can be defeated, the chances of peace will be improved. The Soviet Union, of course, also wants to defeat the ruling powers of Western society, though the resulting Soviet world hegemony will not resemble the peace desired by the peace movement. Most honest members of the movement realize this and, when pressed, try to distinguish between Soviet policies and their own struggle against Western armaments. However, not only are the immediate effects of the two (damage to Western political cohesion and will) the same, but since the movement can only operate freely in the West, its activities by definition lend themselves to exploitation by the Soviets and local communist parties.

Before discussing the challenge to the Western understanding of peace posed by modern totalitarian ideology, especially that of the Soviet Union, let us turn first to the evolution and function of the two traditional types of peace in the Western historical experience, and to the process by which the second, international peace (both as an ideal and as a political condition), developed from the intolerable chaos and violence of the morally charged confrontations of the religious wars of the sixteenth and early seventeenth centuries. The problems of peace in the twentieth century will be discussed in the final section of the chapter.

IMPERIAL PEACE

Although imperial peace and international peace have coexisted as practical and theoretical possibilities throughout modern history, their origins and significance are wholly different. The idea of international peace as the ordered relations of a system of independent sovereign states grew out of the need to put an end to the religious conflicts of the sixteenth and early seventeenth centuries. It was accompanied by a process of consolidation and centralization within the individual states as well; thus the establishment of the European state system can truly be described as the result of a "search for stability" on the local, regional, and national levels as well as the international level.[1] Imperial or hegemonic peace has been a reality, if not necessarily the object of conceptual analysis, ever since large-scale political organizations capable of mobilizing armed forces for the consolidation and expansion of central authority were first established in Egypt and the Near East in the third millennium B.C. Characteristic, indeed constitutive, of the early empires was a conception of world order that legitimated territorial expansion and required the devotion and loyalty of the subject peoples as well as the members of the original "imperial race" or tribe from which the rulers sprang.[2] This conception of order thus implied a fundamental distinction between those already within the empire and those without, who were, at least in theory, subject to tribute, annexation, and integration into the imperial system since recognition of alien and equivalent sovereignties was conceptually impossible. Each of the early empires was in principle a world-empire, and the discrepancy between fact and fiction was concealed by propagandistic language that was not perceived as such. Examples of such an ideology of world hegemony were to be found in the Near Eastern empires and even more consistently in the Chinese empire, in which civilization and peace were assumed to depend exclusively on the power of the emperor, which, in turn, had been bestowed by Heaven. The "foreign devils" and "outer barbarians" represented the forces of chaos and war that it was the task of civilization to tame.

The rise of the city-state, the *polis* (a political entity in the original sense of the term) in Greece in the sixth and fifth centuries B.C. introduced a new element in the evolution of the concepts of peace: the hegemony of a dominant member of a group of otherwise equal powers. One might have expected something resembling the modern European notion of a conflict-ridden balance of power to arise naturally in what in many ways was a microcosm of the modern state system. In fact it did not, and every Greek city that had the opportunity (Athens, Sparta, and Thebes) attempted to establish hegemony (literally, "leadership") over all the others. A potentially stable, if conflict-prone, system therefore never developed; rather, a succession of struggles for supremacy exhausted the social, economic, and moral vigor of each of the *poleis* in turn. Nevertheless, there were organs of potential international, or "inter-political," order (the Olympic games, the oracle at Delphi, and the Amphictyonic League) that, although they did not prevent the successive struggles or provide more than temporary breaks in the conflict, did help to create a certain sense of common Hellenic identity. This common identity survived the destruction of political independence by Philip and Alexander of Macedon and formed an important ideological justification for the Hellenistic empires and the Roman Empire, whose rulers wanted to be seen as bringers of peace and civilization, as indeed they were.[3] Although peace was still primarily understood as a condition to be achieved after world conquest and the establishment of a universal authority, there was, in the later Hellenistic and Roman periods, much emphasis on prosperity and individual happiness as the ends of imperial rule. The philosophical, and even to some extent the religious, outlook of the age was dominated by Stoicism and Epicureanism, both doctrines that, in different ways, proclaimed that a harmonious, self-sufficient soul was the goal of human activity, both public and private.

This emphasis, and its Stoic and Epicurean roots, was clear in the rhetoric and propaganda of the Augustan age; after the physically and morally destructive Roman civil wars of the first century B.C., a new universal social and political order, favorable to the pursuit of spiritual peace, did seem to be in the offing. Just as in the time of Philip and Alexander in the fourth century B.C., generalized violence was ended, not by fragmentation into mutually recognized sovereign units within a common culture, but by the establishment of a model of imperial peace that endured until the modern era. The medieval Holy Roman Empire (see below) in Western Europe was the direct successor of the original empire, and until the eighteenth century, the vast majority of Europeans could simply not conceive of a world without an empire and an emperor, however feeble their authority might be in practice.

In particular, the Roman idea of imperial peace greatly influenced the understanding of peace and political order of early Christianity. The contrast between Roman order and barbarian threat led to varying degrees of identification of the early church with the empire, which was seen as the only reliable guarantee of material peace.[4] The ancient idea of an imperial world order mission was thus not only renewed, but powerfully reinforced, in the Christian Roman and later the Byzantine empires. Nowhere, however, was the idea of peace as dependent exclusively on the victory of a specific religio-political power carried further than in the religious empire of Islam from the seventh century A.D. onward, with its rigorous distinction between the *Dar-al-Islam* (the "abode of submission" to God, the territory and community of the faithful), where peace reigned, and the *Dar-al-Harb* (the rest of the world, the "abode of war").[5]

In the Christian West, after the chaotic period of breakdown and renewal, popularly known as the "Dark Ages," and which lasted, roughly, from the fifth to the tenth centuries A.D., a new stage of political evolution began in which the image of imperial order inherited from Rome and the Christian image of individual repentance and rebirth as the foundation of a perfect society coexisted in uneasy and sometimes contradictory synthesis. No longer was it possible to identify the achievement of universal peace with the victory of a world empire. The identification persisted to some extent in the Eastern successor empire of Byzantium, where the old confusion of religious orthodoxy, global (or "ecumenical" in the original sense of "encompassing the inhabited world") order, and social harmony persisted in a Christian guise.[6]

In the West, the revival of the idea of a universal empire bringing peace and civilization in the Carolingian era (ca. 800), the Ottonian era of the tenth century, and throughout the later Middle Ages was always countered, on the practical level, by the physical and organizational weaknesses that prevented the Frankish and German kings from repeating the achievement of Augustus. On the spiritual level, it was countered by the increasing independence of the church from secular control and by the development of a theology of social and political life, two developments that expressed themselves, on the one hand, as a moral charge or task imposed on the king or the would-be world ruler that his rule be one of moral perfection as well as social harmony; on the other, as a warning to kings that however great their power, it could not rival God's nor put an end to violence. The latter was the result of evil and original sin, which it was not in the power of the king to eradicate. The consequences for the understanding of peace are clear: peace is not primarily a social condition, but rather the result of right action, of acceptance of the divine law. The inevitability of war is assured by the Fall of Man and the consequent power, always, everywhere, and in each individual soul, of evil impulses and demonic temptations. In the case of rulers, these evil impulses meant that they might use their power for their own aggrandizement and not for the common good. The remedy for these evils was found in the sacraments and teaching of the church and, in the secular community, in obedience to the natural law of justice. This is the meaning of St. Augustine's famous saying that "without justice, what are kingdoms but great bands of gangsters?"[7] The Augustinian influence remained a constant counterpoint to the more optimistic idea that a Christian commonwealth of peace was possible in this world. It was eclipsed somewhat in the High Middle Ages, when, in the name of "Roman renewal" (*renovatio imperii*), several of the German kings, from Otto III (983–1002) to Frederick II (1196–1250), used their imperial position as lords of the "Holy Empire" (*sacrum imperium*) to pursue various conceptions of world-rulership, and to attempt to establish a quasi-religious supremacy to which even the popes would be subject.[8] The lack of adequate physical and organizational means of coercion, however, meant that whatever power was achieved in these remarkable attempts was unstable.

Not even within the domain notionally subject to imperial authority (which, from the tenth to the seventeenth centuries, chiefly included modern-day Germany, Austria, Switzerland, northern Italy, and eastern France) was there peace. Local authority was strong and independent and did not recognize any limitations on the right to make war on rivals or on higher authority. Nor was there any developed distinction between conflict within the empire (among local powers or between such powers and the emperor) and conflict with other kings and princes in Europe. The restraint of violence, therefore, could not take the form of imperial pacification (except in theory and hope), but rather was expressed sporadically in attempts to induce the fighting parties to respect "God's peace" or the "truce of God" (*treuga Dei*), mainly by concluding agreements to fight only on certain days of the week or of the year. Restraint of violence in the modern sense of forbidding certain acts or establishing "rules of war" was rudimentary, although an elaborate code of conduct for fighting was developed for use by members of the noble classes, which later played a considerable part in later inspiring such "rules of war."[9]

The Christian empire was ultimately defeated less by inherent material inadequacies than by the breakdown of the uneasy synthesis of the Roman and Christian images of order established a thousand years before. Violence and disorder increased and became endemic in the empire after the middle of the thirteenth century, but elsewhere in Europe, particularly in France and England, royal authority was becoming more effective, and rulers and their ministers were establishing stable institutions of government.[10] As yet, however, the notion of international peace as a stable system of relations between equal sovereignties was undeveloped, and the establishment of such a system was retarded by the great crisis of the West in the fourteenth and fifteenth centuries. This crisis, the most severe in Western history before the wars and tyrannies of the twentieth century, affected all aspects of life, material, political, and spiritual. Materially, it began as a crisis of overpopulation, exacerbated by climatic changes resulting in bad harvests and widespread starvation, in the early fourteenth century. The plague epidemics that began in 1349 and did not subside until the eighteenth century ended overpopulation by reducing the population of Europe by something like 40 percent, a loss that was not made good for over 300 years. At the same time, the political and social changes I have referred to led to a series of wars that caused much destruction and hampered recovery from the ravages of the plague. On the spiritual level, the coherent theological and philosophical world view of the High Middle Ages was being undermined by new and daring ideas about the absolute power of God over man and nature and a renewed emphasis on personal conversion as opposed to loyal obedience to the existing Church.[11] Moreover, the embryonic sovereignty of the new kingdoms was being challenged by new wars and conflicts. Nevertheless, it was in this period that the first serious steps were taken toward limiting war and restraining the apparently inevitable violence of local lords and princes. This occurred primarily in the empire, where by the end of the fifteenth century a fairly elaborate "constitution" had in fact been developed, specifying and delegating the privileges and obligations of the various levels of authority and reserving the right to wage war to the emperor and the council of estates.[12] However, the "imperial constitution," which represented a new stage in the development of political order, could not be tried out in practice to any great extent because its development coincided with the religious and social ferment that preceded the Reformation, and the combination of political and cultural trends and religious change in the early sixteenth century released a series of morally charged violent confrontations that had the double effect of destroying the notion of imperial peace in Europe and ultimately of establishing the two essential pillars of a new kind of peace: the sovereign state and the idea of the balance of power.

SOVEREIGNTY AND THE PRESERVATION OF PEACE

Though the Reformation was not in origin a political movement, it almost immediately became so, and the result was violent conflict. The medieval synthesis of church and empire found its last embodiment in Charles V, Holy Roman emperor from 1519 to 1557, whose vision of world rule and imperial peace clashed directly with the antipapal and, by implication, antiimperial claims and assertions of the Protestant secular princes. The double war waged by the German princes against church power and privilege and against imperial coercion (which was necessarily religious coercion as well) gave the religious wars that were now beginning a moral impulse that rendered ineffective the feeble attempts made thus far to restrain violence. The political enemy was now also, for both sides, a religious enemy and therefore represented a moral evil that had to be eradicated. However, in Germany the confrontation did not immediately lead to a fundamental re-evaluation of the question of peace and limiting war. After the signing of the Peace of Augsburg in 1555, the German lands were divided among the Catholic and the Protestant princes on the condition of mutual noninterference; each local lord gained the right to impose and preserve his faith (Catholic, Lutheran, or Calvinist) in his lands. The imperial authority, a relic of the old synthesis, survived, not without moments of glory and reassertion, until 1806.

In France, however, the religious wars that had begun in 1559 continued to increase in destructiveness and brutality until the social order was severely threatened.[13] In the 1560s and 1570s, for the first time in European history, progressive thinkers (who became known as the *politiques*) proposed a revolutionary solution to the problem of peace and order. The politiques agreed that the old synthesis of political and religious authority was defunct and that it was clearly impossible to establish a new synthesis as long as it was subject to challenge by rivals who not only wished to assert their independence but who fundamentally denied the moral right of any authority not of their own (Catholic or Protestant) faith. They therefore argued for an absolute separation of political sovereignty and faith.[14] Political sovereignty must be absolute and unchallengeable, and should include the right, indeed the obligation, to prevent, if necessary by force, differences of faith from erupting into violence leading to civil war. Whether this definition of sovereignty included a principle of toleration was unclear; the French monarchy did, under certain conditions, tolerate Protestantism from 1598 to 1685. The concept was essentially areligious; the king was to exercise his judgment in deciding whether toleration furthered his interests and those of his realm.

After a long period of quiet, religious war broke out again in Germany in 1618, largely in response to imperial efforts to promote Catholic expansion and control. The resulting Thirty Years' War recalled the fourteenth-century crisis of the Plague and the Hundred Years' War in degree of destruction. Because of changes in the art of war, due in no small measure to the improved organizational and administrative capacities of the new sovereignties, whether national, as in France and Sweden, or local, as in the German states, the Thirty Years' War was an even more terrible ordeal than the earlier crisis in the areas directly affected. Some historians have even argued that the long-term effects of the war were decisive for the social and political evolution of modern Germany. Population loss and economic destruction, on this argument, so enfeebled the empire as a whole that no national state evolved in Germany as it did in France or Britain; furthermore, since the embryonic middle class was the hardest hit of all social groups, it was forced into a position of permanent weakness that was an important cause of the lack of a strong liberal tradition in German politics before 1945.[15] As the fighting intensified and as an end to it began to seem ever more remote, the ideas of the politiques concerning the separation of the problem of political order from that of religious belief and practice gradually gained influence.

Leading political thinkers of the period, from Jean Bodin in France to Johannes Althusius in Germany and Hugo Grotius in the Netherlands, increasingly recognized religious war, organized violence incited by mutual hatred and moral discrimination, as a fatal danger and regarded political order and peace as values in themselves separate from the question of faith.[16] This was perceived most clearly, however, not by any French or German thinker, but by Thomas Hobbes, whose experience of the English Civil War and awareness of the destructive consequences of unbridled politico-religious passions led him unerringly to the recognition that the claim to possess truth and the right to impose it must be excluded from politics, and the determination of law and of the rules governing conduct should be reserved, not to those knowing the "truth," which was subject to individual or group interpretation, but to independent and unchallengeable authority: *auctoritas non veritas facit legem* (authority, not truth, makes the law). This "secularization of the modern state"[17] and the development of the new notion of "national interest" or "reason of state" might on one level be seen as marking a dangerous split between ethics and political behavior; on another level, they represented the only chance of order and peace. However, the idea of absolute sovereignty implicitly excluded imperial peace as a solution to the problem of violence and political confrontation. Thus, a new understanding of peace—international peace among equal partners bound by common rules of conduct above and beyond their denominational affiliation—was born.

THE RE-MORALIZATION OF CONFLICT
IN MODERN IDEOLOGY

The 130 years following the Peace of Westphalia in 1648, which ended the Thirty Years' War, marked, in more than one sense, the "recovery of nerve" of European culture. The failure of the last attempts at imperial pacification in the style of the medieval emperors had not led to chaos but to the peculiar balance-in-tension that was the most original European contribution to political practice.[18] Wars became gradually less destructive, and there was no repetition after 1648 of anything approaching the level of general violence of the Thirty Years' War, in which more than half the population of Germany perished. Armies marched, bivouacked, maneuvered and fought with much less effect on the surrounding countryside than would have been conceivable in the total wars of the sixteenth and early seventeenth centuries. Frederick the Great of Prussia (1740–1786), whose reign combined the limitation of war with an almost total militarization of the economy, once stated that it was his ambition that the peasants should be able to sow and reap their grain while the armies marched and fought.

The many wars of the eighteenth century need not be idealized. Frederick's two wars (1740–1748 and 1756–1763) cost the Prussian people and economy dearly, and they had not yet recovered when he died. Proportionately, the losses were greater than those of the two world wars. It is only in relation to what went before that the eighteenth century in Europe was an era of limited war, but it was precisely this improvement, and the nascent ideals of stable and rationally organized administration, limitation of violence, and absolute rule, that dominated the outlook of the age.[19] Gone was the religious rage, the demonization of the enemy that had made the threat of total war so dangerous in earlier times. Violent confrontations between states occurred now for different reasons, and they were subject to rules of international law that, although they were unenforceable, enjoyed impressive respect.

The prospect of a perpetually stable international order, with no member ever likely to gain the definitive upper hand, led to proposals for permanent peace, such as that of Immanuel Kant, that took as their starting point the reality and sovereignty of individual states. Such proposals had not been unknown before but were now decidedly less utopian than they had formerly seemed. Kant's idea, which he advanced in his essay *Zum ewigen Frieden* (Toward perpetual peace) in 1795, was that since ultimate supremacy was an illusory goal, war could be entirely avoided if all parties to the balance of power recognized their mutual interest in refraining from violent confrontations.[20] Unlike many of those who have claimed to be inspired by his plans and who have exploited his prestige on behalf of a different kind of peace, he was not suggesting or even imagining an inner change of psychological disposition in the rulers of the participating states, much less a change of conviction or opinion by the citizens. His perpetual peace was a strictly political, dispassionate agreement to be concluded in recognition of a common interest in avoiding war.

Just as the imperial reform of the fifteenth century came too late to save the chances of imperial peace in the Reformation era, so Kant's proposal was made too late to have anything but an intellectual impact. With the French Revolution of 1789–1794, political conflict had entered on a new course, one that led inexorably to a re-moralization of confrontation and war and to a demonization of the enemy—one more terrible than the spirit of religious hatred that had been tamed with such effort a century and a half earlier. The new factor was the messianic political ideology of revolution determining not only behavior, but belief and morality as well. That ideology was the extreme form of the humanitarian utopianism of the radical philosophies of the

French Enlightenment, combined with the idea that the mobilization of the disenfranchised masses of the nation would redeem the corrupt nature of existing society and open an era of reason, progress, and happiness for all.[21] In a pattern that was to repeat itself in all subsequent political revolutions, the mobilization took place, but the redemption of society and the promises of harmony and happiness receded ever further into the future. Instead, the most obvious and immediate result of revolution, in France and elsewhere later, was a vast increase in the power of the rulers and in their ability to wage war. The people, the potentially progressive masses hailed by the revolutionary ideologues as the instrument of history, were organized and sent to war as never before.

The paradox of the French Revolution, and by extension of all subsequent revolutions made in the name of humanity, peace, and progress, but in fact culminating in war, has been described by Ernst Topitsch as follows:

> Delegates to the French National Assembly of 1789 believed that an age of "perpetual peace" was dawning . . . History, however, brought the opposite of what the noble illusions had predicted. The intervention of the conservative European powers involved France in critical military conflicts . . . In the revolutionary state, fighting for its survival, the mirage of a "realm of peace" gave way to a new form of that terrible hybrid of war and civil war that had been kept down by absolutism since the great religious struggles. France was forced to a hitherto unheard-of degree of mobilization of its forces; on August 23, 1793, the Convention ordered the *levée en masse*. Whatever the tasks and sufferings the old royal absolutism had required of its subjects for purposes of power, they paled by comparison with this merciless exploitation of military effort. The mobilization of mass armies also entailed an intense emotionalization of war. Passion and the rage of battle were stimulated by ideological propaganda; the merciless practices of civil war were directed against the foreign enemy . . . The nation had marched forth to make an end of royal tyranny and its despicable outgrowth, war, but it found, instead of the war of dynasties, the much more terrible war of peoples.[22]

The two chief characteristics of the new style of war, then, were physical and ideological mobilization of the masses in the name of revolutionary liberation. Although the revolution came to an end with the dictatorship of Napoleon, he exploited the military transformation it had caused to terrible effect. For the first time in nearly three centuries there was a genuine bid for imperial hegemony in Europe, one that required the combined efforts of the conservative powers to defeat. The old order was, superficially, restored, including the principle of international peace among equals and the balance of power, but in actuality the change from the eighteenth century system had been profound. Mass armies, mass mobilization, and political ideologies as instruments of power were permanent features of the European scene, available for exploitation by ruthless leaders. "The nationalization of the masses," as George Mosse called it, meant that the new fervor of nationalism, combined with the attempts at mobilization and the results of the industrial revolution produced armies whose size and spirit were beyond anything hitherto imagined.[23] In 1928, Sir Winston Churchill presciently identified the reasons why war was now total, namely the effective power of modern social, political, and economic institutions on the one hand, and nationalist fervor on the other:

> It was not until the dawn of the twentieth century of the Christian Era that war began to enter into its kingdom as the potential destroyer of the human race. The organization of mankind into great states and empires, and the rise of nations to full collective consciousness, enabled enterprises of slaughter to be planned and executed upon a scale and with a perseverance never before imagined. All the noblest virtues of individuals were gathered together to strengthen the destructive capacity of the mass. Good finances, the resources of worldwide credit and trade, the accumulation of large capital reserves, made it possible to divert for considerable periods the energies of whole peoples to the task of devastation.[24]

The result, when these means were finally deployed to their full extent in World War I, was devastating; it brought about a revision of the understanding of peace, and its implications were at least as profound as that of the sixteenth century, when the vision of imperial peace had given way to the practical solution of international peace and limited war.[25]

The nationalist mobilization of popular sentiment for purposes of confrontation with international rivals for power was not the only force working for an ideological remoralization of political conflict. Nationalism as a social force in the nineteenth century was paralleled by another force: socialism. The former tended to demonize foreigners and aliens, the latter demonized the domestic class enemy and was thus in principle a posture of civil war. However, before 1918 nationalism was generally the stronger force, so that in Germany, for example, the socialists, who had proclaimed the international solidarity of the proletariat against the warmongering capitalists and aristocrats, in the end almost unanimously supported the war in 1914. The result of both was that political confrontation was once again charged with moral overtones and colored by cataclysmic visions, in which morality and justice were reduced to instruments of the ideology, whether nationalist or socialist. War, as Churchill saw, had become total, and the means of waging war were becoming total; consequently, for civilization to survive, peace would have to be total as well.

FROM TOTAL WAR TO TOTAL PEACE

The effort to limit war, characteristic of international relations in the era of the classical European balance of power, was gradually largely replaced by two newer and contradictory forces: the remoralization of conflict and war in the name of social (or national) salvation typical, as we have seen, of modern ideology, and the attempt to outlaw war in the name of morality. These two forces were most evident during and immediately after World War I. There developed on both sides, the German and the Allied, a moralization of the war effort in which one side was charged with a universal mission on behalf of all mankind, and the enemy was seen as not merely a political opponent to be defeated, but as a vile threat to order and morality, who must therefore be destroyed. The result of this tendency was that attitudes and reactions that before 1914 would have seemed callous, ruthless, or immoral were fully acceptable in 1918 and after.[26] The harsh terms that the Germans offered the Bolshevik regime in 1918 gave them no advantage in their pursuit of the war in the West. Similarly, after the final defeat of the Central Powers, the Allies treated them as criminals who were collectively responsible for the war. In the perspective of European history, such an attribution of national guilt for waging war was rather bizarre.[27] It nevertheless prevailed and greatly influenced not only the Treaty of Versailles (1919), but a much wider movement that led to the establishment of the League of Nations and to the Kellogg-Briand Pact of 1928, which outlawed war as an instrument of national policy.

The moralization of war was evident not only in the liberal, bourgeois societies of Germany, France, and Britain but in the Soviet Union as well. Lenin, who successfully established his rule on the ruins of Russian civil society in 1917, proclaimed that war was justified if waged on behalf of the international proletariat (ultimately on behalf of Bolshevism and the Soviet government) and condemned other warfare as simply the expression of contradictions within the imperialist camp. The antiwar movement in the West, therefore, became the unwitting ally of Leninism in its attempt to subvert the defense efforts of democratic Western states. According to Leninist theory, which was not always honored in practice, the just war of the international proletariat against imperialism would end in universal peace.[28] The Western pacifist vision of peace, as it evolved in the 1920s, combined features of earlier ideas of imperial peace with elements of a religious understanding of peace as the consequence of personal conversion and was radically opposed to the revised bourgeois version of international peace between self-contained and independent sovereign states. The influential and important pacifist movement survived, in France and Britain, until World War II. A connection was established between the utopian and apolitical pacifism prevalent, to varying extents, in Western democracies, and the politically effective and consistent hegemonial drive of the Soviet Union, with its ideological message of ultimate and perfect peace, which, however, could come about only as a result of prolonged conflict.

That conflict, the international class struggle, is the prime modern example of the remoralized political confrontation. By a contradiction intrinsic to the doctrines of Karl Marx, the class struggle is both a historical necessity and a moral obligation. In Marx's view, historical progress was the child of conflict; as the bourgeoisie of his own time was, he thought, entitled forcibly to colonize the rest of the world into modernity, so, in the industrialized societies, the proletariat and the progressive intellectuals who transcend their bourgeois class position to join in the struggle were both the instruments and the self-conscious shapers of history, carrying out a task that could not be shirked, but was also a glorious commission on behalf of future generations. Marxists thus took up a posture of civil war, of unremitting hostility, to all aspects of the existing political, economic, and social order. When they came to power, moreover, they required all members of the revolutionary communist movement to engage in aggressive infiltration and subversion of democratic capitalist states, a requirement that has never been denied by the spokesmen and ideologues of that movement.[29] With regard to the issue of peace, we may note that the communist movement by definition denies and cannot but deny the value and the relevance of the old international state system and its associated principle of peace in a balance of power between independent sovereign states. In Western Europe the Bolshevik Revolution forced Social Democrats to decide whether they were primarily for democracy or primarily for communist revolution; the result was a split that separated the democratic socialist majority from the communist minority and made the two factions implacable enemies of each other. The communist parties that arose in the West as a result of that split were loyal to the Soviet Union; their chief purpose was to defeat the Social Democrats and, ultimately, to impose Soviet rule in their respective countries. They were, as the French Socialist leader Léon Blum put it, "nationalists of a foreign power," and the existence, since the 1920s, of such "Soviet parties," organizations committed to the overthrow of the political order in the interests of the Soviet Union, in Western countries is the root of the cold war between East and West, which began long before World War II.[30]

The communist claim that final liberation required a total conversion of minds as well as a total transformation of international relations brought morality back into politics, but as a tool, not an end. According to Lenin, those actions are moral that serve the revolution and the expansion of communist power; actions that have the effect of opposing these ends are evil. Furthermore, only the chosen few, the progressive vanguard, possess the ability to make the distinction between good and evil. Without proper leadership, the revolutionary social class, the workers, will abandon the firm commitment to revolution and will simply form trade unions for the improvement of their condition, thus disobeying the laws of history. It is the task of the communist party, and specifically of its leadership, to enforce those laws.[31]

There were anticipations of Leninism during the French Revolution, but they were outweighed by the inertia of traditional social and political structures and patterns of organization and behavior. Thus, the international revolutionary imperialism of the armed masses in the French Revolution ended as the hegemonic bid for continental supremacy of Napoleon, which was not so different from that of Charles V in the sixteenth century or even of the medieval emperors. By 1917, however, the preconditions of revolution had been drastically modified by the social, intellectual, cultural, and economic transformations of the nineteenth century: revolutionary and reactionary nationalism, socialism, secularization, and philosophical nihilism; the very combination of processes, in short, foreseen and described by Tocqueville and Burckhardt. The explosive power of ideological justifications for violence and war, whether "reactionary," as expressed by the official propaganda of the belligerent states of World War I or by National Socialism, or "revolutionary," as expressed in communism, was the mechanism that released the great "totalitarian pandemic" of the "Second Thirty Years' War" of 1914–1945.[32]

PEACE AS FACT AND AS OBLIGATION
IN THE NUCLEAR AGE

At the end of World War II there was general agreement in the West that the future international order was going to be very different from the system of equal sovereignties, each seeking to serve its own national interest, that had prevailed, with the modifications described above, until 1914. The reasons for the emergence of this consensus were partly sociological and partly ethical and philosophical. The political mobilization of the masses, the rise of political parties divided by sharp ideological differences, and the effects of industrialization represented irreversible changes in the outlook and practice, not only of the masses, but of political leaders as well. These sociological changes, which also made mobilization for total war possible for the first time in history, went hand in hand with changes in ways of thinking and looking at the world. The mentality of the old regime, that of the European state system, with its blend of religion, morality, and Realpolitik, had been undermined by secularization. In one sense, the secularization of politics and culture was partly responsible for the rise of totalitarianism in Europe and hence for the horrors of total war. Another effect of secularization, however, was to deny the state the metaphysical legitimacy and privileges of sovereignty that older philosophers and political thinkers, above all Hegel, had been generally willing to grant. The moral condemnation of war had not been a part of the old system, even in its religious aspect; states had attempted to limit war while claiming the right to go to war as a sovereign privilege and an expression of their "right to be the ultimate judges of what defense of their interests or their honor demands."[33] World War II, while evidently a just and necessary war, waged against an enemy, Hitler, who was not merely a rival for power, but a destroyer of civilization, greatly strengthened the emerging consensus in the democracies that the right to war could no longer be recognized as a universal privilege of sovereignty. As pointed out by Churchill in 1928, social change had made it possible for war to be total, and the consequences of total war, as apparent in 1945, were such that it could not, according to this consensus, be justified under any circumstances. At best, the critics were prepared to grant states a right of self-defense, using means short of total war, as a final recourse. The chief result of this new Western consensus against war as a sovereign right was the creation of the United Nations organization in 1945.

The U.N. idea, however, was vitiated from the start because the organization included the Soviet Union, whose view of war, as we have seen, was incompatible both with the emerging Western consensus against the right of states to go to war and with the survival and well-being of the Western democracies themselves. Stalin and Hitler, both despising constitutional democracy as an inadequate tool of power, destroyed or demoralized their domestic opponents and forced foreign democratic governments to grant them legitimacy. However, after the Soviet Union was attacked by Stalin's erstwhile ally Hitler, it became an ally of the democracies and remained so until Germany was totally defeated. Those who condemned total war and denied that there was any longer an automatic right to go to war had great difficulty in distinguishing between the Soviet Union as an ally against Hitler in a just war, and the Soviet Union as an imperialistic power devoted to a political doctrine incompatible with the new consensus.

Seventeen years before the first nuclear explosion, Churchill wrote:

> It is established that henceforward whole populations will take part in war, all doing their utmost, all subjected to the fury of the enemy . . . It is probable—nay, certain—that among the means which will next time be at their disposal will be agencies and processes of destruction wholesale, unlimited, and perhaps, once launched, uncontrollable.
>
> Mankind has never been in this position before. Without having improved appreciably in virtue or enjoying wiser guidance, it has got into its hands for the first time the tools by which it can unfailingly accomplish its own extermination.[34]

In 1947, after the first use of nuclear weapons in war, and after it was clear that the Soviet Union would soon have the bomb, he added, no less significantly, in reference to the challenge of Soviet power, that the democracies "have only to repeat the same well-meaning, short-sighted behavior towards the new problems which in singular resemblance confront us today to bring about a third convulsion from which none may live to tell the tale."[35]

As those who study his policies and his observations must admit, Churchill was second to none in his prescience and in his understanding of the political problems of peace and war in the twentieth century. Unlike those who believed that the invention of nuclear weapons would automatically force all parties, including both the Soviet Union and its democratic adversaries, to common conclusions regarding future world order, Churchill realized that the power of totalitarian ideology, and after the defeat of Germany this meant Soviet communism, meant that continued global conflict was inevitable if the democracies wished to survive. The ideological confrontation of the cold war, combined with the means of destruction at the disposal of both sides, also meant, however, that the conflict could not be one of violent military confrontation, at least not between the superpowers directly. The Soviet Union appeared to agree to this minimal condition of coexistence, at least after the end of the debate of 1953–1955 in the Kremlin between those who believed in the inevitability of a nuclear war with the West, which the Soviet Union would win, and those who believed that such a war would destroy both sides, and that the Soviet Union must henceforth pursue its global aims in ways that avoided such a holocaust. As Raymond Aron noted in his diagnosis of the East-West conflict as early as 1947, this basic realization made "peace impossible, but war unlikely."[36] The survival of democratic societies would be assured as long as Western statesmen did not forget two crucial facts: that the conflict was real, and that it would lead to disaster unless managed with extreme patience, intelligence, and strategic grasp.

These two facts have not always been equally prominent in public awareness or in political discourse in Western countries, either in Europe or in the United States. For the first two decades after 1945, the first fact—that the conflict was real—tended to dominate the picture, and great efforts were made to secure the political cohesion of the West in the face of the continuing political challenge presented by Soviet power in Europe and elsewhere in the world. Since that time, beginning in public debate, but gradually affecting the analyses of political and strategic specialists as well, the second fact—that the conflict was potentially disastrous—began to dominate. By 1980, most obviously in West Germany, but to a lesser extent in other NATO countries as well, many politicians, and a majority of the intellectuals who habitually discussed East-West issues in public, appeared to believe that, to a very large extent, the conflict was artificial, due to misunderstandings and the ill will of past leaders. The way to defuse its disastrous potential was, on this view, to make brave new proposals for arms control and East-West negotiations, thereby demonstrating good will to the Soviets and starting a process that would shift the relationship from one of opposition to one of neutral coexistence and, perhaps, even to one of positive friendship and mutual understanding.

This shift in perceptions, which was by no means absolute, was partly a generational phenomenon, since many of the leading analysts and politicians of the 1970s and 1980s were too young to remember World War II or the early postwar years, when the Soviet threat was felt to be obvious and immediate. It was also in part a consequence of the final victory of an understanding of peace that owed less to the traditions of the European state system and the balance of power than it did to the utopian ideas of the interwar years or the moralistic revulsion against war that began in the 1920s and was very much strengthened by the realization of the potential destructive power of nuclear weapons. The implications of nuclear weapons were now felt to be so serious that the complementary requirement of care and vigilance in the defense of Western interests was largely forgotten. The "nuclear revolution" was now seen, by an increasing number of political scientists and analysts in the West, as meaning that universal peace was an obligation that must necessarily be as clear to Soviet leaders as it was to those analysts themselves. The problem with this understanding, as its critics saw it, was that the total peace required by the destructive potential of nuclear war was not the same total peace as that envisaged by the Soviet Union.[37] While recognizing the disastrous consequences of a central nuclear war between the superpowers, the Soviet Union had in no way abandoned attempts to expand its own power or to conduct the struggle with the West in all ways short of open and direct challenge. With the West wavering in its equal commitment to the two principles of preservation of peace between the superpowers and vigilant defense of its interests, it was clear that the Soviet Union could only benefit from its continued belief in the seriousness and enduring nature of the East-West conflict.

We have now reached a point where we can evaluate the significance and the implications of various notions of peace in the debate over Western defense in general and in the particular case of West Germany. In the 1980s, I would argue, the defenders of Western democracy and its associated promises of human rights face a double challenge. On the one hand, the Soviet Union, despite the hopes of the 1960s and 1970s, still remains a direct threat to the West. Given the conditions of nuclear balance between the United States and the Soviet Union, the struggle to reduce that threat must still, and for the foreseeable future, be conducted in that shadowy area, analyzed by Aron, between open war and genuine peace in the traditional sense of political peace between equal sovereignties based on mutual respect. On the other, there is the challenge of the utopian idea of peace, born of the pacifist illusions of the 1920s and 1930s and nourished by the fear, realistic enough in its own terms, of nuclear war. The extreme difficulty of the double challenge lies in the fact that the proponents of utopian peace in the West disregard the seriousness of the conflict and thereby make their vision of peace the ally of the wholly different Soviet understanding of peace as the consequence of global Soviet hegemony. The defense of existing peace is attacked by the peace movement, in the name of utopian peace, as a preparation for war. The peace movement, of course, has a point: the peace prevailing between East and West is not satisfactory since it is based in part on the recognition of Soviet power and, therefore, on an acceptance of the denial of human rights and freedom in Eastern Europe. Some few members of the movement do see this point and attack both superpowers as equally guilty of preventing true peace from coming about. The view in this book is somewhat different. True peace, including the rights of East Europeans, is certainly worth striving for, but not at the price of nuclear holocaust. We are driven back to the basic illumination provided by the first atomic flashes of 1945: that the East-West conflict dividing Europe and the world is unique in two ways: in the nature of the adversary, and in the nature of the possible weapons of war. The political and strategic skills and understanding required to carry out this enduring conflict, however, are not unique to the post-1945 era. They are those learned by Western statesmen in the hard school of politics and diplomacy since the seventeenth century, but on a scale, and with ultimate risks, unimaginable to earlier generations.

6

THE DENIAL
OF AUTHORITY

The utopian vision of peace is incompatible with the actual peace established and maintained in Europe by NATO and accepted (conditionally, as we have seen) by the Soviet Union. It is true that this actual peace is imperfect. As many moralists and philosophers have pointed out, and as has been stressed constantly by the teaching authority of the Catholic church, real peace in the sense of harmonious coexistence does not exist when human rights are being violated or denied.[1] Since Soviet power in Eastern Europe is based precisely on the denial of the human and political rights of the East Europeans, the peace prevailing in Europe is certainly an incomplete peace. However, this valid argument is seldom used by the peace movement in the West and its sympathizers. When they deny that there is true peace in Europe, they are not blaming Soviet power, but Western governments, especially the U.S. government, for trying to maintain and improve deterrence.

Behind the revival of utopian pacifism and the belief that the main obstacle to true peace in Europe is NATO and not the Soviet Union, there lies in fact a profound denial of the legitimacy, specifically the legitimate authority, of democratic Western governments. In the world view of the peace movement, governments, whether in Bonn or in Washington, are seen as hostile entities opposed to the true interests of the people. The movement opposes INF modernization, which it considers a dangerous and provocative escalation of the arms race, but that opposition is only part of a more general resistance to any act or decision of the government in power, the democratic character of which is denied. This general resistance and the utopian ideal of worldwide, total peace are, in turn, based on a moralization of politics that, in fact, is a denial of political reality and political action in favor of presumably life-enhancing sentiments. One of the connecting links between the basic sentimental impulse of a wide segment of the successor generation and its intellectual leaders and supporters in West Germany and the particular politics (or antipolitics) of pacifism and neutralism that these groups propound is the idea, to be discussed in this chapter, that authority, hierarchy, rule, and obedience are at best negative elements of past history that must be eliminated if the "soft" society of peace and ecological balance is to be achieved. Usually, these phenomena are condemned as means of oppression used by the ruling classes throughout history to deprive the ruled of their rights and rightful influence.[2]

The view that all established political authority is per se unjust, because it is ultimately coercive, was not, of course, new to the postwar period. It has a long and distinguished ancestry in Western political thought and was quite common, for example, among religious utopian groups in the sixteenth and seventeenth centuries. In the affluent industrial societies of the 1960s and 1970s, however, it was no longer found only among marginal political, social, or ideological minorities, but became the standard view of large parts of the educated younger generation and the academic community generally. This popularity had many causes. One was the so-called Tocqueville effect, according to which increasing prosperity and equality produce a situation in which any remaining inequalities of wealth or of power are seen less as consequences of accident or inevitable elements of any social organization than as affronts to the growing belief in the value and justification of equality. Another was the alliance of antiauthoritarianism with Marxism, which was also, and for partly the same reasons, undergoing a revival in the 1960s. Marxists had not previously been overly concerned with authority as such and were usually content to assert that the result of the class struggle, and of proletarian revolution, would be a rational reorganization of society; presumably, in that society, there would be no inequality of personal wealth, and any inequalities of power would be entirely justified and seen to be so by the people. By the 1960s, this older form of Marxism was on the wane in all Western countries and was being replaced by what Sidney Hook called "existential Marxism," a somewhat heretical variant of the theory, in which the problem of personal alienation from oppressive social and economic structures and the question of ideology were stressed at the expense of the older concentration on economics and the class struggle.[3] Existential Marxism, inspired by the writings of George Lukacs and the German philosophers of the Frankfurt School, most of which dated from the 1920s and 1930s, proved to be very compatible with the diffuse feelings of resistance to and resentment toward authority that were growing among West German, French, and American students in the 1960s.

In West Germany, moreover, as in many other countries, the academic disciplines of sociology, political science, psychology, history, and economics were also changing fast, beginning around 1960. In Chapter 3, I discussed those changes in the historical profession and in historical writing that related to the treatment of German national history and the problem of national division. To an outside observer, however, changes in the social sciences (political science, sociology, and economics) were far more obvious and significant at the time.[4] In political science, the period 1945–1960 had been characterized by a wholesale adoption of American principles and methods, chiefly behaviorism, formal modeling, and what became known as "democracy theory," the main tenet of which is that the natural course of social and political modernization is toward an ever broader extension of civil and political rights and liberties, and toward a liberal organization of the economy. Traditional German types of political science, which focused more on formal legal theory and principles and were based mostly on some form of philosophical idealism, were in almost total eclipse. Their practitioners were either removed from influence in the profession because of their real or alleged collaboration with the Nazi regime—such was the case of Carl Schmitt, for example—or had fled or been exiled. Many of them, such as Leo Strauss or Reinhard Bendix, in fact established long and successful careers in the United States, contributing philosophical sophistication to American political science even while the more technical and mathematical aspects of the latter took over the scene in West Germany.

In the 1960s, the domination of quantitative methods and of democracy theory in West German political science, in which influential elements of the political and cultural elite were trained, was challenged by a revival of older Marxist theory, as in the work of Wolfgang Abendroth, and by existential Marxism in the renewed popularity of the Frankfurt School. The result was a polarization, which began in the mid-1960s and had by no means been resolved twenty years later, between democracy theory and its offshoots and the various forms of neo-Marxism. Of the latter, by far the most important was "critical theory," as developed by Jürgen Habermas and his followers since the early 1960s. Habermas was recognized as the heir to the Frankfurt School–style of thought and to its combination of Marxist economic analysis and Freudian social psychology, although in fact his original training was in the tradition of democracy theory. This early affiliation of his can perhaps best be seen in his enduring belief that societies do indeed share a common course of evolution in the direction of greater freedom. Where he differs from democracy theorists and resembles the neo-Marxists is in his belief that the freedom toward which societies move is not the political freedom of European liberalism, but a "freedom from domination" in a condition of "communicative competence." The latter phrase denotes a state of society in which the members communicate, that is, interact by word, symbol, and deed, free from any irrational overt coercion or psychological obstacles. The achievement of communicative competence and freedom from domination is therefore not only a political, but also a psychological and social task.[5]

It is possible to argue that Habermas is, ultimately, a liberal and not a true Marxist, for whom political freedom is meaningless, and it is true that he spoke out bravely against the fanaticism of student radicals in the late 1960s, for whom even the Frankfurt School was not radical enough. However, the popular effect of Habermas's teaching, and its reception by large numbers of politically interested West German students since around 1970, has been to promote a form of existential Marxism that has led to indiscriminate opposition to every form of political authority and coercion, without regard for any justification they might have. His intellectual prestige added immeasurably to the already rising favor that antiauthoritarianism enjoyed among students, many of whom sought and found employment in the media and in the growing public sector of the 1970s and 1980s, especially in the federal and state ministries of education, housing, and culture.[6] A result of this has been that the attitude of suspicion of authority and automatic belief in its illegitimacy became entrenched in the minds of the majority of politically active younger West Germans, accompanying the radical outbursts of the 1960s, the more localized activism of the 1970s, and the Green movement of the 1980s.

The peace movement is profoundly marked by this antiauthoritarian affect, this emotional belief or prejudice that all authority is by definition bad and action against it is therefore good. It is the only outlook on society and political action that is palatable to the new activists. They have moved from a basic sentimental impulse to the rejection of political compromise and of the decisions of democratically elected governments in the regulation of international peace and to the charge that peace cannot prevail until all "oppressive structures," including all established institutions of production, administration, and coercion, have been eliminated—all institutions, that is, that are not in the hands of the antiauthoritarians. By definition, such institutions have already been reoriented and serve only beneficial purposes.

FREEDOM AND ORDER IN CLASSICAL
GERMAN POLITICAL THOUGHT

As many students of political theory, including the leaders of the Frankfurt School and Habermas himself, have observed, the denial of authority as a general modern problem is a consequence of the Enlightenment and its attempt to produce a rational justification of morality to replace the old justification in terms of transcendent obligation – divine command and natural law.[7] Thus, it is not surprising that this is a problem common to all modern or modernizing countries. In Germany, the denial has been virulent and thorough, and serious attempts to overcome it have been made. A detailed discussion of philosophical history would be out of place here; however, three ideas are significant in the contemporary context: the idea that freedom and order can (and will) be reconciled; the idea of the historical evolution and particularity of law; and the idea of individual autonomy and self-realization.

In idealist philosophy, the reconciliation of freedom and order is most clearly described in Hegel's theory of the state, which also the idea of the historical evolution of law.[8] To Hegel individual freedom has meaning only in a defined context of order – the state. Only the state can guarantee individual freedom; only the free decision of reasonable individuals can be the proper foundation of the state. The idea that law, as the foundation of order, is not something God-given or divinely sanctioned, but rather something that has evolved and is specific to each nation or culture, was not an invention of Hegel's, but was a product of early Romanticism and the discovery in that period of historical particularity and the national spirit or *Volksgeist* of each people or culture. Implicit in this historical understanding of culture and law is a rejection of the rationalist theory of natural law, developed in opposition to Scholastic theology by Thomasius and Pufendorf, which culminated in the Enlightenment and in the idea that natural rights exist independently and are not derived from any national or cultural ground.[9]

The historical understanding of law somewhat contradicts the rationalist element in the idea of the reconciliation of freedom and order (as expressed, notably, by the social contract theories of the Enlightenment) but is consistent with the notion that this reconciliation evolved through a dialectical process as described by Hegel. In this respect, both the historical understanding of law and the reconciliation of freedom and order grew out of the Romantic counter-Enlightenment that began in Germany in the late eighteenth century and with which the young idealist philosophers Fichte, Schelling, and Hegel were very much in sympathy. The Romantic element is even more evident in the idea of individual autonomy and self-expression.[10] Like the idea of reconciliation of freedom and order, the idea of autonomy can be understood and realized in two ways. It might mean that the individual should seek self-fulfilment within the constraints of the organic, historically founded order of his society and nation, which have their own metaphysical legitimacy. Seen in this way, individual self-realization became the apolitical cult of *Bildung* (civilized education) and self-improvement; the ideal represented by Goethe. Or it might mean that the individual should seek autonomy in deliberate conflict with the existing order seen as corrupt and oppressive. Individual self-realization will thus lead directly to revolutionary action—anarchism and ultimately metaphysical nihilism—the path of Marx and Nietzsche. In short, the idea of autonomy can be either socially conservative (bourgeois) or socially revolutionary, depending on whether one views the social order as legitimate and the call to autonomy as a challenge to make the best of life as it is, or as illegitimate, in which case the call to autonomy is a challenge to overthrow the existing order and to initiate a universal response to that challenge by attempting to abolish alienation and oppression.

In the early Romantic period and in the first writings of the idealist philosophers, the revolutionary option was strong, as evidenced in the writings of the younger Fichte and Hegel, for example, and in the general effect the French Revolution had in Germany. Then, however, a change occurred, corresponding to the change from the revolution's aim of universal liberation to Napoleon's national mobilization and imperial expansion. Now that the revolution was no longer a promise but a threat, the philosophers began to emphasize the organic integrity and uniqueness of the national community, thus reducing the reconciliation of freedom and order to a question of allegiance to the German nation and support of its mission to establish a political organization that would symbolize that reconciliation. First, though, national independence had to be wrested from the French occupiers, and this was the theme of the Romantic poets and of Fichte in the period of "national awakening" after the total defeat of Prussia in 1806 and the final abolition of the old imperial authority. In 1813, when this was accomplished, the idealist philosophers (chiefly Hegel) found themselves on the side of the restored Prussian monarchy, believing that it exemplified that unity of freedom and order that had begun as a metaphysical assertion. The revolutionary option survived, however, and was taken up in the 1830s and 1840s by the "left Hegelians" and their most important representative, Marx, as well as by the democratic nationalist revolutionaries of 1848, who looked for the fulfillment of the idealist program in a German national state.

The failure of the revolution of 1848 was a victory for the conservative interpretation of idealist political philosophy.[11] But the idea of autonomy survived as political radicalism and was seen in the Social Democratic workers' movement and in the various versions of utopian rejection of authority that were in evidence in the nineteenth century and that have reappeared in Western society since the 1960s.[12] Around 1900, the Social Democrats, under the guidance of Eduard Bernstein and August Bebel, came to accept of the state as a necessary element of order and departed from the original belief that the revolution would abolish all states and make possible a social system wholly free of domination and coercion. In the Weimar Republic the SPD was firmly within the camp of the democratic parties, and Social Democratic legal thinkers, foremost among them Hermann Heller, were prominent in the defense of the constitutional, democratic state, the *Rechtsstaat*, a notion that earlier Social Democrats would have rejected as an example of bourgeois mystification.

Even during the period of the unified national state (1871–1945), there were occasional signs that the utopian, antistate and antihierarchical element in the organized Social Democratic movement was not wholly extinct. Since 1945, these leftist Social Democrats had a better chance of increasing their influence, especially in the 1960s, when the revolutionary idea of autonomy and rejection of existing institutions began receiving increasing support from the successor generation.

NATURAL LAW AND LEGAL POSITIVISM

The idea of the historical emergence of law had consequences of a different, if no less serious, kind for German political thought than did the idea of revolutionary activism and antiauthoritarianism. The path leading from the early stages of this idea to the denial of authority in contemporary utopian neutralism and radicalism is an indirect one, and it is certainly true, as some have remarked, that affinities of temperament do not constitute evidence of intellectual affiliation. Affinities of temperament in political movements and attitudes, however, are interesting in themselves, if only for purposes of comparison.

One of the consequences of the Romantic search for national identity and originality was, as I have indicated, a view of law that rejected the rationalist theory of natural law and natural rights in favor of an idea of historical evolution. The logical corollary of this view was that laws and the legal system they collectively constituted were unique to each nation—part of its historical identity and part of the particular way in which each nation exemplified the reconciliation of freedom and necessity. In Germany, this was an especially dramatic turn, because it implied a dissociation of Roman law, now seen as largely an alien import, from native German law, which, according to the Romantics, was older, more authentic, and better. The "historical school of law" that began to form in the early nineteenth century sought to develop this theme and to create the basis, in jurisprudence and legal philosophy, for laws and legal practice that would protect and respect this native German law and allow it to continue its organic evolution. In the process, the idea of a natural law that ranked higher than national law, and in cases of conflict overrode it, was lost. The result was the emergence, in the later nineteenth century, of the theory of "legal positivism" from the earlier historical school.[13]

In many ways, legal positivism contradicted the ideas of the historical school of law and was strongly anti-Romantic and anti-idealist; nevertheless, its premises were ultimately drawn from those of the historical school in the sense that both denied the relevance or even the reality of natural law. The idea of natural law implies that there is a set of self-evident moral rules that govern or ought to govern individual and social behavior and to which the legal rules, or laws, established and enforced by states must conform. The value and legitimacy of legal systems and national laws can be judged by the degree to which they correspond to or exemplify the principles of natural law. Conversely, the reason that in any given legal system, some acts are forbidden and there are constraints and rules governing the performance of certain other acts (such as entering into contracts and making wills) is that natural law requires it.

Let us take an extreme example. In natural law, murder is a punishable offense because it is wrong, not because it is forbidden; indeed it is forbidden because it is wrong. Legal positivism, however, dictates that murder is punishable only because it is forbidden, and it is forbidden because the authorities, responding to popular feeling, have decided that it ought to be. Those feelings may be called "moral" or they may not; in neither case are they capable of rational justification. To a legal positivist, moral arguments are simply statements of feeling: to say that something is "morally wrong" is to say "I disapprove of this; so should you," but such disapproval is no more or less rational than any other sentiment.[14] Sentiments are not "true" or "false" by some external standard, they simply reveal facts about the person expressing them.

The legal positivists considered that belief in natural law, however well intentioned, strengthened the despotic possibilities of authorities who used moral arguments to buttress legal measures and sanctions advantageous to themselves. In this sense, legal positivism was an enlightened doctrine. The refusal of legal positivists to consider the question of the justification of moral arguments, however, laid them open to the danger of accepting any given legal system simply because it existed since there was no external standard by which to judge laws and rules. Legal positivists tended by and large to be liberal or socialist; therefore, they were unable to deny the legitimacy of tyrannical laws (for example, the Nazi laws discriminating against Jews) since that would have necessitated an appeal to a higher law, a natural law, whose validity they denied. This was admitted by their most famous spokesman, the Austrian socialist and constitutional specialist Hans Kelsen, ironically enough while he was in exile in the United States.

The problem of justifying moral sentiments (for example, the feeling that the Nazi regime was in some real sense "illegal" and criminal and that its laws were therefore void) by reference to some objective standard was, of course, a very general one and was, as I have said, one that had been endemic to Western culture since the Enlightenment. The legal positivists were the most consistent thinkers of modernity in denying that there was a problem. That most of them happened to be socially progressive and therefore very much committed to policies and practices that others might see as grounded very firmly in a moral commitment to the material improvement of the masses was an irony that might merit further investigation. The problem of Nazism and the fact that legal positivism originated in Germany, although its most famous later representatives were Scandinavian and British, tended to discredit it among members of the younger generation, so that by the late 1960s, the surviving masters of the school were frequently denounced as fascists for refusing to support the antiauthoritarianism of the new utopians.[15] These new utopians, in turn, derived much of their credibility and influence from the revival of natural law that was a direct consequence of Nazism.

Since the idea of natural law implies that moral arguments can be justified and that laws and legal systems derive their legitimacy and validity from some higher principle, it was not surprising that it was abandoned along with all other transcendent principles of political order, in the modern period. If it had not been for the spontaneous moral reaction to the crimes of the Nazi regime, a revival of natural law and of appeals to natural law could hardly have been expected.[16] But the revival was strong, immediate, and sustained. In West Germany particularly, the ideas and premises of natural law were prominent in legislation and especially in the Basic Law of 1949. However, the contradiction between the credibility of metaphysical and transcendent justifications of morality in jurisprudence and legal thought and the lack of credibility of such justifications in the culture as a whole, in philosophy, the social sciences, and in the political culture, made a proper understanding of the content and implications of natural law very difficult.

To be effective, a belief in natural law must not only be universal in a society, it must be part of a generally accepted and durable metaphysical legitimation of the political order. That this is so is, of course, impossible to prove, but it is at least plausible from the evidence of the history of political thought and practice in the West. It seems that the idea of natural law and natural rights cannot long survive unless the society and culture in which it exists are established and justified on positive religious principles, which in the West means Christian, or more particularly Catholic principles. In West Germany, after Hitler, no such legitimation was possible. Nazism had claimed legitimacy in the form of the fanatical loyalty of the people to the Führer—a debased form of Romantic populism. The democratic state that was established in West Germany in 1949 was, by definition, obliged to eschew any such legitimation. Indeed, in a sense the consensus of political thinkers in West Germany eschewed legitimation for the state altogether, preferring that it be justified by its technical, economic, and social accomplishments—by citizen satisfaction and material welfare. The appeal to natural law, thus deprived of any broader foundation, was increasingly restricted to a form of legal moralism, and the fear and suspicion of authority that followed the debacle of Nazism constituted an absolute barrier to any broader reconstruction of the metaphysical foundations of political order. Attempts at such reconstruction, even by philosophers and religious thinkers wholly untainted by any association with the doctrines of National Socialism, were either ignored or denounced as dangerously reactionary.[17] The denial of authority, then, was not just an aspect of the new utopianism of the late 1960s and after; it was an immediate consequence of Hitler's abuse of authority and of the return of political sentiment, after the experience of Nazism, to the general post-Enlightenment path of departure from metaphysical justifications.

THE PROBLEM OF AUTHORITY IN WEST GERMANY

Idealist philosophy was by no means forgotten or unknown in West Germany after 1945; however, it was the object of academic study and analysis and no longer a formative political influence. The old synthesis, including the reconciliation of freedom and order, the idea of the historical evolution of law, and the idea of individual autonomy, was no longer, and its elements survived, if at all, as islands in a sea of vague political sentiments and feelings. The idea of the reconciliation of freedom and order had little real significance in a society based on technical rationality and citizen satisfaction, and one in which the older reality of domination and submission had been forgotten. As we have seen, the idea of the historical emergence of law, which had culminated in legal positivism, was reversed, as a result of the reaction to Nazism, into a superficial revival of natural law in a moralistic form without the metaphysical or religious foundation necessary for solidity. The idea of individual autonomy, which had resulted from the tension between self-assertion and the desire for recognition by others and was based on faith in the possibility of strong, self-reliant individuals, became simple hedonism and "self-actualization" by weak individuals who saw any conflict or constraint as a denial of recognition and not as necessary steps in personal development. This picture of fragmentation was complicated, beginning in the 1950s but increasingly in the 1960s and 1970s, by a new sociology and political science that undermined the credibility of justified authority and the institutions of the democratic constitutional state.

The difficulties of political authority in a modern state are, of course, not unique to West Germany, but, as I have indicated, the experience of totalitarian rule and the exploitation of traditional respect for authority by Hitler and his regime meant that after the fall of Hitler and the defeat of Germany, the problem was virtually insoluble. The answer of idealist philosophy – the reconciliation of freedom and order, the faith in individual autonomy, and the establishment of an organic national system of laws – had been equally discredited by association with the corrupt Nazi form of political Romanticism. There were two other possible answers, each of which offered a solution that was not based on intangible and allegedly "irrational," and therefore dangerous, justifications of authority.

One was Western, specifically American, constitutional liberalism and its form of political science, democracy theory, which evaded the normative question of the best form of rule by asserting that democracy was self-evidently rational and thus indicated by logic, not by morality. The other was Marxism, which answered the normative question of the best form of rule by appealing to a philosophy of history according to which the inevitable, as well as desirable, end of history was a classless society in which authority would be fully rational, predictable, and universally accepted. In both cases, the normative discussion was reduced to interpretation and exegesis of a single form of rule, directly empirical in American political science and assumed to be inevitable in Marxism. These two answers were successively presented in West German political science and in the political speculation and argument on which debate has been based.

The founding generation of West German political scientists and some of its students have maintained, with few real exceptions, that the study of politics according to democracy theory is the just and desirable result of classical European political thought. The younger generation, including some renegades from the generation of the founders, has adopted a "critical" posture based on a revived Marxism, which has been prominent, if not dominant, in the majority of West German universities since the late 1960s and which has had an even greater proportional influence in society at large. Since the mid-1970s there has been a trend toward an anticriticism – the resurrection of democracy theory as a defense of constitutional liberalism against the neo-Marxists and their belief in the illegitimacy of all existing institutions – although the latter still exercise a strong influence.[18] Rarely has the justification of authority and of the power of the state been posed with the urgency of the classical tradition of the period before 1933, nor has the question seriously been posed on the theoretical level of whether the existence of the West German state, as an entity created by historical and political necessity and subject to specific threats and constraints, is justified. Accordingly, in the universities where the successor generation, including the leaders of the peace movement, were educated or employed, a certain abstract quality of debate has developed. Concrete political issues have been shunted aside, by liberals as well as by Marxists, in favor of lengthy discussion of utopian goals or ideal programs, and the very mention of the concept of authority or political rule has been considered suspect, while in the country at large the question of the character and purposes of the West German state has gone unanswered.

It is no wonder that in the late 1970s, when West Germans faced an economic crisis and were having doubts about the value of economic growth, this lack of public debate resulted in a peculiar form of ahistorical and apolitical provincialism and apprehension, one of whose forms is the peace movement.

FROM DEMOCRACY THEORY TO NEO-MARXISM

The neglect of the discussion of authority in modern political science and, by extension, in public debate on political issues is but one instance of a general turning away from the traditional categories and interpretations of Western political thought, in favor of what one might call the neglect of the state.[19] This neglect has been particularly evident in American political science since the 1930s, pioneered by early behaviorists like Harold Lasswell, who defined political science, not as the analysis of concepts like the state, authority, power, and law, but as the study of "who gets what, when, and how." This behavioral and quantitative approach became dominant after 1945 and was seemingly justified by social and political developments: the rise of supranational organizations, the increasing interdependence of countries and social systems, and the decline of the idea of the state as the political community incorporated for defense and survival, which was central to continental European political philosophy from Machiavelli to Hegel. "The era of stateness [Staatlichkeit] is drawing to an end; let no words be wasted on that score." This was the abrupt judgment of Carl Schmitt in 1963, which was justified and expanded by his student Ernst Forsthoff in his work entitled Der Staat der Industriegesellschaft.[20] Both these scholars regretted what they saw as the disappearance of the state, and there can be no doubt that to them it was not just a matter of the reorientation of trends in political science, law, or sociology, but an empirical fact. This is true to an even greater extent of the scholars, publicists, and commentators who have contributed to West German political science since 1950.

As I have indicated, this group can be divided roughly into two camps, a liberal, democratic camp consisting of the founders of postwar political science in West Germany and their loyal students, and a "critical" Marxist camp consisting of a variety of old Marxists, New Leftists, "progressive" liberals, and followers of the Frankfurt School. The liberal camp espoused democracy theory, brought back from America by returning exiles like Ernst Fraenkel, Arnold Bergsträsser, Siegfried Landshut, and Richard Löwenthal and by other exiles who resided in the United States but commuted across the Atlantic in the 1950s and 1960s to help establish and develop political science in West Germany—Eric Voegelin and Carl J. Friedrich are the most notable examples. Voegelin does not fall easily into the liberal camp because his philosophy of politics is fundamentally normative. Those of his students who accept his approach fully (Thilo Schabert, Peter Weber-Schäfer, and Jürgen Gebhardt are the best known) constitute a third category, since they seek a revival of normative political theory. However, this group must still be considered marginal.

In West Germany, the democracy theorists collaborated with anti-Nazi Germans, who welcomed the chance to formulate and present their opinions in freedom, and with the members of the younger generation who had not had a liberal education in political theory. These various groups, though their philosophies ranged from the metaphysical conservatism of Eric Voegelin to the left socialism of Wolfgang Abendroth, shared certain assumptions. All rejected what they saw as irrational justifications of authoritarian rule, and, since idealist philosophy, rightly or wrongly, was seen as largely responsible for support for such justifications in Germany and hence indirectly for National Socialism, they rejected it also. All shared what might be called an "Aristotelian normativism," that is, they viewed politics as the rational assessment of means and ends within a framework of justice based on natural law and natural rights. Their opinions diverged only with regard to the extent and implications of such rights. The liberals, such as Carl Friedrich, Otto von der Gablentz, and Dolf Sternberger, argued that the basic rights (of security, expression, and belief) guaranteed by the *Rechtsstaat* (state based on the rule of law) were sufficient; the socialists, such as Ernst Fraenkel, Richard Löwenthal, and Wolfgang Abendroth, argued that material rights (the right to a job and to a certain standard of living) were equally, if not more, legitimate. Hence they supported a somewhat more egalitarian social and economic policy and spoke of the need for a more fully developed *Sozialstaat* (state guaranteeing social rights). Abendroth left the SPD in the early 1960s and became a radical opponent of the political and social system of the Federal Republic (that is, he effectively joined the Marxist camp).[21] In the early period, the consensus among the founders was nearly complete.

The establishment of Western-style democracy theory was largely complete by the later 1950s. The grand old men of the exiled generation were now heads of institutes at the major universities and of schools of respectful followers and were frequent guest commentators on politics and current events for newspapers, radio, and television. A major task of this period was the analysis of National Socialism and the Third Reich, and despite what left-wing critics said, this task was largely accomplished; young historians and political theorists like Hans Buchheim and Karl Dietrich Bracher laid the foundations with thorough and as yet unsurpassed studies. The only weakness of the new political science in West Germany was its exclusive reliance on democracy theory and its consequent tendency to assume that constitutional democracy was self-reinforcing and self-evidently rational, and that it was a norm that needed no further justification. This engendered an anticommunist attitude critical of the East German and the Soviet regimes as examples of totalitarian rule, but it did not provide a genuinely historical and political justification of the concrete West German state and the purposes, national and international, of its actions. Political scientists tended to focus on domestic issues, on political, social, and economic organization and the problems of the welfare state; "industrial society" was regarded as a type separate from its historical instances and amenable to study without reference to contingent situations and constraints. This relatively narrow focus on an admittedly large and varied subject became a weakness in the later 1960s, when neo-Marxism began its attacks on "bourgeois" political science and "bourgeois" society, with its "false consciousness" of reality, but it was no less a weakness with regard to the national issue. Too often, those committed to democracy theory were unable to explain just why that theory was better than any other, or, more important, why democracy was a superior form of government and political system, in terms that the students in their revolutionary enthusiasm would accept.

The camp of the critical Marxists was not very active in the early postwar years. The most significant early members were the adherents of the Frankfurt School.[22] They had continued their attempt to combine Freud and Marx to provide a general interpretation of modernity and of life in industrial society while in exile in Paris and New York from 1933 to 1950, and they resumed it in Frankfurt (where it had begun) under the leadership of Max Horkheimer and Theodor Adorno. The third founding father, Herbert Marcuse, stayed in America and later inspired the student movement of the 1960s and 1970s. Their formulation, known as "critical theory," was outside the mainstream of democracy theory, but the impressive history and impeccable anti-Nazi credentials of the revived Institute for Social Research were of no small significance in rallying the forces of the left when the assault on the established practices and practitioners of political science and sociology began in 1967–1968. By this time the camp was growing; there had been defections from the founding generation of democracy theorists such as Abendroth, and members of the younger generation had also joined. As it grew, the "critical" camp found increasing favor with the media and with intellectuals outside the universities (such as Heinrich Böll), whose rejection of the established political system was based less on theory than on emotion and resulted in a blend of moralism and revolutionary fervor similar to that of the student radicals.

The basic argument of the critical camp against the democratic constitutional system and its supposedly legitimating doctrine, democracy theory, was simple: West Germany was not, as its defenders claimed, a democratic state or a liberal society. It was a state established by the old ruling classes who, in collaboration with the Western occupiers, had maintained intact the structures of capitalist domination and exploitation. This attempt to arrest historical evolution, however, was doomed to collapse because of its own internal contradictions as well as the revolutionary action of enlightened workers and students. Two features of the neo-Marxist argument appealed immediately to the active members of the successor generation: it promised moral fulfillment through political action, and it gave the successor generation of students a historical significance and a sense of mission, which restored the feeling of importance, of being part of a great movement, that democracy theory because of its rejection of moralism and emotional commitment, could not provide. The argument thus appeared both more realistic (because it "unmasked" the violence and oppression that were "camouflaged" and trivialized by ruling democracy theory and by the social structures it legitimated) and more relevant (because it promised rapid change in the direction of a utopian society beyond authority). Democracy theory had never adequately justified the authority and political power of the democratic state because its practitioners considered any discussion of such issues both irrelevant to modern, technical, and industrial society and likely to be abused for nefarious political purposes. The victory of critical theory and neo-Marxist political science was swift and complete in the majority of the universities and among influential political commentators in the media, many of whom would have denied any direct association or sympathy with Marxist movements.

One of the most successful tactics of the critical camp was its appropriation and use of the term "Enlightenment." Jürgen Habermas (who, as I have indicated, is a serious and much more nuanced thinker than most of his admirers, but who is also the most influential enunciator of critical theory) was the first to use the words "Enlightenment" and "enlightened" to denote practical and theoretical commitment to the neo-Marxist interpretation of the social system (including its moral inadequacy), while retaining the positive connotations (rationality and logic) of the terms. Habermas and many other radical critics of the West German government and its policies quite clearly see themselves as being in some sense the true heirs of the eighteenth-century Enlightenment and seriously believe that their efforts are in the interests of democracy, equality, and human rights. In their interpretation of these desirable goals, however, society is seen as moving toward a final condition of utopian "freedom from rule," which Habermas refers to as "rule-free discourse" (*herrschaftsfreier Diskurs*). The underlying idea is that rule always means domination and domination is always irrational because it depends on violence; since a fully rational society is as clearly preferable to an irrational society as nonviolence is to violence, the task is first to "unmask" and then to destroy domination by a process of revolutionary *praxis* that includes the achievement and the inculcation of "communicative competence"– the skill and the tolerance necessary to conduct "rule-free communication."[23]

The idea that there may be psychological or natural constraints on this utopia of perfect freedom (that is, that people may not act in accordance with "rule-free communication," whatever the social structure) rarely, if ever, occurs to critical theorists. Much more serious than this shortcoming in its consequences, however, is the belief that rule equals domination equals evil, as though political institutions, especially those of a democratic constitutional state, have no justification since they are not needed to guarantee rights and freedoms otherwise threatened.[24] Habermas may not always ignore this necessity, but we can disregard the details of his theory since we are concerned not with political philosophy as such but with the political beliefs and obsessions of a majority of West German intellectuals and educated youth, who provide the bulk of support for the Greens, the peace movement, and the anti-American left of the SPD.

7

THE MORALIZATION
OF POLITICS

The widespread rejection of democracy theory in political science and of the legitimacy of the democratic constitutional state by West German students and by many who were employed by that same state in the 1970s and 1980s was part of a broader change in individual and social psychology and in the political climate. It was foreshadowed in philosophical and cultural thought and debate by the decline of the idealist tradition and of the old views, prevalent until the late nineteenth century, of freedom and order, law and history, and autonomy and order. However, the success of democracy and of liberal capitalism, in the form described as the social market economy, in West Germany, in the period from 1945 to 1973, and the accompanying belief that social and political problems, both international and domestic, were amenable to rational solution concealed the effects of that change. In the same period, as I have mentioned, belief in natural law revived and played an important part in legislation and in public debate. During that time it seemed possible that democracy theory, the social market economy, technocratic government, and a belief in natural law as an ultimate standard were in themselves, without the metaphysical or religious sanction that had been undermined by two centuries of relentless philosophical and political criticism, enough to secure the survival and the material and philosophical well-being of West German society. However, the reaction of the industrial societies to the energy crisis of 1973–1974 and the general economic crisis of inflation and unemployment that, although not entirely caused by the oil shock, was nevertheless drastically exacerbated by it, seemed to many to show that the spiritual resources for dealing with and overcoming public misfortune had been, in fact, dissipated. In West Germany, the direct economic challenges were at first fairly well dealt with, but the effects of the second oil shock and the recession of 1979 and after proved more difficult and coincided in time with the return of the disaffected and alienated members of the successor generation to broad public activism in the form of the Green and peace movements. The two were largely, but not entirely identical; 80 percent of Green voters supported neutralism for West Germany, and a majority identified NATO policies as the major threat to peace. Ideologically and culturally, the beliefs of the peace movement and its intellectual supporters represented a choice of collectivism over democracy theory, of immature autonomy over mature individualism, of antinomianism over respect for law, and of antiauthoritarianism over respect for duly constituted authority and its legitimacy.[1]

Vague and utopian ideas of peace and how to achieve (or keep) it and antiauthoritarianism are both important ingredients in the ideology of the West German left of the 1980s. They are accompanied by a third and equally important ingredient, namely political moralism. Properly understood, political moralism need not be a bad thing; if the survival of the state, the political community of the people, is a good thing per se, it is clearly moral to contribute to it. The relevant actions of government are then properly judged by the extent to which they promote or endanger survival. Political moralism is then simply a somewhat misleading description of the study and exercise of political ethics, the goal of which is the survival of the free and democratic political order. However, the peace movement and its supporters, and the West German left generally, rely on political moralism in a very different sense, namely as an ill-informed and dangerous application of standards of individual behavior to the actions of government. The application is ill-informed, because the activists and ideologues simply do not know, or choose not to know, the conditions and threats under which the West German state and all other democratic states must act to ensure their survival. It is dangerous, because it is based on an idea of peace that is both utopian, ill-defined, and inappropriate since the active pursuit of that idea tends, as I argued in Chapter 5, to undermine the existing, imperfect, but tolerable peace. It is an additional irony that the activities of the peace movement, despite its claims to the contrary, also tend to make the achievement of a more genuine and satisfactory peace in Europe, that is, a peace including respect for the human rights of East Europeans and of all Germans, harder to achieve.

In this chapter, the focus will be on this element of moralism in the politics of the peace movement. To illustrate its origins and its effects, we also turn to aspects of West German culture and political practice that, quite apart from any deliberate intention, have made possible an atmosphere and a set of values in which such political moralism could flourish and be taken seriously. In what follows it is also necessary to bear in mind what was said in the previous chapter about the disappearance of idealist political philosophy in Germany and of the ideological vulnerability of the democracy theory that had supplanted it as the normative consensus of mainstream West German political science and political analysis.

In the prevailing academic climate of the 1970s, respect for facts and recognition of the constraints of reality were classed as unregenerate conservatism — indicative of a politically suspect unwillingness to make a radical break with the Nazi past. Political theorists of the critical camp, as well as social psychologists, educational experts, writers, journalists, and other intellectuals hailed the development of an "enlightened consciousness" as a triumph of democratic commitment, at a time when "enlightened" students were terrorizing insufficiently enlightened professors and fellow students in a manner hardly distinguishable from the behavior of Nazi storm troopers forty years before.[2]

The arrogant treatment meted out to unenlightened professors, including some who were themselves intellectual sources of New Left ideology (such as Theodor Adorno and Jürgen Habermas) was part of a disdain for society, its needs and practices, which was a revival, on a much cruder level, of the anticommercialism and intellectual purism typical of German literary culture in the nineteenth and early twentieth centuries. Thomas Mann called his antibourgeois manifesto *Betrachtungen eines Unpolitischen* (Considerations of an unpolitical man).[3] It would seem that nothing could be more different from Mann's complex and sophisticated argument than the wild barbarism that pervaded West German campuses and common rooms in the 1970s. Yet there was an underlying similarity. The self-styled antiauthoritarians were in their way at least as authoritarian, on behalf of their sentiments, as Mann had been in 1914, and, more important, they were at least as unpolitical. Their belief in the higher value of social spending compared with private consumption and their explicit belief that their own academic degrees and positions made them morally superior to the philistine bourgeois outside the universities, the welfare bureaucracies, or the mass media were fairly direct translations of some of the key "ideas of 1914".[4] While rejecting the "bourgeois," "positivist" principles of scientific and political analysis of their predecessors, they claimed the same right to judge society and in particular its backward members, those in the co-opted working class as well as their own unenlightened colleagues. Ironically, the feeling that an academic position automatically includes the right and the privilege to give authoritative guidance in social and political affairs is no longer accompanied either by a willingness of much of society to be so guided or by the intellectual excellence among academics that might otherwise justify such a feeling. The postwar economic achievements of West Germany are not paralleled in the arts or in academic life. The universal outlook and philosophical wisdom of such figures as Werner Heisenberg, Carl Friedrich von Weizsäcker, Joachim Ritter, and Arnold Bergsträsser, to name only a few from various disciplines who survived into the postwar era, has simply not been matched by their successors.[5]

The rejection of the established order and its residual authority, incorporated in the police and the armed forces, was seen as a noble refusal to be manipulated or disciplined in the service of a not wholly perfect state, whereas the thought that such refusal might objectively serve the interests of states far less perfect crossed the minds of sympathizers, only to be immediately rejected as reactionary. This sympathy for the "critical" mentality has survived more completely in West Germany than in most other countries, notably France and the United States, where for different reasons the activist wave of 1965–1975 has to a large extent died down (although one should not necessarily mistake apathy for common sense). Some commentators, such as the liberal educational theorist Hartmut von Hentig, continue to associate opposition to authority with courage and a progressive outlook, whereas in reality it is sympathy for beleaguered authority and in particular a concern for its security, both foreign and domestic, that now requires courage and a progressive outlook.[6]

Why is this endurance of radicalism and this denial that authority is legitimate more overt and antinomian in West Germany than in other countries? I have sought to provide some reasons: the failure of democracy theory to provide an adequate justification of the raison d'être of the West German state, West Germany's gradual loss of a sense of its historical (and specifically political) origins, its perception of its situation in the 1980s as one of constant exposure to threat, and the existence of a neo-Marxist and "enlightened" utopianism of "rule-free communication" in a situation without authority. The civilizing mission and achievement of political authority, which was the agency of pacification after the wars of religion in Europe, and its function as guarantor of individual rights and liberties were wholly obscured by what the antiauthoritarians saw as its negative and irrational aspects; material prosperity and welfare remained the only commonly accepted justifications for the social system. When these too began to be doubted, beginning in the later 1960s, even this weak and residual justification was ignored by the successor generations (by the mid-1980s, the plural was justified), whose apathy and fear of the future were easily exploited by the professional activists and republic-haters.[7]

The denial of authority, then, is a general phenomenon, observable in the industrial world since the nineteenth century and described and foretold as such by Tocqueville, Burckhardt, and others. In West Germany, it has been a consequence of the combined prejudices of liberal democracy theory and radical neo-Marxism and their failure to provide what West Germany, as a fundamentally threatened political society, needs above all: a dispassionate analysis of its own situation. That failure has resulted from a disparagement of authority and indeed of all the traditional categories of political philosophy that are part of what Gottfried Dietze has called the "Hitler complex"– the pathological fear of contamination of one's own opinions and credibility among colleagues and peers by the mere use of any concept that might conceivably be associated with Nazism.[8] Until legitimate authority can be justified, which will not happen unless some aspects at least of the idealist tradition are rehabilitated, authority will continue to be despised, and the actions taken by any political authority, including especially measures to ensure West German defense against internal or external threats, will be opposed as a matter of moral principle by the "enlightened" class of activists, who, although not a majority, are entrenched in commanding positions in education, left-liberal politics, government, and the media.

THE RETURN OF THE POLITICIZED INTELLECTUAL

The tendency to form harsh judgments of existing political conditions and to assume the worst about the prevailing order has been characteristic of German intellectual culture for centuries. Equally common has been the tendency on the part of certain writers, poets, and philosophers to assume that their position conferred not only a unique ability to analyze national or international politics, but also the right to pass judgments based on that analysis. These assumptions may perhaps be traced to the Reformation. Luther's virulent denunciations of his secular and theological enemies set the pattern for a style of crude and deliberately offensive debate that quickly became part of the national culture. A reason for the virulence was no doubt the despair and frustration felt by all sensitive and perceptive observers of the political scene in Germany. The failure to develop strong national institutions; the constant conflicts between states that were autonomous within the tenuous framework of imperial rule; strong traditions of local autonomy; the rights and claims of estates, free cities, and (in the Catholic states) clergy; and above all the confessional confrontations and bloody civil wars in 1525–1555 and 1618–1648 were certainly enough to discourage any political thinker ambitious on behalf of German national unity, especially in view of the successful national pacification and construction of a stable order that was taking place in neighboring countries, such as France. This ancient rival, which so often in the Middle Ages had been the poorer and weaker nation, began in the seventeenth century a period of supremacy and grandeur that Germans could only envy.

It has often been said that it was the failure to develop a strong central authority and institutions of national sovereignty that inspired the political philosophy for which Germany ultimately became famous; what the Germans could not accomplish, they philosophized about. However, disconsolate observations of political fragmentations and failed plans for unity need not always lead to alienation and hostility. The wave of political moralism in the 1970s and after owes less to the traditions of classical German philosophy or even to Marxism than to the alienation of angry and neurotic intellectuals from their political system. They often justify this moralism by reference to the Weimar years, when a genuine *Kulturkampf* (cultural struggle, or struggle over culture) separated right and left and when there was a genuine and dangerous right with which to contend. It is a dangerous and false analogy, however, since the intellectual left arguably weakened the Weimar Republic as a result of its hatred and contempt for bourgeois society and its political nihilism. Moreover, the grounds for fear and contempt in the 1920s—the existence and growing power of antidemocratic right-wing extremism—no longer exist, except in the hysterical imagination of such writers as Heinrich Böll, whom I discuss more fully presently.

The archetypal left-wing German intellectual of the twentieth century was Bertolt Brecht. Brecht's posthumous power in West Germany is a cultural force that future intellectual historians and cultural critics must find fascinating. A Communist who combined the grossest cynicism and contempt for political opponents with the most saccharine "social realist" propaganda in his songs, he never took any serious notice of the violence and tyranny characteristic of the states and societies he admired, such as the Soviet Union and East Germany, where he spent most of his later years. In this combination of cynicism and contempt, he accurately prefigured the mentality and psychology of the new moralists; his biting sarcasm is an ideologically charged and distorted version of the ruthless verbal massacre of opponents. Even those sympathetic to him or to his politics acknowledged his unpleasant traits. The writer Lion Feuchtwanger, in one of his novels, included a character modeled on Brecht, who is described as follows: "You have been taken in by communism because from birth you have had no social instincts. What for others is a matter of routine throws you when it is novel. Poor man, you cannot empathize with people; you cannot have sympathy with others; that's why you look for artificial communication. Moreover, you are a puritan, you lack the ability to have fun, and you have no charity."[9]

The peace movement and the left of the 1980s especially favored Brecht's postwar ditties denigrating Western defense and supposedly proclaiming an indignant pacifism in the face of senseless warmongering and exploitation of workers. That such a proclamation of pacifism must lose all credibility when made by a man who wholeheartedly supported the offensive military machine and the aggressive ideology of the Stalinist regimes in the Soviet Union and East Germany entirely escaped his millions of admirers, many of whom, during the demonstration in Bonn in October 1982, roared the refrain "say no!" of his poem written against Western intervention in the Korean War, when it was recited by the literary prince of the new moralism, Heinrich Böll. Brecht had achieved a popularity and a political influence in the West German state he so despised, the extent of which even he, the cynic and believer in the inevitability of capitalist self-evisceration, could hardly have dreamed.

The most notable and influential of the new moralists who have adopted Brecht's utter contempt for constitutional democracy, his verbal violence, and his total refusal to respect the common humanity or dignity of those he perceived as enemies (as opposed to "mankind" or, more commonly, "the proletariat") is no doubt Heinrich Böll. Böll's psychology and temper, as revealed by his public behavior and statements, are milder than Brecht's, but they are such a remarkable example of the classic traits of the type of emotional radical who is so committed to the new social religion of refusal as to be almost a caricature. In his revealing analysis of Böll's social criticism and radical rejection of all existing institutions and "corrupt" standards of behavior, Helmut Schelsky describes him as "cardinal and martyr," combining the arrogance of domination with immense self-pity and a "need to suffer" (*Leidensdrang*), or rather a need to seem to suffer, since Böll takes no real risks whatever.[10] Böll sees himself as constantly persecuted and harassed in contemporary West Germany because he dares to criticize what to him is a police state, full of old and new Nazis—ruthless, oppressive, and violent, at best heartless and at worst murderous. Between 1972 and 1975, he took a public stand in favor of "grace" and "sanctuary" for the terrorist Ulrike Meinhof, asserting that the "lies and propaganda" of the "fascist press" were worse than the murders and violence of her gang. Böll presented himself as the long-suffering victim of a war of nerves, then he demanded—and got—numerous media opportunities to complain loudly of the climate of public opinion and of his own helplessness.

A minor event that occurred in the summer of 1972 reveals the quality and political nature of Böll's perceptions. During a general search for terrorists and sympathizers in the region of West Germany where Böll had his summer residence, two policemen appeared at his door and asked to see identification papers. It was an entirely routine matter and thousands of other locals had been the object of identical searches and requests, but to Böll it conjured up visions of Gestapo terror. Within 24 hours, reports of unknown origin had arrived at all major West German newspapers and television and radio networks claiming that "ten to fifteen" policemen armed with machine guns had broken into Böll's home and had subjected him and his guests to brutal interrogation. Böll, it was later disclosed, had actually offered to let the policemen search the house, but they had declined. By this and other tactics, Böll confirmed his image as a powerless intellectual, punished and denigrated by a hostile state. Apparently, at no time did it occur to him or to his admirers that power really lies not with the state, but with those intellectuals and "producers of meaning" (*Sinnproduzenten*, Schelsky's term) who, at any time, can flood the media with their denunciations and assertions and who are wholly immune from criticism simply because any criticism from any source is either official, hence fascist and illegitimate, or unofficial, and thus a product of naiveté or false consciousness. This power to "produce meaning" has vastly increased since 1975; yet the intellectual moralists insist that it does not exist. It is evident in the printed and spoken media, which are largely staffed by sympathizers or members of the "new class" of "producers of meaning," and its effects have been incalculable. The absence of any serious counterweight in the intellectual milieu or in the education provided in schools and universities to those who will in future rule and administer the state and its organs bodes ill for the chances of redressing the balance.

Böll, Günter Grass, Siegfried Lenz, Martin Walser, and virtually all other prominent writers in West Germany, with only few exceptions, such as Peter Schneider and the East German refugee Reiner Kunze, support the peace movement and deny the legitimacy of the authority, the institutions, and the democratic political order in West Germany. Representatives of the movement usually deny or disparage the influence of such men, in a gesture of self-deprecation that exactly parallels Böll's own posture of self-pity and assumed powerlessness. Nevertheless, there can be no doubt that this universal commitment of what Kurt Sontheimer and others call "the literary republic" to utopian ideas of peace and to the abolition of authority is the most extreme example in the Western world of that profound alienation and refusal to identify with the political traditions and practices of one's own state and civilization that is characteristic of twentieth-century intellectuals and their adversary culture.

Grass, who was associated with the SPD and thus was rather to the right of most of his colleagues, began in 1980 to write of "arms race mania" and to become involved with the emerging peace movement. In increasingly hysterical tones, he spoke of the movement as though it were a small, threatened faction oppressed by brutal authority and of the West German government as though its refusal, so far, to yield to the demands of the neutralists and reject INF modernization were a sign of "weak servility" (*feige Anbiederung*) with regard to the United States and socialist France. Grass regarded the

French socialist government as an enemy of peace, because the French president made a public speech in Bonn in February 1983 exhorting the government to stand firm and to accept the missiles. When Grass was asked why he thought the French intellectuals had become overwhelmingly anti-Soviet and anti-Marxist since the mid-1970s, whatever their position on domestic and social issues, he replied that they were merely reacting against the long ascendancy of Jean-Paul Sartre and Marxism. He would not admit, or possibly it did not occur to him, that there might be real grounds for such a change in France and that the same real grounds ought perhaps to influence his own thinking on the subject of East-West relations and Soviet power.[11]

In 1982, Grass stated categorically that the Vietnam war and its attempt to force new missiles on Western Europe had deprived the United States of the right to pass moral judgments on anybody. In December 1983, when the first Pershing IIs arrived in West Germany, he and a large group of political writers signed the Heilbronn Manifesto, which stated that the deployment of Pershing IIs and GLCMs in West Germany "includes the West German Bundeswehr in an offensive strategy directed at the East." Since the Bundeswehr is constitutionally forbidden to engage in offensive actions, the group declared the deployments unconstitutional and concluded that soldiers of the Bundeswehr were now constitutionally obliged either to go on strike or to desert. The arrogance of these intellectuals was perfectly exemplified by Grass when he proclaimed in an interview that "we are the true protectors of the constitution."[12] In the same interview he demonstrated complete ignorance of NATO strategy, of U.S. policy, and of the reasons that people of good faith adduce for INF deployment. Grass had decided that the missiles were immoral and demonstrated the madness, anti-Soviet ideology, and militarism of America, a judgment that he did not feel the least need to justify in detail.

In 1984, leaders of the Greens took the implications of the Heilbronn Manifesto a step further and actually brought suit against the government in the Federal Constitutional Court, alleging that the new U.S. missiles were designed for offensive use and that the West German government was therefore not competent to accept them on its territory without changing the clause of the Basic Law that forbids the preparation of war. The court admitted the suit, but ruled against the Green allegation.

The case of the Heilbronn Manifesto also vividly illustrated Grass's opinion that the West German state is violent and oppressive and a loyal ally of Pentagon warmongers. Government spokesmen suggested that the manifesto represented "an attempt to exercise undue influence on members of the Bundeswehr" in a way designed to weaken the security of the Federal Republic. Such an attempt is expressly forbidden by the West German Criminal Code. The federal prosecutor, however, declined to lay charges against the group on the grounds that there was no subjective intent to harm security. Thus Grass and his fellow travelers stood excused, no matter what the objective consequences of their behavior, because they happened to believe that they were merely opposing preparation of aggressive war and did not subjectively intend to confuse the soldiers or give aid and comfort to the Soviet Union.

The Soviets freely admit that they find great aid and comfort in such actions.[13] However, it is important to note the decision of the prosecutor that subjective intent was more important than objective effect in such attempts to influence public opinion regarding matters affecting national security. This attitude is a consequence, harmful in this case, of natural law moralism as it was revived in West Germany after Nazism. To a legal positivist such a distinction is absurd. In his view, the sentiments and opinions expressed in the manifesto, as well as those of the prosecutor, are legally irrelevant. What matters is that the law of the land forbids any attempt to influence members of the armed forces in any way that might harm national security. The question then can only be: Is the act likely or able to exert such influence? An affirmative answer carries with it the obligation to prosecute, with no alternative allowed.

As indicated in the previous chapter, the idea of natural law does not function well apart from its Christian foundations. If a religious commitment is not overtly accepted as the basis of social order, the use of natural law concepts to legitimize concrete laws and institutions easily becomes superficial. In such a society, a hard-headed legal positivism provides better guidelines for protecting the public interest, despite its shortcomings. Moreover, critics and enemies of existing institutions, such as Grass, are able to legitimize their own, often unfounded opinions and desires by reference to natural law, disguised in this case as a "responsibility to resist." The prosecutor, in failing to apply the provisions of the Basic Law and the Criminal Code, was in effect accepting the moralist claims at face value because the consideration of expediency on which he based his decision implicitly undermined the *Ordnungsdenken* (theory of social order) characteristic of the true natural law tradition. One could easily argue that, in fact, he committed a grave dereliction of duty by refusing to prosecute, although to my knowledge no action alleging this has been brought.

THE ERRORS OF *BERUFSVERBOT*

Natural law moralism outside its proper context in a socially recognized, binding religious commitment is not an adequate guide for policymakers and is an unconvincing justification of existing institutions. This is clear not only from the results of the actions of Böll, Grass, and other intellectuals, but also from the political effects of the application of the principle known as *Berufsverbot*. The term literally means prohibition of the exercise of a calling. In fact it refers to the effects of the provisions in the Basic Law and in other laws and ordinances in preventing known or suspected opponents of constitutional democracy from employment in government, which in West Germany includes the media and education. The most important of these ordinances, and the one that gave rise to the term, which is nowhere used in official language, is the so-called *Radikalenerlass* (Decree on radicals), issued by the chancellor (Brandt) and the prime ministers of the Länder in 1972.[14] This measure was designed to allow the authorities to consider membership in organizations that were regarded as unconstitutional as a reason for denying such members jobs in the public sector. Although the Basic Law explicitly forbade such organizations, the practice, at least since the legalization of the communist party in 1969, had been opportunistic. Organizations regarded as unconstitutional were permitted, in spite of the laws, but their members were still supposed to be kept out of public employment.

Though the Radikalenerlass was thus a weaker measure than direct prohibition, the literary republic seemed to consider it a much worse affront and denounced it as a cover for abuse in the interests of reactionary conformism. In fact, the Radikalenerlass, since it required the authorities to judge the subjective intentions of applicants, and not their overt behavior, as demonstrated, for example, by membership in certain organizations, relied on a moralism not so different from that of Grass. They merely seemed to have opposite purposes. To understand this, it will be helpful to look at the history of official policy in Germany regarding groups or individuals considered to be dangerous to the constitution.

Determined as they were to establish a constitution that would ensure a stable parliamentary government and make it impossible for antidemocratic movements ever again to assume power in the state by exploiting the constitutional process, the founding fathers of the West German republic included the following clause in the Basic Law:

> Associations, the purposes or activities of which are in breach of criminal law or are directed against the constitutional order or against the principle of international understanding, are prohibited.

Note that the clause does not read "may be prohibited" (that is, if the competent authority deems it expedient) but "are prohibited." Similar positive wording is found in the Law of Associations, which establishes the procedure to be followed in taking action against such associations. The

Basic Law designates certain kinds of associations as illegal, so that failure to take action against them, when they are known to exist, is per se a neglect of duty on the part of the authorities. Had the Basic Law and the Law of Associations been respected by politicians and lawyers in the years since 1949, and particularly since the rise of neo-radicalism in the later 1960s, Berufsverbot might never have become such a serious problem.

The Radikalenerlass was designed to clarify existing laws intended to prevent radical enemies of the constitutional order, of any persuasion whatever, from obtaining jobs in public service. The implication of the term "Berufsverbot" is that such prohibition is wrong because anyone who desires it has a right to a job in public service. The idea that the authorities were exploiting their position to prevent activists and others from working for the government arose from the fact that loyalty to the constitution was determined by conviction, not behavior. To understand the importance of this distinction, we go back to the Law to Protect the Republic (*Republikschutzgesetz*) of 1922, which was valid until Hitler's *Machtergreifung* (seizure of power) in 1933. It read in part:

> Any official of the Reich is obliged, in his official activity, to uphold the authority of the constitutional republican state.
>
> He must refrain from any act incompatible with his position as official of the republic. In particular, it is forbidden for him to
>
> 1. abuse his office or the powers available to him in his official capacity in attempts to change the constitutional republican form of government;
>
> 2. in the exercise of his office or abusing his official position, to make any statement concerning the constitutional republican form of government . . . which might tend to disparage [it] in public opinion;
>
> 3. . . . influence subordinates, employees, workers, wards, or students in the direction of derogatory disparagement of the constitutional government of the Reich . . .
>
> 4. tolerate any of the above actions committed by any subordinate in the course of duty.
>
> It is likewise forbidden for any official of the Reich publicly . . . to promote attempts aimed at restoration of the monarchy . . . or to support such attempts by slander, denigration or contemptuous utterances directed against the republic or acting members of the government.[15]

The careful enumeration of detailed acts incompatible with a position in public service clearly shows that the purpose was to define behavior, not attitudes. A civil servant in the Weimar Republic might personally have monarchist convictions; as long as he did not express them or agitate for them, he could not legitimately be accused of wrongdoing or dismissed. The approach taken in the Federal Republic was wholly different. Not individual acts but the ability of the prospective civil servant to "guarantee" his personal loyalty became the criterion by which eligibility was judged. The different merits and implications of the two types of criteria—overt behavior or conviction—can be debated, as they have been, for example, by Ernst-Wolfgang Böckenförde. However, the adoption by lawmakers in West Germany of the criterion of conviction is surprising when its political origins are considered. Böckenförde has pointed out that the requirement of positive commitment to the existing form of government for appointment as a civil servant did not first arise after 1945, but under the Nazi regime. With the Nazi seizure of power, the Republikschutzgesetz was annulled by a series of new ordinances and laws, all of which contained the following clause:

> No one can be called to public service of the Reich who will not undertake to support the national state without reservation [rückhaltslos].

Behavior, defined negatively (by what was forbidden) had been replaced by conviction, defined positively (by what was required). This was only to be expected in a totalitarian regime. It is surprising that the drafters of the Civil Service Law of the Federal Republic, instead of readopting the clear guidelines of the Weimar rule, simply copied the just-quoted Nazi regulation, omitting the words "without reservation" and replacing "national state" with "constitutional order." Perhaps this is simply proof that the natural law approach was sufficiently influential to blind its proponents to the alarming similarities of their new law to the old Nazi law.

The problem of radicals in public service became needlessly complicated. The Radikalenerlass was supposed to clarify matters, but in fact led not to a simplification of procedures but to obfuscations and entanglements that caused defenders of the official position to make the most contorted and intrinsically illogical statements. The totalitarian implications of a test of convictions rather than of behavior allowed enemies of the constitutional order to argue that all they wanted was to "emancipate" and to "educate for freedom" and that they were being prevented from executing these noble tasks by a reactionary and oppressive regime. Had the legislators of the Federal Republic reaffirmed that only overt behavior, and not conviction, which is almost impossible to define or measure, was an acceptable standard of judging loyalty, the antiauthoritarians, peace utopians, and moralists could not argue that their goal was simply more and better democracy, when in fact their actions were incompatible with the interests of the constitutional order. The objections would have been just as loud, but they would have lacked the specious credibility they gained from the ambiguity of the official position. The natural law moralism of the West German Civil Service Law and the considerations of expediency encouraged by the Radikalenerlass were open to abuse by anyone who was willing to assert a sincere commitment to democracy, whereas the legal positivism of the 1922 law, if it had been readopted, would have made it clear that professions of democratic intent could not excuse subversive behavior.

Needless to say, a criterion of behavior would also have required the upholders of the constitution — courts and government agencies — to have been much more strict in their task of enforcement, which they have failed to do, particularly since the Social Democrats took office in 1969. The main reason for this failure, and for the increasing use of arguments of expediency in decisions to allow unconstitutional organizations to flourish, has been the fear of a legal positivist approach and a corresponding inclination, inspired by natural law moralism, to bend over backward in dealing with potential enemies of the constitution. What the politicians and administrators have forgotten, however, is that such tolerance is not really faithful to natural law. Rather, it may allow antidemocratic forces to flourish and ultimately to endanger the constitutional system, a result hardly acceptable to anyone concerned with natural law or justice.

The Radikalenerlass and the resultant problem of Berufsverbot excessively damaged the domestic and international credibility of the West German government and exacerbated the alienation of students. They came to feel, rightly or wrongly, that hypocrisy and coerced conformity (and its counterpart, conspiracy) were characteristic of their society. This feeling was one reason that the strategic and security decisions and arguments of the Schmidt and Kohl governments in the 1980s were met not with a reasonable amount of skepticism but with complete rejection and contempt by a significant and vocal minority of the educated elite.

Literary moralism and the self-inflicted wounds of a Social Democratic government torn between utopian temptations and the imagined constraints of order are two main causes of the malaise and the confrontations of the 1970s and 1980s. A third cause, no less important in social and ideological terms, has been the revival of a moralized religion, a political theology of utopian revolution, pacifism, and anti-institutional egalitarianism.

THE NEW POLITICAL THEOLOGY

"Political theology" is not a term invented by the left, although it is currently taken to mean a theology the subject, methods, and arguments of which are derived from perceived political and social problems. The term was first used by Carl Schmitt in 1922 to refer to the political implications of theology in two senses: first, the nature, history, and function of the Catholic church as a "world-historical form of power"—an institution that, while founded on revelation and with a supernatural mission, had nevertheless a place in the social order and ipso facto political influence; and second, the relationship of absolute and absolutely valid theological statements and definitions of faith to the question of established political order, a relationship Schmitt saw most clearly defined in the writings of Thomas Hobbes.[16] My intention here is not to examine Schmitt's views in detail, but simply to note the fundamental difference between his use of the term "political theology" to describe an objective relation between two independent spheres of thought and action—politics and theology—and the use prevalent since the 1960s. In this newer sense, political theology is an attempt to justify political ideologies, especially those of so-called liberation movements in the Third World, and anti-authoritarian movements in industrial societies such as West Germany and the United States, in theological terms. The moral and ethical force of originally apolitical theological terms and arguments is misappropriated for political agitation, and any sense of an independent intellectual pursuit called "theology," having its own rules, subject, and purpose, is lost in a sea of politicized moralism. The best-known type of political theology, in fact, is called "liberation theology" and is a Latin American invention; the use of the term "political theology" to describe this and other forms of politicized religious thinking, however, originated in West Germany in the 1960s.[17]

This shift, like so many other changes in West Germany, began after 1945. Many Lutherans and Catholics were ashamed that authorities of both churches had complied with Hitler's regime and had failed to denounce practices and policies that had contradicted Christian principles. One result of this shame was the "Heidelberg Confession of Guilt" (1945) of the assembly of the Lutheran Church (Evangelische Kirche in Deutschland, or EKD), which was largely inspired by Martin Niemöller, a theologian who had been imprisoned under Hitler and who later strongly opposed the security policies of the West German government under Adenauer.

In the early postwar years, the defeat of Germany and the collapse of political and economic order in the four occupation zones led a number of Catholic intellectuals and politicians to discuss seriously the possibility of some sort of "Christian socialism" to replace both totalitarian dictatorship and liberal capitalism, which at the time was widely felt to be hopelessly compromised and unworkable. The leading political figure to support this idea was Jakob Kaiser, but he was realistic enough to give up hope for its realization after the Soviets expelled him from their occupation zone, where he had been working. The CDU-CSU parties, founded in 1945, which were largely Catholic, abandoned their emphasis on Christian socialist ideas, and moved to a wholehearted commitment to the concept of the free market economy in 1946–1948, as the latter began to regain credibility as a workable system thanks to the activities and proposals of the group of German liberal economists and thinkers who later became known as the fathers of the "social market economy."[18]

This change of focus was largely the work of Adenauer and his advisors and intellectual supporters in the Western zones, while Jakob Kaiser and the Berlin group of the party remained committed to Christian socialist ideas derived from the criticism of liberal capitalism in Catholic social thought. However, political developments brought Adenauer to power, and Christian socialism lost credibility in the CDU. Fear of any sort of socialism was widespread in West Germany, and Kaiser himself ceased his agitation out of loyalty to the government. The abandonment of Christian socialism by the CDU disillusioned many Catholic intellectuals, such as the young Heinrich Böll or the "conservative anticapitalist" and pacifist Eugen Kogon, who had committed themselves to a moral political order "beyond capitalism." Kogon and Walter Dirks, an ally of Kaiser's, were the editors of the *Frankfurter Hefte*, a journal founded in 1946 that quickly became "the one important example of a serious debate between Christians and Marxists within the CDU," and that in 1946–1949 was undoubtedly the leading cultural and political periodical in the free part of Germany.[19]

Ever since that time, however, the Union parties have had the reputation of being down-to-earth at best and opportunistic at worst, and they have never been able to regain the intellectual following they had in 1945–1950. Because the general orientation of Catholic social thought prevented them from viewing democratic capitalism as a morally adequate framework for political life, and because they were driven by the memory of Nazism to search beyond the economic system under which it gained power, West German Catholic political thinkers of the Christian socialist variety went into hibernation from practical politics from the late 1940s to the 1970s, when an existential, and therefore presumably less anti-Christian, form of Marxism had begun to gain influence in the political culture.

This political asceticism of left-wing Catholics like Kogon was in curious contrast to the revival of political Catholicism during the 1950s, particularly in West Germany and Italy. Adenauer and most of his ministers in West Germany and Alcide De Gasperi and the Christian Democrats in Italy were representative of a brief, but at the time strong, wave of Catholic political commitment to the liberal constitutional order and to European integration. Scores of books were written in those years that purported to demonstrate the continuity of the idea of European unity since the Middle Ages, when spiritual and temporal power were united for the common good. Historically minded analysts of the Common Market did not fail to point out that its area was largely the same as that of the Carolingian Empire during the ninth century, an epoch often hailed as the birth time of European culture and as a model of European unity, a unity that disappeared with the beginnings of national and political differentiation. The message seemed to be that after 1,000 years of restless internecine struggle a Europe shrunken by war and totalitarian expansion had, since 1945, returned to its roots. Cultural unity, a common commitment to democracy, and the requirements of collective security indicated the need for ever closer cooperation and alignment of policies.

These grandiose ideas were later denounced by opponents as constituting an "ideology of Europeanism" (*Abendländlertum*) and their moral and cultural basis and justification were quickly forgotten; instead of speaking of Europe as a civilization worth defending, politicians and publicists restricted themselves to the European Economic Community (EEC) as an economic entity, which they justified exclusively by its ability to promote an ever-increasing material standard of living. The security problem was less prominent in the early 1960s, after the questions of West German membership in NATO and West German rearmament had been resolved. Some theologians had participated actively in these debates; among them was Niemöller. His anti-Nazi past gave him credibility with a wide audience that pardoned his rhetorical excesses, whereas his pacifism reached the point where he asserted that West German defense as a whole was immoral—partly in and of itself, and partly because it prevented the unification of a neutral Germany. He had joined the SPD shortly after the war, and in the mid-1950s he and a few other theologians, such as Helmut Gollwitzer, formed a "Protestant opposition" to rearmament and NATO. Although this group exercised little influence at the time, it was a portent of things to come. A number of younger Protestant clergymen also found themselves drawn in these years to the left wing of the SPD: Erhard Eppler, Heinrich Albertz, Egon Bahr—all of whom have exhibited various degrees of national and pacifist neutralism in the 1980s.[20]

Both Catholicism and Lutheranism in postwar West Germany had a strong current of politicized dissent from and opposition to the social and economic order that was being established after 1948. Lutherans could trace this dissent back to Luther himself, and Catholics could trace it back to such humble medieval models as St. Francis and St. Clare; however, it was primarily a response to Nazism and only secondarily to industrial society and its supposed amorality, although this strain was dominant in the politicization of the churches in other countries. For two decades these dissenters constituted a minority in the churches, but beginning in the later 1960s, when the student revolts erupted and the discussion of the quality of life and the emptiness of the consumer society became popular, these theologians and thinkers found a new and ready audience.

The Second Vatican Council of 1962–1965 and the new emphasis on commitment to this world and to social justice were of inestimable significance for West German Catholics. For the first time, the moral indignation of Eugen Kogon or Josef Pieper seemed legitimated by the highest authority (this meant less to Böll, whose alienation from the Catholic church was complete, although he continued to claim the right, as a member, to attack and denounce it while refusing absolutely to abide by any rules of which he disapproved, which included almost all of them). The published works of theological radicals such as Hans Küng, whose opinions increasingly took on political overtones, had been tolerated, if not approved, during the 1950s and 1960s. By the 1970s, however, the political opinions of Küng were suddenly in great demand, as were those of many younger theologians, such as Johann Baptist Metz or, among the Protestants, Dorothee Sölle, whose understanding of theology had always been primarily political.

In the new political theology developed by these and other radical theologians in the 1960s and 1970s, the kingdom of God is equated with a desirable future condition of the political order.[21] God is "dead" or is at least reduced to a metaphysical concept from which "escape" is necessary. Religion in general is seen in Marxist terms as an ideological distortion of the reality of exploitation, and transcendent reality and the implications of such reality are denied. Political theologians equate the Christian idea of liberation from sin and personal salvation with the Marxist idea of liberation of the human spirit from economic and political oppression. Since such oppression, in their eyes, characterizes the existing order in the West, their call for liberation becomes a call for resistance to that order and, in particular, to the economic and other policies of Western governments. By blurring the radical difference between Christian and Marxist ideas of liberation, the political theologians are able to use the residual moral force of religious arguments for political purposes.

The political theologians thus perpetrate a double hypocrisy or ideological deformation. First, they deny transcendent reality and accept the post-Hegelian view of the human spirit as its own goal and highest purpose, but they nevertheless challenge the policies and decisions of government on grounds that are relevant and admissible only if the transcendent justification is retained. One cannot argue that Christian morality forbids INF modernization if one's position is based on a denial of the divine source and the only legitimation of that morality. Second, they deny that there is any moral value to democratic capitalism, the only existing system that allows the expression of opinions such as those of the new political theologians and the expression of support for unexamined and utopian revolutionary schemes of social transformation or unilateral disarmament. As John Courtney Murray pointed out at a time when many Catholics were using their religious credentials to attack the U.S. government during the Vietnam war: "The danger is lest the very strength of the moral commitment—to peace and against war—may foreclose inquiry into the military and political facts of the contemporary world—the naked facts of power situations and the requirements of law and order in an imperfect world, which may justify recourse to the arbitrament of arms." The government of a constitutional democracy is entitled to a "normal presumption in its favor," especially since it "creates the situation within which the prophetic voice may safely be heard."[22]

Some political theologians insist that their opposition to nuclear deterrence is based on a more loyal interpretation of Christianity than that of earlier generations of clergy, for whom the defense of the West, even with nuclear weapons, was undeniably justified. This argument, too, is specious. It begs the question of how, and by whom, the political implications of Christianity are defined. Since most of the political theologians are Catholic, they are in principle obliged to take their cue from the relevant documents of the magisterium (the teaching authority of the church), that is, from the official statements of the Vatican Council and of the popes and bishops. There is no question that the Bible and the overwhelming consensus of the theological tradition, confirmed by the Vatican Council, supports the legitimacy of defense of a social order, in this case, that of the West, that is not evidently or deliberately unjust against forces representing a social order, in this case, the Soviet Union, that, if victorious, would mean the end of democracy, human rights, and religious freedom.[23] In response to this objection, the political theologians often argue that the threat is not the Soviet Union but the "arms race" as such and the increased chance of nuclear war that allegedly is caused by it. However, it is not enough simply to assert that the Soviet Union is no threat and then to go on to talk exclusively about the arms race; it must be demonstrated that the nature and policies of the Soviet Union are such that they do not threaten the West or justify defense. The political theologians do not attempt to demonstrate this. They are, in fact, more concerned with attacking the social order of which they are a part, democratic capitalism, than with judging an alien social order, which leads one to the suspicion that the real issue is not disapproval of Western defense, but contempt for Western culture, including its religious component. From such a position, disregard of the security needs of countries that, however imperfectly, represent that culture follows logically.

As stated above, the most important element in the new political theology in West Germany was the sense of guilt, especially within the EKD, for having collaborated too much and too easily with the Nazis. The leading

Protestant theologian of the early twentieth century, Karl Barth, lived and worked in Switzerland and thus was not exposed to the Nazi danger. He vigorously denounced collaboration with totalitarianism in Germany, but, being a socialist, he welcomed it with regard to the Soviet Union. To him, it was absurd to compare Hitler and Stalin; whatever the harshness of the Soviet regime, at least its purposes, according to him, were good: economic equality, industrial progress, and the promise of worldwide revolution and an end to exploitation. Barth, in other words, took the ideology and promises of communism seriously without bothering to examine the facts. He also argued that the imposition of communism in Germany or in a part thereof might be seen as just retribution for the failure to resist National Socialism. Such retribution would presumably be painful, and this indicates that, on some level, he understood very well what communism meant, but he did not allow this realization to influence his general judgment that anticommunism was wrong. It was ironic that since Barth distinguished radically between theology and politics, he ought, on his own principles, not to have been regarded with more respect as a political commentator than any other layman; yet his prestige, and the guilt of many German Protestants, legitimated the slowly growing bias against West German defense. Protestant clergy in the Federal Republic have directed their agitation at minor villains, such as South Africa, Rhodesia, and Portugal when it was a colonial power, not against the forces and states much closer to home that represented a real and direct threat to democracy and freedom of religion.

The popularity of political theology has grown commensurately with the strength of the peace movement, in which progressive and politicized theologians—mostly Protestants, such as Albertz, Eppler, and Gollwitzer, but also Catholics, such as Dirks, Kogon, and Metz—have played a leading role.[24] They have given the entrenched radical counterculture of refusal an impetus and a legitimacy that could hardly have been imagined and probably would not even have been welcomed in the 1970s. It would be a mistake, however, to suppose that political theology is typical of the outlook of the majority of West German theologians. What can be said is that the majority of theologians in both West Germany and the United States feel compelled to accept the arguments and the positions of political theology as legitimate and seem to fear denouncing them, as they would have done with considerable vigor until the mid-1960s. The theological consensus according to which the ways and means of collective security, the maintenance of peace and, if necessary, self-defense were left to the competent political and military authorities, ended when political theologians, who, strictly speaking, were not competent, in the 1960s and after applied the moralism of the New Left and the antiauthoritarian movements to the judgment of such ways and means. These critics not only found certain means of defense, notably nuclear weapons, to be unacceptable, but also accused Western governments using nuclear weapons as part of a military deterrent of not being sincerely interested in maintaining peace, while generally ignoring the fact of Soviet nuclear weapons and the Soviet intention to use them in any war with the West.

The theological arms theorists ignored global power relationships and concentrated rather on cheap moralism and an argumentation borrowed from the so-called "critical peace researchers," some of whose ideas I have discussed in Chapter 4.[25] The most important of these ideas is that arms in themselves, not the pursuit by great powers of incompatible interests, cause tension and war. Thus any reduction of arms anywhere must reduce tension and the chances of war. This assumption, combined with the suspicion of Western, as opposed to Soviet, nuclear weapons, is at the root of the rather dramatic shift (Ernst Otto Czempiel speaks of a "Copernican revolution" in Catholic teaching on peace) in the position of many leading West German ecclesiastical bodies on questions of security and deterrence.[26]

Whereas theologians formerly considered the constitutional democratic state in West Germany and in other nations belonging to the Atlantic Alliance as a morally adequate political framework for human life, including religious life, those who espouse the moralism of such movements as liberation theology and the Christian-Marxist dialogue and who claim that unemployment, environmental pollution, and psychological discontent are characteristic features of Western capitalism have come to disparage constitutional democracy to such an extent that they no longer accept the validity of official arguments in favor of collective security and deterrence, but rather view them as ideological camouflage for the nefarious operations of the "military-industrial complex." The old distinction between religion as a way of personal salvation and a guide to individual morality and politics as the organization and maintenance of secular order and security, which had been established after the wars of religion as part of the search for stability and the restraint of violence and sectarian aggression, ceased to exist after a century and a half of movements of cultural secularization and reactions to them. In undermining that distinction in the interests of a secular ideology of progress derived from Marxism, the political theologians were denying that there could be any specific religious purpose in life. To them, religion was an effort to moralize politics, and in their criticism, they indulged in the same enthusiastic impatience with the existing order and faith in a new, perfect order of political, not personal, life, which the statesmen and political thinkers of the seventeenth and eighteenth centuries had successfully defeated.

The difference was that whereas the religious enthusiasts of the seventeenth century used political, mundane force for religious ends, the political theologians of the 1980s are wholly secular in their thinking and instead use the moralism, which is all that is left of traditional religion, to achieve ends that, whether they admit it or not, are strictly political and are incompatible with the survival of constitutional democracy.

This is evident when one considers that the political theologians almost invariably assume that peace and the preservation of life are and ought to be the highest values, a notion that was and is incomprehensible to an older generation of theologians, for whom the salvation of the immortal soul has always been the highest purpose. Since totalitarian regimes have always sought to destroy Christianity because Christianity is directly subversive of the totalitarian goal of total control of mind and body, whereas constitutional democracy, which is concerned mainly with material security and order, allows the free exercise of religion on the organized as well as the individual level, it seems logical that the former must be resisted and the latter supported. If, however, survival is valued more than freedom of the spirit, then constitutional democracy may be preferable, but it cannot be accorded any right to self-defense if such self-defense might involve war and the destruction of life.

Such assumptions and sentiments clearly underlie the rejection by so many in the organized churches of the policies and principles of Western security. The irony is that by their activities and their attempts to regain relevance by using the widespread political moralism to which they subscribe, they are endangering peace and security (to the extent that they actually exist) and are making war and the destruction of life they so abhor more, not less, likely.

8

THE IDEOLOGY
OF EUROPE

The ideology of the peace movement and its sympathizers is, as I have argued, fueled by utopianism, antiauthoritarianism, and a political moralism derived both from political ideas of liberation and autonomy and from a misapplication of the idea of religious liberation to political purposes. As I have also indicated, however, the domestic challenge to security policy in West Germany in the 1980s comes not only from the activists of the peace movement or from disaffected intellectuals and publicists like Günter Grass or Rudolf Augstein, but from a broader change of public opinion regarding defense, security, the United States, and the Soviet Union. This change is especially evident in the SPD, which by 1984 was divided between supporters and opponents of INF modernization and NATO security policies in a way not seen since the 1950s, and with the opponents, led above all by Willy Brandt and Oskar Lafontaine, having the upper hand.[1] In this chapter, I turn from discussing the ideological antecedents of the attack on the West German political system and security policies to a second look at some of the problems and phenomena addressed in the first four chapters. Whereas, however, my focus earlier was primarily on the origins, evolution, and implications of the *Deutschlandpolitik* (national policy) of various parties and political leaders, and on Ostpolitik, especially the Ostpolitik of the social-liberal coalition of 1969–1982, I am concerned here with the nature and effects of the idea that Western Europe has a political interest that is not only different from the interest of the United States in Western Europe, but that can and ought to be defended, as it is often put, "against both superpowers."

I call this idea the "ideology of Europe" because, in my view, it is a belief that the political conditions under which West European democracy will survive are other than they are, and that a struggle that, in fact, directly involves Europeans can be ignored and neglected. It is, therefore, an ideology, and not a reasonable prescription for political action in the true interest of West Europeans. As I see it, the true interest of West Europeans is the survival of constitutional democracy and, if possible, the extension of human rights to East Europeans who are under totalitarian rule.[2] This purpose is not served by the ideology of Europe, which in fact is designed rather to obstruct the considered policies of the West German and other NATO governments for security and defense, policies that, by guaranteeing the freedom of Western Europe, are the necessary precondition for any future pursuit of the true European interest.

At the root of the ideology of Europe is the notion that the United States and the Soviet Union decided at Yalta in February 1945 to divide Europe and to exercise a dominion that, whatever the ideological differences of these two nations, had the effect of preventing the political, economic, or cultural independence, of Western Europe from America, and of Eastern Europe from the Soviet Union. Adherents of the ideology of Europe, though they usually recognize some difference in the political systems and institutions of the United States and the USSR, believe in a separate European identity equidistant from both superpowers and claim that the U.S.-Soviet conflict, which in their eyes is not primarily a conflict between democracy and dictatorship, but a struggle for power, influence, and control of economic resources, should not involve the Europeans. The fact, which Adenauer saw clearly, that, as constitutional democracies, the West European countries constitute a challenge to the Soviet Union and to Soviet hegemony that to the Soviets is intolerable and that the Soviet Union must, given its political aims, seek the separation of Western Europe and the United States in order to extend its hegemony, its form of imperial peace, westwards, is denied. The ideology of Europe, on the contrary, includes the claim that the Soviet Union is not expansionist, but primarily interested in maintaining the status quo. It will defend its security interests (as in Hungary in 1956, Czechoslovakia in 1968, and Poland in 1981), but will not try to expand its influence outside the borders of its empire unless provoked into doing so by the policies of Western governments.

The policy of détente, adopted wholeheartedly by West European governments in the mid-1960s, has, according to this view, stimulated liberalizing tendencies in Eastern Europe and mollified Soviet fears of Western revanchism or "rollback." Détente, both between the United States and the Soviet Union and between Western Europe and the Eastern bloc countries, including the Soviet Union, symbolizes, in the ideology of Europe, the common interest of West and East Europeans in avoiding war and in restraining their respective superpowers from embarking on irresponsible adventures or adopting grand strategies that might lead to war. If only the peaceful policies of contact, negotiation, and mutual concessions can be continued and remain credible, the argument continues, the likelihood of conflict will be decreased and the foundations laid for the emergence, some time in the future, of a "European peace order," in Willy Brandt's phrase, or even a "new European identity," political, cultural, and even economic, reaching from "the Atlantic to the Bug."[3]

As indicated in Chapters 1 to 4, I dispute every one of the assertions and implications of this argument, including the belief that détente between West and East European governments has been achieved in the sense that respect has been established on the official level and individual contacts have been increased and strengthened. Unilaterally revocable agreements obtained by the West in exchange for economic concessions and recognition, which would be described in any other context as bribes or tribute, depending on one's viewpoint, are not useful foundations for a relationship of mutual respect. The East bloc governments know that Western governments, particularly that of West Germany, are more interested in maintaining some level of trade and contact than in confrontation. They are therefore able to treat their subjects more or less as they please without needing to fear anything other than symbolic Western sanctions. Their incentive to moderation and liberalization is probably less than it would be in the absence of the Western credits and other advantages that the Eastern bloc has gained from détente. The fact that East-West détente has not contributed to the well-being of Eastern Europeans and has actually strengthened the regimes is clear from an exhaustive analysis of what the West hoped to achieve by détente and what the actual results have been by Daniel Frei and Dieter Ruloff.[4] The belief that there can or should be a new European identity, or rather the belief that such an identity should be distinct from West European survival within the Alliance, is a fundamental tenet of the new neutralism and is evident in many of the statements of intellectuals, journalistic commentators, and professionals who are by no means directly linked, culturally, socially, or politically, to the Greens or the peace movement. I am thinking particularly of people like Rudolf Augstein, Marion Gräfin Dönhoff, Theo Sommer, Manfred Görtemaker, Günter Gaus, Egon Bahr, and Ralf Dahrendorf—broadly speaking, the FDP and SPD intellectuals and writers who sought to encourage attempts to seek détente in the 1970s. Their articles appeared mostly in *Der Spiegel* and *Die Zeit*, which has often jokingly been called the *Hofblatt* (official court journal) of the Social Democrats. I am not thinking of such intensely suspicious opponents of INF modernization and NATO policies as Oskar Lafontaine, Brandt's possible successor as chairman of the SPD; Gert Bastian, a former general, who was a member of the Bundestag representing the Greens until he left that group in early 1984; or the peace researchers of the Hessische Stiftung Friedens- und Konflikt- forschung (Hessian Foundation for Peace and Conflict Research – HSFK) in Frankfurt.[5]

A remarkable consensus with regard to East-West relations and security policy has, by the mid-1980s, been evident in the writings of these prominent supporters of the foreign and security policies of the social-liberal coalition. According to this consensus, the Reagan administration seeks superiority in nuclear arms, provokes the Soviets by its needlessly hostile rhetoric, is not sincere in seeking arms control, refuses to consider Soviet proposals, and is generally acting in an irresponsible and haughty manner incompatible with a true desire for peace.[6] The Soviet Union, on the other hand, sincerely fears nuclear war and desires only a reliable agreement with the United States, whose unpredictable policy changes make it necessary for the Soviets to con- tinue their otherwise regrettable arms buildup and deployment. The proper role of the West Europeans in all of this is to influence the Americans in the direction of initiating serious negotiations and away from INF moderniza- tion and thereby to demonstrate to the Soviets that the West Europeans, at least, are firmly committed to peace. Accordingly, the resumption of U.S.- Soviet contacts regarding arms control in 1985 was not, on this view, evi- dence that the Reagan administration was truly committed to peace, but that the NATO allies had been successful in getting the United States to support negotiations. This evidence of the commitment of West European govern- ments to détente, whatever the global climate of U.S.-Soviet relations, may in turn induce the Soviets to seek an agreement that will genuinely reduce tensions and the level of arms in Central Europe.[7]

The opposing view (that INF modernization represents a reconfirmation of the American commitment to maintain the security of Western Europe, which is necessary because the aim of Soviet policy is still the destruction of the Western Alliance and the separation – politically, culturally, and mili- tarily – of Western Europe from the United States) is hardly ever granted a hearing by those whose belief in the desirability of a new European order overrides their own earlier reservations about asserting a spurious "European identity." If the political will to defend Western Europe were more certain, the ideology of Europe would by the same token constitute a better guide to pol- icy since the true interest of all Europeans, East and West, is served by the survival of a strong and independent Western Europe. However, the ideology of Europe, as has been indicated, denies that there is any direct Soviet threat to Western Europe. For those who hold that ideology, defense modernization is not a condition of survival, but a needless provocation of the Soviet Union that makes war more, not less, likely. To the extent that its adherents make security policy more difficult, then, the ideology of Europe is useful to the Soviet Union, which is one reason why the Soviets, in the 1980s, have often been heard to claim a common interest with Europe in maintaining peace. The Soviets hope by this means to be able to use the ideology of Europe for their own purposes and to prevent the West Germans, and other Westerners, from thinking too closely about how peace is actually maintained in Europe and who is threatening it. Adherents of the ideology of Europe are well-entrenched in the West German educational, media, and civil service bureaucracies, and they are mostly young and articulate. One must therefore expect a gradual but definite increase of its influence during the coming years. Because the ideology promises something attractive (undisturbed peace in Europe), it is also going to be extremely difficult for its critics to make their case without being denounced as warmongers and provocateurs.

There were, by the mid-1980s, some signs in Western Europe that the ideology was being challenged on its own terms. In France, President Mitterrand has taken an unexpectedly clear anti-Soviet and pro-NATO line in European security matters, while criticizing U.S. policy in Central America and elsewhere. Proposals for an organization similar to the European Defense Community, which the French had rejected in 1954, are frequently debated in France, as is the general question of the threat posed by the Soviet IRBMs, chiefly the SS-20s, and Soviet power in general.[8] In West Germany, the idea that independence of America logically means that Western Europe must do more for its own defense, also, and particularly, in the long-term interest of the East Europeans, whose lot will be much worse if Western Europe is weak, appears to be much less popular than in France. It has less support than the already mentioned contrary idea that independence of America ought to mean less defense since the Soviets would never need to fear the West Europeans. In any case, there is little chance that the West European governments will, in the foreseeable future, seriously consider spending the money necessary for a convincing European conventional deterrent, however desirable a strong European defense organization might be. The elegant, and usually very convincing, arguments for an increased capacity for defense are mostly wishful thinking, for it is neither possible nor likely.[9] What is in fact both possible and likely is that the larger countries in Western Europe will do their best with more or less fixed budgets, and the smaller ones will try hard not to think about the security problem at all, including the probability that American guarantees will lose credibility in direct proportion to the growth of Soviet power and the proliferation of Soviet local, theater, and global nuclear and nonnuclear options.

The challenge is for Western Europe to unite and to realize, in Pierre Hassner's words, that the "fight for Europe, for peace, and for liberty" is the "same fight," and once and for all to lay the foundations for a convincing, and reassuring, conventional and theater-nuclear deterrent as the necessary point of departure for mature and honest relations with the Soviet Union and, perhaps more important, with the captive nations of Eastern Europe, where paradoxically the spirit of European culture sometimes seems more alive and vibrant than in the nerveless West.[10]

The chances that such a realization will occur are slim, however, as long as leading West European spokesmen react with alarm to the observation that the "tragic division of Europe" is the chief obstacle to peace and security on the continent, as they did when that observation was made by Secretary of State George Shultz at the opening of the Stockholm Conference on Disarmament in Europe in January 1984. If the truth may not be spoken in public for fear of offending the sensibilities of those responsible for the tragic division, that is, the Soviets, it is clear that the task of restoring common sense and the memory of recent experience to West European public consciousness is immense and is not one that can reasonably be undertaken in this book.[11] Therefore, in the remainder of this chapter, I shall restrict myself to making some further remarks on the malaise and the perverse as opposed to the healthy solution to the problem of European independence and identity.

SOURCES OF THE NEW EUROPEAN IDEOLOGY

The roots of the ideology of a European identity, as opposed to the idea of Europe as such, can be traced to the immediate postwar period—indeed in some respects even further, to the fierce social and political debates of the 1920s and 1930s. In the earlier period, the idea mainly took the form of a search for some "third way" other than liberal capitalism and authoritarian socialism; in other words, the search was inspired less by the fear of war than by a desire to escape what was felt to be a disastrous and destructive predicament of social unrest, war, and the sense that Western civilization was coming to an end.[12] That communism had failed as a movement of human liberation gradually became clear to many leading intellectuals, at least in France, Britain, and the United States, in the late 1930s and 1940s. That capitalism had failed as well, morally as well as economically, to live up to its claims was also widely believed, in view of the Great Depression and especially in view of the state-controlled war economies that had prevailed in the democratic countries in World War II.

The beliefs that the Depression had been ended mainly by vigorous government action and that in the war that followed, government control of almost all economic activity was not only necessary but desirable led to the almost irresistible convictions, on the part of those who regretted as well as those who favored the development, that industrial economies were now so complex that market forces alone could not guarantee the most favorable outcome for all groups and classes in society and that equality of opportunity and equality of access to goods and to positions could not be achieved except by government intervention and ultimate control. Consequently, when World War II ended, there was almost universal agreement, not just among intellectuals but among politicians, economists, and journalistic commentators, that free market capitalism was dead and that the reconstruction of Europe could take place only under a regime whose nature was as yet unknown, but that would certainly include a much stronger government role than had hitherto been seen. In 1945, the British historian and socialist A. J. P. Taylor noted, with ill-concealed satisfaction, that "nobody in Europe believes in the American way of life—that is, in private enterprise; or rather those who believe in it are a defeated party and a party which seems to have no more future than the Jacobites in England after 1688."[13] This judgment of Taylor's was no more correct than many of his other, more notorious opinions (for example, he believes that Hitler did not plan World War II; rather, war was forced on him by the West). Still, it expressed a state of mind prevalent at the time and enjoying new popularity in the 1980s. In Germany, the SPD was committed to a broad program of nationalization of all major industries; in Britain, the policy of the Labour government of 1945–1951 was one of nationalization and an increase in public consumption. These political and economic measures formed the background of the intellectual arguments heard in these early postwar years that Western Europe could not resist communism as a social force of great moral prestige among the working class and the displaced and miserable millions on the Continent unless it also eschewed capitalism and sought some third way beyond commitment to either system, the American or the Soviet. In France, the idea of a European third way was maintained both by socialists and by Catholic intellectuals such as Emmanuel Mounier and the group associated with the journal *Esprit*, although the third way propounded by Mounier implied sympathy toward communism and hostility toward what he defined as American capitalism.[14] The hostility to liberal capitalism in France declined somewhat among politicians, but continued and even grew among intellectuals during the entire period from 1945 until the rise of the New Left in the 1960s. It was not until the 1980s that there arose in France a group of vigorous and articulate defenders of free enterprise and its political benefits.

In West Germany, the debate of the 1940s combined elements of conservative criticism of the allegedly corrosive effects of capitalism on traditional beliefs and social structures with the socialist view that capitalism represented heartless exploitation and increasing inequality. Stalin was still seen as an anti-Nazi hero and the Soviet Union was still regarded favorably in the West, as was the case until the late 1940s, but hopes for a new European order that was guaranteed, but not controlled, by either super-power were still prevalent and were expressed in vigorous philosophical and political debates that took place in the Western zones of Germany among writers, journalists, and other intellectuals, returning from exile or recover-ing from tyranny. These debates changed character after the establishment of the Federal Republic in 1949 and the institution of the social market econ-omy; for the next twenty years, they had only a modest political significance. The remarkable success of liberal capitalism in producing sustained eco-nomic growth and a rising standard of living proved both the pessimists and the anticapitalists wrong. The defenders of capitalism in West Germany, moreover, had perhaps a stronger intellectual and philosophical foundation for their views than their counterparts in other Western countries.

This foundation had been developed by the German liberal economists of the Freiburg school. Walther Eucken, Alfred Müller-Armack, Ludwig Erhard, and Hermann Röpke had since the 1920s been elaborating and re-fining a philosophical defense and explication of the market economy that came into its own as a counterweight to collectivism and state control after 1945. So convincingly did they present their argument when given the op-portunity, beginning in 1948, that all major political parties, including the SPD, committed themselves to what in the 1950s and later became known as the "social market economy." By this term, Erhard and his colleagues did not mean to imply any particular degree of state intervention, but simply that the market economy as such is automatically "social"–more so than any collectivist system.[15]

The idea of the third way or the third force was eclipsed by the success of the social market economy and the unexpected strength of democratic institutions. It nevertheless continued to be debated in the 1950s and 1960s, particularly in southern Europe, but the focus was now more often the newly independent countries of the so-called Third World. In West Germany, both the conservative argument that capitalism was spiritually empty and inade-quate for human fulfilment and the socialist argument that it was unaccept-able for moral reasons lost ground in the 1950s. Even in those years of rising prosperity and general public contentment, however, both arguments were still occasionally heard. The sense that capitalism is somehow not good enough or not spiritually fulfilling has probably always been the main source of strength of third-way arguments of the cultural type. Such arguments were revived in the 1970s with the rise of student radicalism and of protests against the cult of material satisfaction and the environmental, economic, and alleged psychological consequences of capitalism.

This revival of anticapitalist agitation was, however, more utopian and definitely on a lower intellectual level than the fairly sophisticated discussions of the 1930s and the immediate postwar years. In my view, the success of the new arguments for a third force or third way is attributable not to the influence of the radical movements, but to the cultural pessimism that became increasingly widespread in the late 1970s and that was reminiscent of the cultural despair of the years immediately before and after World War I, as well as to the widely held idea that because American plans and policies were ill-informed and dangerous, Western Europe had a definite mission to fulfill in finding a "third way." This time the goal was not economic cooperation, but cooperation in strategic and political planning.

THE REVIVAL OF THE THIRD WAY

In 1969, the SPD for the first time became the major party of government, and immediately began its new Ostpolitik, based on recognition of the status quo, that is, of Soviet power and control in Eastern Europe. As noted in Chapter 1, the new Ostpolitik was not so new as all that and was anticipated by the gradual opening to the East that was begun during the tenure of Gerhard Schröder as foreign minister in 1961–1966 and continued by Willy Brandt from 1966 on. These years, however, also saw the culmination of the first wave of protest movements and the rapid spread of a new form of anti-capitalist ideology, spurred not by impatience with capitalism, but by fear of its success.[16] It was the Americans who originally proposed, in the early 1960s, that a policy such as the new Ostpolitik, by stabilizing the military and political situation in Europe, would be to the mutual benefit of both East and West. In 1966, the NATO countries officially accepted the recommendations of the Harmel Report that détente and defense should henceforth be the two equally important pillars of Western strategy. The West Germans were at first reluctant to believe such wide claims; for them, Ostpolitik began as a variant of *Deutschlandpolitik*, an attempt to secure better conditions for Germans in the East by negotiations with East Germany and the Soviet Union. By the time Brandt became chancellor in 1969, the originally American idea of détente and of a "security partnership" of East and West, had been taken over wholeheartedly by the West Germans, while Americans, such as Henry Kissinger, began having doubts about the effects of détente on the security policies of the West German government. Kissinger feared that the apparent success of détente in drawing the Soviets into a "web of negotiations" would engender excessive optimism in West Germany concerning what could be achieved in this regard and would lead to a neglect of the strong defense without which détente was simply another form of appeasement. The skepticism of some Americans, subdued though it was until the election of Ronald Reagan, had the curious effect of lending official West

German policy under Brandt and Schmidt a credibility, as perceived by the radical left, that it might not otherwise have had—simply, or chiefly, because it appeared to imply a certain degree of opposition to official U.S. policies. By the mid-1970s, West German liberals and Social Democrats were often heard to argue that perhaps West Germany might be the model of a third way in a political role as mediator between East and West or, more specifically, as a critic of American policies and sympathetic to "legitimate Soviet security interests."

This new semiofficial West German obligation to mediate and to "save détente," as it was often put, strongly influenced Willy Brandt and several of his aides, such as Egon Bahr or Günter Gaus, who continued to play a role in official policy formation after his resignation as chancellor. After the election of Ronald Reagan in 1980, it began to spread well beyond the SPD into the ranks of FDP and CDU politicians, spokesmen, and analysts. This sense of obligation should not be confused with another political line of thought that also implied a third way for Europe, but placed more emphasis on national sovereignty and security; the "Gaullist" path of Franz-Josef Strauss and certain other members of the Union parties, particularly the CSU.[17] They supported the national policy of maintaining a claim to the Eastern provinces and of seeking unification, but they rejected the Social Democratic notion that the demand for reunification should be surrendered to allow discussions, negotiations, and contacts. In particular, West German "Gaullists" refused to recognize positions that the West German government, before 1969, had considered illegal and illegitimate, such as the recognition of the East German regime as a sovereign state and the acceptance of the Oder-Neisse line as the official frontier between Germany and Poland. The implication of this West German "Gaullism" was that since unification was clearly impossible, it was better to continue to refuse to recognize the Soviet-controlled status quo in Eastern and Central Europe and to encourage a West German national consciousness (Staatsbewusstsein) in order to attempt to guarantee the will to maintain security and stability. The next higher goal of European integration could not be pursued without a strong national consciousness and national will, because integration, in Strauss's view, was possible only among patries (fatherlands)—not among technocratic societies lacking national solidarity and cultural vigor.

The pure Straussian line never became very popular in West Germany, mostly because of the reputation Strauss had and has in the leftist-liberal media and even among some Christian Democrats, as an authoritarian conservative or (as perceived by the left) a neo-Nazi oppressor. However, his belief in the need for a West German national consciousness was adopted by many in the center of West German politics and gradually became the more or less official position of the Union parties. The argument that West Germany needed its own *Staatsbewusstsein*, however, was not in itself likely to have much effect as long as the other elements in the "Gaullist" outlook, namely the insistence on national unity as a principle and European political integration, were neglected.

West German Gaullism never included the anti-Americanism of de Gaulle himself, nor was there much talk by Strauss of a European "third way" between the superpowers. Nevertheless, there has been a definite, if not very significant reorientation, since the later 1970s, on the part of those who formerly supported a Straussian or Gaullist position on the national issue. Helmut Diwald, Armin Mohler, Hans-Dietrich Sander, and certain elements of the student generation (such as Henning Eichberg) who move with conspicuous ease from right to left, have adopted an anti-Western (specifically anti-American) and yet conservative and anti-Marxist stance.[18]

THE IDEOLOGY OF NEW EUROPEAN IDENTITY

The arms control debates of the early 1980s have frequently been described as "a battle for the mind of Europe." For this phrase to have meaning, there must be a European mind to be fought over, presumably by the United States and the Soviet Union in demonstrating their commitment to peace. As foreseen by Kissinger in 1969, the prescriptions of the Harmel Report and the popularity of the détente, as opposed to the defense, side of security policy, led to a state of mind among politicians and commentators in West Germany in which peace, not freedom, has become the final aim of policy. Kissinger argues that the two are not separable and that the maintenance and improvement of peace depends directly on the will to preserve freedom.

It is this "European mind" and the attitudes and policies entailed that are the basis of what is becoming known as the "new European identity." That there is some common character to the culture, polities, and societies of Western Europe is not in doubt. What is at issue here is not the actual similarities among West European nations, but the claims to greater sophistication, sensibility, and rationality in the pursuit of peace made on behalf of Western European peoples and governments by certain politicians and commentators, above all in West Germany. Generally, these claims involve the following two assumptions: first, that there is a specific European interest, as well as a European idea of how to maintain peace and security that differs from U.S. policy in important respects, notably in being less bellicose and more reasonable towards the Soviet Union. However, there is often an ambiguity in the notion of this European identity since it is not always clear whether it is meant to include Soviet-occupied Europe as well. If the notion is to be descriptive rather than emotive, it must, of course, include the East Europeans, whose interests must then be ascertained and taken into account. The real or supposed interests of East Europeans are occasionally included in the discussion of a European identity. The conclusion usually is that support of those interests entails a continuation of détente policies, which for West Germany means Ostpolitik, since to break off Ostpolitik would, on this argument, harm the East European peoples as much as it would irritate their governments. The other possible conclusion, which, in fact, is supported by spokesmen for East European democratic movements, such as Solidarity in Poland, is that the interests of the East Europeans and their governments are radically opposed and that if Western Europe genuinely wants to support the true interests of East Europeans, as opposed to the interests of the communist regimes, it must first improve its defenses and move towards greater political unity. Détente and Ostpolitik, at least as practiced by the SPD-FDP governments of 1969–1982 should, according to these East Europeans, be pursued only from a position of strength. This answer to the question of how to help the East Europeans, however, is almost never heard in West Germany.

The idea of a European identity was gradually revived in the 1970s in a context very different from that of the early postwar years or the interwar years, when it first flourished. Détente was now the basis of official policy in all Western countries, and any doubts about its significance or beneficial effects were ruled illegitimate and unreasonable. Helmut Schmidt revived the notion of a "security partnership," and in the United States the so-called "Sonnenfeldt Doctrine," which stated that the West had a strategic interest in the stability of the Soviets, became popular among policymakers and analysts. The members of the successor generation, many of whom were at university during the Vietnam war, and who felt resentment of and hostility toward American administrations and practices, began moving into professional and academic positions or into the ranks of the unemployed academics.[19]

There were other reasons for the alienation of West German youth from the United States and American policies. America, too, has a successor generation serving in the policy elite, and by the mid-1980s it was well on its way to replacing the old guard with direct experience of World War II or the years of European reconstruction. No longer do all American policymakers feel that the United States and Western Europe are bound in a *Gefahrengemeinschaft* (a community of shared danger and shared exposure to a common threat). Rather, Western Europe is simply regarded as one of many areas of potential danger and conflict. This shift is largely generational, but it has also been influenced by domestic economic changes in the United States, the

decreasing importance of the Eastern seaboard, and the increasing importance of the Pacific Basin for American trade and strategic interests.

Personal contacts between the United States and West Germany are
changing character as well. Fewer Germans are emigrating to America.
Almost a million emigrated between 1950 and the mid-1960s, barely 125,000
in 1961–1980. Most Germans living in America have now lived there long
enough to be fully Americanized; they have fewer friends and relations in the
old country, and West Germans as a whole are thus less often personally and
directly exposed to the American perspective of the emigrants. One should
not underestimate the significance of such contacts, or the lack of them, in
the shaping of public feelings. The gratitude felt by older West Germans
toward the United States is a consequence of their close relations with
American troops after 1945 and, in part, of contacts with American friends
and relatives that had been cut off by the war. Opinion surveys clearly show
a strong correlation of age and sympathy for the United States; in the
mid-1980s, almost a third of all West Germans described their feelings as
anti-American in an extensive and careful poll, with the younger cohorts
(born 1946–1955) being over twice as anti-American as their elders.[20] The
value of this particular survey is that it is part of a long-term analysis of generational opinion changes in Western Europe since 1970, and it is clear that
the tendency towards more anti-Americanism and opposition to the Atlantic Alliance is growing, particularly, but not exclusively, among the young.
During the 1970s, many West Germans observed the drug- and crime-related
problems of U.S. servicemen in West Germany, their lack of discipline, and
their failure to respect the customs of the community where they were
stationed. Although these problems have largely been solved since the late
1970s, they have contributed to an unfavorable image of Americans in the
eyes of many Germans.

Also in the 1970s, social scientists of the New Left created the science of
peace research at the HSFK and elsewhere, claiming to have solved the problem of conflict in the world by demonstrating that wars were caused by
Western industrial society and its effects on the rest of the world; ecology
became an issue, and political moralism invaded debate. The clear distinction among pro-American, neutralist, and pro-Soviet was replaced by an
emphasis on the difference between "security conservatism" (a belief and
trust in the need for and relevance of deterrence) and "alternative security,"
which ranged from support for nuclear-free zones and unilateral disarmament to wholly utopian aspirations for a new order without authority and
conflict. The Republican victory in the United States in 1980, the NATO
double-track decision on INF modernization in 1979, and a mixture of Soviet
blandishments and pressure increased the sense of unease and opposition to
established security policy in the successor generation and among the many

academics and professional commentators who had been critical of the
United States, of NATO, and of industrial society generally since the 1960s
or early 1970s.

The combination of these factors with the prevalent utopianism, antiauthoritarianism, and moralism referred to earlier resulted in a new ideology.
In this ideology, old radical ideas from the 1930s or 1940s of an anticapitalist
Europe, the belief in the possibility and even the reality of change in Eastern
Europe resulting from Ostpolitik, Gaullist or semi-Gaullist visions of a revived European style and weight in global politics, and Social Democratic
ideas for "change through convergence" away from the Atlantic and toward
the East were combined. The consequence was a shift in public and political
attitudes that could not but affect U.S.–West German relations. To many
people, including many politicians and official or semiofficial spokesmen, the
West-West crisis now appeared more fraught with danger than any possible
East-West crisis. While the official line in general still was that the greatest
danger was the decoupling of U.S. and West European security, for example,
by the failure to carry out INF modernization, which would leave Western
Europe without a countervailing Eurostrategic (theater-nuclear) deterrent to
the Soviet IRBMs, the peace movement and the peace researchers welcomed
decoupling as a strategy for peace. Their argument was that since the Soviet
threat was largely an American invention anyway, the deployment of new
NATO missiles was both unnecessary and provocative. If these new missiles
were not deployed, the Soviet Union would not itself feel threatened and
would, they asserted, be willing to negotiate further disarmament. The
resulting lessening of tensions would benefit both Western and Eastern
Europe and contribute to world peace.[21]

While not believing, or professing not to believe, in a Soviet threat, the
peace researchers alleged that U.S. administrations were unable or unwilling
to understand the European situation. Their interpretation of the superpower conflict was that it arose not from the incompatibility of democracy
and dictatorship or the refusal of the Soviet Union to concede an equal right
of existence to democratic societies, but from what they called "the international system" itself and primarily from U.S. attempts to extend and secure
global hegemony.[22] Accordingly, Western Europe was not directly concerned
in that conflict and could indeed pursue its own policies of disarmament and
negotiation with the Soviets to reduce the chances of conflict caused by
American-inspired confrontations.

The danger inherent in the West-West crisis was seen very differently by
the "security conservatives" and the proponents of "alternative security"
policies. To the former, it was the danger of Soviet hegemony or even of war
resulting from decoupling theater and strategic deterrence and from the possibility that the United States would not risk strategic nuclear war to defend

an indefensible Europe. To the latter, it was the danger that American provocations and misconceived policies would "force" the Soviets to war. This difference resulted from radically divergent views of the nature, intent, and policies of the Soviet Union and of the causes and course of global political developments since 1945.

For the security conservatives like Adenauer and his intellectual and political heirs in the 1980s, such as Alois Mertes, peace was the consequence of the military strength of the Atlantic Alliance. Strength was relevant because the Soviet Union relied for its power, prestige, and influence on armed force, and, as Michael Howard put it, "societies which continue to see armed force as an acceptable means for attaining their political ends are likely to establish a dominance over those which do not. Indeed they will not necessarily have to fight for it."[23] The West, therefore, while rejecting war as an instrument of policy, had to demonstrate a credible will to fight if attacked, precisely in order to avoid being attacked.

In this view, the East-West conflict not only affects Europe, but Europe cannot escape from it even if the Europeans should want to. The belief of the peace movement and its supporters that Europe can indeed escape from the conflict is therefore, in the eyes of security conservatives, extremely dangerous. What makes the belief truly paradoxical is that it is so often accompanied by another belief, namely that this imaginary peaceful Europe can and should play a role of moral guidance in the world. One might say that the belief in the possibility of withdrawal from the East-West conflict represents one aspect of a failure of realism. The other aspect is the rise of the political moralism represented by the belief in a European role as peacemaker and moralizer to the world. While generally confined, in its more extreme forms, to the peace movement and the left fringe of the SPD, this failure of realism was also apparent in the acts and pronouncements of leading mainstream politicians in the SPD (Willy Brandt) and the FDP. In the latter party, Foreign Minister Hans-Dietrich Genscher, who continued in office under Helmut Kohl after the dissolution of the SPD-FDP coalition in 1982, spoke repeatedly of the dangers of abandoning Ostpolitik and of the "European patriotism of peace" that must be displayed in order to restrain both superpowers (but especially the United States) from letting their differences get out of hand.[24]

At the semiofficial level, some of the continental European Social Democratic parties (the Dutch, Belgian, and Danish Social Democrats and the Norwegian Labor Party, with the SPD represented by Egon Bahr) held discussions, beginning in 1980, on security and foreign policy; these consultations became known as the "Scandilux" talks, referring to the geographical area, from Scandinavia to Luxembourg, represented by these parties. The common theme of these consultations was the need to negotiate, to "save détente," to avoid confrontations, and increase aid to the Third World.[25] Spokesmen of these parties often referred to such aid as "humanitarian defense," their idea presumably being that government-subsidized loans or gifts to Third-World countries such as Tanzania or Zimbabwe would prevent a North-South war, which was seen by many Scandiluxians as a more threatening and immediate danger, if the North did not mend its ways, than war with the Soviet Union.

During his visit to China in early 1982, the then Danish prime minister and leader of the Social Democrats since 1973, Anker Jørgensen, was lectured publicly by his Chinese communist hosts, in front of reporters, on the need for Western Europe to stand together, to resist aggression, and to be wary of the illusion that Soviet goals and interests corresponded to their own. No American cold warrior could have put the case for vigilance better. Jørgensen's response was typical of the Scandilux attitude. He rejected what he evidently believed was an "attitude," rather than a conclusion based on hard Chinese experience of the Soviets, and stated that "negotiations must be possible," as though this belief in negotiations would automatically solve all problems. He thought that negotiations, not improved defenses, ought to be enough to keep the peace, therefore they do keep the peace. Similarly, his foreign minister Kjeld Olesen expressed public alarm in late 1981 over American plans to build and deploy 100 new ICBMs (the MX missiles). No such alarm had been registered by the Social Democrats in the Scandilux countries during the deployment of the many hundreds of ICBMs and IRBMs by the Soviet Union over the preceding decade and a half.

A paradoxical feature of the new ideology of Europe is that it is predominantly, but not exclusively, popular among forces, groups, and interests of the participants in "alternative" movements, that is, socialists, anarchists, and others who term themselves progressive. In the late 1940s and 1950s, the movement for European integration was also extremely popular among the young, but it was centrist and liberal (in the European, not the American sense), a part of the democratic revival that followed World War II. In the 1960s and 1970s, the idea of European integration lost its fascination for the younger generation. Its leftist-liberal origins were forgotten, and by the time of the rise of the new social movements in West Germany, European federalism was no longer seen as a progressive idea. The New Left and its descendant, the peace movement, only wished European integration under socialist and collectivist auspices. Accordingly the old Europeanists, on the right wing of the SPD, in the FDP, and in the Union parties, resisted, in the name of security and Atlantic concerns, the new European ideology espoused by the left.

It is probably true, as Zbigniew Brzezinski pointed out in a 1983 interview, that the older generation could afford to be Atlanticist precisely because it was "politically Americanized while culturally non-Americanized," whereas the successor generation, as represented by the Greens, "tends to be culturally more Americanized than ever before and politically more de-Americanized than ever before."[26] It was partly a question of identity. The founding fathers of the Federal Republic, and their contemporaries throughout Western Europe, were secure in their identities as Europeans and were committed to the Atlantic Alliance and to friendship with America precisely because their ultimate concern was Europe. Their children, but even more their grandchildren, are much less sure of what Europe is or of its value. They, not the founders, were affected by the Americanization of European culture and daily life that began in the 1950s. Americanization undermined their identity as Europeans and thereby, paradoxically, made them less sure of why they were supposed to be committed to the Atlantic Alliance. To this one must add the increasing tendency, reinforced during the Vietnam war, to criticize and attack U.S. policies. This tendency, so far from originating in Europe, began in America and was taken over rapidly in Western Europe in part because young Europeans were now Americanized and attuned to American political fashions and beliefs.

THE NEW EUROPEAN IDEOLOGY AND THE REAL SITUATION OF EUROPE

It is remarkable that the center of gravity of the new ideology of Europe is West Germany, formerly considered the most Atlantic and the least Europeanist of the major NATO allies. Its premise, as stated in 1981 by Peter Bender, one of the most articulate advocates of "the Europeanization of Europe," is that the East-West issue no longer is what it was:

> No longer are East and West separated by a conflict of competing faiths or enthusiasms, but only by routine differences of interest. The problem of détente in Europe is no longer the possible undermining of the West, but the inner collapse of the East. No longer does ideology determine conduct in the East, but the drive for modernization . . . Europe is no longer divided ideologically, only politically.[27]

This theory, presented by Bender as a great discovery concerning the political realities of the early 1980s, seems, in the perspective of postwar history and of political analysis, incredibly outdated. I recall from my days in the *Gymnasium* in Denmark in the late 1960s how it was considered popular and imaginative to talk of the East-West conflict as "just traditional power politics," that ideological factors were ritually discounted, that U.S. economic and political presence in Western Europe was seen less as protection and more as hegemony, as the security purposes of the Alliance were being forgotten, and that the "legitimate interests" of the Soviet rulers in Eastern Europe were acknowledged by teachers and others who could in no sense be called Marxists or even leftists. Certainly, like any other reasonably intelligent young European, I was partly if not wholly convinced that there was substance to the hopes for détente and for the "disintegration of a secular faith" (the subtitle of Richard Lowenthal's book on world communism after Khrushchev), that the "end of ideology" was at hand, and that purely technical means and principles of planning, both domestic and international, were the means to achieve global stability and world peace.[28] Progress, an emphasis on reason, and the self-evidence of common principles—all these things were in the air at the time, and only reactionary fools, it was felt, could fail to be aware of them.

Bender's visions of a "Europe from the Atlantic to the Bug," his belief that the social and economic patterns of West and East European societies were converging, his notion that there was a correspondence between the "unwillingness of both Europes to obey their respective superpowers" when each power attempted to coerce allegiance in order to strengthen its position in its (irrational and anachronistic) conflict with the other, could have been copied directly from any number of editorials, political speeches, or even high school essays that were written in Northern Europe in the 1960s. If his book had been published fifteen years earlier, it would have been an entirely typical contribution to the debate on the future of Europe, a bit optimistic and facile perhaps, yet not too far removed from reality. For such ideas to have been presented in 1981, however, is simply astonishing. The author, one feels, must be in the grip of a powerful ideology. Bender writes as though nothing has happened: no invasion of Czechoslovakia, no sustained Soviet arms buildup, no increase in Soviet actions directed against Western interests and security in Africa, Asia, and Latin America, no domestic and international terrorism and violence of "liberation" regimes sustained by Soviet power, no increased repression of dissidents in the Soviet Union and Eastern Europe, no Solidarity and no martial law in Poland.

These changes, which ought to have made it impossible for the Bender who published *Offensive Entspannung* (Offensive détente) in 1964 to proclaim an "end of the ideological age" and a new role for Germany as "a bridge to the East" in the 1980s, were, in the ideology of which his views are representative, overshadowed by changes in attitudes toward America and the West. The Vietnam war shattered confidence in American wisdom and leadership at the same time that neo-Marxist and collectivist passions were invading the universities, the media, the publishing houses, and other institutions affecting ideological orientation of the successor generation. The majority of my contemporaries marched resolutely in the direction formerly known as "left," which by the early 1970s was entirely without historical continuity with the traditions and even the beliefs of the old European left of the nineteenth and early twentieth centuries. Being left-wing implied little more than strict adherence to a narrow range of beliefs and behavior, including patterns of speech and dress, classified as "progressive," "working-class," "anti-imperialist," "emancipatory" and above all morally binding and sentimentally convincing. Meanwhile, others stood back in alarm, fearing that they were witnessing another act in the drama of the Western failure of nerve, this time caused not by economic disaster, widespread cultural despair, or nihilistic moral anarchy, but by prosperity, impatience, and moralism.[29] Certainly, for those who followed these trends, beliefs such as Bender's were useful as lending support to arguments against Western defense. They do not, however, correspond very well to reality.

An example is the crucial contention, not only of Bender and many others with ties to the left wing of the SPD but of conservatives such as the Americans George F. Kennan or George Liska, that "ideology" has been replaced by mere "conflicts of interest" and that some form of the classic model of great-power relations can be applied to the U.S.-Soviet case.[30] Kennan and Liska are by no means leftists; their personal preferences and moral standards are clearly conservative. Kennan, for example, finds contemporary American culture distasteful because it seems to him materialistic and uncivilized. He has been quoted as saying that he found many aspects of Russian society (he rarely uses the word Soviet) more worth defending than much of what he sees in the West. The Soviet Union seems to remind him of the way America used to be. Oddly enough, this somewhat authoritarian conservatism of Kennan's is no obstacle to the popularity of his views on U.S.-Soviet relations in the peace movement, whose members dress, behave, and speak in ways otherwise distasteful to Kennan.

The argument that U.S.-Soviet relations are merely a power struggle and that the nature and policies of the Soviet Union are comparable to those of Western states is thus made by adherents of the traditional right, like Kennan, as well as by leftists of all kinds. It finds particular favor among young people, both in West Germany and, as polls taken in 1984 show, in the United States.[31] The common denominator in the support for this view is the lack of a sense of the importance of ideology. It is noteworthy that some of the most acute analysts with the best record of predicting Soviet behavior have been those men and women who, in the past, had themselves been

Communists or who, at least, believed in the Soviet promise of equality, justice, and progress.[32] This circumstance indicates, as a hypothesis, that some degree of past infection by the virus of ideology helps, as an immunization against naiveté and misunderstanding, if one is to evaluate properly the exact nature of the threat posed by the Soviet Union. Since the 1950s, however, ideological distinctions have lost much of their importance or relevance in Western societies. The generations born since 1945 have not, in their political experience, been exposed to clear ideological choices for or against communism, or for or against constitutional democracy. The most important ideological choice, in fact, has been the choice against the United States as a political, social, and cultural model for other Western societies. The successor generation has not, in general, had occasion to gain direct and immediate understanding of the alien character of the Soviet Union and its fundamental hostility to the West. In fact, instead of respecting the genuine differences between the Soviet system and the Western world, a majority of young people on both sides of the Atlantic have withdrawn into a parochial concern with the problems of their own society.

Such parochialism is dangerous in a democracy, where popular errors of judgment are reflected in the results of elections and in the options of elected leaders. If the perception that the Soviet Union was just another great power and that U.S.-Soviet tension could be relieved if the West changed its policies was correct, the danger would be manageable. The problem is that the perception is wrong, and even if it were not wholly wrong, it would certainly be dangerous to act as if it were true, as the West German government did under Brandt and, to a lesser degree, under Schmidt and Kohl. The fact is, as Robert Conquest has pointed out, "that the Soviet leaders are not just reasonable men who chance to hold certain views, but men totally determined by their Marxist-Leninist attitudes . . . that concessions made to them will not buy goodwill, and that weakness will be exploited by expansionism."[33]

If, then, the Soviet Union remains an alien element on the European scene, however, the ideas of a symmetry of East and West and the possibility of a "Europeanization" of Europe become untenable. The ultimate interest of Europe, whether East or West, is, on this view, the ultimate end of the Soviet empire. Only then will there be a genuine chance of a world order of stability and peace. There is no chance of this interest being achieved in the near future.[34] The secondary interest of Europe, therefore, is to maintain such peace and security as is possible as long as the Soviet Union exists. This interest is in all essentials identical for the United States and the West European allies and indeed for the East Europeans as well, since a weakened, defeated, or intimidated West will no longer be for them even a symbolic counterweight to or escape from Soviet control, and the incentive for the

Soviets to treat Eastern Europeans slightly better to gain political and financial credit in the West will be lost. Moreover, as Russian and East European dissidents often point out, there can be no separation of peace and human rights:

> There are 400 million people in the East whose freedom was stolen from them and whose existence is miserable. It so happens that peace is impossible while they remain enslaved, and only with them (not with their executioners) should you work to secure real peace in our world.[35]

States that respect human rights are, for sociological, psychological, and political reasons, more peaceable than totalitarian dictatorships. Contrary to the ideology of Europe, that new wisdom of the West, therefore, the peace that Western Europe has enjoyed since 1945 is a function of restraint, not appeasement, of the Soviet Union.

If that restraint is to continue, military preparedness and a defense posture sufficiently credible to be a deterrent to the enemy (the Soviet Union) and reassuring to friends (the peoples of the Western Alliance and the subject peoples of Eastern Europe, fulfillment of whose hopes is bound up with the fate of the West) are required. The ways and means of establishing and maintaining such deterrence and the relative merits of improved conventional, modernized theater-nuclear, and American strategic nuclear weapons should be debated. It is more important, however, to maintain the essential distinctions between constitutional democracy and totalitarian rule and between the enlightened solution of political problems by the use of reason and the suppression of dissent and criticism by the use of force. By doing so, one is not making debate with critics of this view, including the believers in the ideology of European identity, more difficult. On the contrary, the debate will benefit from more honesty on both sides. Those who, because of ideological commitment, wishful thinking, misconceived moralism, or a sentimentally based disinclination to face facts, deny that peace, in the context of East-West relations, is preserved primarily by the political and defensive will of Western countries or who, influenced by older, conservative arguments, maintain that there is a correspondence between the two superpowers will not change their minds just because we, their critics, assure them that we respect their good will and share their commitment to peace. Such assurances merely add to the confusion.

To summarize, the ideology of a European identity is a mixture of basically incompatible elements: neo-Marxist anticapitalist arguments and older Gaullist and conservative arguments for European independence—

arguments closely related to the conservative world-order thinking of Kennan, Liska, Hedley Bull, and others. In this chapter my primary purpose has been to point out the fallacies of the ideology and to show not only that it fails to take into consideration some important facts, but also that, if adopted as a guideline for policy, it could have dire consequences for the Europe it pretends to support.

9

ELEVEN NEUTRALIST PROPOSITIONS

Changes in the national and security policies of West German parties and governments, changes in the arguments used by opponents of NATO and of nuclear or conventional deterrence, beliefs and illusions about peace, authority, morality, the Soviet threat, and the conditions of survival of constitutional democracy in Western Europe are all elements that must be considered in any evaluation not merely of the peace movement and the overt agitation against NATO and the United States but of the entire drift and content of academic and journalistic debate on the security and the domestic political system of the Federal Republic and on the problem of national division. In the preceding chapters, I have touched on all these factors. In this chapter I summarize the ideology of the peace movement and its intellectual sympathizers in eleven propositions that, I think, express the core of their beliefs. These propositions fall into three groups: general philosophical principles; theories and assertions about the nature of the East-West conflict; and beliefs about how to achieve the desired goals. I discuss these groups in order.

GENERAL PHILOSOPHICAL PRINCIPLES

At the root of the neo-pacifist argument is an assumption that is so widely held that it may seem incorrect to consider it to be specific to the peace movement. However, the assumption cannot be ignored since in the new pacifism it is part of a moral argument whose validity is held to be self-evident, and it is precisely these allegedly self-evident qualities that I wish to examine. This first proposition can be formulated as follows:

> 1. Physical survival is the highest good. Any attitude or policy that is believed to threaten or can be presented as threatening this good is morally objectionable.

That this is, in fact, a proposition to which those who describe themselves as part of the peace movement adhere is abundantly evident from the rhetoric of their demonstrations, the language of their posters and proclamations, and the titles of such characteristic publications of the peace movement as the anthology *Friedenszeichen — Lebenszeichen* (Signs of peace — signs of life).[1] It is also clear from the use by the peace movement and the Greens of symbols of organic growth and fertility that evoke a favorable response in virtually everyone. However, the idea that physical survival is the highest good has been adhered to, to some extent, by all significant political forces that have played a role in the West since the secularization of the European mind was completed in the nineteenth century. It implies that it is the task of individuals and governments to secure the material means of life, to guarantee as far as possible the survival of citizens, and to undertake no act that might threaten that survival.

It should be borne in mind that the notion that ensuring physical survival is the chief task of governments was not part of classical European thought, at least not until the eighteenth century. The classical tradition was well aware of the danger of making any single value, like survival, the absolute standard of all political action. More important, the classical tradition knew that physical survival was not guaranteed simply by being made infinite in importance, but that it was sometimes necessary to put other values, honor, for example, first, in order to secure not only honor, but survival as well. However, this notion was a logical consequence of the disappearance of the belief in an immortal soul whose salvation depended in greater or lesser part on the voluntary actions of the individual.[2] Given the universal acceptance in the modern West of physical survival as the highest goal, disagreement arises chiefly over the means to this end. The importance of this proposition for my present purpose is the moral value imputed to it. A possible position might be that physical survival is in fact the highest possible good (if only because it is universally held to be so), but this conclusion does not in and of itself justify the importance attributed to physical survival. Or one might be neutral as to the moral value of physical survival and thus make no *a priori* moral judgment of policies that might, in theory or in fact, threaten the survival of oneself or others. One might also apply other criteria in judging such policies—whether they promote liberty or equality, for example. The peace movement, however, perceives survival as a moral necessity; anyone or anything that can be presented as threatening survival is ipso facto considered immoral, and one is morally obliged to oppose such a person or policy.

The difference between the peace movement's belief in the ultimate value of survival and the general belief in it characteristic of modern societies lies in how survival is perceived and the means used to ensure it. Paradoxically, it seems that the pursuit of other goals, such as freedom, can guarantee survival under better conditions than the single-minded pursuit of survival at any cost. "Better red than dead" in practice often means "red as well as dead," but the logical course to follow is "neither red nor dead." This, however, may require that physical survival be put aside as the only objective in a time of emergency. As Vladimir Bukovsky puts it, "Peace has never been preserved by a hysterical desire to survive at any price." To quote Sidney Hook's statement of his moral beliefs:

> It is better to be a live jackal than a dead lion—for jackals, not men. Men with the moral courage to fight intelligently for freedom have the best prospects of avoiding the fate of jackals as well as lions. Survival is not the be-all and end-all of a life worthy of man. Sometimes the worst thing we can know of a man is that he has survived. Those that say life is worth living at any cost have already written for themselves an epitaph of infamy, for there is no cause and no person they will not betray in order to survive. Man's vocation should rather be the use of the arts of intelligence in behalf of human freedom.[3]

The second proposition is almost as basic as the first and is subject to some of the same logical considerations:

2. Peace is the highest political good; any attitude or policy that is believed to threaten it is morally objectionable, and those proposing such a policy are wicked.

This proposition, like the preceding one, consists of an assertion and a moral qualification. The assertion is clearly in line with the main thrust of Western political thought since the late sixteenth century, as I have shown in Chapter 5; in particular, it is consistent with the ideas for a rational, per-

petual peace propounded by Kant and other philosophers. The moral qualification that peace is necessarily the highest political good, however, stems
rather from a confusion of the Christian tradition of a "peace that passeth all
understanding" as a grace of God with a possible condition of society achievable by political action. The moralized definition of peace was a constant
undercurrent in millenarian and other heretical and marginal movements
throughout the Christian era. In the nuclear age, however, it has gained unprecedented public acceptance and has become inextricably intertwined
with the first proposition, that physical survival is the highest good and that
policies that threaten, or seem to threaten, survival are morally objectionable. If physical survival is held to be the highest good, and nuclear war is
seen as an ultimate disaster that, if it were ever to occur, would, in fact,
threaten the survival of all human life, the dramatic popular response of the
peace movement to what it believes to be the increased chances of nuclear
war is perfectly understandable.

THE NEUTRALIST SYNDROME:
OPPOSITION TO CURRENT POLICIES

The next eight propositions imply a certain view of East-West relations, of the
Soviet Union, of the likely causes of conflict in Europe, and of the constitutional democratic system itself. In combination with the ideas of propositions 1 and 2, they provide the premises of the agitation of the peace movement and of the arguments of its academic supporters and sympathizers.

The first three of these address the question of what the West, especially
Western Europe, should do to achieve or to keep peace. The first two concern
the nature and intentions of the Soviet Union. The third is a claim about
what causes wars. They are closely related, and the first can be stated as
follows:

3. The Soviet Union, whatever the qualities of its regime, is not an
aggressive power and does not seek to dominate Western Europe.

The evidence offered for this proposition consists of statements by
Soviet leaders to the effect that the Soviet Union is a peace-loving state, that
it is not conducting an arms buildup, and that its foreign relations are based
on principles of mutual respect and noninterference. The peace movement's
refusal to examine these statements closely to determine their actual meaning contrasts strangely with its determination not to accept at face value the

statements by Western leaders that they neither want war nor seek to destroy the Soviet Union by force and that the purpose of Western arms is deterrence and, if necessary, defense, but never attack.

The following proposition, which is often advanced in the same breath as proposition 3 in arguments against the need for Western defense efforts, is in fact somewhat contradictory:

4. The U.S.-Soviet struggle is not a fight between constitutional democracy and totalitarian tyranny. It is simply a struggle between two structurally similar and morally equivalent great powers for the territory and resources of the rest of the world.

To say that the Soviet Union is not a threat to Western Europe, and then to say that the U.S.-Soviet struggle is a fight for power and influence in the world, is a contradiction since Western Europe is presumably one of the stakes in this fight. Yet both propositions are frequently advanced as evidence that there is no need to worry about Soviet capabilities or intentions. In fact, this contradiction is less important than what the two propositions together reveal about the assumptions and logic of those who believe them.

The next proposition we have encountered before, mainly in Chapter 4. Combined with the two preceding propositions, it provides what its adherents think is a decisive argument against Western defense and for unilateral disarmament:

5. The very existence of nuclear arms and, to a lesser extent, conventional arms is inevitably a source of tension, ultimately leading to war.

All three propositions, if true, would absolve West Europeans from doing more to ensure their defense and from thinking seriously about the value and potential of their own political system as compared with that of the Soviet Union. If the Soviet Union is no direct threat, and, in fact, feels threatened itself by NATO and the United States, then propositions 3–5 indicate that the way to reduce tension is for the West to disarm. The effect of Western disarmament would be to encourage the Soviet Union to take similar steps, thus initiating a process of progressive, mutual disarmament. This is, in fact, the course suggested by the U.S. Catholic bishops in their pastoral letter on nuclear arms and peace, "The Challenge of Peace."[4] The argument, however, ignores the fact that the United States did, in fact, reduce the size of its nuclear arsenal and its conventional forces, both absolutely and relative to Soviet forces, in the years 1969–1979. These steps by the United States had no perceptible influence on the rate or nature of the Soviet arms buildup, which, by the mid-1980s, had been going on at a very steady rate, both in nuclear and in conventional forces, for some twenty years. The so-called "arms race," in fact, turns out on closer inspection to be a very one-sided race, in which one side, the United States, was "ambling back," as Albert Wohlstetter put it, while the other, the Soviet Union, was "racing forward." The Soviets, who in the early 1960s were clearly weaker than the United States, insofar as comparisons could be made between very dissimilar systems, force structures, and operational doctrines, were twenty years later just as arguably equal or superior.[5]

One might think that those who accept proposition 3 would have some difficulty in explaining this considerable Soviet arms buildup. Some, in fact, deny that it has occurred and use extremely specious means of counting men, weapons, and warheads to make their case. Others argue that the many threats facing the Soviets in the world justify the buildup. These threats are supposed to come primarily from the United States and to a lesser extent from China or from NATO. Yet if the United States were really such a threat to the Soviets, why then did the Americans not attack when they were superior, as all admit they were until the mid-1960s at least? The reason can only be that the United States is not really that much of a threat or as aggressive as the peace movement claims. But if the United States is perhaps not as aggressive or threatening as all that, why, then, the Soviet buildup?

At this point in the argument, psychological factors are usually introduced: the Soviets are by nature paranoid, secretive, and mistrustful of foreigners, and Russian history is full of invasions, oppression, and violence. While we in the West might think Soviet armaments a sign of insufficiently peaceable intent, says the peace movement, they are actually only a sign of insecurity. Moreover, the mere fact that the United States has never directly attacked the Soviet Union does not mean that many Americans, especially in the Reagan administration, would not like to, and the Soviets are justifiably worried by the hard-liners in Washington.

Proposition 4, that the U.S.-Soviet struggle is a fight for power and not a confrontation of democracy and totalitarianism, is often advanced to support the argument that the Soviets feel threatened, but are not themselves a threat to the West. The peace movement knows that it is important to claim that the Soviet Union is not a totalitarian dictatorship and not bent on a drive for global hegemony if its criticism of Western defense is to be credible. However, it is not entirely clear why the Soviet Union would be less dangerous if it were only an ordinary great power bent on protecting and expanding its interests in competition with the United States. George Kennan, for example, makes a great deal of his belief that Soviet leaders have not believed in the principles of Marxism-Leninism for a long time and that they are basically frightened old men who simply want to maintain their empire undisturbed. Yet the sufferings of Afghan villagers and Polish democrats are no less real, whatever the motivations of their oppressors. The assertion that the Soviets are no threat because the Soviet Union is not driven by Marxism-Leninism is incoherent. The point is that the Soviets are doing certain things at home and abroad; whether they are doing them because they are afraid or because they are arrogant and aggressive is less important than the actions themselves and what they tell us about what to expect if Soviet power should continue to grow. We live in a dangerous world, and on the principle of better safe than sorry one might reasonably argue that even a defensive or nonideological Soviet Union can and ought to be resisted. On the other hand, the broad consensus of reputable Soviet specialists in the West is that while the regime has certainly become somewhat less harsh since the days of Stalin, nothing fundamental has changed. Marxist-Leninist ideology and a simple drive for power are inextricably intertwined in Soviet domestic and foreign policy. Western Europe, therefore, should not rely on the hopes of George Kennan or of the peace movement as a guide for policy, but should instead improve its defenses and move toward greater political unity "as the essential ingredient of a new and viable world order."[6]

What proposition 4 basically says is that since the peace movement cannot or does not want to believe in the reality of totalitarianism, its adherents will simply assume that the Soviets are rather like people in the West and will let us, that is, the West, exist if the West lets them exist. The idea that the Soviet Union might be a very different phenomenon from a Western constitutional democracy and that in fact its ideology is such that it is unable and unwilling to concede an equal right of existence to constitutional democracies is simply too complicated for most in the peace movement to grasp. When they are presented with that idea, they do not argue against it, but instead denounce its supporters as fascists and warmongers. It means, however, that the East-West struggle, the cold war, is not only not over, but that it will go on for a very long time yet and that the West European nations, being constitutional democracies, are directly involved in that struggle. The peace movement's alienation from the democratic system (proposition 10, below), its refusal to accept the possibility that the Soviet Union might be totalitarian and expansionist (propositions 3 and 4), and its simplistic belief that more weapons mean more chance of war (proposition 5) add up to a monumental failure of political imagination. Whether that failure is due to inadequate education, psychological immaturity, or a lack of experience is another matter that I shall not discuss here.

Given the belief that arms, not men, cause war, the attempts of NATO to secure the deterrent on the Central Front by modernizing INF and improving conventional preparedness have naturally been greeted with hostility:

6. The desire of political and military leaders of NATO to place more arms in Central Europe is both irrational and immoral.

It is clearly irrational to want more arms if, as the peace movement claims, there is no Soviet threat and Western defenses are in any case strong enough already, and it is immoral since, according to proposition 5, more arms automatically increase the risk of war. If, however, the Soviets and their Warsaw Pact satellites have become too superior in conventional weapons and INF in Europe, the Western deterrent, based on the doctrine of flexible response, is in danger of losing its credibility, which depends on the perceived will of SACEUR (Supreme Allied Commander Europe) to request, and of the U.S. president to order, first use of INF to avert conventional defeat. Soviet nuclear superiority in Europe, as well as the Soviet strategic threat to the U.S. homeland, might well make such a decision impossible, leaving no option but surrender. It was precisely to restore flexibility to the doctrine of flexible response that SACEUR in 1982 began calling for increased conventional defense in Europe and presented the so-called FOFA (Follow-On Forces Attack) concept, which involves retaliation with conventional, precision-guided munitions against enemy troop concentrations, communications centers and choke-points, airfields, and other military installations behind the front lines. Unlike earlier NATO operational doctrines, which did not foresee striking behind enemy lines, FOFA is a threat not merely to enemy troops in action but to the preparations for an attack. It was adopted as part of NATO's declared strategy of flexible response in late 1984 on the explicit grounds that it would improve deterrence by making an attack more dangerous and difficult.[7] If deterrence is improved, war is less likely.

The peace movement's opposition to Western defense, however, is based not only on a denial of the need for such defense, but on a denial of its rationale even if there were an attack:

7. Even if the Soviet Union did attack the West, it would be immoral to use force to oppose such an attack, for the reasons stated in propositions 1 and 2.

This assertion is not shared by all Greens or all peace activists since some support ideas of "civilian" or "alternative" defense such as those outlined in

Chapter 4. All agree, however, that nuclear defense is meaningless and must never be contemplated. According to the logic of the peace movement, this leads to the demand that the means of nuclear defense must be removed. From the early 1950s to the mid-1960s, NATO strategy relied more or less overtly on the threat of massive nuclear retaliation by U.S. strategic forces. The growth of the Soviet nuclear arsenal and of Soviet retaliatory capabilities made massive retaliation increasingly less credible. After much debate, the concept of flexible response was adopted by NATO in 1967.[8] Since that time, the principle of Western deterrence has been that Soviet attack is deterred above all by uncertainty as to the Western response: nuclear war is so terrible that no Soviet planner would recommend an attack that might bring on nuclear retaliation. Both the peace movement and the West German and other NATO governments condemn and fear nuclear war; the difference lies in their evaluation of the role of a nuclear threat that "one is not, and one should not be, prepared to implement," as Henry Kissinger said in 1961.[9] To the peace movement, the very existence of nuclear weapons is as morally evil as their use would be; to NATO officials, the existence of the Western nuclear deterrent makes use of nuclear weapons by any nation, including the Soviet Union, less likely.

If the peace movement believed in the existence of a Soviet threat, its spokesmen might be more inclined to agree that an inadequate, or even an adequate, conventional defense might be likely to invite a Soviet attack and that, if the attack were not immediately successful, the temptation for the Soviets to use nuclear weapons if the West had no nuclear deterrent would be overwhelming. However, they usually advance some argument based on propositions 3–5 in the attempt to prove that the only threat of nuclear war is that posed by Western attempts to strengthen deterrence. Even adherents of alternative territorial defense schemes, such as those discussed in Chapter 4 and practiced in Austria and Switzerland, who view the Soviet threat seriously, do not recognize that such schemes are unlikely to deter the Soviet Union and would moreover require a degree of militarization of West German society that is entirely incompatible with the antimilitary and antiauthoritarian outlook of the peace movement and of younger West Germans generally.

In propositions 8 and 9, the political arguments against the need for defense (propositions 3–5), and the moral arguments against defense with nuclear weapons (propositions 6–7), are developed into a criticism of the United States as chiefly responsible for the increase in East-West tension.

8. In its attempt to compel West Europeans to accept more arms, the United States is behaving just like the Soviet Union in Eastern Europe,

imposing its colonial hegemony without regard for the interests of the inhabitants.

The idea that Western Europe, and West Germany in particular, is some sort of U.S. colony that the Americans are defending only to serve some obscure strategic purpose of their own or to serve their economic interests is not new to the 1980s. It was popular among both socialists and some conservatives in Western Europe in the 1940s and became virtually the reigning orthodoxy of the French left in the 1950s and 1960s. In West Germany, it had few supporters outside the extreme left until the 1970s; even during the Vietnam war years anti-American protest was not generally directed against alleged U.S. hegemony in West Germany itself. In the mid-1970s, however, both the left and the much smaller right began to accuse the United States of being an occupying power in Germany just like the Soviet Union and to attack the West German government for being excessively compliant and obedient to U.S. interests. The influential weeklies, *Stern* and *Der Spiegel*, began arguing that West and East Germans and, in particular, the West and East German governments had common interests different from those of the United States and the Soviet Union. Almost invariably, U.S. policies and interests were criticized, while Soviet interests were generally respected. The arguments of propositions 3–5 and 8 became increasingly popular, reaching a high point in Günter Grass's denunciation of the Bonn government for its "weak servility" in allowing the United States to deploy the Pershing IIs in West Germany.[10] As explained in Chapter 3, a certain rehabilitation of German nationalism and real or alleged national characteristics took place also, not, as one would have expected, on the right, but primarily on the left. Frequently, as in the writings of Peter Brandt or Helmut Diwald, it seemed as though these neo-nationalists viewed the Soviet Union, despite its oppressive regime, with more sympathy and understanding than they viewed the United States. Educated professionals, including academics, who were by no means Marxists or otherwise radically opposed to constitutional democracy, asserted that there was really "no difference" between Soviet and American society, that Americans were just as "oppressed" by their "social structures" as the Soviets, and that racial and other discrimination and poverty in the United States was somehow equivalent to or even worse than political oppression in the USSR. The greater degree of social discrimination and poverty and the regular occurrence of shortages, which are a result of the economic system in the Soviet Union, were ignored and perhaps even unknown.

It does not seem as though the predicament of Eastern Europe, and in particular the events in Poland since 1980, has had any lasting influence on this trend of opinion. In fact, when martial law was imposed on Poland in

December 1981, socialist politicians in West Germany and Scandinavia justified the oppression on the grounds that Solidarity, a workers' movement, had made unreasonable demands on a political system that ought not to have to live up to such demands. Such cynical disregard, even contempt, for the true aspirations of East Europeans had not, I think, been heard before from representatives of the mainstream West European left, which appeared more concerned for the security of the Soviet Union than for that of the democratic countries of the West.

The next proposition follows logically from the preceding:

9. Since the Soviet Union is a European power, it has a legitimate security interest in Eastern Europe and shares a commitment to peace with Western Europe that U.S. policies now threaten. To this extent, American behavior is actually more dangerous than Soviet behavior.

The reasons for the belief in a common interest in peace of the Soviet Union and Western Europe are psychological and political in nature. Some people, perhaps a majority of the Greens, may actually believe that the Soviet Union simply wishes to exist as it is, without expanding its influence (proposition 3) and that any improvements in NATO defenses are therefore dangerous and ought to be rejected. Others, and here I would place the SPD opponents of the double-track decision, like Oskar Lafontaine, Egon Bahr, and Erhard Eppler, and most professional academics and commentators, may have other motives, for example, what Hans-Peter Schwarz defines simply as "an inclination, in view of the decline of American power, to accommodate oneself to the new lord and master."[11] Perhaps a combination of various impulses is the most common reason for the prevalence of opinions based on proposition 9: on the one hand, a realistic view of Western weakness and a more or less conscious desire to avoid trouble; on the other, a gradual loss of a sense of why constitutional democracy might be threatened and, if it is, why it might be worth defending.

Those who distrust the United States and its policies and refuse to believe that the East-West conflict is not just a struggle for power and influence but an unavoidable ordeal with serious implications for citizens of a democratic state also tend to disregard the achievements and advantages of constitutional democracy and hence to believe that their own society is not worth defending. In a poll taken in 1982 asking citizens of various democratic countries whether they were proud of their country and whether they were willing to fight to defend it, the affirmative response in the United States was 95 percent to the first, and 71 percent to the second question, whereas in West Germany it was 59 and 35 percent, respectively.[12] These figures are evidence of considerable alienation from the West German political system and society. Within the ranks of the Greens and the peace movement and among their supporters, this alienation is often expressed as follows:

10. The Western political and social system does not embody the values of life and peace.

If this is accepted, action against Western governments and their policies is legitimated by precisely the moral arguments of the first two propositions. The proposition is essentially a product of the anticonstitutional and anti-institutional radicalism of the 1960s, but whereas that radicalism was usually charged with an optimistic belief that revolutionary change in the desired direction was inevitable, the more recent wave of opposition to institutions and official policies includes a large measure of pessimism and is thus reminiscent of the radicalism of the Weimar Republic.[13]

The Greens are known more for what they are against than for what they hope to achieve, as their "nonnegotiable demands" on any negotiating point indicate. Nuclear energy, a military deterrent based on nuclear weapons, environmental pollution, and increased consumption and mechanization are all evils to be combated, but the vision of the "Green" society of "mass democratic involvement" is vague in the extreme. The utopian dreams of the 1960s, which were at least specific, seem to have been replaced by resentment of current trends and policies because they are threatening—but threatening to what? The Green program is vague if only because the moral premises and purposes of the movements themselves are vague. If one does not know clearly what one values enough to fight for, it is also hard to judge when it is threatened, or by what.[14]

The lack of faith in Western constitutional democracy and in its decisionmaking institutions is not unique to West Germany, but it has been a constant characteristic of radicalism there since the 1960s, though, as I have said, the pessimism of the 1980s marks something of a new mood. The notion of Western intellectuals that their own governments are more of an immediate danger to peace and sanity than any possible enemy is at least as old as the cold war. By the 1980s, however, this notion had grown in influence, strengthened by the fears of economic crisis and a general sense of being at the "end of history," having no future, and being incapable of daring to plan ahead.[15] The question is whether this fear of the future is based on an objective evaluation of factual dangers, so that elimination of those dangers might lead to a more optimistic or calm attitude, or whether the evaluation is so subjective that no conceivable change in conditions could assuage the fears. I think the political psychology of the leaders of the Greens and of the peace movement makes the latter case more likely. The majority of these leaders are professional intellectuals: teachers, journalists, psychologists, and social workers, committed to the therapeutic view of society and of perceived social ills. Their self-perception and legitimacy as publicly respected commentators and analysts of social and political problems depend on their ability to justify the need for continual attack on what is, in the name of what ought to be. If a rational debate could be held on the dangers alleged by the peace movement to exist, real, if imperfect, solutions might be proposed and even implemented, and the movement might be deprived of its raison d'être. The movement is a cultural force with considerable popularity—virtually a subculture with its own language, behavior patterns, and dress codes and its own mutual intimacy, and it has no interest in finding such solutions. Official spokesmen, however sympathetic, therefore have great difficulty in making contact with those committed to the worldview and the strategies of the peace movement. The movement's apocalyptic belief in the imminence of nuclear war and in the aggressive intentions of Western governments means that professions of good will and commitment to peace by outsiders, especially by representatives of those governments, are simply ignored or denounced as dishonest attempts at camouflage.

The fact is that a large proportion of the successor generation, from which the Greens and the peace movement draw their support, does not share the values and beliefs on which the West German political system and society were built.[16] This group, which comprised about 20 percent of the population in the mid-1980s, has hopes, beliefs, and expectations that sociologists have called "postmaterialist." Postmaterialists value collectivism over individualism, equality over liberty, and environmental quality over economic growth. On the crucial issue of peace, they believe, as we have seen, that there is no need for continual defensive efforts, for one or more of three reasons: either because there is no threat, or because defense is immoral, or because they do not think their own society worthy of defense. It may be, as some have argued, that consistently held postmaterialist values are incompatible with the long-term survival of modern industrial societies and of constitutional democracy.[17] However, even if postmaterialism were not as dangerous as all that, it is nevertheless clear that postmaterialism in the 1980s in West Germany was premature: the conditions of political survival and economic prosperity that prevailed from 1945 onward had not changed, and if postmaterialist attitudes were to influence policy in any decisive way, the result might well be the destruction, rather than the peaceful transformation, of society.

As Günther Gillessen, an editor of the *Frankfurter Allgemeine Zeitung*, puts it:

> The Federal Republic was not founded for the purpose of producing wealth and a comfortable life for its citizens. It was designed as

a structure of defense for a part of the nation that was allowed to build this structure for itself. The foundation implied a mutual commitment to an association of solidarity in the face of the dangers facing each individual. In the Atlantic Association, this process was repeated on the national level. There is no security of possession or use of basic rights and liberties without individual sacrifice for the common good . . . Refusal of sacrifice and parasitic appropriation of the results of the work of others have for long been gnawing away at the bonds of community that maintain the state. The interpretation of those bonds has deteriorated: instead of a threatened community of danger, we had, first the welfare state, then the provident state of total social care. Such a state commands no loyalties, only claims at the expense of others.[18]

Remarks of this kind are a source of fear and worry among so-called progressive political scientists and others who share the postmaterialist outlook and who seem to fear that Gillessen and Schelsky and those who think like them are using a nonexistent danger, namely the Soviet threat, to argue the need for an authoritarian state. Richard Saage, Jürgen Habermas, and others, who have routinely overestimated the power and influence of neoconservative thought in West Germany since the mid-1970s, assert that the intention of such reactionary arguments is to discredit the "Enlightenment," as interpreted by Habermas, and to oppose progress toward postmaterialist goals, namely more economic equality, an end to corporate capitalism and environmental pollution, and, finally, the "rule-free dialogue" and "communicative competence" that, for Habermas, are the characteristics of a truly democratic society.[19] The notion that there might be some real reason to worry about social cohesion and the loyalty of younger generations, alienated as a result of bad education and fifteen years of "critical" social analysis, is wholly foreign to the intellectual postmaterialists. Because they do not accept the reality of any outside threat, except that posed by American policies and reactionary domestic forces, they are not prepared to grant that the West German state must be prepared to defend itself, much less the necessity for any type of military deterrent.

THE WORLD AS IT SHOULD BE

The ten propositions are based on a worldview in which there are no political conflicts except those caused by the dynamics of capitalism or by the momentum of the arms race; in which a quiescent and defensive Soviet Union is being threatened by new American weapons and strategies that constitute an imminent danger of war; in which constitutional democracy as it exists is illegitimate or at best grossly imperfect, and in neither case worth defending (certainly not in the way proposed by NATO). Therefore, it is the task of all truly democratic and peace-loving forces to oppose those weapons and strategies, reassure the Soviets, and proceed to the construction of a new and better world.

The details of this effort are, as I have said, rarely elaborated since the Greens, the peace movement, and the politically committed younger generation are characteristically against a great number of things, specific and general, but not in favor of anything very concrete. However, their aspirations can perhaps be described somewhat as follows:

11. Ultimately, Europe, both East and West, must free itself of both superpowers. This will release energy and resources for the solution of the world's real problems: hunger, poverty, economic inequality, and environmental pollution.

The beliefs that if only the arms race could be ended, vast amounts of money and resources will suddenly become available and that there are only four problems to be solved are the final illusion of these unpolitical or anti-political new social movements. Perhaps because they have never been exposed to any very serious threats to their survival and material well-being, postmaterialists, including the peace movement, do not understand the seriousness of political conflicts, such as that between constitutional democracy and totalitarian rule. Postmaterialism is by nature apolitical, but its potential consequences, for social cohesion, political stability, and defense, are highly political indeed.

The postmaterialists' prescription for achieving the world they want is, ultimately, unrealistic as well as undesirable. It is unrealistic, first, because the mere listing of problems is not the same as a serious proposal for their solution. The belief that poverty in the Third World is chiefly, or even primarily, a result of exploitation by industrial capitalism disregards both the history of industrial capitalism and the social structure, culture, and political problems of Third World countries themselves. Only thorough study in a spirit of hard-headed realism, and not misplaced indignation, can help to solve the problems that offend conservatives no less than they do postmaterialists. It is unrealistic, second, because the unpolitical men and women of the new movements deny the usefulness of history and political experience, except such history as is or can be made ideologically useful to their cause. Finally, it is undesirable because it so totally lacks the dimension of liberty, either individual or collective. Maybe the postmaterialists are not worried about threats to their freedom because it has always been so well protected that no threats were apparent. If so, one must again deplore their lack of historical and political awareness, for personal freedom is threatened in many places and was in fact taken away from Germans from 1933 to 1945. The absence of concern for the collective freedom of their society and their country is equally alarming. Nowhere in the agitation of the peace movement or in the writings of its supporters does one find a serious understanding of the importance of the defense of free political institutions. This is ironic, since postmaterialists are supposed to be more concerned with values and the quality of life than ordinary "materialists." In fact, it seems that it is the materialists, including the "security conservatives" who loyally defend NATO and support Western defense, who have the greater sense of values and of the quality of life, and the postmaterialists who seem more concerned with the preservation of their own material prerogatives than with the preservation of the political order that makes freedom and economic growth possible.

It is, perhaps, this loss of a sense of why freedom is important that is the saddest feature of the new neutralism.

10

CONCLUSION

The first Pershing II missiles arrived in the Federal Republic in December 1983, and, as Walter Laqueur put it, "the sky did not fall."[1] Yet it would be incorrect and even hazardous to assume that since the beginning of 1984, the political health of the Alliance in general has been restored and, in particular, that the uncertainty over the direction of national and security policy and debate in West Germany has ended.

The first reason for continued apprehension is the scheduling of deployment itself. Deployment, in batches, of the 108 Pershing IIs reserved for West German territory is not supposed to be completed before the end of 1988. The SPD, the Greens, the peace movement, the influential leftist-liberal media, and other groups are bound to keep up the pressure on the government to make a formal request for a suspension or an interruption *sine die* of the deployment. If the SPD should return to power in the 1987 elections, it is indeed virtually certain that the party will make such a request, inasmuch as it is committed to halting and reversing deployment. The interest of the Soviet Union in promoting such a moratorium is, of course, evident, and it is almost inevitable that some proposal to this effect will be forthcoming from the Soviets long before deployment is complete. Pressure to comply with such a request on the governments of NATO countries that are receiving INF will be intense, not only from the Soviets, but from important domestic constituencies as well.

Second, the peace movement may have suffered a defeat in 1983, but it has certainly not lost the war against NATO. The widespread criticism of deterrence, of the U.S. government, and of the foreign and security policies of the Kohl government will continue. According to one well-informed analyst, the failure to stop deployment meant that a majority, perhaps as much as three-fourths, of the movement will cease taking an active part in its work. However, the remaining 25 percent or so will be committed activists who may see their only chance to fight against NATO defense efforts in direct action. This may take the form of obstructing troop movements and maneuvers, or it may escalate to outright attacks on U.S. personnel.[2] In 1984, there was at least one case of attempted obstruction of movements of U.S. troops in the strategically crucial Fulda area. Some of the terrorist organizations of the 1970s, the Red Army Fraction in West Germany, the Italian Red Brigades, and the French Action Directe, also resumed their activities in 1984, killing three high officials associated with NATO defense procurement in France and West Germany. While these terrorist actions were not on the same scale as those of the 1970s, they were much more overtly directed against NATO, and terrorist spokesmen openly proclaimed their purpose to be the defeat of NATO defense plans in the interests of the Soviet Union.

Direct and indirect Soviet support and exploitation of the peace movement is also likely to continue. There is some evidence that the Soviet Union may have provided as much as a billion dollars, mostly via East Germany or via Soviet-controlled companies in West Germany, to organizations within the peace movement dominated by Communists. While most of those who took part in peace movement activities in 1980–1983 were certainly not Communists, the latter played a disproportionate role in setting agendas, organizing demonstrations, and controlling the public posture of peace movement organizations. Very probably, the hard core of activists remaining after the falling away of the uncommitted is dominated by Communists as well. Though the DKP, the official West German communist party, only has some 25,000 members, even such a small number of highly motivated, disciplined, and committed individuals, backed by the resources of the Soviet Union, are more than sufficient to make life quite difficult for the government.

The third reason to avoid complacency is that, as a result of the peace movement and of the rising influence of the successor generation, the broad consensus on defense policy that included most of the SPD, the FDP, and the CDU-CSU, has been shattered. There is little hope that the SPD will ever return to the Atlanticist position of 1969–1982. The belief that security is best served by a combination of military preparedness and negotiations (the prescription of the Harmel Report of 1966), which was held strongly by Helmut Schmidt, has been replaced in the SPD by a deep division between a large majority of party leaders and activists highly critical of NATO, of U.S. security policies, and of nuclear deterrence; only a small minority continues to believe in the validity of the old policy.[3] The abandonment of the Atlanticist line by the SPD is, without question, the most dramatic and portentous development in West German politics since the inauguration of the Ostpolitik of the social-liberal coalition in 1969. It is true that even in 1969 there were radicals in the SPD influenced by the student movement who insisted that Ostpolitik was not enough and that the SPD should be less pro-American and pro-NATO, but, at least until the later 1970s, their influence was fairly marginal. During the 1970s, however, there took place a gradual radicalization of the party as a whole, as former leaders of the SPD youth organization rose to power within it. At the same time, the social base of the party was changing. The blue-collar working class was shrinking, and in its place the new class of white-collar bureaucrats, educators, civil servants, and academic intellectuals began to impose its values and outlook on the SPD. Its opinions were disproportionately postmaterialist; in fact the successor generation, characterized by postmaterialist values, was largely made up of the younger elements of the new class. In foreign and defense policy, the new class was far more likely to be anti-American and to be sympathetic to Soviet interests.

Until his resignation in 1982, Helmut Schmidt had been able to compel the loyalty of the Bundestag group and of the annual party congresses to the Atlanticist line and to a security policy based on the recommendations of the Harmel Report. In 1983, however, following the defeat of the SPD in the federal election of March 6, the Schmidt forces lost all control of party policy. The defeat of the SPD, and especially the success of the Greens, was seen by the new class as evidence of the bankruptcy of Atlanticism and of the need for a reorientation of SPD defense policy toward the positions of the peace movement. During 1983, Willy Brandt, the party chairman and elder statesman of the left wing of the SPD, reasserted the full control of the party that he had been obliged to share with Schmidt and with the now-retired leader of the Bundestag group, Herbert Wehner. This was amazing not only because of his age (70), but because his resignation as chancellor in the wake of the Guillaume spy scandal of 1974 had seemed permanently to discredit him as a strong party leader. He was strongly assisted in his recovery by Oskar Lafontaine, whom many saw as Brandt's heir; so rapid was Lafontaine's rise to prominence in 1983–1984, and so effective was his anti-American agitation in gaining support both in the party organization and among voters that some commentators by mid-1984 were speaking of a "Lafontainization" of the SPD.[4]

Brandt's emotional commitment to what he believes to be the cause of peace is intense. Even so, his own stature and idealism would not have been enough to give him direction of party policy had it not been for the devoted help of close aides and supporters who had been opposing Schmidt's Atlanticist line at least since 1976. Some of them were of the successor generation and shared its postmaterialist values and its tendency to believe the claims of peace researchers politically committed to opposing U.S. and NATO policies on the grounds that they were needless and dangerous since there was, in fact, no Soviet threat. Others, like Egon Bahr, belonged to the older group on the SPD left who had been neutralist in the 1950s and who had believed since the early 1960s that SPD policy should accommodate itself to the status quo in Europe and seek "change through rapprochement" with the Soviet Union and East Germany. It was a 1979 article by Bahr in *Die Zeit* that, more than any other single statement, turned influential West German opinion against the enhanced radiation warhead or "neutron bomb," which had been supported by Schmidt. In 1982, Bahr produced a proposal for a nuclear-free zone in Central Europe, which strongly resembled the Soviet-inspired Rapacki Plan of 1956–1957. The SPD at that time could not yet openly sponsor such a plan, so it was instead brought up at the "Scandilux" discussions (mentioned in Chapter 8), where Bahr had observer status, and presented by Swedish prime minister Olof Palme as a serious and original contribution to the discussion of peace in Europe. It was typical not only of the lack of realism and responsibility of the Scandilux discussions but of the strength of neutralism in the SPD itself that the immediate support by the Soviets of the proposal was seen not as a warning, but as an advantage. The notion that Soviet and West European political interests were compatible was no longer questioned by the majority of SPD leaders.

Bahr's attitude on the national issue is similarly difficult to reconcile with a sincere commitment to Western security as the precondition for the protection of the ultimate interests of all Germans and all Europeans, including those under Soviet rule. Most West Germans in the mid-1980s believed that the main political problem in Europe was East-West tension as such, which was expressed in, or even caused by, an "arms race" that could lead to war and the devastation of Germany. They no longer considered that the tension itself was in fact a result of the division of Germany (and of Europe) caused by the Soviet Union and maintained in its sole interest. Egon Bahr played a great part in bringing about this change of view in his role as a spokesman for Ostpolitik and for negotiations with the East European regimes. In the 1980s, he criticized support for Solidarity on the grounds that democratic movements in Eastern Europe were liable to irritate the Soviet Union and endanger the stability of the communist regimes, and since he also believed that the stability of those regimes was in the Western interest as well, Westerners should refrain from encouraging movements of resistance to them. When the former Czech socialist leader Jiri Pelikan told an SPD gathering in May 1983 that there can be no peace in Europe without national self-determination of peoples—a fundamental tenet of the East European resistance movements—Bahr exclaimed that anyone making such a statement was a disturber of the peace; the Germans had given up the right to self-determination in the interests of peace, and so should the East Europeans.[5] Similarly, when Secretary of State George Shultz stated at the opening of the Conference on Security and Disarmament in Europe in Stockholm in January 1984 that "the division of Europe is unacceptable" and a threat to peace, Bahr strongly objected. It is clear that the East Europeans, the Catholic church, and George Shultz do not share Bahr's and the present-day SPD's understanding of what peace in Europe means and how to achieve it. For them, peace based on accepting the division of Europe is at best tentative and always fragile, precisely because the West is faced with a threat from a state, the Soviet Union, that is by nature violent and aggressive in both its domestic policies and its foreign relations. For Bahr, the relation between the internal structure and character of the Soviet Union and its international behavior is unimportant. However, it is quite clear that peace is not simply the result of diplomatic treaties; the endurance of peace between states is at least as much a function of the character of those states as such. The argument that certain kinds of society are peaceful and are likely to respect peace in their foreign affairs and that others are not peaceful and not likely to respect international peace is a powerful and a logical one. It is a pity that it is so little understood in the SPD.

Bahr, whose example illustrates the dominant views of the SPD, simultaneously insists that Germans, including East Germans, should protect their interests, which are not those of the United States or the Soviet Union, and ignores the causes and consequences of national division. The appeal to an alleged German national interest different from the common interest of the West in restraining the Soviet Union, and even the appeal to patriotism, is deliberately made by those who want to blame the United States for the failure, in 1983, of negotiations for the control of INF deployments by both sides and who want to argue that American INF deployment represents an escalation of the arms race and a preparation for nuclear war in Europe. To summarize the position of those who now shape SPD policy, I can do no better than to quote one of the sharpest critics of the new line, Professor Gesine Schwan of Berlin, herself a Social Democrat of the old school:

> Why do so many Social Democratic activists close their eyes to these threats [to peace]? . . . Because their understanding of the Soviet Union is ambivalent. They respectively trivialize and dramatize Soviet policy, two attitudes that are not contradictory. Behind the superficial trivialization lies resignation and a deep fear of Soviet military power . . . Soviet political and economic weakness is pointed out only to serve as an argument for Soviet touchiness, so that the Polish struggle for freedom is denounced as both hopeless and a danger to peace . . .

Only those who close their eyes to the Soviet threat can depart
from the policy of the double decision as easily as the decisive elements of the SPD have done. Those who do so, moreover, can no
longer be overly concerned with the maintenance of Western
freedom . . .

The dynamic thrust in the shaping of SPD policy now comes
from Oskar Lafontaine, Erhard Eppler, and Egon Bahr. Their
common denominator is critical distance to the West, suspicion
verging on hostility toward the policy of the United States and the
promotion of nationalist resentments against the superpowers
and especially against America . . .

This recently developing shift is tending directly to make
German social democracy, founded in the name of freedom,
one of the most effective instruments of the Soviet policy
of domination.[6]

The growing distrust of American policies and fear of nuclear weapons,
a trend that is clear in the SPD, does, of course, have its perfectly understandable reasons. It is a fourth reason, closely related to the preceding, why
complacency regarding West Germany's role in the Western defense effort
after the beginning of INF deployment is misplaced. The continued dependence on nuclear weapons and on the threat of first use for deterrence has,
under conditions of global nuclear parity and Soviet Eurostrategic (theater
nuclear) superiority, alienated informed public opinion from that strategy
and those responsible for it. Using Michael Howard's felicitous distinction,
the Soviet Union may still be deterred, but the West European population is
less and less reassured, by the existing posture. Increasingly, the public fears
nuclear war

not . . . arising out of a Soviet attack on Western Europe, but
rather from some self-sustaining process of escalation . . . essentially caused by the whole apparatus of nuclear weapons in some
way "getting out of control" . . . It is therefore against the prospect
of nuclear war itself, rather than that of Soviet attack, that Europeans now require *reassurance*, and any measures taken to deal
with the latter that make the former seem more likely will continue to be deeply disruptive. The explanation that any measures
effective in deterring Soviet attack make nuclear war *less* likely is
no longer, for many Europeans, altogether persuasive.[7]

If Howard is right, and there is much evidence to show that he is, then
the West Europeans might be more reassured with a defense posture relying
more on conventional weapons and less explicitly on the threat of first use
of nuclear weapons. It has been objected, for example, by Carl Friedrich von

Weizsäcker, that increased reliance on conventional forces in Europe would make war more conceivable and therefore more likely. However, this objection rests on assumptions about Soviet doctrine and intentions that are necessarily unprovable. If Soviet operational doctrine reflects the notion, popular in the West, that once nuclear weapons of any size are used in a war, no further control is possible, and the result will be a total holocaust, then, indeed, eschewing first use and relying on conventional weapons will, in some sense, make a war in Europe less destructive and therefore more conceivable. But a war in Europe is not necessarily more likely because it is more conceivable. The fact is, first, that we cannot be sure what Soviet operational doctrine for war in Europe is; the evidence we do have can be taken to imply either a combined-arms approach, including tactical nuclear weapons from the outset, or reliance on conventional forces and chemical warfare. Second, the question of Soviet doctrine is in any case less important than the political will of the West to defend itself. The Soviets go to war only when the political circumstances, in their view, compel them to do so. An enfeebled, quarreling, neutralistic, and disorganized Western Europe might well, in some future crisis, constitute a circumstance inviting attack. A well-prepared, confident, realistic, and more united West, on the other hand, is not only the best overall deterrent in itself, it is the foundation of all deterrence.

To make Western Europe, and especially West Germany, better prepared, more confident, more realistic, and more committed to greater political unity in Europe, requires sophisticated leadership. It is not enough simply to rehearse the arguments for flexible response, the recommendations of the Harmel Report, or even the far more important argument, presented in this book, that the chief political problem for Europeans is not the threat of war as such, but the division of their continent effected and maintained in the interests of the Soviet Union. It is also not enough simply to follow public opinion if that opinion is ill-informed or dominated by dangerous and simplistic ideas, such as the idea that abandoning the threat of first use will automatically, without a compensating improvement in conventional forces, make war less likely.

The task of securing the freedom and independence of Western Europe, and thereby keeping alive the promise of freedom for Eastern Europe, is made harder by the breakdown of consensus, not only on how to accomplish this task, but even on whether the task is an appropriate one, in the political elite. This breakdown has, as we have seen, been stimulated by, and has itself in turn stimulated, a breakdown of popular consensus on security and defense matters in all West European countries, but primarily in West Germany. Not only are the policymakers in disagreement, but the public is no longer prepared to accept their policies without argument, even if they all agreed on what those policies should be.

By the mid-1980s, there seemed to be quite an extensive consensus in informed West European circles that increased conventional defense was indeed necessary, although few leaders were willing openly to recommend abandoning the threat of first use of nuclear weapons, such as was suggested by the "Gang of Four" (McGeorge Bundy, George Kennan, Robert McNamara, and Gerard Smith) in a *Foreign Affairs* article in 1982 and by Herman Kahn twenty years earlier.[8] Both the Gang of Four and Kahn qualified their recommendation; the former by making it contingent on an increase in conventional forces, and the latter by tying it to what he called "guaranteed second use." Both stressed that a no first use policy would cost more, not less, than the existing defense posture. These qualifications were largely ignored in Western Europe and West Germany in particular. The Gang of Four's article was widely praised by leading political commentators, but it was represented to the public as being primarily a moral condemnation of the nuclear arms race (which is barely touched on in the article) and of the first-use doctrine. It was strongly implied that these four former leading U.S. policymakers were primarily interested in accusing the Reagan administration of an arms buildup and of rejecting arms control, and this alleged fact was then taken to show that U.S. policy was dangerous and that the Europeans ought to oppose it. The example shows how serious contributions to the debate on policy at a high level are distorted and manipulated by media with a vested interest in certain policies and positions, and in particular how the West German media, in the early 1980s, seemed more concerned to find reasons for attacking the Reagan administration than to understand the reasons and the content of that administration's policy toward the Soviet Union.

The consensus on the need for conventional defense is nevertheless clear, and by the mid-1980s was manifested in several NATO decisions to increase conventional forces and improve their readiness. The FOFA concept of targeting rear-echelon enemy forces, communication centers and choke-points, airfields, and missile sites with accurate conventional warheads and air strikes, while opposed by those who think that a more credible conventional defense makes war more likely, was gaining ground among informed West Europeans, even in West Germany. With some luck and a political leadership not tempted by complacency in the wake of the first INF deployments, it seemed possible to achieve some combination of reassurance and deterrence for West Germany and Western Europe, at least in the short and medium term.

The challenge of establishing genuine West European defense cooperation and greater political unity, however, goes far beyond West Germany. Nevertheless, the West German response to it will be decisive. If the West German government continues its theoretical reliance on a deterrent posture (flexible response, including the threat of first use) criticized, and even feared, by a majority of citizens and moreover refuses to consider bold initiatives to restore public faith not only in the value of NATO (in general, this faith has not weakened seriously) but in NATO's ability to keep the peace without nuclear weapons, official policy will be increasingly opposed not just by a few activists but by broad sectors of the public, especially the growing post-materialist segment of the successor generation.

These people tend to see peace and survival as threatened by Western and chiefly American actions and, above all, by reliance on the nuclear de-terrent. What better purpose for statesmen and strategists on both sides of the Atlantic than to cooperate in the elaboration and execution of strategies that will guarantee peace and also attempt to gain the support of those whose fear (forgivable if ill-founded) and ignorance threaten not only peace but survival and liberty as well?

In the end, the consequences of the actions of the peace movement, of the "Lafontainization" of the SPD, and of anti-Americanism generally in West Germany may be determined less by the rise of postmaterialist values and the decline of faith in constitutional democracy than by the behavior and policies of the Soviet Union. Few will dare to predict them with confi-dence. Increased military power and the idea that the Soviet Union is a "security partner" in Europe (and not, rather, the adversary against whom security is maintained) have given the Soviets a leverage on Western policies they did not have in the 1960s. All that can be said with certainty is that Soviet efforts to divide the Alliance and to convince West Europeans that American policies are a threat to them will continue, as will the Soviet mili-tary buildup in all categories. The only counsel one can offer those who wish to guarantee the freedom of Western Europe and to uphold the principles of constitutional democracy is that they prepare for a long struggle not only against Soviet efforts to exert overt and subversive influence but also to eliminate the confusion and combat the ignorance of increasing numbers of their own fellow citizens.

NOTES

INTRODUCTION

1. Quoted by Uwe Nerlich, "Theatre Nuclear Forces in Europe," in Kenneth A. Myers, ed., *NATO—The Next Thirty Years* (Boulder, Colo.: Westview Press, 1980), 69. The best analysis of the problem is Karl-Peter Stratmann, *NATO-Strategies in der Krise* (Baden-Baden: Nomos, 1981). For further references, see the notes to Chapter 4.

2. The question of direct or indirect Soviet influence on and exploitation and control of Western peace movements is a vast subject beyond the scope of this study. The Soviet view of the movements is analyzed in Gerhard Wettig, *Die Funktion der westeuropäischen Friedensbewegung in sowjetischer Sicht*, Berichte des Bundesinstituts für ostwissenschaftliche und internationale Studien, 1983, no. 49. For a polemical analysis of the peace movements as assemblages of "useful idiots," see Vladimir Bukovsky, "The Peace Movement and the Soviet Union," *Commentary* (May 1982); reprinted in Francis Schaeffer, Vladimir Bukovsky, and James Hitchcock, *Who Is for Peace?* (Nashville, Tenn.: Thomas Nelson, 1983). For facts on and interpretation of the connections between the USSR and these movements, see chap. 6 of John Barron, *KGB Today: The Untold Story* (New York: Reader's Digest Press, 1983); Wynfred Joshua, "Soviet Manipulation of the European Peace Movement," *Strategic Review* 11, no. 1 (Winter 1983): 9–18; J. A. E. Vermaat, "Moscow Fronts and the European Peace Movement," *Problems of Communism* 31, no. 6 (November–December 1982): 43–56; and, specifically for the connections between communist organizations and the peace movement in West Germany, Gerd Langguth, *Protestbewegung: Entwicklung, Niedergang, Renaissance. Die Neue Linke seit 1968* (Cologne: Wissenschaft & Politik, 1983), 256–61. On the relationship of the SPD to such communist organizations and the peace movement, see Horst Niggemeier, "Wie stellt sich die

SPD ihre Abgrenzung gegenüber Kommunisten vor?" in Jürgen Maruhn and Manfred Wilke, eds., *Wohin treibt die SPD?* (Munich: Olzog, 1984), 87–97; and Jürgen Maruhn, "Sozialdemokratisches Selbstbewusstsein gegen schiefe Bündnisse," in ibid., 98–111.

3. See Paul Johnson, *Modern Times* (New York: Harper & Row, 1983), 577–87; and Robert Mayne, *Postwar* (London: Thames & Hudson, 1983). See also the portraits of Konrad Adenauer, Alcide De Gasperi, Robert Schuman, and others in Thomas Jansen and Dieter Mahncke, eds., *Persönlichkeiten der europäischen Integration* (Bonn: Europa Union, 1981).

4. Karl Dietrich Bracher, *Zeit der Ideologien* (Stuttgart: Deutsche Verlags-Anstalt, 1982), 349, with references; and Theodor Eschenburg, *Jahre der Besatzung, 1945–1949*, vol. 1 of *Geschichte der Bundesrepublik Deutschland* (Stuttgart: Deutsche Verlags-Anstalt, 1983), 424–28. For the principles of German neo-liberalism and the social market economy, see the entry "Marktwirtschaft, soziale," by Wolfgang Schmitz in *Katholisches Soziallexikon*, 2d ed. (Innsbruck: Tyrolia, 1980), cols. 1709–720, with full references.

5. Stephen F. Szabo, "Brandt's Children: The West German Successor Generation," *Washington Quarterly* 7, no. 1 (Winter 1984): 50–59, summarizes the author's detailed surveys, for which see Stephen F. Szabo, ed., *The Successor Generation: International Perspectives of Postwar Europeans* (London and Woburn, Mass.: Butterworths, 1983). The basic sociological clues to an interpretation of the phenomenon can be found in Daniel Bell, *The Cultural Contradictions of Capitalism*, 2d ed. (New York: Harper Colophon, 1978); and in Ronald Inglehart, *The Silent Revolution: Changing Values and Political Styles Among Western Publics* (Princeton, N.J.: Princeton University Press, 1977). In his important book on the new social movements, including the peace movement and the Greens, *Neue soziale Bewegungen* (Opladen: Westdeutscher Verlag, 1982), Karl- Werner Brand provides an overview and critique of various interpretations, including Bell's. Two detailed surveys of long-term changes in values, behavior, and attitudes toward important political institutions and policy issues are Heiner Meulemann, "Value Changes in West Germany, 1950–1980: Integrating the Empirical Evidence," *Social Science Information* 22 (1983): 777–800; and Heinz Rausch, "Politisches Bewusstsein und politische Einstellungen im Wandel," in Werner Weidenfeld, ed., *Die Identität der Deutschen* (Munich: Hanser, 1983), 119–53. They should be read along with the sociological interpretations of Helmut Schelsky, "Die Generationen der Bundesrepublik," in Walter Scheel, ed., *Die andere deutsche Frage* (Stuttgart: Klett, 1981), 158–78; and Friedrich H. Tenbruck, "Alltagsnormen und Lebensgefühle in der Bundesrepublik," in Richard Löwenthal and Hans-Peter Schwarz, eds., *Die zweite Republik* (Stuttgart: Seewald, 1974), 289–310. For changes in the political vocabulary as indicators of changing perceptions of vital issues such as defense, security, and Ostpolitik, see the fascinating study by Wolfgang Bergsdorf, *Herrschaft und Sprache* (Pfullingen: Neske, 1983). For changes in public opinion on defense throughout Western Europe in the early 1980s, an indispensable source is Gregory A. Flynn and Hans Rattinger, eds., *The Public and Atlantic Defense* (Totowa, N.J.: Rowman & Allanheld, 1984). For interpretations, see Michael R. Gordon, "Mood Contrasts and NATO," *Washington Quarterly* 8, no. 1 (Winter 1985): 107–30;

and, on generational change of opinion and attitudes toward international politics, Ronald Inglehart, "Generational Change and the Future of the Atlantic Alliance," *PS* 17 (1984): 525–35.

6. Allan Bloom in "Our Listless Universities," *National Review*, December 13, 1982; and Herman Kahn, in personal conversation.

7. For example, Hedley Bull, "European Self-Reliance and the Reform of NATO," *Atlantic Quarterly* 1 (1983): 25–43; Henry A. Kissinger, "A Plan to Reshape NATO," in Walter Laqueur and Robert E. Hunter, eds., *European Peace Movements and the Future of the Atlantic Alliance* (New Brunswick, N.J.: Transaction Books, forthcoming); and Pierre Hassner, "Pacifisme et terreur," in Pierre Lellouche, ed., *Pacifisme et dissuasion* (Paris: Institut Français des Relations Internationales, 1983), 156–76. See further in Chapters 4 and 10.

CHAPTER 1

1. A valid case can be made that the actual turning point came in 1941, specifically on June 22, when Hitler launched the German invasion of the Soviet Union. Its failure sealed Germany's fate and admitted Soviet rule to the heart of the old continent. On the importance of the period 1941–1949 as a whole compared to that of 1945, see Hans-Peter Schwarz, "Die aussenpolitischen Grundlagen des westdeutschen Staates," in Löwenthal and Schwarz, *Die zweite Republik*, 29–36.

2. On Niekisch, see Friedrich Kabermann, *Widerstand und Entscheidung eines deutschen Revolutionärs* (Cologne: Wissenschaft & Politik, 1973). Westphal's work is *Weltgeschichte der Neuzeit, 1750–1950* (Stuttgart: Kohlhammer, 1953). On postwar attitudes to the national issue in historical writing generally, see Chapter 3; and on the "basic emotions" in Germany in 1945, see Ernst Nolte, *Deutschland und der Kalte Krieg* (Munich: R. Piper Verlag, 1974), 190–96.

3. Friedrich Meinecke, *Die deutsche Katastrophe* (Wiesbaden: F. A. Brockhaus, 1946); and Hellmuth Plessner, *Die verspätete Nation*, rev. ed. (Frankfurt: Suhrkamp, 1980).

4. Manfred Schlenker, quoted in George G. Iggers, *The German Conception of History*, 2d ed. (Middletown, Conn.: Wesleyan University Press, 1983), 264.

5. Odo Marquard, *Abschied vom Prinzipiellen* (Stuttgart: Reclam, 1980), preface.

6. Helmut Schelsky, *Die skeptische Generation*, rev. ed. (Frankfurt: Ullstein, 1975). See also his survey of the distinctive characteristics of the several generations that were politically active in the first thirty years of the Federal Republic, "Generationen der Bundesrepublik." On "political generations" specifically, see Hans-Peter Schwarz, "Die westdeutsche Aussenpolitik—historische Lektionen und politische Generationen," in Walter Scheel, ed., *Nach dreissig Jahren* (Stuttgart: Klett, 1979), 145–73.

7. Adam B. Ulam, *Expansion and Coexistence: Soviet Foreign Policy, 1917–73* (New York: Praeger, 1974), 398–404; and Chapter 8 *passim*. The best study of Soviet plans and policies regarding Germany is Renata Fritsch-Bournazel, *L'Union Soviétique et les*

Allemagnes (Paris: Presses de la Fondation Nationale des Sciences Politiques, 1979). The reasons, origins, and course of the U.S.-Soviet conflict and the role of Germany as a focal point of that conflict are the main theme of Ernst Nolte's magisterial *Deutschland und der Kalte Krieg*; for the first stages of the conflict, see 183–230. The revised edition of this work (Stuttgart: Klett, 1985) appeared too late for me to use, so all references are to the first edition. The two editions are in any case substantially identical for the period concerned here; the most important new material consists of Nolte's responses to criticism of the first edition and of a continuation of the narrative to the early 1980s. For Churchill's views at the time, see Winston S. Churchill, *The Second World War*, vol. 6 , *Triumph and Tragedy* (Boston: Houghton Mifflin, 1953), 570–74; a passage that includes the text of the famous "Iron Curtain" telegram of May 12, 1945, to President Truman.

8. The subject of the mass expulsion of ethnic Germans from German national territory or from the territory of other states at the end of World War II has long been taboo. The fundamental collection of evidence is Theodor Schieder, ed., *Dokumentation der Vertreibung der Deutschen aus Ost-Mitteleuropa*, vols. 1–5 (n.p.: Bundesministerium für Vertriebene, 1954–1961; reprinted, Munich: Deutscher Taschenbuch Verlag, 1983). The first comprehensive work to be published in English was Alfred M. de Zayas, *Nemesis at Potsdam: The Anglo-Americans and the Expulsion of the Germans*, rev. ed. (London: Routledge & Kegan Paul, 1979). See especially chaps. 4 and 6. Of the approximately 10 million expelled, about 2 million only escaped Soviet occupation and possible death because the German Navy during the last months of the war and indeed for even a few days after the formal surrender, although it was under constant Soviet bombardment and submarine attack that were in violation of the laws of war, continued to ferry refugees from the eastern Baltic ports westward to areas occupied or about to be occupied by the Western Allies. With a casualty rate of 1 percent, this was the largest, and arguably the most successful, evacuation in history.

9. See Alfred Weber, "Haben wir Deutschen nach 1945 versagt?" in Alfred Weber, *Haben wir Deutschen nach 1945 versagt?* (Munich: Piper, 1979). The beliefs of Alfred Weber (1868–1959), brother of the more famous Max, represented a uniquely German blend of socialist political commitment and cultural conservatism, and in his last years, he declared his sympathy for nationalist-neutralist ideas similar to those of Peter Brandt and others in the 1980s; see Nolte, *Deutschland und der Kalte Krieg*, 190–96. Although some West Germans are dreaming of a restored *Mitteleuropa*, the true tragedy of the division of Europe is perceived most clearly by some East Europeans. See especially Milan Kundera, "L'Occident kidnappé," in *Le Débat* (Paris), 27 (September 1983); an English translation, entitled "The Tragedy of Central Europe," appeared in *New York Review of Books*, April 26, 1984. As pointed out in Chapter 2 and elsewhere, the political split in Western Europe, including West Germany, in the 1980s was not so much between an ill-defined "left" and an equally ill-defined "right," but between those who followed the Polish, Czech, Hungarian, and Russian dissidents in regarding the Soviet Union and its control of Eastern Europe as the political problem par excellence and those, such as most leading politicians and official

analysts in Western Europe, who insisted that the division of Europe and Germany was, on the contrary, a foundation of stability and détente.

10. Two detailed works on the first postwar years in Germany are Eschenburg, *Jahre der Besatzung*; and Christoph Klessmann, *Die doppelte Staatsgründung* (Göttingen: Vandenhoeck & Ruprecht, 1982). Eschenburg, a distinguished political scientist born in 1904, describes ideas and events positively and sympathetically. Klessmann, a much younger man, takes a far more critical line and is thus representative of a good deal of the writing on West German history since around 1970. One advantage of his work is that he quotes a number of important documents in full. For brief general views, see Hans-Adolf Jacobsen, "The Division of Germany"; and Karl Hardach, "Germany Under Western Occupation, 1945–1949," both in Charles Burdick, Hans-Adolf Jacobsen, and Winfried Kudszus, eds., *Contemporary Germany: Politics and Culture* (Boulder, Colo.: Westview Press, 1984), 60–76. Many good insights are to be found in Henry M. Pachter, *Modern Germany: A Social, Cultural, and Political History* (Boulder, Colo.: Westview Press, 1978), 268–92.

11. On conditions in Western Europe in 1947–1948, see Alan S. Milward, *The Reconstruction of Western Europe, 1945–1951* (Berkeley and Los Angeles: University of California Press, 1984), 1–125; and Alfred Grosser, *The Western Alliance* (New York: Random House, 1981), chap. 2.

12. See Hans Herzfeld, *Berlin in der Weltpolitik, 1945–1970*, Veröffentlichungen der Historischen Kommission zu Berlin, no. 38 (Berlin: Walter de Gruyter, 1973), chaps. 2–3.

13. On Kaiser and the struggle in the CDU between the Westerners, led by Adenauer, and the Christian socialist wing, under Kaiser, see Hans-Peter Schwarz, *Vom Reich zur Bundesrepublik*, 2d ed. (Stuttgart: Klett, 1980), chap. 6; Eschenburg, *Jahre der Besatzung*, 130–36 (an excellent summary of the issues); and Herzfeld, *Berlin*, 167–70.

14. On Schumacher and the SPD, see the more detailed discussion in Chapter 2.

15. See Ulam, *Expansion and Coexistence*, 435–40. Ulam regards the implementation of the ERP as "a watershed in the cold war . . . It was no longer a question of this or that political difference . . . it was the totality of foreign policies of each side that became the object of attack by the other." Milward, *Reconstruction of Western Europe*, is a comprehensive history of the period based on full use of documentary evidence.

16. On the beginnings of West German foreign policy, see Schwarz, "Die aussenpolitischen Grundlagen" (see note 1); Schwarz, *Vom Reich zur Bundesrepublik*; Waldemar Besson, *Die Aussenpolitik der Bundesrepublik* (Munich: Piper, 1970), the best work overall; Frank R. Pfetsch, *Die Aussenpolitik der Bundesrepublik, 1949–1980* (Munich: Fink, 1981); Hans-Adolf Jacobsen, "The Role of the Federal Republic of Germany in the World, 1949–1982," in Burdick et al., *Contemporary Germany*, 128–76; and an anthology of critical assessments and original sources, Helga Haftendorn, ed., *Die Aussenpolitik der Bundesrepublik Deutschland* (Berlin: Wissenschaftlicher Autoren-Verlag, 1982). Haftendorn's own introductory overview, 2–29, is especially useful. Jacobsen, "Role of the FRG," provides, on 129 and 131–32, useful and original

original diagrammatic representations of the structure and determinants of West German foreign policy. A brilliant synopsis of the differing approaches to foreign policy is the chapter "Die aussenpolitischen Denkschulen," in Hans-Peter Schwarz, *Die Ära Adenauer, 1949–1957,* vol. 2 of *Geschichte der Bundesrepublik Deutschland* (Stuttgart: Deutsche Verlags-Anstalt, 1981), 453–64.

17. The inside story of the founding of NATO was told by Sir Nicholas Henderson, *The Birth of NATO* (London: Weidenfeld & Nicolson, 1982).

18. On military and political developments affecting West Germany in 1945–1950, see Norbert Wiggershaus, "Vom Potsdam zum Pleven-Plan: Deutschland in der internationalen Konfrontation, 1945–1950," in Roland G. Foerster et al., *Von der Kapitulation bis zum Pleven-Plan* (Munich: Oldenbourg, 1982), 1–118. On Allied discussions on rearming West Germany, see, in the same volume, Norbert Wiggershaus, "Die Entscheidung für einen westdeutschen Verteidigungsbeitrag 1950," 325–402; and, for the domestic West German debate, the contribution by Roland G. Foerster, "Innenpolitische Aspekte der Sicherheit Westdeutschlands, 1947–1950," 403–575. The book as a whole is the first of three volumes commissioned by the West German Office of Military History and entitled *Anfänge westdeutscher Sicherheitspolitik, 1945–1956.* Vols. 2 and 3, not yet published in 1984, deal with the plans and negotiations for the EDC and with the decision to form the Bundeswehr, respectively.

19. For the history of the EDC, see Edward Fursdon, *The European Defence Community: A History* (New York: St. Martin's Press, 1979).

20. Hans Speidel, *Aus unserer Zeit* (Berlin: Propyläen, 1977), chap. 12 *passim.* Speidel, whose importance in the establishment of a West German defense force can hardly be overrated, not only describes his own views at the time, but also includes the text of the most important of his speeches and proposals of the period 1946–1950 concerning the defense and security of West Germany. For analysis of the rearmament debate in an international and intellectual context, see Nolte, *Deutschland und der Kalte Krieg,* 287–329.

21. Adam Ulam, *Expansion and Coexistence,* 534–37; for the legend of "lost opportunities," see Hans-Peter Schwarz, *Die Ära Adenauer, 1949–1957,* 149–60; Wilhelm G. Grewe, *Rückblenden, 1976–1951* (Berlin: Propyläen, 1979), 149–51 and 323–25; and, for the most detailed dissection, Hermann Graml, "Die Legende von der verpassten Gelegenheit: Zur sowjetischen Notenkampagne des Jahres 1952," *Vierteljahrshefte für Zeitgeschichte* 29 (1981): 307–41. The issues are well summed up by Pachter, *Modern Germany,* 287–92. On Winston Churchill's abortive plan to obtain German unification as part of an arrangement with the post-Stalin Soviet leadership as revealed in documents released in 1984 under the British thirty-year rule, see Anthony Glees, "Churchill's Last Gambit," *Encounter,* April 1985, pp. 27-35.

22. Adenauer's views of the Soviet Union and the policy that followed from them are discussed by Boris Meissner, "Adenauer und die Sowjetunion von 1955 bis 1959," in Dieter Blumenwitz, ed., *Konrad Adenauer und seine Zeit* (Stuttgart: Deutsche Verlags-Anstalt, 1976), 2:192–219; for his national policy, see Hans-Peter Schwarz, "Das Spiel ist aus und alle Fragen offen, oder: Vermutungen zu Adenauers Wiedervereinigungspolitik," in Helmut Kohl, ed., *Konrad Adenauer, 1876–1976* (Stuttgart:

Belser, 1976), 140–56; for the general principles of his foreign policy, see Hans-Peter Schwarz, "Das aussenpolitische Konzept Adenauers," in Klaus Gotto, ed., *Konrad Adenauer: Seine Deutschland- und Aussenpolitik, 1955–1963* (Munich: Deutscher Taschenbuch Verlag, 1975), 97–155. Helga Haftendorn, *Sicherheit und Entspannung* (Baden-Baden: Nomos, 1983), 69–78, denies that reunification was a "real goal" for Adenauer or that it was integrally connected with his Western policy.

23. On the Hallstein doctrine, see Grewe, *Rückblenden*, 251–62.

24. On the various legal interpretations of the postwar situation of Germany, see H. W. Koch, *A Constitutional History of Germany* (London: Longman, 1984), 318-52; and, for more detail, Otto Kimminich, "Die Rechtslage Deutschlands nach Grundgesetz und Grundvertrag," *Politische Studien* 31 (1980): 367–78; and Wilhelm Kewenig, "Deutschlands Rechtslage heute," *Europa-Archiv* 29 (1974): 71–82. The latter two reflect the situation after recognition of East Germany in 1972.

25. On the unitary citizenship, see Ernst-Wolfgang Böckenförde, "Die Teilung Deutschlands und die deutsche Staatsangehörigkeit," in Hans Barion et al., eds., *Epirrhosis: Festgabe für Carl Schmitt* (Berlin: Duncker & Humblot, 1968), 423–63, the most thorough legal and political analysis, reflecting the situation on the eve of Brandt's Ostpolitik; Ulrich Scheuner, "Die deutsche einheitliche Staatsangehörigkeit: Ein fortdauerndes Problem der deutschen Teilung," *Europa-Archiv* 34 (1979): 345–56; and Jens Hacker, "Stand und Perspektiven der deutsch-deutschen Beziehungen," in Wilhelm G. Grewe et al., *Die aussenpolitische Lage Deutschlands am Beginn der achtziger Jahre* (Berlin: Duncker & Humblot, 1981), 86–89. Hacker provides full references for further study of the legal, constitutional, and procedural issues involved.

26. On 1955 as a watershed year see Haftendorn, *Sicherheit und Entspannung*, 26–32.

27. Hans-Peter Schwarz, *Die Ära Adenauer, 1957–1963*, vol. 3 of *Geschichte der Bundesrepublik Deutschland* (Stuttgart: Deutsche Verlags-Anstalt, 1983), 381.

28. On the second Berlin crisis, see Herzfeld, *Berlin*, chap. 7 (good on the broader implications); Hannes Adomeit, *Soviet Risk-Taking and Crisis Behavior* (London: George Allen & Unwin, 1982), 183–311 (the most detailed study); Grosser, *Western Alliance*, 246–55; and Haftendorn, *Sicherheit und Entspannung*, 123–41. Nolte, *Deutschland und der Kalte Krieg*, 473–500, has a global perspective.

29. Grosser, *Western Alliance*, 255–58.

30. Schwarz, *Die Ära Adenauer, 1957–1963*, 288–90.

31. Ibid., 304. On the "Gaullism" of Strauss see also Klaus Hildebrand, *Von Erhard zur Grossen Koalition 1963-1969*, vol. 4 of *Geschich te der Bundesrepublik Deutschland* (Stuttgart: Deutsche Verlags-Anstalt, 1984), 97, and remarks in chapter 8 below.

32. For a discussion of the "new politics," see Kendall Baker et al., *Germany Transformed: Political Culture and the New Politics* (Cambridge, Mass.: Harvard University Press, 1981); and scattered remarks in Klaus von Beyme, "The Power Structure in the Federal Republic of Germany," in Burdick et al., *Contemporary Germany*, 77–102. Pachter, *Modern Germany*, 351–62, puts the new politics in a broader social and

cultural context. On the reflection of "new politics" in political language and programmatic statements of policy, see Bergsdorf, *Herrschaft und Sprache*, 243–59.

33. The ideas are restated and justified by Herbert Hupka; see his "Die Einheit der Nation: Der Auftrag des Grundgesetzes und die politisch-rechtliche Situation in der Gegenwart," in Klaus Weigelt, ed., *Heimat und Nation*, Studien zur politischen Bildung 7 (Mainz: von Hase & Koehler, 1984), 255–71, especially 260.

34. The essentials of Bahr's speech are reprinted in Peter Brandt and Herbert Ammon, eds., *Die Linke und die nationale Frage* (Reinbek: Rowohlt, 1981), 235–40. On the road to a new Ostpolitik in the 1960s see the exhaustive treatment by Hildebrand, *Von Erhard zur Grossen Koalition*, 3 01-39. For Bahr's vision of Ostpolitik to succeed, the cooperation of the East German regime was necessary, and it has always been clear that it can and will oppose any policy that might counteract the effects of national division. See Hacker, "Stand und Perspektiven," 97–99 and 104–7; Jens Hacker, "Das nationale Dilemma der DDR," in Boris Meissner and Jens Hacker, *Die Nation in östlicher Sicht* (Berlin: Duncker & Humblot, 1979), 40–68. The obvious fact, which is too often forgotten, is that for the East German regime, national division is a condition of survival. This point is made by Hupka in "Einheit der Nation," 259.

35. The "ideology of Ostpolitik" is displayed, for instance, by Manfred Görtemaker in *Die unheilige Allianz* (Munich: C. H. Beck, 1979). T he author of this useful account of East-West relations since 1943, a specialist in international politics with close ties to the right wing of the SPD, repeatedly asserts, in the final chapters, that East and West have the same purposes, that each side has in fact agreed to respect the security interests of the other, and that the West's relations with Eastern Europe have been to the advantage of all parties—including the East Europeans. For analysis of this position, see Pierre Hassner, "Arms Control and the Politics of Pacifism in Protestant Europe," in Uwe Nerlich, ed., *Soviet Power and Western Negotiating Policies*, vol. 2, *The Western Panacea: Constraining Soviet Power Through Negotiations* (Cambridge, Mass.: Ballinger, 1983), 117–50; Falk Bomsdorf, "Arms Control as a Process of Self-Constraint: The Workings of Western Negotiating Policy," in Nerlich, *Soviet Power*, 2:67–116, especially 98–101; Pierre Hassner, "Zwei deutsche Staaten in Europa: Gibt es gemeinsame Interessen in der internationalen Politik?" in Weidenfeld, *Identität der Deutschen*, 294–323; Hans-Peter Schwarz, "Die Alternative zum kalten Krieg? Bilanz der bisherigen Entspannung," in Hans-Peter Schwarz and Boris Meissner, eds., *Entspannungspolitik in Ost und West* (Cologne: Heymann: 1979), 147–91; Karl Kaiser, "Prioritäten sozialdemokratischer Aussen- und Sicherheitspolitik," in Maruhn and Wilke, *Wohin treibt die SPD?* 9–27; Gesine Schwan, "Die SPD und die westliche Freiheit," in ibid., 38–52; and, more specifically for criticism of the argument that increased trade leads to lessening of tensions, Daniel Frei and Dieter Ruloff, "Entspannungserwartungen und Entspannungsfolgen: Eine Bilanz anhand politischer und wirtschaftlicher Indikatoren," *Zeitschrit fuř Politik* 29 (1982): 295–310. In his analysis of the new Ostpolitik, Nolte speaks of the "unequal dismantling of the Cold War," *Deutschland und der Kalte Krieg*, 579–89. For a suggestion of what an Ostpolitik conducted in the true interests of East Europeans (and not their rulers) might look like, see Timothy Garton Ash, *The Polish Revolution: Solidarity* (New York: Scribner's, 1984), 316–31.

36. For an assessment by Atlanticist Social Democrats of the turn to neutralism and anti-Americanism in SPD security policy in the 1980s, see Maruhn and Wilke, *Wohin treibt die SPD?* For Schmidt's position, see his speech "Zur Lage der Sicherheitspolitik," given at the extraordinary SPD party congress in November 1983 and reprinted in ibid., 129–64.

CHAPTER 2

1. On neutralism as an issue of public debate in the 1950s, see Hans-Peter Schwarz, *Die Ära Adenauer, 1949–1957*, 122–26, 260–61; Nolte, *Deutschland und der Kalte Krieg*, 296 307; and, more generally, Pachter, *Modern Germany*, 287–92. Niemöller's long and fascinating life is the subject of James Bentley, *Martin Niemöller* (New York: Free Press, 1984). On the origins of *Der Spiegel*, see Eschenburg, *Jahre der Besatzung*, 167–70.

2. One of the few who would was the historian Alfred Heuss; see his *Versagen und Verhängnis: Vom Ruin deutscher Geschichte und ihres Verständnisses* (Berlin: Siedler, 1984), 210–11. On the far left there were also a few who, out of an equal dislike of U.S. and Soviet behavior and policies, returned to the fact of division as the basic problem of Europe; see the introduction to Brandt and Ammon, *Die Linke und die nationale Frage*, especially 27–28. In general, though, the West German left, in radical opposition to the French left and to its own former position, tended to see division as a precondition, and not as an obstacle, to stability. This was the reason for the extraordinary efforts at "understanding" Soviet and Polish communist policies during the Polish crisis of the 1980s, which were heavily criticized in other countries and in West Germany by the lone voice of Peter Schneider, "Warnung vor diesem Frieden," *Kursbuch*, no. 68 (June 1982): 181–87. See Garton Ash, *Polish Revolution*, 332-37; and Sigrid Meuschel, "Neo-Nationalism and the West German Peace Movement's Reaction to the Polish Military Coup," *Telos*, no. 56 (Summer 1983): 119–30.

3. Helga Haftendorn, herself a Social Democrat, describes SPD foreign policy principles in her *Sicherheit und Entspannung*, 87–104. See also Schwarz, *Die Ära Adenauer, 1949–1957*, 457–61; and, for a broader perspective comparing Social Democratic with other variants of Ostpolitik, his "Supermacht und Juniorpartner: Ansätze amerikanischer und westdeutscher Ostpolitik," in Schwarz and Meissner, *Entspannungspolitik*, 147–91. Ingemar Dörfer, a Swedish defense expert, in an article on Scandinavian attitudes to security, refers to "the well-known inability of Social Democrats to conceive international politics in terms of power relationships." See Ingemar Dörfer, "La Scandinavie ou la défense de la virginité nucléaire," in Lellouche, *Pacifisme et dissuasion*, 115. A similar observation might be made of American liberals, who in this as in other respects are the counterparts of European left-wing Social Democrats.

4. For an analysis of real versus perceived interests in regard to the German question, see Pierre Hassner, "Zwei deutsche Staaten in Europa."

5. See Frei and Ruloff, "Entspannungserwartungen und Entspannungsfolgen." This behavioristic model confirms the political analysis of Schwarz, "Die Alternative

zum kalten Krieg," in Schwarz and Meissner, *Entspannungspolitik*, 275–303.

6. On this point I agree with Brandt and Ammon, *Die Linke und die nationale Frage*, 54–55.

7. The standard work on nationalism in West Germany until 1960 is Kurt P. Tauber, *Beyond Eagle and Swastika*, 2 vols. (Middletown, Conn.: Wesleyan University Press, 1967). After that time, old-style nationalism virtually disappeared. There was a certain revival of arguments justifying nationalism, but not so much of nationalism itself, beginning in the late 1970s; see Bernard Willms, *Die deutsche Nation* (Cologne: Edition Maschke, 1982); and my comments in Chapter 3.

8. For a critique of the revival of *Heimat* ideas, see Wilfried von Bredow and Hans-Friedrich Foltin, *Zwiespältige Zufluchten: Zur Renaissance des Heimatgefühls* (Berlin: Dietz, 1981); and, for a moderate justification of them, Klaus Weigelt, "Heimat – der Ort personaler Identitätsfindung und sozio-politischer Orientierung," in Weigelt, *Heimat und Nation*, 15– 25. In an acerbic piece, "Eine Zukunft für die Vergangenheit," in Wolfgang Pohrt, *Endstation: Über die Wiedergeburt der Nation* (Berlin: Rotbuch Verlag, 1982), 51–68, Pohrt, himself a man of the radical left, pointed out the similarity of neo-romantic anticapitalism and *Heimat* ideology to certain aspects of Nazism. Cf. also Russell A. Berman, "The Peace Movement Debate: Provisional Conclusions," *Telos*, no. 57 (Fall 1983): 129–44.

9. The figures and an interpretation of them can be found in Erwin K. Scheuch, "Die deutsche Nation im Bewusstsein der Bevölkerung der Bundesrepublik Deutschland," in Weigelt, *Heimat und Nation*, 161–88. See also Elisabeth Noelle-Neumann, "Who Needs a Flag?" *Encounter*, January 1983, 72–80. Concerning the increase in popularity of the Bundeswehr, see the remarks by Lewis Gann, "Reflections on the Western European Peace Movement," in Dennis L. Bark, ed., *To Promote Peace* (Stanford: Hoover Institution Press, 1984), 98. On West German attitudes to security policy seen in relation to the level of public knowledge of the issues involved, see Ralf Zoll, "Public Opinion and Security Policy: The West German Experience," *Armed Forces and Society* 5 (1978–79): 590–605.

10. On what for want of a better term has been called neo-nationalism in the Green Party and the peace movement, see Pierre Hassner, "The Shifting Foundation," *Foreign Policy*, Fall 1982, 19–32; Elim Papadakis, *The Green Movement in West Germany* (New York: St. Martin's Press, 1984), 146–50; and Meuschel, "Neo-Nationalism." On hopes for a socialist reunification of Germany from the West, see the texts in Brandt and Ammon, *Die Linke und die nationale Frage*, 351–55; and the anthology *Die deutsche Einheit kommt bestimmt*, ed. Wolfgang Venohr (Bergisch Gladbach: Lübbe, 1983). Historians and others who look back at Nazism and see only the organized regime, the terror, and the Holocaust sometimes forget that Nazism was also a "social movement" with elements of anti-Western and anticapitalist romanticism and irrationalism. See Othein Rammstedt, *Soziale Bewegung* (Frankfurt: Suhrkamp, 1978), 11–27.

11. One might pursue the roots of Social Democratic nationalism further back, to the nationalism of the liberals of 1848 and to the legacy of centuries of political fragmentation of Germany. The idea that Germany was backward and despised by the

West and thus needed to assert itself to disprove these attitudes affected all political groups; among Social Democrats it led to the desire for a progressive and enlightened Germany with social, economic, and political equality. The SPD regarded national unity as essential for attaining these goals. Interestingly, Kurt Schumacher's doctoral dissertation, presented in 1920, was primarily an analysis of the debate in the SPD on the value and legitimacy of a strong national state. It was published for the first time with an introduction by the Social Democratic political philosopher Carlo Schmid; see Kurt Schumacher, *Der Kampf um den Staatsgedanken in der deutschen Sozialdemokratie* (Stuttgart: Kohlhammer, 1972).

12. See, for instance, Heinrich Freiherr Jordis von Lohausen, *Mut zur Macht*, 2d ed. (Berg am See: Vowinckel, 1980). Vowinckel was a publisher of nationalist and neo-Nazi literature in the 1950s.

13. On Kaiser, see remarks in Chapter 1; and, specifically on his ideas of a united, neutral Germany as a "bridge between East and West," Werner Conze, *Jakob Kaiser: Politiker zwischen Ost und West, 1945–1949* (Stuttgart: Kohlhammer, 1969).

14. Except where noted, all further quotes in this chapter have been culled from Brandt and Ammon, *Die Linke und die nationale Frage*, where they will be found in chronological order. All translations are mine. On the internal history of the SPD, its relations with other parties, and the evolution of its policies in general in the period 1945–1960, two works in particular stand out: Hartmut Soell, *Fritz Erler—Eine politische Biographie* (Berlin: Dietz, 1976); and Kurt Klotzbach, *Der Weg zur Staatspartei: Programmatik, praktische Politik und Organisation der deutschen Sozialdemokratie 1945 bis 1965* (Berlin: Dietz, 1982), an extensively annotated survey of the programs, policies, and organization of the SPD from 1945 to 1965, based on intimate familiarity with leading figures and access to otherwise closed sources.

15. For official East German attitudes to the national issue, see the official statements in Brandt and Ammon, *Die Linke und die nationale Frage*; and, for analysis, Peter Christian Ludz, *Die DDR zwischen Ost und West* (Munich: C. H. Beck, 1977), 221–63; and Klaus Motschmann, "Deutschlandpolitik im Wandel: Von Ulbricht zu Honecker," in Weigelt, *Heimat und Nation*, 272–85.

16. Emphasis in original.

17. See Haftendorn, *Sicherheit und Entspannung*, 381–84.

18. Ibid., 99–104.

19. On Reuter's views, see Herzfeld, *Berlin*, 178–84 and chap. 5 *passim*.

20. See Soell, *Fritz Erler*, 344–51.

21. On the nuclear debate, the best overview is Schwarz, *Die Ära Adenauer, 1957–1963*, 50–57.

22. See Diethelm Prowe, "Die Anfänge der Brandtschen Ostpolitik in Berlin, 1961–1963," in Wolfgang Benz and Hermann Graml, eds., *Aspekte deutscher Aussenpolitik im 20. Jahrhundert* (Stuttgart: Deutsche Verlags-Anstalt, 1976), 249–86; and Herzfeld, *Berlin*, 481–84. For Brandt's own feelings, see Willy Brandt, *Begegnungen und Einsichten* (Hamburg: Hoffmann & Campe, 1976), 9–41.

23. On the notion that the Wall was primarily an expression of the political bank-ruptcy of the East, rather than a drastic humiliation of the United States and an insult to West Germany, see Adomeit, *Soviet Risk-Taking*, 304.

24. Brandt, *Begegnungen*, 246–48. See also his other speeches and articles from the period 1965–1968 on the "European peace order" that he hoped to construct, based on acceptance, and not denunciation, of existing conditions, that is, Soviet domi-nation of Eastern Europe and the division of Germany; Willy Brandt, *Friedenspolitik in Europa* (Frankfurt: S. Fischer, 1968). On Brandt's changing views and the rise of the New Left in the SPD, see also the polemic by Hans Erler (son of Fritz), *Fritz Erler contra Willy Brandt* (Stuttgart: Seewald, 1976).

25. On the Erfurt meeting, see Haftendorn, *Sicherheit und Entspannung*, 363–73.

26. Motschmann, "Deutschlandpolitik im Wandel," 283–84, does not see as clear a break in East German national policy in 1970. On official East German attitudes to the changes in SPD security policy in the 1980s, see the very interesting overview by Manfred Wilke, "Die SPD im Zerrspiegel der SED," in Maruhn and Wilke, *Wohin treibt die SPD?* 112–28.

27. Haftendorn, *Sicherheit und Entspannung*, 380.

28. Günter Gaus, *Wo Deutschland liegt* (Hamburg: Hoffmann & Campe, 1983).

29. Bomsdorf, "Arms Control," 89. Bomsdorf attributes this view specifically to Egon Bahr, though it was also expressed by Chancellor Helmut Schmidt, normally considered an opponent of the Bahr–Gaus–Oskar Lafontaine line, for example in his Bundestag address of June 17, 1979, where he asserted that "in the eyes of others, the German division is today part of the European balance of power that secures peace in Europe." Quoted by Gordon A. Craig, *The Germans* (New York: G. P. Putnam's Sons, 1982), 309. For a rare leftist critique of this preference for what is believed to be peace over the rights of East Europeans, see Schneider, "Warnung"; and for sharp criticism of the logical fallacies involved in claiming a "security partnership" with the Soviet Union, see Bomsdorf, "Arms Control," 98–101. Notwithstanding these falla-cies, which he does not recognize, Bahr has since the mid-1970s been trumpeting the notion that security is possible only "with," and not "against," the Soviet Union. By the mid-1980s, Bahr had thoroughly disseminated this idea among the social demo-cratic parties of northwestern Europe via the so-called Scandilux meetings, on which see Nikolaj Petersen, "The Scandilux Experiment: Towards a Transnational Social Democratic Security Perspective?" *Cooperation and Conflict* 20 (1985): forthcoming. For the decline of "Munich 1938" as an image of danger, see Schwarz, "Westdeutsche Aussenpolitik," 157–60 and 172–73. Hassner, "Zwei deutsche Staaten," 299–313 and 316–20, distinguishes between alleged common interests of the West and East German governments, the existence of which he doubts, and the evident common interests of the entire German people, which are unlikely to be realized as long as the Soviet Union, despite claims to the contrary, remains implacably opposed to them. On the difficulty of defining the foreign policy interests of the East German regime, see Ludz, *DDR*, 259 and 261–63. See also Alois Mertes, "Friedenserhaltung–Frieden-sgestaltung: Zur Diskussion über 'Sicherheitspartnerschaft,'" *Europa-Archiv* 35 (1983): 187–96.

30. The people, events, and ideas that, in 1976–1981, destroyed the hegemony of Marxism in French intellectual life and spurred the rise of an anti-Soviet, antitotalitarian left in France are themselves material enough for a book. Two important examples of the new, or rather revived, views are Claude Lefort, *L'Invention de la démocratie* (Paris: Livre de Poche, 1983); and André Glucksmann, *La Force du vertige* (Paris: Grasset, 1983). The former consists of a series of essays and articles on democratic movements in Eastern Europe and the nature of the Soviet Union; the latter is a philosophical defense of the strategy of deterrence and an attack on the West German peace movement. For Aron's views, see Raymond Aron, *In Defense of Decadent Europe* (South Bend, Ind.: Regnery Gateway, 1979), originally published as *Plaidoyer pour l 'Europe décadente*, 2d ed. (Paris: Livre de Poche, 1978); and Raymond Aron, *Les dernières années du siècle* (Paris: Commentaire Julliard, 1984).

31. For evidence on changing attitudes, see the articles by Gordon, Inglehart, Meulemann, and Rausch quoted in note 5 to the Introduction.

CHAPTER 3

1. The standard work on the protest movements in West Germany from the 1960s to the early 1980s is Langguth, *Protestbewegung*; pp. 277–86 contain Langguth's interpretation of their causes and character.

2. The debate over Ostpolitik and the involvement of the Constitutional Court are described by Haftendorn, *Sicherheit und Entspannung*, 381–402.

3. On generational change in the West German political elite, see Schwarz, "Westdeutsche Aussenpolitik." For the notion of a pragmatic, problem-oriented "new politics" replacing the "old politics" consisting of the conflict of deeply held philosophical beliefs about the basic questions of society and human existence, see Baker et al., *Germany Transformed*.

4. On the Greens, see Kim R. Holmes, "The Origins, Development, and Composition of the Green Movement," in Clay Clemens et al., *The Greens of West Germany: Origins, Strategies and Transatlantic Implications* (Cambridge, Mass.: Institute for Foreign Policy Analysis, 1983), 15–46; Gerd Langguth, *Der grüne Faktor: Von der Bewegung zur Partei?* (Zürich: Interfrom, 1984); and Papadakis, *Green Movement*. Almost all Green supporters regard themselves as part of the peace movement, but the latter does not consist solely of Greens. On the origins and political context of the peace movement as such, see Papadakis, *Green Movement*, 132–56; and Langguth, *Protestbewegung*, 256–61.

5. Among the best known of these writings are Peter Bender, *Das Ende des ideologischen Zeitalters* (Berlin: Severin & Siedler, 1981); and Venohr, *Die deutsche Einheit*. Both will be discussed more fully below. By no means all left-wingers were sympathetic to such ideas; see Wolfgang Pohrt, "Ein Volk, ein Reich, ein Frieden"; and "Endstation: Über die Wiedergeburt der Nation"; both in Pohrt, *Endstation*, 71–76 and 95–128. For an outsider's evaluation of these tendencies, see Pierre Hassner, "The Shifting Foundation," *Foreign Policy*, no. 48 (Fall 1982): 19–32.

6. Statement at a hearing of the Committee for Inter-German Relations of the Bundestag, the proceedings of which were published as *Deutsche Geschichte und politische Bildung* in *Zur Sache*, no. 2, 1981.

7. For postwar German historiography, see the following: George G. Iggers, *The German Conception of History*, rev. ed. (Middletown, Conn.: Wesleyan University Press, 1983); Günther Heydemann, *Geschichtswissenschaft im geteilten Deutschland*, Erlanger historische Studien, no. 6 (Frankfurt: Peter D. Lang, 1980); Werner Conze, "Die deutsche Geschichtswissenschaft seit 1945," *Historische Zeitschrift* 225 (1973): 1–28; Konrad Repgen, "Methoden- oder Richtungskämpfe in der deutschen Geschichtswissenschaft seit 1945?" *Geschichte in Wissenschaft und Unterricht* 30 (1979): 591–610; Wolfgang J. Mommsen, "Gegenwärtige Tendenzen in der Geschichtsschreibung der Bundesrepublik," *Geschichte und Gesellschaft* 7 (1981): 149–88; and the polemical but extremely useful and stimulating piece by Hans-Ulrich Wehler, "Zur Lage der Geschichtswissenschaft in der Bundesrepublik, 1949–1979," in his *Historische Sozialwissenschaft* (Göttingen: Vandenhoeck & Ruprecht, 1980), 13–41. Wehler's opinion of what is important in history and why is not mine, and for that reason I wish especially to emphasize how useful I found his article.

8. On historians under Nazism, see Karl F. Werner, *Das NS-Geschichtsbild und die deutsche Geschichtswissenschaft* (Stuttgart: Kohlhammer, 1967). Werner's little book is a good survey, but the subject needs renewed and broader treatment.

9. The rise of modern historical study is the subject of Herbert Butterfield, *Man on His Past* (Cambridge, Eng.: Cambridge University Press, 1969); on the influence of state-centered nationalism on historical thought in Germany, see Iggers, *German Conception*, 29–43.

10. On the impact of the events of 1866 on public political discussion in Germany, see Hans-Joachim Schoeps, *Ja–Nein–und Trotzdem* (Mainz: von Hase & Koehler, 1974), 216–23.

11. On historiography in the Wilhelmian period, see Elisabeth Fehrenbach, "Rankerenaissance und Imperialismus in der wilhelminischen Zeit," in Bernd Faulenbach, ed., *Geschichtswissenschaft in Deutschland* (Munich: C. H. Beck, 1974), 54–65.

12. The influence of the idea of a "German path" on historians has been studied by Bernd Faulenbach, *Die Ideologie des deutschen Weges* (Munich: C. H. Beck, 1980).

13. On Weimar historiography, see Bernd Faulenbach, "Deutsche Geschichtswissenschaft zwischen Kaiserreich und NS-Diktatur," in Faulenbach, *Geschichtswissenschaft*, 66–85. Possibly the best study ever done of Meinecke's philosophical, political, and historiographical role and significance in German culture is Henry M. Pachter, "Friedrich Meinecke and the Tragedy of German Liberalism," in his *Weimar Etudes* (New York: Columbia University Press, 1982), 135–70. For studies of Meinecke and other historians from a viewpoint within the historical discipline, see Ernst Schulin, "Friedrich Meinecke," in Hans-Ulrich Wehler, ed., *Deutsche Historiker*, vol. 1 (Göttingen: Vandenhoeck & Ruprecht, 1971), 39–57; on Ritter, Andreas Dorpalen, "Gerhard Ritter," in ibid., 86–99; on Rothfels, Hans Mommsen, "Hans Rothfels," in Hans-Ulrich Wehler, ed., *Deutsche Historiker*, vol. 9 (Göttingen: Vandenhoeck &

Ruprecht, 1982), 127–47; and Werner Conze, "Hans Rothfels," *Historische Zeitschrift* 237 (1983): 311–60. Conze's piece, an extensive biographical and philosophical portrait of Rothfels, who had been his teacher, shows that epithets such as "conservative nationalist" do not apply to him and that the wholesale rejection of his style and approach by younger historians, which began long before his death in 1976, was in many ways unfair and unenlightened.

14. See Werner, *NS-Geschichtsbild*; and Wehler, "Zur Lage," 16–17.

15. Meinecke, *Deutsche Katastrophe*; and "Ranke und Burckhardt," in Friedrich Meinecke, *Werke*, vol. 7, *Zur Geschichte der Geschichtsschreibung* (Munich: Oldenbourg, 1968), 93–121.

16. Gerhard Ritter, *Die Dämonie der Macht* (Munich: Oldenbourg, 1948); and Gerhard Ritter, *Lebendige Vergangenheit* (Munich: Oldenbourg, 1958), contain the most important of these writings.

17. For some examples of such attempts at philosophical reorientation, see Gerhard Ritter, *Das deutsche Problem*, 2d ed. (Munich: Oldenbourg, 1966); Peter Rassow, *Die geschichtliche Einheit des Abendlandes* (Cologne: Böhlau, 1960); Hermann Heimpel, "Entwurf einer deutschen Geschichte," in Hermann Heimpel, *Der Mensch in seiner Gegenwart* (Göttingen: Vandenhoeck & Ruprecht, 1954), 162–95; Albert Mirgeler, *Geschichte Europas* (Freiburg: Herder, 1954); Michael Seidlmayer, *Weltbild und Kultur Deutschlands im Mittelalter*, vol. 1, part 6, of Leo Just, ed., *Handbuch der deutschen Geschichte* (Darmstadt: Akademische Verlagsgesellschaft Athenaion, 1957), English trans. as *Medieval Culture and Civilization in Germany* (Oxford: Blackwell, 1960); Friedrich Heer, *Der Aufgang Europas* (Vienna: Europa Verlag, 1949); Friedrich Heer, *Quellgrund dieser Zeit* (Einsiedeln: Johannes Verlag, 1956); Friedrich Heer, *Europäische Geistesgeschichte* (Stuttgart: Kohlhammer, 1953).

18. Albert Mirgeler, "Vielfalt und Einheit der deutschen Lande," in his *Geschichte und Gegenwart* (Freiburg: Alber, 1965), 85–86.

19. Conze, "Rothfels," 353. For a contemporary assessment, with wide perspectives, of the directions of historical study in the later 1950s, see Gerhard Ritter, "Zur Problematik gegenwärtiger Geschichtsschreibung," in Ritter, *Lebendige Vergangenheit*, 255–83. Even then, Ritter noted that political history was being neglected and that social and cultural history enjoyed increasing prestige.

20. Fritz Fischer, *Germany's War Aims in the First World War* (New York: Norton, 1967). On the impact of Fischer's work, see Wehler, "Zur Lage," 23–25, and cf. A. J. P. Taylor, "Fritz Fischer and His School," *Journal of Modern History* 47 (1975): 120–24.

21. Wehler, "Zur Lage," 38–41, a polemic against "neo-traditionalists." The notes to the article on 313–16 contain references to the debate and Wehler's reply to responses to the first publication of his article. The most important of these responses is Karl-Georg Faber, "Geschichtswissenschaft als retrospektive Politik?" *Geschichte und Gesellschaft* 6 (1980): 574–85. Interestingly, in view of their very different approaches, Wehler considers Bracher "unquestionably our leading *Zeithistoriker*" (contemporary historian) , "Zur Lage," 306–19.

22. See Wilfrid von Bredow, "Geschichte als Element der deutschen Identität?" in

Weidenfeld, *Identität*, 102–18; and Rudolf von Thadden's "ten points" in his testimony to the Bundestag Committee on Inter-German Affairs, *Zur Sache*, no. 2 (1981): 17–20.

23. For a spirited defense of the argument that historical study is a unique sort of enterprise, see Geoffrey Elton, "The Historian's Social Function," *Transactions of the Royal Historical Society*, 5th ser., 27 (1977): 197–211; and Geoffrey Elton, "Two Kinds of History," in Robert W. Fogel and Geoffrey Elton, *Which Road to the Past?* (New Haven and London: Yale University Press, 1983).

24. Golo Mann, *Wallenstein* (Frankfurt: S. Fischer, 1971); and Joachim Fest, *Hitler* (Berlin: Propyläen, 1973).

25. Quoted by Wehler, "Zur Lage," 37–38. The device of a reverse chronology used by Diwald in *Geschichte der Deutschen* (Berlin: Propyläen, 1978) was employed far more gracefully and with more logic by Norman Davies, *The Heart of Europe* (Oxford: Oxford University Press, 1984).

26. Hellmut Diwald, "Deutschland—Was ist es?" in Venohr, *Deutsche Einheit* , 31. For an extension of the argument, see Diwald's *Mut zur Geschichte* (Bergisch-Gladbach: Lübbe, 1983), 202–12.

27. Peter Brandt and Herbert Ammon, "Patriotismus von links," in Venohr, *Deutsche Einheit*, 118–59.

28. On the importance of the 1977 exhibition for the question of German national identity, see Arno Borst, "Barbarossas Erwachen: Zur Geschichte der deutschen Identität," in Odo Marquard and Karlheinz Stierle, eds., *Identität* (Munich: Wilhelm Fink, 1979), 17–60. On the renewed interest in Prussia, see Hans-Ulrich Wehler, *Preussen ist wieder chic* (Frankfurt: Suhrkamp, 1982). Apart from the almost forgotten work by Hans-Joachim Schoeps, *Preussen: Geschichte eines Staates* (Berlin: Propyläen, 1966), published at a time when the very idea of Prussia was both out of fashion and out of favor, the first complete history appeared precisely in the year of the exhibition: Gerd Heinrich, *Geschichte Preussens: Staat und Dynastie* (Berlin: Propyläen, 1981).

29. Peter Brandt, ed., *Zur Sozialgeschichte eines Staates*, vol. 3 of *Preussen—Versuch einer Bilanz* (Reinbek: Rowohlt, 1981); and Peter Brandt and Herbert Ammon, "Die deutsche Linke und die nationale Frage," in Brandt and Ammon, *Die Linke und die nationale Frage*, 29–57.

30. Lothar Gall, *Bismarck—Der weisse Revolutionär* (Berlin: Propyläen, 1981); and Theodor Schieder, *Friedrich der Grosse* (Berlin: Propyläen, 1983).

31. On this realization, see James J. Sheehan, "What Is German History? Reflections on the Role of the *Nation* in German History and Historiography," *Journal of Modern History* 53 (1981): 1–23. An example of a history of Germany deliberately eschewing emphasis on the nation-state, while maintaining the priority of political history, is Rudolf Buchner, *Deutsche Geschichte im europäischen Rahmen* (Darmstadt: Wissenschaftliche Buchgesellschaft, 1975).

32. David P. Calleo, *The German Problem Reconsidered* (New York: Cambridge University Press, 1978); and Gordon A. Craig, *The Germans* (New York: G. P. Putnam's Sons, 1982).

33. Calleo, *German Problem*, 158–59.

34. Nolte, *Deutschland und der Kalte Krieg*, 50.

35. Craig, *The Germans*, 10–11.

36. Ibid., 299.

37. On Schmitt's thought and influence in the last years of the Weimar Republic, see Joseph W. Bendersky, *Carl Schmitt: Theorist for the Reich* (Princeton, N.J.: Princeton University Press, 1983). Schmitt expressed his ideas in short, pithy essays, of which the most important are *Der Begriff des Politischen*, rev. ed. (Berlin: Duncker & Humblot, 1963), English edition with introduction by George L. Schwab, Carl Schmitt, *The Concept of the Political* (New Brunswick, N.J.: Rutgers University Press, 1975); and *Der Nomos der Erde*, rev. ed. (Berlin: Duncker & Humblot, 1974).

38. Bernard Willms, *Selbstbehauptung und Anerkennung* (Opladen: Westdeutscher Verlag, 1977), and *Einführung in die Staatslehre* (Paderborn: UTB/Schöningh, 1979).

39. Bernard Willms, *Die Deutsche Nation* (Cologne: Edition Maschke, 1982).

40. Ibid., 207–8.

41. Ibid., 288 and 321.

CHAPTER 4

1. Bernard Brodie, "The Development of Nuclear Strategy," *International Security* 2, no. 4 (Spring 1978): 77.

2. For the history of this debate, see Lawrence Freedman, *The Evolution of Nuclear Strategy* (London: Macmillan, 1981); and, for an example, see "A Garthoff-Pipes Debate on Soviet Strategic Doctrine," *Strategic Review* (Fall 1982): 36–63.

3. On the prehistory of INF modernization, see Ib Faurby, Hans-Henrik Holm, and Nikolaj Petersen, "Introduction: The INF Issue – History and Implications," in Hans-Henrik Holm and Nikolaj Petersen, eds., *The European Missiles Crisis: Nuclear Weapons and Security Policy* (New York: St. Martin's Press, 1983), 1–42; and Freedman, *Evolution*, 383–87. For analysis of the strategy and political purposes of the Soviet Union and the West, see Michel Tatu, *La Bataille des Euromissiles*, Les Sept Epées, Cahier no. 29 (Paris: Fondation pour les Etudes de Défense Nationale, 1983), 27–35.

4. For the numbers, see *The Military Balance, 1984–1985*. Writing in July 1984, the editors stated that the number of SS-20 launchers west of the Urals was "being increased" and that "2 more sites, 18 launchers may be operational shortly" (17). If correct, this information means that $18 \times 3 \times 2 = 108$ additional 150-kiloton warheads were being made available to Soviet forces in Europe in late 1984. For the overall Eurostrategic nuclear balance in mid-1984, see table 2, 136–37, in the same issue. Tatu, *Bataille*, 9–24, provides a strategic analysis of Soviet purposes in deploying the SS-20. On the "arms race," see Laurence W. Martin, *The Two-Edged Sword* (London: Macmillan, 1982), 10–11 and 64. The classic criticism of the notion of a self-sustaining arms race was made by Albert Wohlstetter in three articles, "Is There a Strategic Arms Race?" *Foreign Policy*, no. 15 (Summer 1974): 3–20, "Rivals, but No

'Race,'" *Foreign Policy*, no. 16 (Fall 1974): 48–81; and "Racing Forward? Or Ambling Back?" *Survey*, nos. 100–101 (Summer–Autumn 1976): 163–217. *Foreign Policy*, nos. 16 and 19 (Summer 1975) contained reactions to Wohlstetter; for his reply, see "Optimal Ways to Confuse Ourselves," *Foreign Policy*, no. 20 (Fall 1975): 170–98. For a perspective on Wohlstetter's arguments, see Freedman, *Evolution*, 347–51.

5. *International Herald Tribune*, November 29, 1983; and for the complete poll data, Flynn and Rattinger, *The Public and Atlantic Defense*. See also Elisabeth Noelle-Neumann, "Are the Germans 'Collapsing' or 'Standing Firm'?" *Encounter*, February 1982, pp 69–81.

6. Schwarz, *Die Ära Adenauer, 1957–1963*, 320.

7. Schelsky, *Die Arbeit tun die anderen*, 333–40.

8. See Mertes's op-ed piece defending Ostpolitik as a national policy, *New York Times*, October 12, 1984.

9. For a more detailed account of the views I have labeled "new Ostpolitik" and "neo-neutralism," with examples, see Jeffrey Herf, "The Center Left Could Not Hold: The SPD and West German Security," in Laqueur, *European Peace Movements*.

10. Peter Bender, *Das Ende des ideologischen Zeitalters* (Berlin: Severin & Siedler, 1981). Bender's book was seen by many foreign observers as the archetypal statement of the Europeanist wing of the peace movement, that is, of those who rejected great power politics and believed that East and West Europeans could and should unite in a neutral, peaceful, ecologically balanced *Gemeinschaft*. See, for example, Herf, "Center Left."

11. See Oskar Lafontaine, *Angst vor den Freunden* (Reinbek: Rowohlt, 1983). The publishing house of Rowohlt provided much of the neo-neutralist, anti-U.S., and anti-NATO literature of the 1970s and 1980s. For analogous rhetoric from an SPD disarmament specialist, see Hans Günter Brauch, *Die Raketen kommen!* (Cologne: Bund Verlag, 1983).

12. See Bogislav von Bonin, *Opposition gegen Adenauers Sicherheitspolitik* (Hamburg: Verlag Neue Politik, 1976).

13. Carl Friedrich von Weizsäcker, *Wege in der Gefahr*; Horst Afheldt, *Verteidigung und Frieden*; Emil Spannocchi and Guy Brossolet, *Verteidigung ohne Schlacht* (all Munich: Hanser, 1976). Horst Afheldt later identified closely with the peace movement; see his *Defensive Verteidigung* (Reinbek: Rowohlt, 1983). In his *Atomkrieg. Das Verhängnis einer Politik m it militärischen Mitteln* (Munich: Hanser, 1984), Afheldt expanded his analysis to a condemnat ion of arms control as understood by U.S. policymakers and argued that it had only made war more likely. Like George Kennan and most liberal or leftist West German analysts, however, Afheldt believes firmly that war by accident on the model of 1914 is the only peril; he is therefore unable to provide a truly political analysis of the Soviet threat in Europe. Cf. also the remarks in Herf, "Center Left."

14. For Galtung's views, see his *Environment, Development and Military Activity: Towards Alternative Security Doctrines* (Oslo: Universitetsforlaget, 1982). Galtung and Dieter Senghaas between them provide most of the intellectual arguments used by

the peace movement. Galtung, however, is even more removed from the real, political world than Senghaas; his opinions, though propounded with a certain verve, display an extreme eccentricity characteristic of much of what passes for political analysis in Scandinavia. Possibly this is because the small size and long history of political stability of these countries have led to a loss of political realism; see Dörfer, "La Scandinavie." On "critical peace research" as promoted by Galtung and Senghaas, see also Schelsky, *Die Arbeit tun die anderen*, 290–97; Herf, "Center Left"; and Friedrich H. Tenbruck, "Frieden durch Friedensforschung?" in Manfred Funke, ed., *Friedensforschung—Entscheidungshilfe gegen Gewalt* (Munich: List, 1975), 425–39.

15. See the final pages of Freedman, *Evolution.*

16. On Soviet war-fighting doctrine against the Western Alliance, see the collection of Soviet statements in Harriet F. Scott and William F. Scott, eds., *The Soviet Art of War: Doctrine, Strategy and Tactics* (Boulder, Colo.: Westview Press, 1982); the best analyses are Nathan Leites, *Soviet Style in War* (New York: Crane Russak, 1982); and Peter H. Vigor, *The Soviet View of War, Peace and Neutrality* (London: Routledge & Kegan Paul, 1975). Cf. also John Erickson, "The Soviet View of Deterrence: A General Survey," *Survival* 24 (1982): 242–51. An excellent summary and evaluation of the conflicting beliefs and arguments of Western analysts concerning Soviet military doctrine is Douglas M. Hart, "The Hermeneutics of Soviet Military Doctrine," *Washington Quarterly* 7, no. 2 (Spring 1984): 77–88. On the likelihood that a Soviet assault on Western Europe would use nuclear weapons from the outset, see Viktor Suvorov, *Inside the Soviet Army* (London: Hamish Hamilton, 1982); Graham F. Vernon, "Soviet Options for War in Europe: Nuclear or Conventional?" *Strategic Review* 7, no. 1 (Winter 1979): 52–56; and Christopher N. Donnelly, "Soviet Operational Concepts in the 1980s," in *Strengthening Conventional Deterrence in Europe: Proposals for the 1980s*, Report of the European Security Study (New York: St. Martin's Press, 1983), 105–36. For Soviet INF doctrine, see David Holloway, "The INF Policy of the Soviet Union," in Holm and Petersen, *European Missiles Crisis*, 92–114, an invaluable analysis of a highly obscure subject. For considerably more detail, see Stephen M. Meyer, *Soviet Theatre Nuclear Forces*, part 1, *Development of Doctrine and Objectives*, and part 2, *Capabilities and Implications*, Adelphi Papers 187–88 (London: International Institute for Strategic Studies, 1984). For Soviet conceptions of the political uses of power, see Hannes Adomeit, "The Political Rationale of Soviet Military Capabilities and Doctrine," in *Strengthening Conventional Deterrence* , 67–104; and Robert Conquest, "Soviet Foreign Policy," in Bark, *To Promote Peace*, 201–14. A more popular view, with which neither Adomeit nor I can agree, is presented by Robert Legvold, "Military Power in International Politics: Soviet Doctrine on Its Centrality and Instrumentality," in Nerlich, *Soviet Power*, 1:123–59. For the perceptions and effects of Soviet power on Western negotiators, strategists, and public opinion, see Lothar Ruehl, "The Threat Perceived? Leverage of Soviet Military Power in Western Europe," in *Soviet Power*, 1:195–205; and Hassner, "Arms Control and the Politics of Pacifism."

17. For a definition and description of the ULV, see Christian Brünner, "Verteidigung," in *Katholisches Soziallexikon*, cols. 3203–19.

18. The latter reaffirmed this in *Die Zeit*, February 18, 1983.

19. The view that the East-West conflict is due to mutual misunderstanding or even to deliberate U.S. policies was popular in the late 1940s, then disappeared, only to return in the 1960s under the name "revisionism." See Nolte, *Deutschland und der Kalte Krieg*, 34–38, on revisionist histories of the cold war, and 536–51, on the context of that revisionism in revived left-wing politics in the United States and West Germany. On the belief in a spiraling arms race, see the articles by Albert Wohlstetter cited in note 2. As noted in 1965 by Aaron Wildavsky (quoted in Freedman, *Evolution*, 204–5), and in 1979 by Hans-Peter Schwarz ("Westdeutsche Aussenpolitik," 158), those who, like George Kennan or many West Germans, saw the U.S.-Soviet conflict as essentially meaningless (a "delusion"), also tended to see 1914 (war by accident) rather than 1938 (war as a consequence of the appeasement of a totalitarian power) as the main image of danger. In the summer of 1982, Helmut Schmidt publicly referred to what he must have considered the valid analogy of 1914 as an illustration of the European and global situation. That Kennan sees the image of 1914 as increasingly applicable to the world of the 1980s, and that he wants it to be so seen by the public, is clear from the stated implications of his historical writings, and by their public reception. See, for example, the reviews of his *The Fateful Alliance: France, Russia, and the Coming of the First World War* (New York: Pantheon, 1984) by Paul Kennedy (*New York Times Book Review*, October 21, 1984), and by Alastair Horne (*New Republic*, November 5, 1984). On unilateral disarmament, "gradualism" (gradual unilateral disarmament, an example of which is the notion, popular in the United States, of a "nuclear freeze"), and civilian defense as strategies for securing peace, see Daniel Frei, "Friedenssicherung durch Gewaltverzicht?" *Aus Politik und Zeitgeschichte: Beilage zur Wochenzeitung Das Parlament*, April 16, 1983. Frei's study is the most painstaking analytical and substantive examination of these ideas known to me.

20. Frei, "Friedenssicherung," 7–8. The most sophisticated philosophical and strategic argument for the possibility and efficacy of civilian defense is that of Gene Sharp, who applied his theories to Europe in his *Making Europe Unconquerable* (London and Philadelphia: Taylor & Francis, 1985). Cf. Michael Walzer, *Just and Unjust Wars* (New York: Basic Books, 1977), 329–35.

21. Frei, "Friedenssicherung," 12–14 and 16–18.

22. Gottfried Greiner, "Pazifismus und Sicherheitspolitik," *Europäische Wehrkunde* 31 (1982): 433–36.

23. On Soviet strategy toward West Germany, see Gerhard Wettig, "Germany, Europe, and the Soviets," in Herbert J. Ellison, ed., *Soviet Policy Toward Western Europe* (Seattle and London: University of Washington Press, 1983), 31–60; Karen Dawisha, "Soviet Ideology and Western Europe," in Edwina Moreton and Gerald Segal, eds., *Soviet Strategy Toward Western Europe* (London: George Allen & Unwin, 1984), 19–38; Hannes Adomeit, "Soviet Decision-Making and Western Europe," in ibid., 39–84 (comprehensive survey of domestic Soviet policy formation); Edwina Moreton, "The German Factor," in ibid., 110–37; and Adomeit, "Political Rationale."

24. On the Soviet interpretation of "peace," see Paul H. Nitze, "Living With the Soviets," *Foreign Affairs* 63 (1984–85): 360–74; Vigor, *Soviet View*, 160–77; Rolf Geyer,

"Das sowjetische Friedenskonzept," *Politische Studien* 33 (1982): 47–56; and, for further implications and perspective, Chapter 5 below.

25. Among the many presentations of this view, that of Jeffrey Herf, "Western Strategy and Public Discussion: The Double Decision Makes Sense," *Telos*, no. 52 (Summer 1982): 114–28, deserves to be mentioned because it was specifically directed at the arguments of the peace movement. Herf was subjected to a set of vicious attacks by supporters of the West German peace movement in *Telos*, no. 56 (Summer 1983): 130–55, and responded in the same issue, 156–71.

26. Karl-Peter Stratmann, *NATO-Strategie in der Krise* (Baden-Baden: Nomos, 1981), 228–32; and Tatu, *Bataille*, 17–24.

27. Sir John Hackett, *The Third World War* (London: Sidgwick & Jackson, 1978), is probably the most thorough as well as the best known of these; equally if not more important is his elaboration of this scenario in *The Third World War: The Untold Story* (London: Sidgwick & Jackson, 1982); Robert Close, *Europe Without Defense* (London: Pergamon, 1979); Robert Close, *Encore un effort et nous aurons définitivement perdu la troisième guerre mondiale* (Brussels: Belfond, 1981); "François" (Guy Doly), *Si les Russes attaquent* (Paris: Laffont, 1980); see also the scenarios in Löser, *Weder rot noch tot*, 22–45, and in Ferdinand Otto Miksche, *Bis 2000* (Stuttgart: Seewald, 1979), 222–59.

28. On U.S. targeting policy and the role of counterforce strikes, see Desmond Ball, *Targeting for Strategic Deterrence*, Adelphi Paper 185 (London: International Institute for Strategic Studies, 1983), especially 17–25; and Lew Scott and Marc Dean Millot, "U.S. Nuclear Strategy in Evolution," *Strategic Review* 12, no. 1 (Winter 1984): 19–28. On the relationship of strategy to social change, see Michael Howard, "Social Change and the Defense of the West," "War and the Nation-State," "The Forgotten Dimensions of Strategy," and "Reassurance and Deterrence," all in his *The Causes of Wars*, 2d ed. (Cambridge, Mass.: Harvard University Press, 1984).

29. Stratmann, *NATO-Strategie*, 232.

30. Schwarz, "Alternative zum Kalten Krieg?" 302.

31. That strength, in this case the strength of a more united Western Europe, would deter, and not provoke, Soviet expansionism, is a basic theme of what one might call "realistic," as opposed to "optimistic," Sovietology. The realistic school, as it happens, includes most of the recognized experts on Soviet history and society; see, for example, Adam B. Ulam, *Dangerous Relations* (New York: Oxford University Press, 1982), 315–16, on Western strength "as the essential ingredient of a new and viable world order." Cf. also Hugh Seton-Watson, *The Imperialist Revolutionaries* (Stanford: Hoover Institution Press, 1978); and two informative and witty articles by Peter Wiles, "Leninism and *Weltinnenpolitik*," *Survey*, nos. 100–101 (Summer–Autumn 1976): 154–62; and "Is an Anti-Soviet Embargo Desirable or Possible?" in *The Conduct of East-West Relations in the 1980s*, pt. 2, Adelphi Paper 190 (London: International Institute for Strategic Studies, 1984), 37–50.

32. Howard, "Reassurance and Deterrence," in *The Causes of Wars*, 263.

33. Freedman, *Evolution*, 285–302.

34. On the Rogers plan, see Bernard W. Rogers, "Greater Flexibility for NATO's Flexible Response," *Strategic Review* 11, no. 2 (Spring, 1983): 11–19; and "Prescriptions for a Difficult Decade: The Atlantic Alliance in the 1980s," *Foreign Affairs* 60 (1981–82): 1145–156; and *The Economist*, July 31, 1982. General Rogers surveyed the general problems of the Alliance in "NATO: The Next Decade," in Christopher Coker, *The Future of the Atlantic Alliance* (London: Macmillan and the Royal United Services Institute, 1984), 131–40. On the FOFA concept, see Boyd D. Sutton et al., "New Directions in Conventional Defence?" *Survival* 26 (1984): 50–78; and D. R. Cotter and N. F. Wikner, "NATO's Forward Defence: New Strategy," in Coker, *Atlantic Alliance*, 188–94. The term "conventional retaliation" was devised by Samuel P. Huntington; see his "The Renewal of Strategy," in Samuel P. Huntington, ed., *The Strategic Imperative: New Policies for American Security* (Cambridge, Mass.: Ballinger, 1982), 9–51; and his "Broadening the Strategic Focus," a reply to Michael Howard's "Reassurance and Deterrence," in *Defence and Consensus: The Domestic Aspects of Western Security*, pt. 3, Adelphi Paper 184 (London: International Institute of Strategic Studies, 1983), 27–32. Mearsheimer's view is found in chap. 6 of his *Conventional Deterrence* (Ithaca, N.Y.: Cornell University Press, 1983); for a critical response, see Josef Joffe, "Stability and Its Discontent: Should NATO Go Conventional?" *Washington Quarterly* 7, no. 4 (Fall 1984): 136–47. On NATO's conventional deterrent and its desirable future development in general, see in particular the "Report of the Steering Group," in *Strengthening Conventional Deterrence*, 6–35; but see also the criticism of these recommendations, which heavily stress emerging technologies, in *Survival* 26 (1984): 283–84; and James M. Garrett, "Conventional Force Deterrence in the Presence of Nuclear Weapons," *Armed Forces and Society* 11 (1984–85): 59–83. On the political need and advantages of improving NATO's conventional forces in the context of a greater West European role, see William Wallace, "European Defence Co-operation: The Reopening Debate," *Survival* 26 (1984): 251–61; Hedley Bull, "European Self-Reliance and the Reform of NATO," *Atlantic Quarterly* 1 (1983): 25–43; Laurence Radway, "Towards the Europeanisation of NATO," *Atlantic Quarterly* 1 (1983): 129–47; and the contributions to Robert E. Hunter, ed., *NATO: The Next Generation* (Boulder, Colo.: Westview Press, 1984). A skeptical view of the possibilities of a greater European role in its own defense is Coker, *Atlantic Alliance*, 50–75, the chapter entitled "The Lilliputian Senate: The Failure of European Cooperation," but see also 121–30, "The Need for an Atlantic Community." Coker also warned against using the peace movement's agitation as an argument against the nuclear deterrent since "conventional retaliation" and similar ideas are, in his view, more likely to provoke a public reaction against NATO; see his "The Peace Movement and Its Impact on Public Opinion," *Washington Quarterly* 8, no. 1 (Winter 1985): 93–105.

CHAPTER 5

1. See Theodore K. Rabb, *The Search for Stability in Early Modern Europe* (New York: Oxford University Press, 1975).

2. Since the sharp separation of spiritual and temporal power is a uniquely

Western invention, imperial expansion and world-rule in the early high cultures were also and especially religious forces. See in general on the concept of order and empire, Eric Voegelin, *Order and History*, 4 vols. (Baton Rouge: Louisiana State University Press, 1956–1974). It is hoped that this interpretation of world history will be completed with volume 5, *The Search For Order*, in the near future.

3. For a comparison of the peace brought by the Roman Empire to the international peace of the modern European state system, see Albert Mirgeler, "Die geschichtlichen Friedensschlüsse," in his *Geschichte und Gegenwart*, 64–77.

4. See W. H. C. Frend, *The Rise of Christianity* (Philadelphia: Fortress Press, 1984), for a general and wide-ranging introduction to all the aspects – political, theological, social, cultural – of the subject.

5. See the entries on Dar-al-Harb and Dar-al-Islam in *Encyclopedia of Islam*, new ed. (Leiden: Brill, 1965), 2:126–27.

6. See Francis Dvornik, *Early Christian and Byzantine Political Philosophy*, Dumbarton Oaks Studies 12 (Washington, D.C.: Dumbarton Oaks Center, 1966).

7. *City of God*, book IV, chap. 4.

8. On the idea of the "holy empire" and medieval Christian conceptions of social order, see Alois Dempf, *Sacrum Imperium*, rev. ed. (Darmstadt: Wissenschaftliche Buchgesellschaft, 1954).

9. See James T. Johnson, *Ideology, Reason, and the Limitation of War: Religious and Secular Concepts, 1200–1740* (Princeton, N.J.: Princeton University Press, 1975). On medieval ideas of peace and order in general, see Hermann Conrad, "Rechtsordnung und Friedensidee im Mittelalter und in der beginnenden Neuzeit," in Alexander Hollerbach and Hans Maier, eds., *Christlicher Friede und Weltfriede* (Paderborn: Schöningh, 1971), 9–34.

10. See Joseph R. Strayer, *On the Medieval Origins of the Modern State* (Princeton, N.J.: Princeton University Press, 1970). On the revolution in thought and practice that made establishment of royal power and hence of the modern state possible, see Harold J. Berman, *Law and Revolution: The Formation of the Western Legal Tradition* (Cambridge, Mass.: Harvard University Press, 1983). Berman's idea that the "legal revolution" of the decades around 1100 was the decisive caesura in Western history before the democratic and industrial revolutions of around 1800 parallels Dietrich Gerhard's suggestion that the period 1000–1800 is best viewed as a whole and that the conventional division of Western history at around 1500 is misleading; see his *Old Europe: A Study of Continuity* (New York: Academic Press, 1981). The unity of the period 1000–1800 was also an argument of Christopher Dawson's; see his *The Making of Europe* (London: Sheed & Ward, 1932).

11. On these ideas, see Francis Oakley, *Omnipotence, Covenant, and Order* (Ithaca, N.Y.: Cornell University Press, 1983); and Stephen Ozment, *The Age of Reform, 1250–1550* (New Haven and London: Yale University Press, 1980).

12. See Otto Brunner, *Land und Herrschaft*, 5th ed. (Darmstadt: Wissenschaftliche Buchgesellschaft, 1965). On warfare in general in the late medieval–early modern period, see Michael Howard, *War in European History* (London: Oxford Uni-

versity Press, 1976), chap. 1; and John R. Hale, *War and Society in Renaissance Europe* (London: Fontana, 1985). On the Renaissance origins of the view of politics as the task of securing the survival of the city (or the state) in a world not organized into a single, authoritative hierarchy, see the chapter "Renaissance Republicanism and the *Respublica Christiana*," in William J. Bouwsma, *Venice and the Defense of Republican Liberty* (Berkeley and Los Angeles: University of California Press, 1968); and, more generally, Quentin Skinner, *The Foundations of Modern Political Thought*, vol. 1, *The Renaissance* (Cambridge, Eng.: Cambridge University Press, 1978).

13. See John H. M. Salmon, *Society in Crisis* (New York: St. Martin's Press, 1975).

14. See Skinner, *Foundations*, vol. 2, *The Age of Reformation* (Cambridge, Eng.: Cambridge University Press, 1978), 249–54.

15. On the effects of the Thirty Years' War, see Rudolf Vierhaus, *Staaten und Stände 1648–1763*, vol. 5 of *Propyläen Geschichte Deutschlands (Berlin: Propyläen, 1984)*, 54–75.

16. For thorough introductions to the thought and lives of Althusius and Grotius, see the chapters devoted to them in Erik Wolf, *Grosse Rechtsdenker der deutschen Geistesgeschichte*, 4th ed. (Tübingen: Mohr, 1963); on Grotius's contribution to international law, see Wilhelm G. Grewe, "Grotius–Vater des Völkerrechts?" *Der Staat* 23 (1984): 161–78.

17. On Hobbes in general, see John P. Plamenatz, *Man and Society*, vol. 1 (London: Routledge & Kegan Paul, 1963). On Hobbes's theory of authority, see Schmitt, *Begriff des Politischen*, esp. 65–67; and Ernst-Wolfgang Böckenförde, "Die Entstehung des modernen Staates als Vorgang der Säkularisation," in his *Staat und Gesellschaft* (Frankfurt: Suhrkamp, 1976).

18. On the theory and practice of the balance of power, see Georges Livet, *L'équilibre européen de la fin du XVe à la fin du XVIIIe siècle* (Paris: Presses Universitaires de France, 1976). A lucid assessment of classical balance of power theory in relation to contemporary changes in international relations is Robert K. Gilpin, *War and Change in World Politics* (New York: Cambridge University Press, 1981). Less convincing is Gilpin's argument that East-West relations today are essentially of the same kind as relations between states in the classical system. On the changes in warfare, see Howard, *War*, chap. 3; André Corvisier, *Armies and Societies in Europe, 1494–1789* (Bloomington: Indiana University Press, 1979); and, specifically on the limitation of war, Johnson, *Ideology*.

19. On ideals of government and administration in Germany in the seventeenth and eighteenth centuries, ideals that prefigured the belief in the strong, benevolent state and in state control of the economy in Wilhelmian Germany, see Marc Raeff, *The Well-Ordered Police State* (New Haven and London: Yale University Press, 1983).

20. An optimistic view of the effect of Kant's *On Perpetual Peace* is F. H. Hinsley, "Immanuel Kant and the Pattern of War and Peace Since His Time," in Helmut Berding et al., eds., *Vom Staat des Ancien Regime zum modernen Verfassungsstaat* (Munich: Oldenbourg, 1978), 91–101. On tension, conflicts, peace, and the idea of the balance of power in the age of absolutism, see in general Heinz Durchhardt, ed., *Gleichgewicht der Kräfte, Convenance, Europäisches Konzert: Friedenskongresse und Friedensschlüsse*

vom Zeitalter Ludwigs XIV. bis zum Wiener Kongress (Darmstadt: Wissenschaftliche Buchgesellschaft, 1976); Johannes Kunisch, *Staatsverfassung und Mächtepolitik: Zur Genese von Staatskonflikten im Zeitalter des Absolutismus* (Berlin: Duncker & Humblot, 1979). On international peace in relation to Christian ideals of peace, see Hans Maier, "Der christliche Friedensgedanke und der Staatenfriede der Neuzeit," in Hollerbach, *Christlicher Friede*, 35–51.

21. See Jacob L. Talmon, *The Origins of Totalitarian Democracy* (1952; reprinted New York: W. W. Norton, 1974), and Hannah Arendt, *On Revolution* (New York: Viking, 1970), for the interpretation borrowed here. A good recent introduction to the changes in warfare during this period is Geoffrey Best, *War and Society in Revolutionary Europe, 1770–1870* (London: Fontana, 1982). Ernst Topitsch, "Machtkampf und Humanität," in his *Gottwerdung und Revolution* (Pullach bei München: UTB/Verlag Dokumentation, 1973), 135–217, is a wide-ranging and very stimulating analysis of the relationship of political power, violence, and humanitarian ideals throughout European history. I have drawn repeatedly on it in this section.

22. Topitsch, "Machtkampf und Humanität," 171–72. On the change in the ideological, political, and cultural aspects of war that began in the French Revolution, see also Roman Schnur, "Weltfriedensidee und Weltbürgerkrieg, 1791/92," in his *Revolution und Weltbürgerkrieg*, Schriften zur Verfassungsgeschichte, vol. 35 (Berlin: Duncker & Humblot, 1983), 11–32. The other essays in this volume by Schnur are also relevant. Cf. the remarks on democratization, the idea of popular sovereignty, and war, in Robert Leckie, *Warfare* (New York: Harper & Row, 1970), quoted in Robert L. Phillips, *War and Justice* (Norman: University of Oklahoma Press, 1984), xiii–xiv.

23. George L. Mosse, *The Nationalization of the Masses* (New York: Howard Fertig, 1975). On war in the nineteenth century see also Howard, *War*, chap. 4; and his essay "War and the Nation-State," in his *Causes of Wars*; and Theodore S. Hamerow, *The Birth of a New Europe* (Chapel Hill: University of North Carolina Press, 1983), 363–88.

24. Winston S. Churchill, *The Second World War*, vol. 1, *The Gathering Storm* (Boston: Houghton Mifflin Co., 1948), 38.

25. By accident rather than by design actual combat operations in World War I were quite limited geographically, so that civilian losses, compared to the devastation of the Thirty Years' War or even to the wars of Frederick the Great were relatively small. In this specific sense World War I was the last limited major war. Cf. Brian Bond, *War and Society in Europe, 1870–1970*, chap. 4; and Keith Robbins, *The First World War* (Oxford: Oxford University Press, 1984).

26. On the effects of World War I, see Geoffrey Best, *Humanity in Warfare* (New York: Columbia University Press, 1980), 216–62; Howard, *War*, chap. 5; and Bond, *War and Society*, chap. 5.

27. A spirited introduction to the question is found in Calleo, *The German Problem*, chap. 3. See also Ritter, *Das deutsche Problem*, chap. 5.

28. See Bertram D. Wolfe, "Communist Ideology and Soviet Foreign Policy," in his *An Ideology in Power* (New York: Stein & Day, 345–61); and Topitsch, "Machtkampf und Humanität," 192–95.

29. See Seton-Watson, *Imperialist Revolutionaries.*

30. Blum, quoted in Jacob L. Talmon, *The Myth of the Nation and the Vision of Revolution* (Berkeley and Los Angeles: University of California Press, 1981), 445. See also Nolte, *Deutschland und der Kalte Krieg*, 73–88 and 122–23, on the profound ideological origins of the Cold War.

31. Sidney Hook discusses the Leninist form of Marxism in "Marxism: A Synoptic Exposition," in his *Marxism and Beyond* (Totowa, N.J.: Rowman & Littlefield, 1983), 23–53, on 34–46. See also Leszek Kolakowski, *Main Currents of Marxism*, vol. 2, *The Golden Age* (Oxford: Oxford University Press, 1978).

32. For an examination of the "totalitarian pandemic" as the result of changes in the social psychology of certain groups and classes, see Emmanuel Todd, *Le fou et le prolétaire*, 2d ed. (Paris: Livre de Poche, 1981). A less provocative attempt to define the specific temper as well as the causes of the ideological confrontations of the 1920s and the 1930s is Bracher, *Zeit der Ideologien*, especially part 2.

33. Raymond Aron, *On War* (New York: W. W. Norton, 1968), 86, quoted in Phillips, *War and Justice*, 73.

34. Churchill, *Gathering Storm*, 40.

35. Ibid., 41.

36. Quoted by Pierre Hassner in his introduction to Aron, *Les dernières années*, 8. On the turn to the doctrine of "peaceful coexistence" in the Soviet Union, see Michel Heller and Aleksandr Nekrich, *L'Utopie au pouvoir* (Paris: Calmann-Lévy, 1982), 466–69; and Bertram D. Wolfe, "The Age of the Diminishing Dictators," in his *Ideology in Power*, 224–25.

37. On the "nuclear revolution," see Michael Mandelbaum, *The Nuclear Revolution: International Politics Before and After Hiroshima* (New York: Cambridge University Press, 1981); and Gilpin, *War and Change*, 213–19 and 231–44. On the Soviet view of peace, see Vigor, *Soviet View*, 160–77; and Nitze, "Living With the Soviets."

CHAPTER 6

1. See Valentin Zsifkovits, "Friede," *Katholisches Soziallexikon*, cols. 781–93.

2. See the characteristic statements in Freimut Duve, Heinrich Böll, and Klaus Staeck, eds., *Kämpfen für die sanfte Republik* (Reinbek: Rowohlt, 1980). In *Das Gotteskomplex* (Reinbek: Rowohlt, 1979), the psychologist Horst Eberhard Richter assumes that the problem of contemporary West German society is still the drive to be tough and perfect, and not, as I argue, the *Wehleidigkeit* (whining self-pity) and *Angst* of the new sentimentalists.

3. See Hook, "Marxism."

4. Two surveys of West German political science and sociology by practitioners critical of neo-Marxism and antiauthoritarianism are Hans-Joachim Arndt, *Die Besiegten von 1945: Versuch einer Politologie für Deutsche samt Würdigung der Politikwissenschaft in der Bundesrepublik Deutschland* (Berlin: Duncker & Humblot, 1978); and Helmut Schelsky, *Rückblicke eines 'Anti-Soziologen'* (Opladen: Westdeutscher

Verlag, 1981). On democracy theory in general, see the survey by its most prominent West German follower, Karl Dietrich Bracher, in his *Zeit der Ideologien*, 331-50.

5. The main work is Jürgen Habermas, *Theorie des kommunikativen Handelns*, 2 vols. (Frankfurt: Suhrkamp, 1981). The political implications of Habermas's position, however, are much more clear in other works, especially in his *Legitimationsprobleme im Spätkapitalismus* (Frankfurt: Suhrkamp, 1973). For his support of the peace movement, see Jürgen Habermas, "Recht und Gewalt—Ein deutsches Trauma," *Merkur* 38 (1984): 15-28; and the reply by Martin Kriele, "Friedenspolitik am Scheideweg," ibid., 803-12.

6. This is the basic thesis of Schelsky, *Die Arbeit tun die anderen*. I shall be drawing repeatedly on Schelsky's work in this chapter. For a very similar analysis, see Thomas A. Spragens, Jr., *The Irony of Liberal Reason* (Chicago: University of Chicago Press, 1981), 150-77. It is only fair to note that Schelsky's book has been vigorously attacked, not just by intellectuals of the type targeted by him, but by others who, like him, criticize the romanticism and the sentimental antipolitical mentality with which I am concerned; see, for example, Richard Löwenthal, "Neues Mittelalter oder anomische Kulturkrise?" in his *Gesellschaftswandel und Kulturkrise* (Frankfurt: Fischer, 1979), 37-57. A positive conception of authority that can be opposed to the negative neo-Marxist and other "critical" theories is found in Carl J. Friedrich, *Tradition and Authority* (London: Pall Mall Press, 1972).

7. See Alastair MacIntyre, *After Virtue* (Notre Dame, Ind.: Notre Dame University Press, 1981), 35-59. MacIntyre, however, fails to discuss the German idealist attempt to justify morality.

8. See George A. Kelly, *Hegel's Retreat from Eleusis* (Princeton, N.J.: Princeton University Press, 1978).

9. See Heinrich Rommen, *Die ewige Wiederkehr des Naturrechts*, 2d ed. (Munich: Kösel, 1947), 76-127, on individualist natural rights theories of the seventeenth and eighteenth centuries and the rise of the historical school of law; and Spragens, *Irony of Liberal Reason*, 203-13.

10. On the idea of autonomy in Hegel, see Charles Taylor, *Hegel and Modern Society* (Cambridge: University Press, 1979).

11. See Nipperdey, *Deutsche Geschichte, 1800-1866*, 504-8 and 531-33 (on Hegelianism), and 663-70 (on the failure of the revolution of 1848).

12. On the history of revolutionary utopianism, nationalism, and organized socialism from the mid-nineteenth century to World War I, see Talmon, *The Myth of the Nation*. On the development of Marxism particularly, see Kolakowski, *Main Currents*, vol. 2.

13. See Rommen, *Ewige Wiederkehr*, 128-39; and Roland Girtler, "Rechtspositivismus," *Katholisches Soziallexikon*, cols. 2362-68, a first-rate overview.

14. For a classic statement of the legal positivist position on the rationality of value judgments, see Hans Kelsen, "What Is Justice?" in his *What Is Justice?* (Berkeley and Los Angeles: University of California Press, 1957), 1-24. See also 159, 174, 266-67, 295-97, and 390. On legal positivism in Germany in general, see Kenneth H.

F. Dyson, *The State Tradition in Western Europe* (Oxford: Martin Robertson, 1980), 107–10 and 175–79. See also the wise remarks on natural law, rights, and positivism by Maurice Cranston, *What Are Human Rights?* (New York: Taplinger, 1973), 9–24.

15. The late Alf Ross (1899–1979), a student of Kelsen's and for many years the dean of Scandinavian legal theorists, aroused the violent ire of the New Left by publishing two feature articles in the leading Danish daily in 1969 on Herbert Marcuse, whom he called "the herald of left fascism." What the left fascists did not know and probably never suspected was that Ross, who had been denied his doctorate of law in Copenhagen in the 1930s by the reigning school of legal theorists, was a committed social democrat and known in his youth as "Alf the Red."

16. On the revival of natural law, see Johannes Messner, "Naturrecht," *Katholisches Soziallexikon*, col. 1901; and the relevant articles in Werner Maihofer, ed., *Naturrecht oder Rechtspositivismus* (Darmstadt: Wissenschaftliche Buchgesellschaft, 1962). For a legal positivist response, see Hans Kelsen, "A 'Dynamic' Theory of Natural Law," in his *What Is Justice?* 174–97.

17. An example of such a reconstruction is Helmut Kuhn, *Der Staat* (Munich: Kösel, 1967).

18. Arndt, *Die Besiegten von 1945*, provides statistical evidence on the strength in the different university departments of various methodological and political orientations within political science. For examples of the anticriticism, see Karl Dietrich Bracher, *Zeitgeschichtliche Kontroversen*, 4th ed. (Munich: Piper, 1980); and the same author's *Zeit der Ideologien*.

19. On the "neglect of the state," see Dyson, *State Tradition*, 282–87; and the various articles in *Daedalus* 108, no. 4 (Fall 1979), a special issue entitled *The State*. See also Rüdiger Altmann, "Staats- und Geschichtsbewusstsein in der politischen Kultur der Bundesrepublik Deutschland," in Weigelt, *Heimat und Nation*, 220–26; and Willms, *Einführung in die Staatslehre*.

20. Schmitt, *Begriff des Politischen*, vi; and Ernst Forsthoff, *Der Staat der Industriegesellschaft* (Munich: Beck, 1971), especially chap. 1.

21. On the distinction of *Rechtsstaat* and *Sozialstaat*, see the articles in Ernst Forsthoff, ed., *Rechtsstaatlichkeit und Sozialstaatlichkeit* (Darmstadt: Wissenschaftliche Buchgesellschaft, 1968). For background on the history of the distinction, see Dyson, *State Tradition*, 117–34.

22. On its early history until its return to Germany, see Martin Jay, *The Dialectical Imagination* (New York: Basic Books, 1973); in general, see the chapter on Herbert Marcuse in Kolakowski, *Main Currents*, vol. 3, *The Breakdown*.

23. For an excellent summary of Habermas's complex thought, see Geoffrey Hawthorn, *Enlightenment and Despair* (Cambridge, Eng.: Cambridge University Press, 1976), 240–45.

24. The fundamental problem democracy theorists and other non-Marxist political scientists have in dealing with the Frankfurt School and Habermas, namely the lack of respect of the latter for institutional rationality and the significance of institutions in general, was emphasized in the two most important public confrontations

between these groups that have hitherto taken place. The first was the Popper-Adorno debate at the ninth congress of the German Sociological Association in 1961, which expanded to include several other thinkers as well in subsequent years, and which became known as the *Positivismusstreit*; it is recorded in Theodor W. Adorno et al., *Der Streit um den Positivismus in der deutschen Soziologie* (Neuwied: Luchterhand, 1969). The second was the Hennis-Habermas debate on the notion of legitimacy at the sixteenth congress of the German Sociological Association in 1975; see Wilhelm Hennis, "Legitimität: Zu einer Kategorie der bürgerlichen Gesellschaft," in his *Politik und praktische Philosophie* (Stuttgart: Klett, 1977), 198–242; and cf. Dyson, *State Tradition*, 183.

CHAPTER 7

1. Two exceptional analyses of the longer-term value changes in West Germany, which may help to explain the rise of the peace movement, are Arnold Gehlen, *Moral und Hypermoral* (Frankfurt: Athenäum, 1969); and Tenbruck, "Alltagsnormen und Lebensgefühle." On Green support for neutralism, see Inglehart, "Generational Change."

2. For some choice examples, see Hermann Lübbe, *Endstation Terror* (Stuttgart: Seewald, 1978); and Arndt, *Die Besiegten von 1945*, 361–77.

3. Thomas Mann, *Betrachtungen eines Unpolitischen*, first published 1918, now reissued in the new Frankfurt Edition of separately available volumes of his works, ed. Peter de Mendelssohn (Frankfurt: S. Fischer, 1983). On the context and circumstances of its composition in 1914–1918, see Peter de Mendelssohn, *Der Zauberer* (Frankfurt: S. Fischer, 1975), 975–1181; and for its significance, Erich Heller, *Thomas Mann: The Ironic German* (Chicago: Henry Regnery, 1959; reprinted Cambridge: Cambridge University Press, 1979), chap. 3.

4. On the evolution of these "ideas," see Heinrich Lübbe, *Politische Philosophie in Deutschland*, 2d ed. (Munich: Deutscher Taschenbuch Verlag, 1975).

5. Except possibly by one or two historians; Hans-Peter Schwarz (*Die Ära Adenauer*) and Thomas Nipperdey (*Deutsche Geschichte 1800–1866*) both have a breadth of vision and an ease of style reminiscent of the grand tradition.

6. See his essays collected in *Die entmutigte Republik* (Munich: Hanser, 1979).

7. On current attitudes of West German youth, see the German Shell Foundation's report *Jugend '81* (Leverkusen: Leske, 1981), and more generally, Meulemann, "Value Changes." On the protest movements of the late 1960s and 1970s in general, see Langguth, *Protestbewegung*. On the ideology of the Greens, see Langguth, *Grüne Faktor*; and Papadakis, *Green Movement*.

8. See Gottfried Dietze, *Deutschland – Wo bist Du?* (Munich: Olzog, 1980), chap. 3.

9. Quoted in Henry M. Pachter, "Brecht's Personal Politics," in his *Weimar Etudes*, 232. The whole piece, 225–45, though much more sympathetic to Brecht than I think he deserves, is of great value for understanding him and his work. Cf. also the recep-

tion of Ronald Hayman, *Brecht: A Biography* (London: Weidenfeld & Nicolson, 1983) by Timothy Garton Ash in *Times Literary Supplement*, January 20, 1984, and the ensuing correspondence in subsequent issues (especially letters from Sidney Hook and Melvin J. Lasky, February 3, 1984).

10. Schelsky, *Die Arbeit tun die anderen*, 342–63, a case study of Böll's behavior in 1972–1974 as an example of the attitudes and mentality of what Schelsky calls "the new priesthood."

11. See Günter Grass, "Vom Recht auf Widerstand," in his *Widerstand lernen* (Neuwied: Luchterhand, 1984), 58–67.

12. The Heilbronn Manifesto is reproduced in ibid., 97–98. For the interview with Grass, see *Die Zeit*, March 2, 1984.

13. Gerhard Wettig, *Die Funktion der westeuropäischen Friedensbewegung in sowjetischer Sicht*, Berichte des Bundesinstituts für ostwissenschaftliche und internationale Studien, no. 49, 1983.

14. See Ernst-Wolfgang Böckenförde, "Rechtsstaatliche politische Selbstverteidigung als Problem," in Ernst-Wolfgang Böckenförde, Christian Tomuschat, and Dieter C. Umbach, eds., *Extremisten und öffentlicher Dienst* (Baden-Baden: Nomos, 1981), 9–33. I am heavily indebted to this incisive essay.

15. For the passages quoted, see Ernst-Wolfgang Böckenförde, *Der Staat als sittlicher Staat*, Wissenschaftliche Abhandlungen und Reden zur Philosophie, Politik und Geistesgeschichte 14 (Berlin: Duncker & Humblot, 1978), 24–30.

16. Schmitt, *Begriff des Politischen*; and Carl Schmitt, *Politische Theologie* 1, 2d ed., and 2 (Leipzig and Berlin: Duncker & Humblot, 1934 and 1970).

17. Liberation theologians were criticized in 1984 by the pope for their tendency to adopt Marxist ideology, an event that led to a good deal of media attention; see *The Economist*, October 13, 1984. A thorough, critical discussion of the origins and implications of liberation theology is James V. Schall, S.J., "Liberation Theology in Latin America," in James V. Schall, S.J., ed., *Liberation Theology* (San Francisco: Ignatius Press, 1982), 3–126. See also Edward Norman, *Christianity and the World Order* (Oxford: Oxford University Press, 1979); Michael Novak, *Freedom with Justice: Catholic Social Thought and Liberal Institutions* (San Francisco: Harper & Row, 1984), 183–94; and Martin Kriele, *Befreiung und politische Aufklärung* (Freiburg: Herder, 1980), 218–55.

18. On the shift from Christian socialism to the social market economy in the CDU, see Klessmann, *Doppelte Staatsgründung*, 142–47, with official party statements of 1945–1949 reprinted on 421–28.

19. Eschenburg, *Jahre der Besatzung*, 164–65. See also Schwarz, *Die Ära Adenauer, 1949–1957*, 446–48.

20. On the evolution of the EKD, see Klaus Motschmann, *Herrschaft der Minderheit* (Munich: Langen-Müller, 1983), 125–64. On Protestant pacifism and opposition to rearmament in the 1950s, see the sources collected, with sympathetic commentary, in Christian Walther, ed., *Atomwaffen und Ethik: Der deutsche Protestantismus und die atomare Aufrüstung, 1954–1961* (Berlin: Christian Kaiser, 1981). This work is highly

relevant for the study of West German Protestant pacifism in general, not just opposition to nuclear weapons. On the Catholic Church in West Germany, the background survey by Karl Forster, "Der deutsche Katholizismus in der Bundesrepublik Deutschland," in Anton Rauscher, S.J., ed., *Der soziale und politische Katholizismus* (Munich: Olzog, 1981), 1:209–64, is indispensable for an understanding of the state of West German Catholicism before the politicization that began in the late 1960s. Some later developments are included in Hans Maier, "Der Weg der deutschen Katholiken seit 1945," in his *Stellungnahmen* (Munich: Kösel, 1978), 134–51.

21. See Norman, *Christianity and the World Order*; Michael Novak, *The Spirit of Democratic Capitalism* (New York: Simon & Schuster, 1982), 235–95; and, for a sympathetic view of radical theology, Harvey Cox, *Religion in the Secular City* (New York: Simon & Schuster, 1984), 85–171. For brief presentations by two leading adherents of the new political theology, see the contributions by Johann Baptist Metz and Dorothee Sölle to Jürgen Habermas, ed., *Stichworte zur "Geistigen Situation der Zeit"* (Frankfurt: Suhrkamp, 1979). On Sölle see also Michael Novak, "What German Theology Teaches America: The Case of Dorothee Sölle," *Catholicism in Crisis* 2, no. 6 (May 1984): 27–32.

22. John Courtney Murray, S.J., "War and Conscience," in James Finn, ed., *A Conflict of Loyalties: The Case for Selective Conscientious Objection* (New York: Pegasus, 1968), 22–24; quoted in James E. Dougherty, *The Bishops and Nuclear Weapons: The Catholic Pastoral Letter on War and Peace* (Hamden, Conn.: Archon Books, 1984), 96.

23. This was specifically pointed out by the French, and with somewhat less vigor by the West German, bishops in their pastoral letters on war and peace; see the English translations in James V. Schall, S.J., ed., *Bishops' Pastoral Letters* (San Francisco: Ignatius Press, 1984). The issue was skirted in the pastoral of the U.S. bishops, *The Challenge of Peace: God's Promise and Our Response* (Washington, D.C.: United States Catholic Conference, 1983). See the criticism in Dougherty, *Bishops and Nuclear Weapons*, esp. 136–41 and 185–90; Philip F. Lawler, *The Ultimate Weapon* (Chicago: Regnery Gateway, 1984); and Michael Novak, ed., *Clarity in the Nuclear Age* (Nashville, Tenn.: Thomas Nelson, 1983). Both the strategic and the moral arguments of the U.S. bishops were criticized by Herman Kahn, *Thinking About the Unthinkable in the 1980s* (New York: Simon & Schuster, 1984), 46–49 and 211–17; and by Albert Wohlstetter, "Bishops, Statesmen, and Other Strategists on the Bombing of Innocents," *Commentary*, July 1983, 15–35. A West German response to the U. S. pastoral by two leading Catholic policymakers directly charged that it "makes war and oppression in Europe more likely": Georg Leber and Alois Mertes, "Eine Herausforderung an unser christliches Gewissen," in Hans-Joachim Veen, ed., *Argumente für Frieden und Freiheit*, Forschungsbericht Konrad-Adenauer-Stiftung 25 (Melle: Ernst Knoth, 1983), 25–32. On the relevance of the just-war doctrine in the nuclear age in general, see Dougherty, *Bishops and Nuclear Weapons*; James T. Johnson, *Can Modern War Be Just?* (New Haven and London: Yale University Press, 1984); and William V. O'Brien, "Just-War Doctrine in a Nuclear Context," *Theological Studies* 44 (1983): 191–220. The foundation for all debate on just-war teaching in the nuclear era is the classic work by John Courtney Murray, S.J., *We Hold These Truths* (New York: Sheed & Ward, 1960), 221–73.

24. In Europe, the tendency has been far more pronounced in Protestant bodies; see Jean Klein, "Les chrétiens, les armes nucléaires et la paix," in Lellouche, *Pacifisme et dissuasion*, 199–222; and Hassner, "Arms Control and the Politics of Pacifism."

25. See Chapter 4 and note 3 to Chapter 8.

26. For a summary of important statements by Catholic bodies, primarily in West Germany, see Heinz Theo Risse and Hans Jürgen Müller, "Zum Stand der kirchlichen Friedensarbeit," in Norbert Glatzel and Ernst Josef Nagel, eds., *Frieden in Sicherheit* (Freiburg: Herder, 1981), 176–212; and for the traditional position, the two contributions in section I, "Die Antwort der katholischen Tradition," of that work. Czempiel's statement dates from 1967 and is found in his "Die Christen und die auswürtige Politik: Lehre vom gerechten Krieg oder Praxeologie des Friedens," *Civitas* 6 (1967): 20–45.

CHAPTER 8

1. See Kaiser, "Prioritäten sozialdemokratischer Aussen- und Sicherheitspolitik," in Maruhn and Wilke, *Wohin treibt die SPD?* 9–27.

2. For some suggestions as to what a dynamic Western policy toward the Soviet Union might look like, see Aaron Wildavsky, ed., *Beyond Containment* (San Francisco: Institute for Contemporary Studies, 1983).

3. The Bug is a river that forms part of the post-1945 Polish-Soviet border. The phrase is Peter Bender's more modest version of de Gaulle's ambitious vision of a *Europe des patries* stretching from the Atlantic to the Urals, in which a nationalistic, but no longer Marxist-Leninist, Russia, would be the Eastern anchor of a system of states with common interests and perceptions. For Bender's ideas, see his *Das Ende des ideologischen Zeitalters*; his "Die Wirklichkeit Europas," *L'80*, no. 25 (Spring 1983): 15–25; and his article on Germany, "Fest im Westen—Eine Brücke zum Osten," *Die Zeit*, February 17, 1984.

4. Frei and Ruloff, "Entspannungserwartungen und Entspannungsfolgen."

5. The results of research at HSFK are published by Suhrkamp in the series Friedensanalysen, which had reached eighteen volumes by late 1984. Volume 16 is an anthology of studies of various aspects of the peace movement from the perspective of peace research; see Reiner Steinweg, ed., *Die neue Friedensbewegung* (Frankfurt: Suhrkamp, 1982). Suhrkamp has played an important role as a conduit for political writings and politically committed research supporting the ideas of the peace movement and the New Left. For a comprehensive statement of the beliefs and arguments of "critical peace research" by one of its inventors, see Galtung, *Environment, Development and Military Activity*. Tenbruck, "Frieden durch Friedensforschung?" exposes the scientific pretensions of critical peace research for what they are, a faith in utopian social organization masquerading as science.

6. See, for example, Gaus, *Wo Deutschland liegt*, 281–86. For further examples, and an excellent critique, of such attitudes in the SPD and the peace movement, see Friedrich-Wilhelm Baer-Kaupert, "Frieden—Das ist die einzige Alternative: Über die

Schwierigkeiten, zwischen Desinformation und Drohpolitik eine Politik zur Sicherung des Friedens zu entwickeln," in Maruhn and Wilke, *Wohin treibt die SPD?* 53–78.

7. For typical expressions of this line, see Dönhoff's front-page editorial in *Die Zeit*, April 1, 1983; and Theo Sommer's reports from Moscow in ibid., March 18 and 25, 1983.

8. See especially Manel, *L'Europe face aux SS 20*, with a preface by Raymond Aron, which is also a first-rate summary of the whole problem; and Tatu, *Bataille des Euromissiles*.

9. See Huntington, "Broadening the Strategic Focus"; Radway, "Toward the Europeanisation of NATO"; and Howard, "Reassurance and Deterrence."

10. Hassner, "Pacifisme et terreur," 176; and, for an East European view, Kundera, "The Tragedy of Central Europe."

11. Since the late 1970s, Americans and Frenchmen have been much more willing than most West Germans to look objectively at the relationship of political division and conflict in Europe; see, for example, Zbigniew Brzezinski, "The Future of Yalta," *Foreign Affairs* 63 (1984–85): 279–302; Glucksmann, *La Force du vertige*; and Aron, *Les dernières années*.

12. For an overview of these ideas and for some comments on the weakness of arguments for constitutional democracy as a source of the defeats of democracy in the interwar period, see Bracher, *Zeit der Ideologien*, 239–52. See also his *Geschichte und Gewalt* for further perspectives on the common patterns of both left- and right-wing arguments against constitutional democracy and belief in reason and progress.

13. Quoted in Charles S. Maier, "The Two Postwar Eras and the Conditions for Stability in Twentieth-Century Western Europe," *American Historical Review* 86 (1981): 327. The sense that comprehensive economic planning and some degree of socialism were inevitable was widespread even among liberals in the 1940s. The best statement of this belief is Joseph A. Schumpeter, *Capitalism, Socialism and Democracy*, 3d ed. (London: George Allen & Unwin, 1950), esp. 131–63 . That this sense gave way to a revival of belief in free enterprise and democratic capitalism was due in no small measure to the arguments of Friedrich A. Hayek, *The Road to Serfdom* (1944; rev. ed., London: Routledge & Kegan Paul, 1976). An overview of the course of this revival and of the democratic consensus in West Germany in the 1950s is given by Schwarz, *Die Ära Adenauer, 1949–1957*, 439–53.

14. On Mounier and *Esprit*, see Michel Winock, *Histoire politique de la revue "Esprit," 1930–1950* (Paris: Seuil, 1975). Mounier died in 1950.

15. The philosophical justification of the tenet that the free market contributes more than any collectivist system to pluralism, equality of opportunity, and social development has been the lifelong task of Friedrich A. Hayek. For a brief summary of his argument, see his "The Principles of a Liberal Social Order," in the selection from his work entitled *The Essence of Hayek* (Stanford: Hoover Institution Press, 1984), 363–81.

16. On the fear of progress in the material, technical sense as a root of the new ideology, see Bracher, *Zeit der Ideologien*, especially the last three chapters; and

Hermann Lübbe, *Zwischen Trend und Tradition* (Zürich: Interfrom, 1981). On the early stages of the protest movement, see Langguth, *Protestbewegung*, 36–56, and, on the Greens in particular, Holmes, "Origins of the Green Movement."

17. Strauss's "Gaullism" and concern for the independence and sovereignty of Western Europe has not prevented him from conducting his own personal Ostpolitik after he was refused the post of foreign minister in Kohl's cabinet in 1982. It consisted of arranging several $300 million loans to East Germany in 1983–1984, and, to the degree that it provides aid to a regime he formerly regarded as illegitimate, it contradicts his professed principles as stated, for instance, in his "The Manifesto of an Atlanticist," *Strategic Review* 10, no. 3 (Summer 1982): 11–15.

18. For the views of Diwald, Mohler, and Sander, see their contributions to the journal *Criticón*, no. 60 (March–April 1982); and for the neo-nationalism of the students organized in the Bund Deutscher Burschenschaften, see Henning Eichberg, *Nationale Identität* (Munich: Langen-Müller, 1978); and the contributions in Helmut Grosser, ed., *Das Volk ohne Staat* (Neustadt: Pfaehler, 1981). See also Eichberg's declaration "National ist revolutionär" in Brandt and Ammon, *Die Linke und die nationale Frage*, 351–52.

19. See Szabo, *The Successor Generation*; and, for conclusions regarding the political impact of the successor generation in positions of influence, Szabo, "Brandt's Children."

20. Inglehart, "Generational Change."

21. See Stratmann, *NATO-Strategie*, 228–40.

22. The classic statements of this crucial assumption of peace research are Dieter Senghaas, *Rüstung und Militarismus* (Frankfurt: Suhrkamp, 1972); and Galtung, *Environment, Development and Military Activity*. For a critical analysis of its presuppositions and implications, see Karl-Peter Stratmann, "Vom Autismus kritischer Friedensforschung," in Funke, *Friedensforschung*, 397–423. I should note that Funke's anthology consists primarily of arguments for, not against, peace research and its alleged benefits.

23. Howard, *Causes of Wars*, 22.

24. Hassner, "The Shifting Foundation," 30.

25. On the Scandilux ideas, see Petersen, "Scandilux Experiment."

26. Zbigniew Brzezinski, "The Atlantic Crisis: A Personal View," *Atlantic Quarterly* 1 (1983): 97.

27. Bender, *Das Ende des ideologischen Zeitalters*, 18. Quoted with critical comments by Bracher, *Zeit der Ideologien*, 352.

28. Richard Lowenthal, *World Communism: The Disintegration of a Secular Faith* (New York: Oxford University Press, 1965).

29. See Bracher, *Zeit der Ideologien*, 351–71.

30. See George F. Kennan, *Nuclear Delusions* (New York: Harper & Row, 1982). Kennan is popular among certain West German commentators, notably Theo Sommer and Marion Gräfin Dönhoff of *Die Zeit*, where Kennan's writings themselves also often appear in German translation. For Liska's extraordinary views, the popu-

larity of which is directly proportional to their opacity and vagueness, see his *Russia and the Road to Appeasement* (Baltimore: Johns Hopkins University Press, 1982); and "The West at the Crossroads: The Case for U.S.-Soviet Appeasement," *SAIS Review* 3, no. 1 (Winter–Spring, 1983): 169–81. Note that Liska takes appeasement in a positive sense, as a necessary step to defuse tension.

31. See Daniel Yankelovich and John Doble, "The Public Mood: Nuclear Weapons and the USSR," *Foreign Affairs* 63 (1984–85): 33–46.

32. See, for two notable examples, Bertram D. Wolfe, *Revolution and Reality* (Chapel Hill: University of North Carolina Press, 1981); and Robert Conquest, "Soviet Foreign Policy."

33. Robert Conquest, "Relating to Russia," *Survey*, nos. 100–101 (Summer–Autumn 1976): 139.

34. The contributors to Wildavsky, ed., *Beyond Containment*, and Richard Pipes, *Survival Is Not Enough* (New York: Simon & Schuster, 1984), all suggest various policies that would both decrease the danger of war and promote the general Western interest in a weakening of Soviet expansionism.

35. Bukovsky, "The Peace Movement and the Soviet Union," 84. Cf. Garton Ash, *Polish Revolution*, 332–37.

CHAPTER 9

1. Helmut Donat and Johann P. Tammen, eds., *Friedenszeichen — Lebenszeichen: Pazifismus zwischen Verächtlichmachung und Rehabilitierung. Ein Lesebuch zur Friedenserziehung* (Bremerhaven: Die Horen, 1982); and Jonathan Schell, *The Fate of the Earth* (New York: Vintage Press, 1982). On Schell, see also Leon Wieseltier, *Nuclear War, Nuclear Peace* (New York: Holt, Rinehart & Winston, 1983); and Kahn, *Thinking About the Unthinkable in the 1980s*, 207–8.

2. See Hannah Arendt, *The Human Condition* (Chicago: University of Chicago Press, 1958).

3. Bukovsky, "The Peace Movement and the Soviet Union," 84. For Sidney Hook's "thumbnail credo," see his "On Western Freedom," in his *Marxism and Beyond*, 207.

4. For detailed criticism of the position of the U.S. bishops on both strategic and moral grounds, see Kahn, *Thinking About the Unthinkable in the 1980s*, esp. 46–49 and 211–17.

5. Wohlstetter, "Racing Forward? Or Ambling Back?"

6. Ulam, *Dangerous Relations*, 315.

7. On FOFA, see Sutton et al., "New Directions in Conventional Defence?"

8. See Freedman, *Evolution*, 285–302.

9. Quoted by Nerlich, "Theatre Nuclear Forces," 67.

10. Grass, *Widerstand lernen*, 64.

11. Schwarz, "Alternative zum Kalten Krieg?" 302.

12. Elisabeth Noelle-Neumann, "Do We Need a Flag?" *Encounter,* January 1983, 72–80. See also the broad survey of young people's opinions and attitudes carried out by the German Shell Foundation, *Jugend '81* (Leverkusen: Leske, 1982); and Meulemann, "Value Change."

13. On differences between the radicalism of the 1960s and the Green and peace movements of the 1980s, see Bracher, *Zeit der Ideologien,* 306–30; and, from a viewpoint inspired by 1960s leftism itself, Berman, "Peace Movement Debate."

14. On the demands of the Greens, see Papadakis, *Green Movement,* 18–62.

15. For an analysis of this malaise and its social and psychological origins, see Christopher Lasch, *The Minimal Self* (New York: W. W. Norton, 1984). While critical of excessive pessimism, Lasch nevertheless accepts certain assumptions of the peace movement, particularly the idea that peace and stability will not come about as long as nuclear weapons exist.

16. See Inglehart, "Generational Change"; and Meulemann, "Value Change." On the contrast between postmaterialist values and the survival requirements of industrial society in general, see Daniel Bell, *The Cultural Contradictions of Capitalism,* 2d ed. (New York: Basic Books, 1978). The psychology of postmaterialism and the interactions between value change and cultural change are the subject of Bernice Martin, *A Sociology of Contemporary Cultural Change* (New York: St. Martin's Press, 1981), which contains a number of observations relevant to an understanding of the genesis of the peace movement and its outlook. Bernice Martin has applied her theory of cultural change to the psychology of antinuclear pacifism directly in "Invisible Religion, Popular Culture and Anti-nuclear Sentiment," in David Martin and Peter Mullen, eds., *Unholy Warfare* (Oxford: Blackwell, 1983), 108–40.

17. Schelsky, *Die Arbeit tun die anderen;* and Walter Künneth, "Die Ideologie des Pazifismus: Eine Staatsgefährdung?" *Zeitschrift für Politik* 29 (1982): 282–94.

18. *Frankfurter Allgemeine Zeitung,* May 31, 1980, quoted with disapproval by Richard Saage, *Rückkehr zum starken Staat?* (Frankfurt: Suhrkamp, 1983), 255–56.

19. See the introduction to Habermas, *Stichworte;* and two pieces by Richard Saage, "Rückkehr zum starken Staat? Zur Renaissance des Freund-Feind-Denkens in der Bundesrepublik," and "Neokonservatives Denken in der Bundesrepublik," both in his *Rückkehr.*

CHAPTER 10

1. Walter Laqueur, "Post-Pershing Germany," *The New Republic,* March 5, 1984.

2. The observer is Alexei Alexeiev of the Graduate School of the RAND Corporation. His analysis, on which this paragraph is based, was provided at a Hoover Institution seminar. The full details are found in a report compiled by Alexeiev in 1984 for government use.

3. Despite the hopes of Karl Kaiser and others as reported by James Markham in the *New York Times,* March 12, 1984, there was no sign by early 1985 of a serious revival of Atlanticism in the SPD. For some troubled assessments and occasional

harsh words by Atlanticist Social Democrats, see Maruhn and Wilke, *Wohin treibt die SPD?*; especially Kaiser, "Prioritäten"; Winkler, "Wohin treibt die SPD?"; and Hartmut Jäckel, "Offener Brief an den Oppositionsführer," 79–86.

4. Winkler, "Wohin treibt die SPD?"

5. Schwan, "Die SPD und die westliche Freiheit," 43.

6. Ibid., 43–51. See also Richard Löwenthal's criticism of the views of leading Social Democrats, who, in his words, feared "reideologization and anticommunism" rather than "the danger presented by the Soviet bloc" and who had forgotten that the East-West conflict is unavoidably ideological and that "German identity can only be realized in the defense of Western values," and not in any spurious neutralism, in *Die Zeit*, May 25, 1984. Löwenthal's tough talk and his willingness to point out dangerous tendencies in the SPD in this article contrast curiously with his almost Bahr-like admonitions to the U.S. government of the "urgent need for steps to overcome the confrontation," as though such steps were either possible or in the Western interest, in "The German Question Transformed," *Foreign Affairs* 63 (1984–85): 315. It would seem that Löwenthal is worried enough to criticize the SPD, but only in a German forum; in international journals, he stands by his party against reckless U.S. and NATO policies. His loyalty does him credit, but one wonders whether maintaining it to such an extent is truly "im deutschen Interesse."

7. Howard, "Reassurance and Deterrence," in his *The Causes of Wars*, 257. Emphasis in original.

8. McGeorge Bundy, George Kennan, Robert McNamara, and Gerard Smith, "Nuclear Weapons and the Atlantic Alliance," *Foreign Affairs* 60 (1981–82): 753–68; and Kahn, *Thinking About the Unthinkable in the 1980s*, 212 and 218–20. On prospects for improving the political stability of NATO, see also two articles by Henry Kissinger, "Nuclear Weapons and the Peace Movement," *Washington Quarterly* 5, no. 3 (Summer 1982): 31–39; and "A Plan to Reshape NATO," in Laqueur and Hunter, *European Peace Movements*.

BIBLIOGRAPHY

Adomeit, Hannes. "The Political Rationale of Soviet Military Capabilities and Doctrine." In *Strengthening Conventional Deterrence in Europe*. Report of the European Security Study. New York: St. Martin's Press, 1983, pp. 67–104.

_____. "Relations Between Eastern and Western Europe: Prospects for Change, I." In *The Conduct of East-West Relations in the 1980s*. Part 1. Adelphi Paper 190. London: International Institute for Strategic Studies, 1984, pp. 1–11.

_____. "Soviet Decision-Making and Western Europe." In Edwina Moreton and George Segal, eds., *Soviet Strategy Toward Western Europe*. London: George Allen & Unwin, 1984, pp. 39–84.

_____. *Soviet Risk-Taking and Crisis Behavior: A Theoretical and Empirical Analysis*. London: George Allen & Unwin, 1982.

Afheldt, Horst. *Atomkrieg. Das Verhängnis einer Politik mit militärischen Mitteln*. Munich: Hanser, 1984.

_____. *Verteidigung und Frieden*. Munich: Hanser, 1976.

_____. *Defensive Verteidigung*. Reinbek: Rowohlt, 1983.

Altmann, Rüdiger. "Staats- und Geschichtsbewusstsein in der politischen Kultur der Bundesrepublik Deutschland." In Klaus Weigelt, ed., *Heimat und Nation*. Studien zur politischen Bildung 7. Mainz: von Hase und Koehler, 1984, pp. 220–26.

Arndt, Hans-Joachim. *Die Besiegten von 1945: Versuch einer Politologie für Deutsche samt Würdigung der Politikwissenschaft in der Bundesrepublik Deutschland*. Berlin: Duncker und Humblot, 1978.

Aron, Raymond. *Les Dernières années du siècle*. Paris: Commentaire Julliard, 1984.

_____. *Paix et guerre entre les nations*. 8th ed. Paris: Calmann-Lévy, 1984.

Baer-Kaupert, Friedrich-Wilhelm. "Frieden – Das ist die einzige Alternative: Über die Schwierigkeiten, zwischen Desinformation und Drohpolitik eine Politik zur Sicherung des Friedens zu entwickeln." In Jürgen Maruhn and Manfred Wilke, eds., *Wohin treibt die SPD?* Munich: Olzog, 1984, pp. 53–78.

Baker, Kendall; Dalton, Russel J.; and Hildebrandt, Kai. *Germany Transformed: Political Culture and the New Politics.* Cambridge, Mass.: Harvard University Press, 1981.

Ball, Desmond. *Targeting for Strategic Deterrence.* Adelphi Paper 185. London: International Institute for Strategic Studies, 1983.

Baring, Arnulf. *Machtwechsel: Die Ära Brandt-Scheel.* Stuttgart: Deutsche Verlags-Anstalt, 1982.

Barron, John. *KGB Today: The Hidden Hand.* New York: Reader's Digest Press, 1983.

Bender, Peter. *Das Ende des ideologischen Zeitalters.* Berlin: Severin und Siedler, 1981.

———. "Die Wirklichkeit Europas," *L'80,* no. 25 (February 1983): 15–25.

Benz, Wolfgang; Plum, Günther; and Röder, Werner. *Einheit der Nation: Diskussionen und Konzeptionen zur Deutschlandpolitik der grossen Parteien seit 1945.* Stuttgart: Frommann, 1978.

Benz, Wolfgang, and Graml, Hermann, eds. *Aspekte deutscher Aussenpolitik im 20. Jahrhundert.* Stuttgart: Deutsche Verlags-Anstalt, 1976.

Berghahn, Volker R. *Modern Germany: Society, Economy and Politics in the Twentieth Century.* Cambridge, Eng.: Cambridge University Press, 1982.

Bergsdorf, Wolfgang. *Herrschaft und Sprache.* Pfullingen: Neske, 1983.

Berman, Russell A. "The Peace Movement Debate: Provisional Conclusions." *Telos,* no. 57 (Fall 1983): 129–44.

Berschin, Helmut. *Deutschland – Ein Name im Wandel.* Munich: Olzog, 1981.

Besançon, Alain, and Gann, Lewis. "The Churches, Peace and Communism." In Dennis L. Bark, ed., *To Promote Peace.* Stanford: Hoover Institution Press, 1984, pp. 25–40.

Besson, Waldemar. *Die Aussenpolitik der Bundesrepublik.* Munich: Piper, 1970.

Beste, Hans Dieter. "Offensive gegen die Angst." *Europäische Wehrkunde* 31 (1982): 387–89

Beyme, Klaus von. *The Political System of the Federal Republic of Germany.* New York: St. Martin's Press, 1982.

———. "The Power Structure in the Federal Republic of Germany." In Charles Burdick, Hans-Adolf Jacobsen, and Winfried Kudszus, eds., *Contemporary Germany: Politics and Culture.* Boulder, Colo.: Westview Press, 1984, pp. 77–102.

Biedenkopf, Kurt. "Domestic Consensus, Security and the Western Alliance." In *Defence and Consensus: The Domestic Aspects of Western Security.* Part 1. Adelphi Paper 182. London: International Institute for Strategic Studies, 1983, pp. 6–13.

Böckenförde, Ernst-Wolfgang. "Rechtsstaatliche politische Selbstverteidigung als Problem." In Ernst-Wolfgang Böckenförde, Christian Tomuschat, and Dieter C. Umbach, eds., *Extremisten und öffentlicher Dienst.* Baden-Baden: Nomos, 1981, pp. 9–33.

_____. *Der Staat als sittlicher Staat.* Berlin: Duncker und Humblot, 1978.

_____. *Staat, Gesellschaft, Freiheit.* Frankfurt: Suhrkamp, 1976.

Bomsdorf, Falk. "Arms Control as a Process of Self-Constraint: The Workings of Western Negotiating Policy." In Uwe Nerlich, ed., *Soviet Power and Western Negotiating Policies.* Cambridge, Mass.: Ballinger, 1983, 2:67–116.

Bond, Brian. *War and Society in Europe, 1870–1970.* London: Fontana, 1984.

Bonin, Bogislav von. *Opposition gegen Adenauers Sicherheitspolitik.* Hamburg: Verlag Neue Politik, 1976.

Borst, Arno. "Barbarossas Erwachen: Zur Geschichte der deutschen Identität." In Odo Marquard and Karlheinz Stierle, eds., *Identität.* Munich: Wilhelm Fink, 1979, pp. 17–60.

Boyens, Armin, ed. *Kirchen in der Nachkriegsgeschichte.* Göttingen: Vandenhoeck und Ruprecht, 1979.

Bracher, Karl Dietrich. *Geschichte und Gewalt.* Berlin: Severin und Siedler, 1981.

_____. *Zeit der Ideologien: Eine Geschichte politischen Denkens im 20. Jahrhundert.* Stuttgart: Deutsche Verlags-Anstalt, 1982.

_____. *Zeitgeschichtliche Kontroversen.* 4th ed. Munich: Piper, 1980.

Brand, Karl-Werner. *Neue soziale Bewegungen: Entstehung, Funktion und Perspektive neuer Protestpotentiale.* Opladen: Westdeutscher Verlag, 1982.

Brandt, Peter, ed. *Preussen—Versuch einer Bilanz,* vol. 3, *Zur Sozialgeschichte eines Staates.* Reinbek: Rowohlt, 1981.

Brandt, Peter, and Ammon, Herbert, eds. *Die Linke und die nationale Frage.* Reinbek: Rowohlt, 1981.

Brandt, Willy. *Begegnungen und Einsichten.* Hamburg: Hoffmann und Campe, 1976.

_____. *Friedenspolitik in Europa.* Frankfurt: S. Fischer, 1968.

Bredow, Wilfrid von. "Geschichte als Element der deutschen Identität?" In Werner Weidenfeld, ed., *Die Identität der Deutschen.* Munich: Hanser, 1983, pp. 102–18.

Brodie, Bernard. "The Development of Nuclear Strategy." *International Security* 2, no. 4 (Spring 1978): 65–83.

Brünner, Christian. "Verteidigung." In *Katholisches Soziallexikon.* 2d ed. Verlag Tyrolia: Innsbruck, 1980, cols. 3203–20.

Brzezinski, Zbigniew. "The Atlantic Crisis: A Personal View." *Atlantic Quarterly* 1 (1983): 95–104.

_____. "The Future of Yalta." *Foreign Affairs* 63 (1984–85): 279–302.

Bukovsky, Vladimir. "The Peace Movement and the Soviet Union." *Commentary* (June 1982). Reprinted in Francis Schaeffer, Vladimir Bukovsky, and James Hitchcock, *Who Is for Peace?* Nashville, Tenn.: Thomas Nelson, 1983.

Bull, Hedley. "European Self-Reliance and the Reform of NATO." *Atlantic Quarterly* 1 (1983): 25–43.

_____. "The State in the Modern World." *Daedalus* 108, no. 4 (Fall 1979): 111–123.

Bundy, McGeorge; Kennan, George; McNamara, Robert; and Smith, Gerard. "Nuclear Weapons and the Atlantic Alliance." *Foreign Affairs* 60 (1981– 82): 753–68.

Burdick, Charles; Jacobsen, Hans-Adolf; and Kudszus, Winfried, eds. *Contemporary Germany: Politics and Culture*. Boulder, Colo.: Westview Press, 1984.

Burrows, Bernard, and Edwards, Geoffrey. *The Defence of Western Europe*. London: Butterworths, 1982.

Calleo, David P. "The Atlantic Alliance: An Enduring Relationship?" *SAIS Review*, no. 4 (Summer 1982): 27–39.

_____. *The German Problem Reconsidered*. New York: Cambridge University Press, 1978.

The Challenge of Peace: God's Promise and Our Response. Washington, D.C.: United States Catholic Conference, 1983.

Childs, David, and Johnson, Jeffrey. *West Germany: Politics and Society*. New York: St. Martin's Press, 1981.

Churchill, Winston S. *The Second World War*. Vol. 1: *The Gathering Storm*. Vol. 6: *Triumph and Tragedy*. Boston: Houghton Mifflin Co., 1948, 1953.

Clemens, Clay. "The Green Program for German Society and International Affairs." In Robert L. Pfaltzgraff, Jr., Kim R. Holmes, Clay Clemens, and Werner Kaltefleiter, *The Greens of West Germany*. Cambridge, Mass.: Institute for Foreign Policy Analysis, 1983, pp. 47–85.

Coker, Christopher. *The Future of the Atlantic Alliance*. RUSI Defence Studies Series. London: Macmillan, 1984.

_____. "The Peace Movement and Its Impact on Public Opinion." *Washington Quarterly* 8, no. 1 (Winter 1985): 93–105.

Conquest, Robert. "Soviet Foreign Policy." In Dennis L. Bark, ed., *To Promote Peace*. Stanford: Hoover Institution Press, 1984, pp. 201–214.

Conze, Werner. "Die deutsche Geschichtswissenschaft seit 1945." *Historische Zeitschrift* 215 (1973): 1–28.

_____. "Hans Rothfels." *Historische Zeitschrift* 237 (1983): 311–60.

_____. *Jakob Kaiser: Politiker zwischen Ost und West, 1945–1949*. Stuttgart: Kohlhammer, 1969.

Craig, Gordon A. *The Germans*. New York: G. P. Putnam's Sons, 1982.

Craig, Gordon A., and George, Alexander. *Force and Statecraft*. New York: Oxford University Press, 1983.

Czempiel, Ernst-Otto. "Die Zukunft der Atlantischen Gemeinschaft." *Aus Politik und Zeitgeschichte: Beilage zur Wochenzeitung Das Parlament*, April 2, 1983.

Dalton, Russell J., ed. *Electoral Change: Realignment and Dealignment in Western Societies*. Princeton, N.J.: Princeton University Press, 1985.

de Zayas, Alfred M. *Nemesis at Potsdam: The Anglo-Americans and the Expulsion of the Germans*. Rev. ed. London: Routledge & Kegan Paul, 1979.

Dietze, Gottfried. *Deutschland–Wo bist Du?* Munich: Olzog, 1980.

Diner, Dan. "Die 'nationale Frage' in der Friedensbewegung." In Reiner Steinweg, ed., *Die neue Friedensbewegung: Analysen aus der Friedensforschung*. Friedensanalysen 16. Frankfurt: Suhrkamp, 1982, pp. 88–95.

Diwald, Hellmut. "Deutschland—Was ist es?" In Wolfgang Venohr, ed., *Die deutsche Einheit kommt bestimmt*. Bergisch Gladbach: Lübbe, 1983, pp. 16–33.

————. *Geschichte der Deutschen*. Berlin: Propyläen, 1978.

————. *Mut zur Geschichte*. Bergisch Gladbach: Lübbe, 1983.

Donat, Helmut, and Tammen, Johann P., *Friedenszeichen—Lebenszeichen: Pazifismus zwischen Verächtlichmachung und Rehabilitierung. Ein Lesebuch zur Friedenserziehung*. Bremerhaven: die horen, 1982.

Donnelly, Christopher N. "Soviet Operational Concepts in the 1980s." In *Strengthening Conventional Deterrence in Europe*. New York: St. Martin's Press, 1983, pp. 105–36.

Dörfer, Ingemar. "La Scandinavie ou la défense de la virginité nucléaire." In Pierre Lellouche, ed., *Pacifisme et dissuasion*. Paris: Institut Français des Relations Internationales, 1983, pp. 107–39.

Dorpalen, Andreas. "Gerhard Ritter." In Hans-Ulrich Wehler, ed., *Deutsche Historiker*, vol. 1. Göttingen: Vandenhoeck und Ruprecht, 1971, pp. 86–99.

Dougherty, James E. *The Bishops and Nuclear Weapons: The Catholic Pastoral Letter on War and Peace*. Hamden, Conn.: Archon Books, 1984.

Draper, Theodore. "The Phantom Alliance." In Robert W. Tucker and Linda Wrigley, eds., *The Atlantic Alliance and Its Critics*. New York: Praeger, 1983, pp. 1–27.

————. "The Western Misalliance." *Washington Quarterly* 4, no. 1 (Winter 1981): 13–69. Also in his *Present History*. New York: Random House, 1983, pp. 51–114.

Duve, Freimut; Böll, Heinrich; and Staeck, Klaus, eds. *Kämpfen für die sanfte Republik*. Reinbek: Rowohlt, 1980.

Dyson, Kenneth H. F. *The State Tradition in Western Europe*. Oxford: Martin Robertson, 1980.

Edinger, Lewis J. *Politics in West Germany*. 2d ed. Boston: Little, Brown, 1977.

Eichberg, Henning. *Nationale Identität*. Munich: Langen-Müller, 1978.

————. "National ist revolutionär." In Peter Brandt and Herbert Ammon, eds., *Die Linke und die nationale Frage*. Reinbek: Rowohlt, 1981, pp. 351–52.

Ellison, Herbert J., ed. *Soviet Policy Toward Western Europe*. Seattle and London: University of Washington Press, 1983.

Ericsson, John. "The Soviet View of Deterrence: A General Survey." *Survival* 24 (1982): 242–51.

Erler, Hans. *Fritz Erler contra Willy Brandt*. Stuttgart: Seewald, 1976.

Eschenburg, Theodor. *Jahre der Besatzung, 1945–1949*, vol. 1 of *Geschichte der Bundesrepublik Deutschland*. Stuttgart: Deutsche Verlags-Anstalt, 1983.

Faber, Karl-Georg. "Geschichtswissenschaft als Retrospektive Politik?" *Geschichte und Gesellschaft* 6 (1980): 574–85.

Farwick, Dieter. "Weder rot noch tot?" *Europäische Wehrkunde* 31 (1982): 210–14.

Faulenbach, Bernd. "Deutsche Geschichtswissenschaft zwischen Kaiserreich und NS-Diktatur." In Bernd Faulenbach, ed., *Geschichtswissenschaft in Deutschland*. Munich: Beck, 1974.

————. *Die Ideologie des deutschen Weges*. Munich: Beck, 1980.

Faurby, Ib; Holm, Hans-Henrik; and Petersen, Nikolaj. "Introduction: The INF Issue — History and Implications." In Hans-Henrik Holm and Nikolaj Petersen, eds., *The European Missiles Crisis: Nuclear Weapons and European Security*. New York: St. Martin's Press, 1983, pp. 1–42.

Flynn, Gregory A., and Rattinger, Hans, eds. *The Public and Atlantic Defense*. Totowa, N.J.: Rowman & Allanheld, 1984.

Foerster, Roland S. "Innenpolitische Aspekte der Sicherheit Westdeutschlands, 1947–1950." In Roland G. Foerster et al., *Anfänge westdeutscher Sicherheitspolitik, 1945–1956*, Vol. 1, *Von der Kapitulation bis zum Pleven-Plan*. Munich: Oldenbourg, 1982, pp. 403–575.

Foerster, Roland S.; Greiner, Christian; Meyer, Georg; Rautenberg, Hans-Jürgen; and Wiggershaus, Norbert. *Anfänge westdeutscher Sicherheitspolitik, 1945–1956*, Vol. 1, *Von der Kapitulation bis zum Pleven-Plan*. Munich: Oldenbourg, 1982.

Forsthoff, Ernst. *Der Staat der Industriegesellschaft*. Munich: Beck, 1971.

Freedman, Lawrence. *The Evolution of Nuclear Strategy*. London: Macmillan, 1981.

Frei, Daniel. "Friedenssicherung durch Gewaltverzicht?" *Aus Politik und Zeitgeschichte: Beilage zur Wochenzeitung Das Parlament*. April 16, 1983.

Frei, Daniel, and Ruloff, Dieter. "Entspannungserwartungen und Entspannungsfolgen: Eine Bilanz anhand politischer und wirtschaftlicher Indikatoren." *Zeitschrift für Politik* 29 (1982): 295–310.

Friedrich, Carl J. *Tradition and Authority*. London: Pall Mall Press, 1972.

Fritsch-Bournazel, Renata. "L'Allemagne et l'Europe de l'Est." In Renata Fritsch-Bournazel, André Brigot, and Jim Cloos, *Les Allemands au coeur de l'Europe*. Cahiers de la Fondation pour les Etudes de Défense Nationale, no. 28. Paris: Stratégique, 1983.

————. *L'Union Soviétique et les Allemagnes*. Paris: Presses de la Fondation Nationale des Sciences Politiques, 1979.

Füllenbach, Josef, and Schulz, Eberhard, eds. *Entspannung am Ende?* Munich: Oldenbourg, 1980.

Fursdon, Edward. *The European Defence Community: A History*. New York: St. Martin's Press, 1979.

Galtung, Johan. *Environment, Development and Military Activity: Towards Alternative Security Doctrines*. Oslo: Universitetsforlaget, 1982.

Gann, Lewis H. "Reflections on the Western European Peace Movement." In Dennis L. Bark, ed., *To Promote Peace*. Stanford: Hoover Institution Press, 1984, pp. 97–114.

Garthoff, James A., and Pipes, Richard. "A Garthoff-Pipes Debate on Soviet Strategic Doctrine." *Strategic Review* 10, no. 4 (Fall 1982): 36–63.

Garton Ash, Timothy. *The Polish Revolution: Solidarity.* New York: Scribner's, 1984.

Gaus, Günter. *Wo Deutschland liegt.* Hamburg: Hoffmann und Campe, 1983.

Gehlen, Arnold. *Moral und Hypermoral.* Frankfurt: Athenäum, 1969.

Geyer, Rolf. "Das sowjetische Friedenskonzept." *Politische Studien* 33 (1982): 47–56.

Gilpin, Robert G. *War and Change in World Politics.* New York: Cambridge University Press, 1981.

Glatzel, Norbert, and Nagel, Ernst Josef, eds. *Frieden in Sicherheit: Zur Weiterentwicklung der katholischen Friedensethik.* Freiburg: Herder, 1981.

Glucksmann, André. *La Force du vertige.* Paris: Grasset, 1983 .

Gordon, Michael R. "Mood Contrasts and NATO." *Washington Quarterly* 8, no. 1 (Winter 1985): 107–30.

Graml, Hermann. "Die Legende von der verpassten Gelegenheit: Zur sowjetischen Notenkampagne des Jahres 1952." *Vierteljahrshefte für Zeitgeschichte* 29 (1981): 307–41.

Grass, Günter. *Widerstand lernen.* Neuwied: Luchterhand, 1984.

Greiner, Gottfried. "Pazifismus und Sicherheitspolitik." *Europäische Wehrkunde* 31 (1982): 433–36.

Grewe, Wilhelm G. *Rückblenden, 1976–1951.* Berlin: Propyläen, 1979.

Grewe, Wilhelm G.; Hacker, Jens; Meissner, Boris; von Raven, Wolfram; Thalheim, Karl C.; and Zieger, Gottfried. *Die aussenpolitische Lage Deutschlands am Beginn der achtziger Jahre.* Studien zur Deutschlandfrage, no. 5. Berlin: Duncker und Humblot, 1982.

Griffith, William E. *The Ostpolitik of the Federal Republic of Germany.* Cambridge, Mass.: MIT Press, 1978.

Grosser, Alfred. *The Western Alliance.* New York: Viking, 1980.

Grosser, Hubert, ed. *Das Volk ohne Staat.* Neustadt an der Saale: Pfaehler, 1981.

Habermas, Jürgen, ed. *Stichworte zur "Geistigen Situation der Zeit."* Frankfurt: Suhrkamp, 1979.

Hacker, Jens. "Das nationale Dilemma der DDR." In Boris Meissner and Jens Hacker, eds., *Die Nation in östlicher Sicht.* Berlin: Duncker und Humblot, 1979, pp. 40–68.

————. "Stand und Perspektiven der deutsch-deutschen Beziehungen." In Wilhelm G. Grewe et al., *Die aussenpolitische Lage Deutschlands am Beginn der achtziger Jahre.* Berlin: Duncker und Humblot, 1982, pp. 61–114.

Hackett, Sir John. *The Third World War.* London: Sidgwick & Jackson, 1978.

————. *The Third World War: The Untold Story.* London: Sidgwick & Jackson, 1982.

Haftendorn, Helga. *Sicherheit und Entspannung.* Baden-Baden: Nomos, 1983.

Haftendorn, Helga; Wilker, Lothar; and Wörmann, Claudia, eds., *Die Aussenpolitik der Bundesrepublik Deutschland.* Berlin: Wissenschaftlicher Autoren-Verlag, 1982.

Hart, Douglas M. "The Hermeneutics of Soviet Military Doctrine." *Washington Quarterly* 7, no. 2 (Spring 1984): 77–88.

Hassner, Pierre. "Arms Control and the Politics of Pacifism in Protestant Europe." In

Uwe Nerlich, ed., *Soviet Power and Western Negotiating Policies*. Cambridge, Mass.: Ballinger, 2:117–50.

———. "Pacifisme et terreur." In Pierre Lellouche, ed., *Pacifisme et Dissuasion*. Paris: Institut Français des Relations Internationales, 1983, pp. 155–76.

———. "Recurrent Stresses, Resilient Structures." In Robert W. Tucker and Linda Wrigley, eds., *The Atlantic Alliance and Its Critics*. New York: Praeger, 1983, pp. 61–94.

———. "Was geht in Deutschland vor?" *Europa-Archiv* 37 (1982): 517–26; English version "The Shifting Foundation," *Foreign Policy*, no. 48 (Fall 1982): 19–32, without notes.

———. "Zwei deutsche Staaten in Europa: Gibt es gemeinsame Interessen in der internationalen Politik?" In Werner Weidenfeld, ed., *Die Identität der Deutschen*. Munich: Hanser, 1983, pp. 294–323.

Hättich, Manfred. "Einheit der Nation und Nationalbewusstsein im geteilten Deutschland." In Klaus Weigelt, ed., *Heimat und Nation*. Studien zur politischen Bildung 7. Mainz: von Hase und Koehler, 1984, pp. 206–19.

Hayek, Friedrich A. "The Principles of a Liberal Social Order." In *The Essence of Hayek*. Stanford: Hoover Institution Press, 1984, pp. 363–81.

Heimpel, Hermann. "Entwurf einer deutschen Geschichte." In his *Der Mensch in seiner Gegenwart*. Göttingen: Vandenhoeck und Ruprecht, 1954, pp. 162–95.

Henderson, Nicholas. *The Birth of NATO*. London: Weidenfeld & Nicolson, 1982.

Hennis, Wilhelm. "Legitimität." In his *Politik und praktische Philosophie*. Stuttgart: Klett, 1977, pp. 198–242.

Hennis, Wilhelm; Kielmansegg, Peter Graf von; and Matz, Ulrich, eds. *Regierbarkeit: Studien zu ihrer Problematisierung*. 2 vols. Stuttgart: Klett, 1977, 1979.

Hentig, Hartmut von. *Die entmutigte Republik*. Munich: Hanser, 1980.

Herf, Jeffrey. "The Center Left Could Not Hold: The SPD and the Peace Movement in West Germany." In Walter Laqueur and Robert E. Hunter, eds., *European Peace Movements and the Future of the Atlantic Alliance*. New Brunswick, N.J.: Transaction Books, 1985.

———. "The Double Decision Still Makes Sense." *Telos*, no. 56 (Summer 1983): 156–71.

———. "Western Strategy and Public Discussion: The Double Decision Makes Sense." *Telos*, no. 52 (Summer 1982): 114–28.

Herzfeld, Hans. *Berlin in der Weltpolitik, 1945–1970*. Veröffentlichungen der Historischen Kommission zu Berlin, no. 38. Berlin: de Gruyter, 1973.

Heuss, Alfred. *Versagen und Verhängnis: Vom Ruin deutscher Geschichte und ihres Verständnisses*. Berlin: Siedler, 1984.

Heydemann, Günther. *Geschichtswissenschaft im geteilten Deutschland*. Erlanger historische Studien 6. Frankfurt: Peter Lang, 1980.

Hildebrand, Klaus. *Von Erhard zur Grossen Koalition 1963–1969*, vol. 4 of *Geschichte der Bundesrepublik Deutschland*. Stuttgart: Deutsche Verlags-Anstalt, 1984.

Holloway, David. "The INF Policy of the Soviet Union." In Hans-Henrik Holm and Nikolaj Petersen, eds., *The European Missiles Crisis: Nuclear Weapons and Security Policy*. New York: St. Martin's Press, 1983, pp. 92–114.

Holm, Hans-Henrik, and Petersen, Nikolaj. "Conclusion: The INF Problem and the Choices Ahead." In Hans-Henrik Holm and Nikolaj Petersen, eds., *The European Missiles Crisis: Nuclear Weapons and Security Policy*. New York: St. Martin's Press, 1983, pp. 232–59.

Holmes, Kim R. "The Origins, Development, and Composition of the Green Movement." In Robert L. Pfaltzgraff, Jr., et al., *The Greens of West Germany: Origins, Strategies and Transatlantic Implications*. Cambridge, Mass.: Institute for Foreign Policy Analysis, 1983, pp. 15–46.

Hook, Sidney. "Marxism." In *Dictionary of the History of Ideas*. New York: Scribner's, 1973, 3:146–61. Also in his *Marxism and Beyond*. Totowa, N.J.: Rowman & Littlefield, 1983, pp. 23–53.

Howard, Michael. *The Causes of Wars*. 2d ed. Cambridge, Mass.: Harvard University Press, 1984.

_____. "The Causes of Wars." *Encounter*, March, 1982. Also in his *The Causes of Wars*, pp. 7–22.

_____. "The Forgotten Dimensions of Strategy." *Foreign Affairs* 57 (1978– 79): 975–86. Also in his *The Causes of Wars*, pp. 101–15.

_____. "On Fighting a Nuclear War." *International Security* 5, no. 4 (Spring 1981): 3–17. Also in his *The Causes of Wars*, pp. 133–50.

_____. "Reassurance and Deterrence: Western Defence in the 1980s." In *Defence and Consensus: The Domestic Aspects of Western Security*. Part 3. Adelphi Paper 184. London: International Institute for Strategic Studies, 1983, pp. 17–26. Also in his *The Causes of Wars*, pp. 245–64.

_____. "War and the Nation-State." *Daedalus* 108, no. 4 (Fall 1979): 101–10. Also in his *The Causes of Wars*, pp. 23–35.

_____. *War in European History*. Oxford: Oxford University Press, 1976.

Hunter, Robert E., ed. *NATO: The Next Generation*. Boulder, Colo.: Westview Press, 1984.

Huntington, Samuel P. "Broadening the Strategic Focus: Comments on Michael Howard's Paper." In *Defence and Consensus: The Domestic Aspects of Western Security*. Part 3. Adelphi Paper 184. London: International Institute for Strategic Studies, 1983, pp. 27–32.

_____. "The Renewal of Strategy." In Samuel P. Huntington, ed., *The Strategic Imperative: New Policies for American Security*. Cambridge, Mass.: Ballinger, 1982, pp. 9–51.

Hupka, Herbert. "Die Einheit der Nation: Der Auftrag des Grundgesetzes und die politisch-rechtliche Situation in der Gegenwart." In Klaus Weigelt, ed., *Heimat und*

Nation. Studien zur politischen Bildung 7. Mainz: von Hase und Koehler, 1984, pp. 255–71.

Iggers, George G. *The German Conception of History*. 2d ed. Middletown, Conn.: Wesleyan University Press, 1983.

Inglehart, Ronald. "Generational Change and the Future of the Atlantic Alliance." *PS* 17 (1984): 525–35.

Jacobsen, Hans-Adolf. "The Division of Germany." In Charles Burdick, Hans-Adolf Jacobsen, and Winfried Kudszus, eds., *Contemporary Germany: Politics and Culture*. Boulder, Colo.: Westview Press, 1984, pp. 60–65.

————. "The Role of the Federal Republic of Germany in the World, 1949–1982." In Charles Burdick, Hans-Adolf Jacobsen, and Winfried Kudszus, eds., *Contemporary Germany: Politics and Culture*. Boulder, Colo.: Westview Press, 1984, pp. 128–76.

Jäckel, Hartmut. "Offener Brief an den Oppositionsführer." In Jürgen Maruhn and Manfred Wilke, eds., *Wohin treibt die SPD?* Munich: Olzog, 1984, pp. 79–86.

Jens, Walter, ed. *In letzter Stunde: Aufruf zum Frieden*. Munich: Kindler, 1982.

Joffe, Josef. "Stability and Its Discontent: Should NATO Go Conventional?" *Washington Quarterly* 7, no. 4 (Fall 1984): 136–47.

Johnson, James T. *Can Modern War Be Just?* New Haven and London: Yale University Press, 1984.

Joshua, Wynfred. "Soviet Manipulation of the European Peace Movement." *Strategic Review* 11, no. 1 (Winter 1983): 9–18.

Kahn, Herman. *Thinking About the Unthinkable in the 1980s*. New York: Simon & Schuster, 1984.

Kaiser, Karl. "Prioritäten sozialdemokratischer Aussen- und Sicherheitspolitik." In Jürgen Maruhn and Manfred Wilke, eds., *Wohin treibt die SPD?* Munich: Olzog, 1984, pp. 9–27.

Kaiser, Karl; Leber, Georg; Mertes, Alois; and Schulze, Franz-Josef. "A German Response to No First Use," *Foreign Affairs* 60 (1981–82): 1157–70.

Karber, Phillip A. "To Lose an Arms Race: The Competition in Conventional Forces Deployed in Central Europe, 1965–1980." In Uwe Nerlich, ed., *Soviet Power and Western Negotiating Policies*. Cambridge, Mass.: Ballinger, 1983, 1:31–88.

Kelsen, Hans. *What Is Justice?* Berkeley and Los Angeles: University of California Press, 1957.

Kewenig, Wilhelm. "Deutschlands Rechtslage heute." *Europa-Archiv* 29 (1974): 71–82.

Kimminich, Otto. "Die Rechtslage Deutschlands nach Grundgesetz und Grundvertrag." *Politische Studien* 31 (1980): 367–78.

Kissinger, Henry A. "The Future of NATO." *Washington Quarterly* 2, no. 4 (Fall 1979): 3–12.

————. "A Plan to Reshape NATO." *Time*, March 5, 1984. Also in Walter Laqueur and Robert E. Hunter, eds., *European Peace Movements and the Future of the Atlantic Alliance*. New Brunswick, N.J.: Transaction Books, 1985.

Klein, Jean. "Les chrétiens, les armes nucléaires et la paix." In Pierre Lellouche, ed., *Pacifisme et dissuasion*. Paris: Institut Français des Relations Internationales, 1983, pp. 199–222.

Klessmann, Christoph. *Die doppelte Staatsgründung: Deutsche Geschichte, 1945–1955*. Göttingen: Vandenhoeck und Ruprecht, 1982.

Klotzbach, Kurt. *Der Weg zur Staatspartei: Programmatik, praktische Politik und Organisation der deutschen Sozialdemokratie 1945 bis 1965*. Berlin: Dietz, 1982.

Koch, H. W. *A Constitutional History of Germany in the Nineteenth and Twentieth Centuries*. London: Longman, 1984.

Kolakowski, Leszek. *Main Currents of Marxism*, vols. 2–3, *The Golden Age* and *The Breakdown*. Oxford: Oxford University Press, 1978.

Kriele, Martin. *Befreiung und politische Aufklärung*. Freiburg: Herder, 1980.

Kundera, Milan. "L'Occident kidnappé," *Le Débat*, no. 27 (September 1983); translated as "The Tragedy of Central Europe." *New York Review of Books*, April 26, 1984.

Künneth, Walter. "Die Ideologie des Pazifismus—Eine Staatsgefährdung?" *Zeitschrift für Politik* 29 (1982): 282–94.

Lafontaine, Oskar. *Angst vor den Freunden*. Reinbek: Rowohlt, 1983.

Langguth, Gerd. *Der grüne Faktor: Von der Bewegung zur Partei*. Zürich: Interfrom, 1984.

———. *Protestbewegung: Entwicklung, Niedergang, Renaissance*. Cologne: Verlag Wissenschaft und Politik, 1983.

Laqueur, Walter. *America, Europe, and the Soviet Union*. New Brunswick, N.J.: Transaction Books, 1983.

———. *Germany Today. A Personal Report*. Boston: Little, Brown, 1985.

———. *The Political Psychology of Appeasement*. New Brunswick, N.J.: Transaction Books, 1980.

Laqueur, Walter, and Hunter, Robert E., eds. *European Peace Movements and the Future of the Atlantic Alliance*. New Brunswick, N.J.: Transaction Books, 1985.

Legvold, Robert. "Military Power in International Politics: Soviet Doctrine on Its Centrality and Instrumentality." In Uwe Nerlich, ed., *Soviet Power and Western Negotiating Policies*. Cambridge, Mass.: Ballinger, 1983, 1:123–59.

Leinemann, Jürgen. *Die Angst der Deutschen*. Reinbek: Rowohlt, 1982.

Leites, Nathan. *Soviet Style in War*. New York: Crane Russak, 1982.

Lellouche, Pierre. "Does NATO Have a Future?" In Robert W. Tucker and Linda Wrigley, eds., *The Atlantic Alliance and Its Critics*. New York: Praeger, 1983, pp. 129–54.

———. "La contestation pacifiste et l'avenir de la sécurité en Europe." In Pierre Lellouche, ed., *Pacifisme et dissuasion*. Paris: Institut Français des Relations Internationales, 1983, pp. 13–55.

———, ed. *Pacifisme et dissuasion*. Paris: Institut Français des Relations Internationales, 1983.

Liska, George. *Russia and the Road to Appeasement.* Baltimore: Johns Hopkins University Press, 1982.

Livet, Georges. *L'Equilibre européen de la fin du XVe à la fin du XVIIIe siècle.* Paris: Presses Unive rsitaires de France, 1976.

Löser, Jochen. *Weder rot noch tot.* Munich: Olzog, 1981.

Löwenthal, Richard. "Die Deutschen sind keine Pendler." *Die Zeit,* May 25, 1984.

_____. "The German Question Transformed." *Foreign Affairs* 63 (1984–85): 303–15.

_____. *Gesellschaftswandel und Kulturkrise.* Frankfurt: Fischer Taschenbuch Verlag, 1979.

_____. "Vom kalten Krieg zur Ostpolitik." In Richard Löwenthal and Hans-Peter Schwarz, eds., *Die zweite Republik.* Stuttgart: Seewald, 1974, pp. 604–99.

Löwenthal, Richard, and Schwarz, Hans-Peter, eds. *Die zweite Republik: 25 Jahre Bundesrepublik Deutschland – Eine Bilanz.* Stuttgart: Seewald, 1974.

Lübbe, Hermann. *Endstation Terror: Rückblick auf lange Märsche.* Stuttgart: Seewald, 1978.

Ludz, Peter C. *Die DDR zwischen Ost und West.* Munich: Beck, 1977.

Lunn, Simon. "INF and Political Cohesion in NATO." In his -Henrik Holm and Nikolaj Petersen, eds., *The European Missiles Crisis: Nuclear Weapons and Security Policy.* New York: St. Martin's Press, 1983, pp. 208–24.

Maier, Hans. "Der Weg der deutschen Katholiken seit 1945." In his *Stellungnahmen.* Munich: Kösel, 1978, pp. 134–51.

de Maizière, Ulrich. "Verteidigungspolitik in der Demokratie." In Wilhelm Hennis et al., eds. *Regierbarkeit: Studien zu ihrer Problematisierung.* Vol. 2. Stuttgart: Klett, 1979, pp. 254–78.

Mandelbaum, Michael. *The Nuclear Revolution: International Politics Before and After Hiroshima.* New York: Cambridge University Press, 1981.

Manel, Michel. *L'Europe face aux SS 20.* 2d ed. Paris: Stratégies, 1983.

Mann, Thomas. *Betrachtungen eines Unpolitischen.* Berlin: S. Fischer, 1918; reissued Frankfurt: S. Fischer, 1983.

Martin, Bernice. "Invisible Religion, Popular Culture and Anti-nuclear Sentiment." In David Martin and Peter Mullen, eds., *Unholy Warfare.* Oxford: Blackwell, 1983, pp. 108–40.

_____. *A Sociology of Contemporary Cultural Change.* Oxford: Blackwell, 1981.

Martin, Laurence W. *The Two-Edged Sword.* London: Macmillan, 1982.

Maruhn, Jürgen. "Sozialdemokratisches Selbstbewusstsein gegen schiefe Bündnisse." In Jürgen Maruhn and Manfred Wilke, eds., *Wohin treibt die SPD?* Munich: Olzog, 1984, pp. 98–111.

Maruhn, Jürgen, and Wilke, Manfred, eds. *Wohin treibt die SPD? Wende oder Kontinuität sozialdemokratischer Sicherheitspolitik.* Munich: Olzog, 1984.

Mearsheimer, John J. *Conventional Deterrence.* Ithaca, N.Y.: Cornell University Press, 1983.

Meinecke, Friedrich. *Die deutsche Katastrophe*. Wiesbaden: Brockhaus, 1946. Also in his *Gesammelte Werke*, vol. 8. Stuttgart: Koehler und Amelang, 1965.

———. "Ranke und Burckhardt." In his *Gesammelte Werke*, vol. 7: *Zur Geschichte der Geschichtsschreibung*. Munich: Oldenbourg, 1968, pp. 93–121.

Meissner, Boris. "Adenauer und die Sowjetunion von 1955 bis 1959." In Dieter Blumenwitz et al., eds., *Konrad Adenauer und seine Zeit*, vol. 2. Stuttgart: Deutsche Verlags-Anstalt, 1976, pp. 192–219.

———. "Die Bundesrepublik Deutschland und die Sowjetunion – Entwicklung, Stand und Perspektiven ihrer Beziehungen." In Wilhelm G. Grewe et al., *Die aussenpolitische Lage Deutschlands am Beginn der achtziger Jahre*. Berlin: Duncker und Humblot, 1982, pp. 115–35.

———. "Das Entspannungskonzept der Hegemonialmacht: Entspannungsbegriff und Entspannungspolitik aus der Sicht der Sowjetunion." In Hans-Peter Schwarz and Boris Meissner, eds., *Entspannungspolitik in Ost und West*. Cologne: Heymann, 1979, pp. 1–35.

Meissner, Boris, and Hacker, Jens, eds. *Die Nation in östlicher Sicht*. Berlin: Duncker und Humblot, 1979.

Mertes, Alois. "Friedenserhaltung – Friedensgestaltung: Zur Diskussion über 'Sicherheitspartnerschaft.'" *Europa-Archiv* 35 (1983): 187–96.

Meulemann, Heiner. "Value Change in West Germany, 1950–1980: Integrating the Empirical Evidence." *Social Science Information* 22 (1983): 777–800.

Meuschel, Sigrid. "Neo-Nationalism and the West German Peace Movement's Reaction to the Polish Military Coup." *Telos*, no. 56 (Summer 1983): 119–30 .

Meyer, Stephen M. *Soviet Theatre Nuclear Forces*. Part 1: *Development of Doctrine and Objectives*. Part 2: *Capabilities and Implications*. Adelphi Papers 187–88. London: International Institute for Strategic Studies, 1983, 1984.

The Military Balance, 1984–1985. London: International Institute for Strategic Studies, 1984.

Milward, Alan S. *The Reconstruction of Western Europe, 1945–1951*. Berkeley and Los Angeles: University of California Press, 1984.

Mirgeler, Albert. "Die geschichtlichen Friedensschlüsse." In his *Geschichte und Gegenwart*. Freiburg: Karl Alber, 1965, pp. 64–77.

———. "Vielfalt und Einheit der deutschen Lande." In his *Geschichte und Gegenwart*. Freiburg: Karl Alber, 1965, pp. 78–92.

Mommsen, Wolfgang J. "Gegenwärtige Tendenzen in der Geschichtsschreibung der Bundesrepublik." *Geschichte und Gesellschaft* 7 (1981): 149–88.

Moreton, Edwina. "The German Factor." In Edwina Moreton and George Segal, eds., *Soviet Strategy Toward Western Europe*. London: George Allen & Unwin, 1984, pp. 110–37.

Moreton, Edwina, and Segal, George, eds. *Soviet Strategy Toward Western Europe*. London: George Allen & Unwin, 1984.

Morgan, Roger. "The Federal Republic and the United States." In Charles Burdick,

Hans-Adolf Jacobsen, and Winfried Kudszus, eds., *Contemporary Germany: Politics and Culture.* Boulder, Colo.: Westview Press, 1984, pp. 177 –202.

Motschmann, Klaus. "Deutschlandpolitik im Wandel: Von Ulbricht zu Honecker." In Klaus Weigelt, ed., *Heimat und Nation.* Studien zur politischen Bildung 7. Mainz: von Hase und Koehler, 1984, pp. 272–85.

————. *Herrschaft der Minderheit.* München: Langen-Müller, 1983.

————. *Sozialismus und Nation.* Munich: Langen-Müller, 1979.

Münch, Ingo von, ed. *Dokumente des geteilten Deutschland.* Stuttgart: Kröner, 1968.

Myers, Kenneth A., ed. *NATO–The Next Thirty Years.* Boulder, Colo.: Westview Press, 1980.

Nerlich, Uwe. "Alliance Strategy in the 1980s and the Political Approach to Soviet Power." In Uwe Nerlich, ed., *Soviet Power and Western Negotiating Policies.* Cambridge, Mass.: Ballinger, 1983, 1:331–41.

————. "Arms Negotiations and the Process of Political Change in Europe: Reordering Priorities of Western Security Policies." In Uwe Nerlich, ed., *Soviet Power and Western Negotiating Policies.* Cambridge, Mass.: Ballinger, 1983, 2:391–408.

————. "Theatre Nuclear Forces in Europe: Is NATO Running Out of Options?" In Kenneth A. Myers, ed., *NATO–The Next Thirty Years.* Boulder, Colo.: Westview Press, 1980, pp. 63–93.

————, ed. *Soviet Power and Western Negotiating Policies.* Vol. 1: *The Soviet Asset: Military Power in the Competition over Europe.* Vol. 2: *The Western Panacea: Constraining Soviet Power Through Negotiations.* Cambridge, Mass.: Ballinger, 1983.

Niggemeier, Horst. "Wie stellt sich die SPD ihre Abgrenzung gegenüber Kommunisten vor?" In Jürgen Maruhn and Manfred Wilke, eds., *Wohin treibt die SPD?* Munich: Olzog, 1984, pp. 87–97.

Nipperdey, Thomas. *Deutsche Geschichte, 1800–1866.* Munich: C. H. Beck, 1983.

————. "Wehlers Kaiserreich." *Geschichte und Gesellschaft* 1 (1975): 539–60.

Nitze, Paul H. "Living with the Soviets." *Foreign Affairs* 63 (1984–85): 360–74.

Noelle-Neumann, Elisabeth. "Are the Germans 'Collapsing' or 'Standing Firm'?" *Encounter,* February 1982.

————. "Do We Need a Flag?" *Encounter,* January 1983.

————, ed. *The Germans: Public Opinion Polls, 1967–1980.* Westport, Conn.: Greenwood, 1981.

Nolte, Ernst. *Deutschland und der Kalte Krieg.* 1st ed. Munich: Piper, 1974. 2d ed. Stuttgart: Klett, 1985.

Norman, Edward. *Christianity and the World Order.* Oxford: Oxford University Press, 1978.

Novak, Michael. "Moral Clarity in the Nuclear Age." *Catholicism in Crisis* 1, no. 4 (March 1983). Also in Michael Novak, ed., *Moral Clarity in the Nuclear Age.* Nashville, Tenn.: Thomas Nelson, 1983.

Ortlieb, Heinz-Dietrich. *Vom totalitären Staat zum totalen Egoismus.* Zürich: Interfrom, 1978.

Oudenaren, John van. "The Soviet Conception of Europe and Arms Negotiations." In Uwe Nerlich, ed., *Soviet Power and Western Negotiating Policies*. Cambridge, Mass.: Ballinger, 1983, 1:161–94.

Pachter, Henry M. "Brecht's Personal Politics." In his *Weimar Etudes*. New York: Columbia University Press, 1982, pp. 225–45.

_____. "Friedrich Meinecke and the Tragedy of German Liberalism." In his *Weimar Etudes*. New York: Columbia University Press, 1982, pp. 135–70.

_____. *Modern Germany: A Social, Cultural, and Political History*. Boulder, Colo.: Westview Press, 1978.

Papadakis, Elim. *The Green Movement in West Germany*. New York: St. Martin's Press, 1984.

Paz, Octavio. "Alemania: Nacionalismo y pacifismo." *Vuelta*, no. 86 (January 1984): 22–24.

_____. "Pacifismo, nihilismo, eterno ritorno." *Vuelta*, no. 81 (August 1983): 44–46.

Peisl, Anton, and Mohler, Armin, eds. *Die deutsche Neurose: Über die beschädigte Identität der Deutschen*. Berlin: Ullstein, 1980.

Petersen, Nikolaj. "The Scandilux Experiment: Towards a Transnational Social Democratic Security Perspective." *Cooperation and Conflict* 20 (1985), forthcoming.

Plessner, Hellmuth. *Die verspätete Nation*. Rev. ed. Frankfurt: Suhrkamp, 1980.

Pohrt, Wolfgang. *Endstation: Über die Wiedergeburt der Nation*. Berlin: Rotbuch, 1982.

Prowe, Diethelm. "Die Anfänge der Brandtschen Ostpolitik in Berlin, 1961–1963." In Wolfgang Benz and Hermann Graml, eds., *Aspekte deutscher Aussenpolitik im 20. Jahrhundert*. Stuttgart: Deutsche Verlags-Anstalt, 1976, pp. 249–86.

Rabb, Theodore K. *The Search for Stability in Early Modern Europe*. New York: Oxford University Press, 1975.

Radway, Laurence. "Towards the Europeanisation of NATO." *Atlantic Quarterly* 1 (1983): 129–47.

Rammstedt, Othein. *Soziale Bewegung*. Frankfurt: Suhrkamp, 1978.

Rausch, Heinz. "Politisches Bewusstsein und politische Einstellungen im Wandel." In Werner Weidenfeld, ed., *Die Identität der Deutschen*. Munich: Hanser, 1983, pp. 119–53.

Repgen, Konrad. "Methoden- oder Richtungskämpfe in der deutschen Geschichtswissenschaft seit 1945?" *Geschichte in Wissenschaft und Unterricht* 30 (1979): 591–610.

Risse, Heinz Theo, and Müller, Hans Jürgen. "Zum Stand der kirchlichen Friedensarbeit." In Norbert Glatzel and Ernst Josef Nagel, eds., *Frieden in Sicherheit*. Freiburg: Herder, 1981, pp. 176–212.

Ritter, Gerhard. *Das deutsche Problem*. 2d ed. Munich: Oldenbourg, 1966.

_____. "Zur Problematik gegenwärtiger Geschichtsschreibung." In Gerhard Ritter, *Lebendige Vergangenheit*. Munich: Oldenbourg, 1958, pp. 255–83.

Roberts, Adam. "The Critique of Nuclear Deterrence." In *Defence and Consensus: The*

Domestic Aspects of Western Security. Part 2. Adelphi Paper 183. London: International Institute for Strategic Studies, 1983, pp. 2–18.

Rogers, Bernard W. "Greater Flexibility for NATO's Flexible Response." *Strategic Review* 11, no. 2 (Spring 1983): 11–19.

————. "Prescriptions for a Difficult Decade: The Atlantic Alliance in the 1980s." *Foreign Affairs* 60 (1981–82): 1145–56.

Rommen, Heinrich. *Die ewige Wiederkehr des Naturrechts.* 2d ed. Munich: Kösel, 1947.

Rose, Clive. *Campaigns against Western Defence. NATO's Adversaries and Critics.* RUSI Defence Studies Series. London: Macmillan, 1985.

Rostow, W. W. *The Division of Europe After World War II, 1946.* Austin: University of Texas Press, 1981.

Royen, Christoph. *Die sowjetische Koexistenzpolitik gegenüber Westeuropa.* Internationale Politik und Sicherheit 2. Baden-Baden: Nomos, 1978.

Ruehl, Lothar. "The Media and the Image of Defence Policy: Europe." In *Defence and Consensus: The Domestic Aspects of Western Security.* Part 1. Adelphi Paper 182. London: International Institute for Strategic Studies, 1983, pp. 36–44.

————. "The Threat Perceived? Leverage of Soviet Military Power in Western Europe." In Uwe Nerlich, ed., *Soviet Power and Western Negotiating Policies.* Cambridge, Mass.: Ballinger, 1983, 1:195–205.

Saage, Richard. "Neokonservatives Denken in der Bundesrepublik." In his *Rückkehr zum starken Staat?* Frankfurt: Suhrkamp, 1983, pp. 228–82.

————. "Rückkehr zum starken Staat? Zur Renaissance des Freund-Feind-Denkens in der Bundesrepublik." In his *Rückkehr zum starken Staat?* Frankfurt: Suhrkamp, 1983, pp. 7–42.

Schall, James V., S.J., ed. *Bishops' Pastoral Letters.* San Francisco: Ignatius Press, 1984.

Schelsky, Helmut. *Die Arbeit tun die anderen.* Opladen: Westdeutscher Verlag, 1975.

————. "Die Generationen der Bundesrepublik." In Walter Scheel, ed., *Die an dere deutsche Frage.* Stuttgart: Klett, 1981, pp. 178–98.

————. *Rückblicke eines "Anti-Soziologen."* Opladen: Westdeutscher Verlag, 1981.

————. *Die skeptische Generation.* 2d ed. Berlin: Ullstein, 1975.

Scheuch, Erwin K. "Die deutsche Nation im Bewusstsein der Bevölkerung der Bundesrepublik Deutschland." In Klaus Weigelt, ed., *Heimat und Nation.* Studien zur politischen Bildung 7. Mainz: von Hase und Koehler, 1984, pp. 161–88.

————. "Politischer Extremismus in der Bundesrepublik." In Richard Löwenthal and Hans-Peter Schwarz, eds. *Die zweite Republik.* Stuttgart: Seewald, 1974, pp. 433–69.

Scheuner, Ulrich. "Die deutsche einheitliche Staatsangehörigkeit: Ein fortdauerndes Problem der deutschen Teilung." *Europa-Archiv* 34 (1979): 345–56.

Schlaga, Rüdiger, and Spanger, Hans-Joachim. "Die Friedensbewegung und der War-schauer Pakt: Ein Spannungsverhältnis." In Reiner Steinweg, ed., *Die neue Friedens-bewegung: Analysen aus der Friedensforschung.* Friedensanalysen 16. Frankfurt: Suhrkamp, 1982, pp. 54–85.

Schmidt, Helmut. "Zur Lage der Sicherheitspolitik." In Jürgen Maruhn and Manfred Wilke, eds., *Wohin treibt die SPD?* Munich: Olzog, 1984, pp. 129–64.

Schmitt, Carl. *Der Begriff des Politischen.* Rev. ed. Berlin: Duncker und Humblot, 1963. Eng. trans. with intro. by George Schwab, *The Concept of the Political.* Brunswick, N.J.: Rutgers University Press, 1975.

Schmitz, Kurt Thomas. *Deutsche Einheit und europäische Integration: Der sozialdemokratische Beitrag zur Aussenpolitik der BRD.* Bonn: Neue Gesellschaft, 1978.

Schmitz, Wolfgang. "Marktwirtschaft, Soziale." In *Katholisches Soziallexikon.* 2d ed. Innsbruck and Graz: Tyrolia and Styria Verlag, 1980, cols. 1709–20.

Schneider, Peter. "Warnung vor diesem Frieden." *Kursbuch*, no. 68 (June 1982): 181–87.

Schulz, Eberhard. *Die deutsche Nation in Europa.* Bonn: Europa Union, 1982.

Schwan, Gesine. "Die SPD und die westliche Freiheit." In Jürgen Maruhn and Manfred Wilke, eds., *Wohin treibt die SPD?* Munich: Olzog, 1984, pp. 38–52.

Schwarz, Hans-Peter. "Die Alternative zum Kalten Krieg? Bilanz der bisherigen Entspannung." In Hans-Peter Schwarz and Boris Meissner, *Entspannungspolitik in Ost und West.* Cologne: Heymann, 1979, pp. 275–303.

———. *Die Ära Adenauer, 1949–1957,* vol. 2 of *Geschichte der Bundesrepublik Deutschland.* Stuttgart: Deutsche Verlags-Anstalt, 1981.

———. *Die Ära Adenauer, 1957–1963,* vol. 3 of *Geschichte der Bundesrepublik Deutschland.* Stuttgart: Deutsche Verlags-Anstalt, 1983.

———. "Das aussenpolitische Konzept Adenauers." In Klaus Gotto, ed., *Konrad Adenauer: Seine Deutschland- und Aussenpolitik, 1953–1963.* Munich: Deutscher Taschenbuch Verlag, 1975, pp. 97–155.

———. "Die aussenpolitischen Grundlagen des westdeutschen Staates." In Richard Löwenthal and Hans-Peter Schwarz, eds. *Die zweite Republik.* Stuttgart: Seewald, 1974, pp. 27–63.

———. "Das europäische Konzert der gelähmten Leviathane: Variationen zum Thema Unregierbarkeit und Aussenpolitik." In Wilhelm Hennis et al., eds., *Regierbarkeit: Studien zu ihrer Problematisierung.* Vol. 1. Stuttgart: Klett, 1977, pp. 296–312.

———. "Das Spiel ist aus und alle Fragen offen, oder: Vermutungen zu Adenauers Wiedervereinigungspolitik." In Helmut Kohl, ed., *Konrad Adenauer, 1876–1976.* Stuttgart: Belser, 1976, pp. 140–56.

———. "Supermacht und Juniorpartner: Ansätze amerikanischer und westdeutscher Ostpolitik." In Hans-Peter Schwarz and Boris Meissner, *Entspannungspolitik in Ost und West.* Cologne: Heymann, 1979, pp. 147–91.

———. *Vom Reich zur Bundesrepublik: Deutschland im Widerstreit der aussenpolitischen Konzeptionen in den Jahren der Besatzungsherrschaft, 1945–1949.* 2d ed. Stuttgart: Klett, 1980.

———. "Die westdeutsche Aussenpolitik—Historische Lektionen und politische Generationen." In Walter Scheel, ed., *Nach dreissig Jahren.* Stuttgart: Klett, 1979, pp. 145–73.

———. "What Is Wrong with U.S.-German Relations?" *SAIS Review*, no. 4 (Summer 1982): 53–71.

Schwarz, Hans-Peter, and Meissner, Boris, eds. *Entspannungspolitik in Ost und West*. Cologne: Heymann, 1979.

Scott, Harriet F., and Scott, William F., eds., *The Soviet Art of War: Doctrine, Strategy and Tactics*. Boulder, Colo.: Westview Press, 1982.

Seebacher-Brandt, Brigitte. *Ollenhauer – Biedermann und Patriot*. Berlin: Siedler, 1984.

Seton-Watson, Hugh. *The Imperialist Revolutionaries: Aspects of International Communism in the 1960s and 1970s*. Stanford: Hoover Institution Press, 1978.

Sharp, Gene. *Making Europe Unconquerable*. London and Philadelphia: Taylor & Francis, 1985.

Sheehan, James J. "What Is German History? Reflections on the Role of the *Nation* in German History and Historiography." *Journal of Modern History* 53 (1981): 1–23.

Skinner, Quentin. *The Foundations of Modern Political Thought*. 2 vols. Cambridge, Eng.: Cambridge University Press, 1978.

Sloss, Lew, and Millot, Marc Dean. "U.S. Nuclear Strategy in Evolution." *Strategic Review* 12, no. 1 (Winter 1984): 19–28.

Soell, Hartmut. *Fritz Erler – eine politische Biographie*. Berlin: Dietz, 1976.

Sontheimer, Kurt. *Grundzüge des politischen Systems der Bundesrepublik Deutschland*. Munich: Piper, 1980.

———. *Die verunsicherte Republik*. Munich: Piper, 1979.

———. *Zeitwende*. Hamburg: Hoffmann und Campe, 1983.

Spannocchi, Emil, and Brossolet, Guy. *Verteidigung ohne Schlacht*. Munich: Hanser, 1976.

Speidel, Hans. *Aus unserer Zeit*. Berlin: Propyläen, 1977.

Spieker, Manfred. "Die Verteidigung des Friedens gegen den Pazifismus." *Aus Politik und Zeitgeschichte: Beilage zur Wochenzeitung Das Parlament*. April 30, 1983.

Spragens, Thomas A., Jr. *The Irony of Liberal Reason*. Chicago: University of Chicago Press, 1981.

Steinweg, Reiner, ed. *Die neue Friedensbewegung: Analysen aus der Friedensforschung*. Friedensanalysen 16. Frankfurt: Suhrkamp, 1982.

Stent, Angela. *From Embargo to Ostpolitik: The Political Economy of Soviet-West German Relations, 1955–1980*. Cambridge, Eng.: Cambridge University Press, 1981.

Stratmann, Karl-Peter. "Modernization and Deployment of Nuclear Forces in Europe: Agreed Constraints in the Stabilization of Deterrence." In Uwe Nerlich, ed., *Soviet Power and Western Negotiating Policies*. Cambridge, Mass.: Ballinger, 1983, 2:325–45.

———. *NATO-Strategie in der Krise?* Internationale Politik und Sicherheit, no. 5. Baden-Baden: Nomos, 1981.

_____. "Vom Autismus kritischer Friedensforschung." In Manfred Funke, ed., *Friedensforschung – Entscheidungshilfe gegen Gewalt*. Munich: List, 1975, pp. 397–423.

Strauss, Franz Josef. "Manifesto of an Atlanticist." *Strategic Review* 10, no. 3 (Summer 1982): 11–15.

Strengthening Conventional Deterrence in Europe: Proposals for the 1980s. Report of the European Security Study. New York: St. Martin's Press, 1983.

Stürmer, Michael. "Kein Eigentum der Deutschen: Die deutsche Frage." In Werner Weidenfeld, ed., *Die Identität der Deutschen*. Munich: Hanser, 1983, pp. 83–101.

Sutton, Boyd D.; Landry, John R.; Armstrong, Malcolm B.; Estes, Howell M., III; and Clark, Wesley K. "New Directions in Conventional Defence?" *Survival* 26 (1984): 50–78.

Szabo, Stephen F. "Brandt's Children: The West German Successor Generation." *Washington Quarterly* 7, no. 1 (Winter 1984): 50–59.

_____, ed. *The Successor Generation: International Perspectives of Postwar Europeans*. London and Woburn, Mass.: Butterworths, 1983.

Talmon, Jacob L. *The Myth of the Nation and the Vision of Revolution*. Berkeley and Los Angeles: University of California Press, 1981.

Tatu, Michel. *La Bataille des Euromissiles*. Paris: Seuil, 1983. Also published as Cahiers de la Fondation pour les Etudes de Défense Nationale, no. 29. Paris: Stratégique, 1983.

Tauber, Kurt P. *Beyond Eagle and Swastika: German Nationalism Since 1945*. Middletown, Conn.: Wesleyan University Press, 1967.

Telos, no. 51 (Spring 1982). Special issue on European Peace Movements.

Telos, no. 52 (Summer 1982). Special issue on Social Movements.

Telos, no. 56 (Summer 1983). Further debate on Peace Movements.

Tenbruck, Friedrich H. "Alltagsnormen und Lebensgefühle in der Bundesrepublik." In Richard Löwenthal and Hans-Peter Schwarz, eds., *Die zweite Republik*. Stuttgart: Seewald, 1974, pp. 289–310.

_____. "Frieden durch Friedensforschung?" In Manfred Funke, ed., *Friedensforschung – Entscheidungshilfe gegen Gewalt*. Munich: List, 1975, pp. 425–39.

Tiedtke, Stephan. "Wider den kurzen Atem: Thesen zur sicherheitspolitischen Strategie der Friedensbewegung." In Reiner Steinweg, ed., *Die neue Friedensbewegung: Analysen aus der Friedensforschung*. Friedensanalysen 16. Frankfurt: Suhrkamp, 1982, pp. 34–53.

Todd, Emmanuel. *Le Fou et le prolétaire*. 2d ed. Paris: Livre de Poche, 1980.

Topitsch, Ernst. "Machtkampf und Humanität." In his *Gottwerdung und Revolution*. Pullach bei München: UTB/Verlag Dokumentation, 1973, pp. 135–217.

Tucker, Robert W. "The Atlantic Alliance and Its Critics." In Robert W. Tucker and Linda Wrigley, eds., *The Atlantic Alliance and Its Critics*. New York: Praeger, 1983, pp. 155–89.

Ulam, Adam B. *Dangerous Relations: The Soviet Union and the World, 1970–1982*. New York: Oxford University Press, 1983.

_____. *Expansion and Coexistence: Soviet Foreign Policy, 1917–73.* 2d ed. New York: Praeger, 1974.

Venohr, Wolfgang, ed. *Die deutsche Einheit kommt bestimmt.* Bergisch Gladbach: Lübbe, 1982.

Vermaat, J. A. Emerson. "Moscow Fronts and the European Peace Movement." *Problems of Communism* 31, no. 6 (November–December 1982): 43–56.

Vetschera, Heinz. "Soziale Verteidigung und ziviler Widerstand: Zum theoretischen Konzept der alternativen Wehrpolitik." *Europäische Wehrkunde* 31 (1982): 307–12 and 351–56.

Vigor, Peter H. *The Soviet View of War, Peace and Neutrality.* London: Routledge & Kegan Paul, 1975.

Wallace, William. "European Defence Co-operation: The Reopening Debate." *Survival* 26 (1984): 251–61.

Walther, Christian, ed. *Atomwaffen und Ethik: Der deutsche Protestantismus und die atomare Aufrüstung, 1954–1961.* Berlin: Christian Kaiser, 1981.

Weber, Alfred. *Haben wir Deutschen nach 1945 versagt?* Munich: Piper, 1979.

Wehler, Hans-Ulrich. *Preussen ist wieder chic.* Frankfurt: Suhrkamp, 1982.

_____. "Zur Lage der Geschichtswissenschaft in der Bundesrepublik Deutschland, 1949–1979." In his *Historische Sozialwissenschaft.* Göttingen: Vandenhoeck und Ruprecht, 1980, pp. 13–41.

Weidenfeld, Werner. "Die Bundesrepublik Deutschland: Kein Provisorium – aber was sonst?" *Aus Politik und Zeitgeschichte: Beilage zur Wochenzeitung Das Parlament.* March 17, 1983.

_____. *Die Frage nach der Einheit der deutschen Nation.* Munich: Olzog, 1981.

_____, ed. *Die Identität der Deutschen.* Munich: Hanser, 1983.

Weigelt, Klaus, ed. *Heimat und Nation.* Studien zur politischen Bildung 7. Mainz: von Hase und Koehler, 1984.

Wettig, Gerhard. *Die Funktion der westeuropäischen Friedensbewegung in sowjetischer Sicht.* Berichte des Bundesinstituts für ostwissenschaftliche und internationale Studien, no. 49, 1983.

_____. "Germany, Europe, and the Soviets." In Herbert J. Ellison, ed., *Soviet Policy Toward Western Europe.* Seattle and London: University of Washington Press, 1983, pp. 31–60.

Wiggershaus, Norbert. "Die Entscheidung für einen westdeutschen Verteidigungsbeitrag, 1950." In Roland G. Foerster et al., *Anfänge westdeutscher Sicherheitspolitik, 1945–1956.* Vol. 1. Munich: Oldenbourg, 1982, pp. 325–402.

_____. "Von Potsdam zum Pleven-Plan: Deutschland in der internationalen Konfrontation, 1945–1950." In Roland G. Foerster et al., *Anfänge westdeutscher Sicherheitspolitik, 1945–1956.* Vol. 1. Munich: Oldenbourg, 1982, pp. 1–118.

Wildavsky, Aaron, ed. *Beyond Containment.* San Francisco: Institute for Contemporary Studies, 1983.

Wildenmann, Rudolf. "Public Opinion and the Defence Effort: Trends and Lessons. Europe." In *Defence and Consensus: The Domestic Aspects of Western Security.* Part 1. Adelphi Paper 182. London: International Institute for Strategic Studies, 1983, pp. 24–28.

Wiles, Peter. "Is an Anti-Soviet Embargo Desirable or Possible?" In *The Conduct of East-West Relations in the 1980s.* Part 2. Adelphi Paper 190. London: International Institute for Strategic Studies, 1984, pp. 37–50.

_____. "Leninism and *Weltinnenpolitik.*" *Survey,* nos. 100–101 (Summer–Autumn 1976): 154–62.

Wilke, Manfred. "Die SPD im Zerrspiegel der SED." In Jürgen Maruhn and Manfred Wilke, eds., *Wohin treibt die SPD?* Munich: Olzog, 1984, pp. 112–28.

Willms, Bernard. *Die deutsche Nation.* Cologne: Edition Maschke, 1982.

Winckler, Hans Heinrich. "Über die Blöcke hinaus." *Europäische Wehrkunde* 31 (1982): 491–98.

Windsor, Philip. "Arms Control in Europe as a Framework for Political Change in Eastern Europe." In Uwe Nerlich, ed., *Soviet Power and Western Negotiating Policies.* Cambridge, Mass.: Ballinger, 1983, 2:375–90.

_____. *Germany and the Western Alliance: Lessons from the 1980 Crises.* Adelphi Paper 170. London: International Institute for Strategic Studies, 1981.

Winkler, Heinrich A. "Wohin treibt die SPD?" In Jürgen Maruhn and Manfred Wilke, eds., *Wohin treibt die SPD?* Munich: Olzog, 1984, pp. 28–37.

Winkler, Theodor H. *Arms Control and the Politics of European Security.* Adelphi Paper 177. London: International Institute for Strategic Studies, 1982.

Winning the Peace: Joint Pastoral Letter of the French Bishops. English translation with an introduction by James V. Schall, S.J., in *Bishops' Pastoral Letters.* San Francisco: Ignatius Press, 1984.

Wohlstetter, Albert. "Bishops, Statesmen and Other Strategists on the Bombing of Innocents," *Commentary,* June 1983.

_____. "Is There a Strategic Arms Race?" *Foreign Policy,* no. 15 (Summer 1974): 3–20.

_____. "Optimal Ways to Confuse Ourselves." *Foreign Policy,* no. 20 (Fall 1975): 170–98.

_____. "Racing Forward? Or Ambling Back?" *Survey,* nos. 100–101 (Summer–Autumn 1976): 163–217.

_____. "Rivals, but No 'Race.'" *Foreign Policy,* no. 16 (Fall 1974): 48–81.

Wolfe, Bertram D. "Communist Ideology and Soviet Foreign Policy." In his *An Ideology in Power.* New York: Stein & Day, 1969, pp. 345–61.

Yankelovich, Daniel, and Doble, John. "The Public Mood: Nuclear Weapons and the USSR." *Foreign Affairs* 63 (1984–85): 33–46.

Zoll, Ralf. "Public Opinion and Security Policy: The West German Experience." *Armed Forces and Society* 5 (1978–79): 590–605.

INDEX